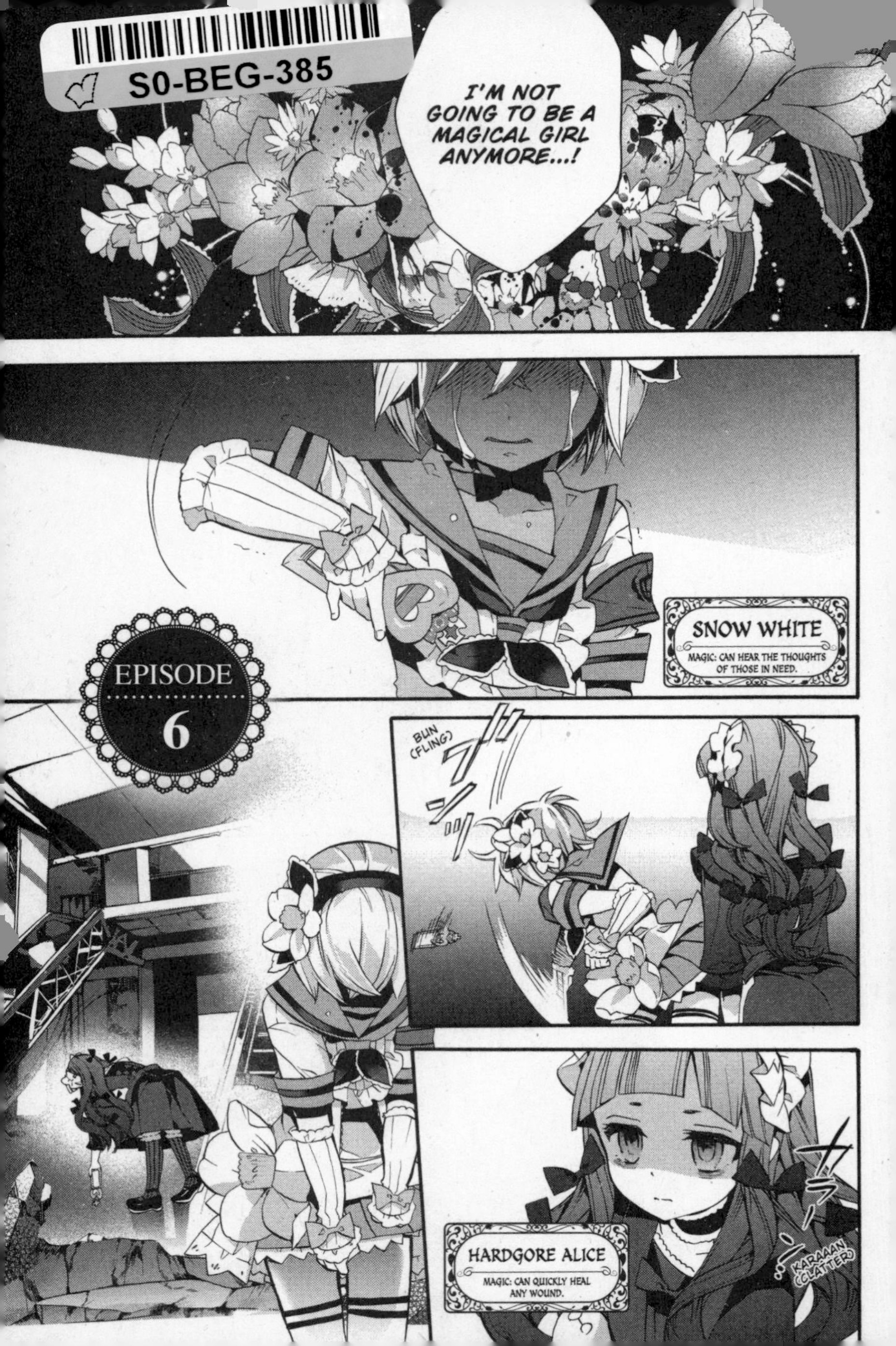
I'M NOT GOING TO BE A MAGICAL GIRL ANYMORE...!
SNOW WHITE
MAGIC: CAN HEAR THE THOUGHTS OF THOSE IN NEED.
EPISODE 6
BUN (FLING)
HARDGORE ALICE
MAGIC: CAN QUICKLY HEAL ANY WOUND.
KARAAAN (CLATTER)

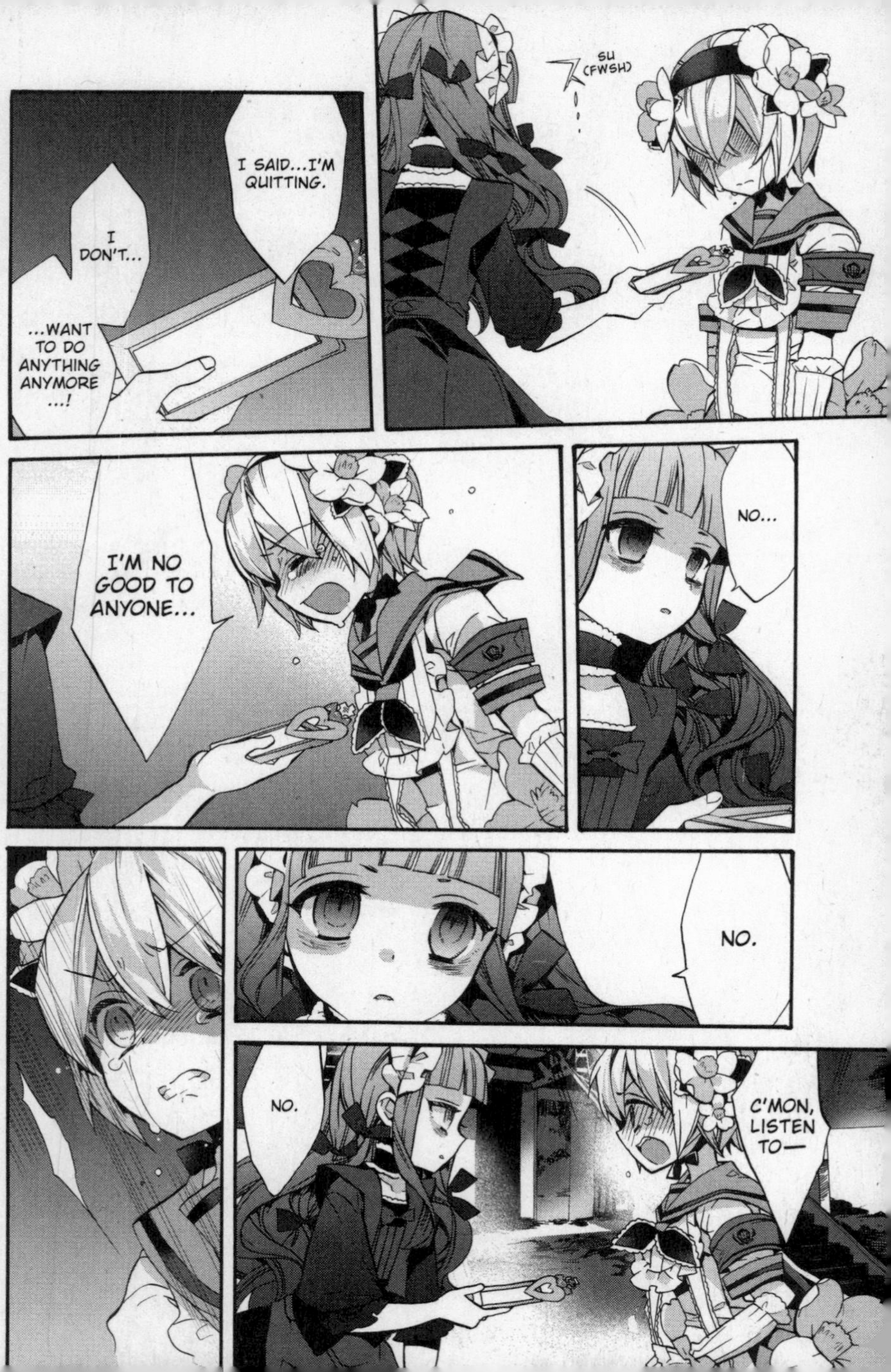
SU (FWSH)
I SAID...I'M QUITTING.
I DON'T...
...WANT TO DO ANYTHING ANYMORE ...!
NO...
I'M NO GOOD TO ANYONE...
NO.
C'MON, LISTEN TO—
NO.

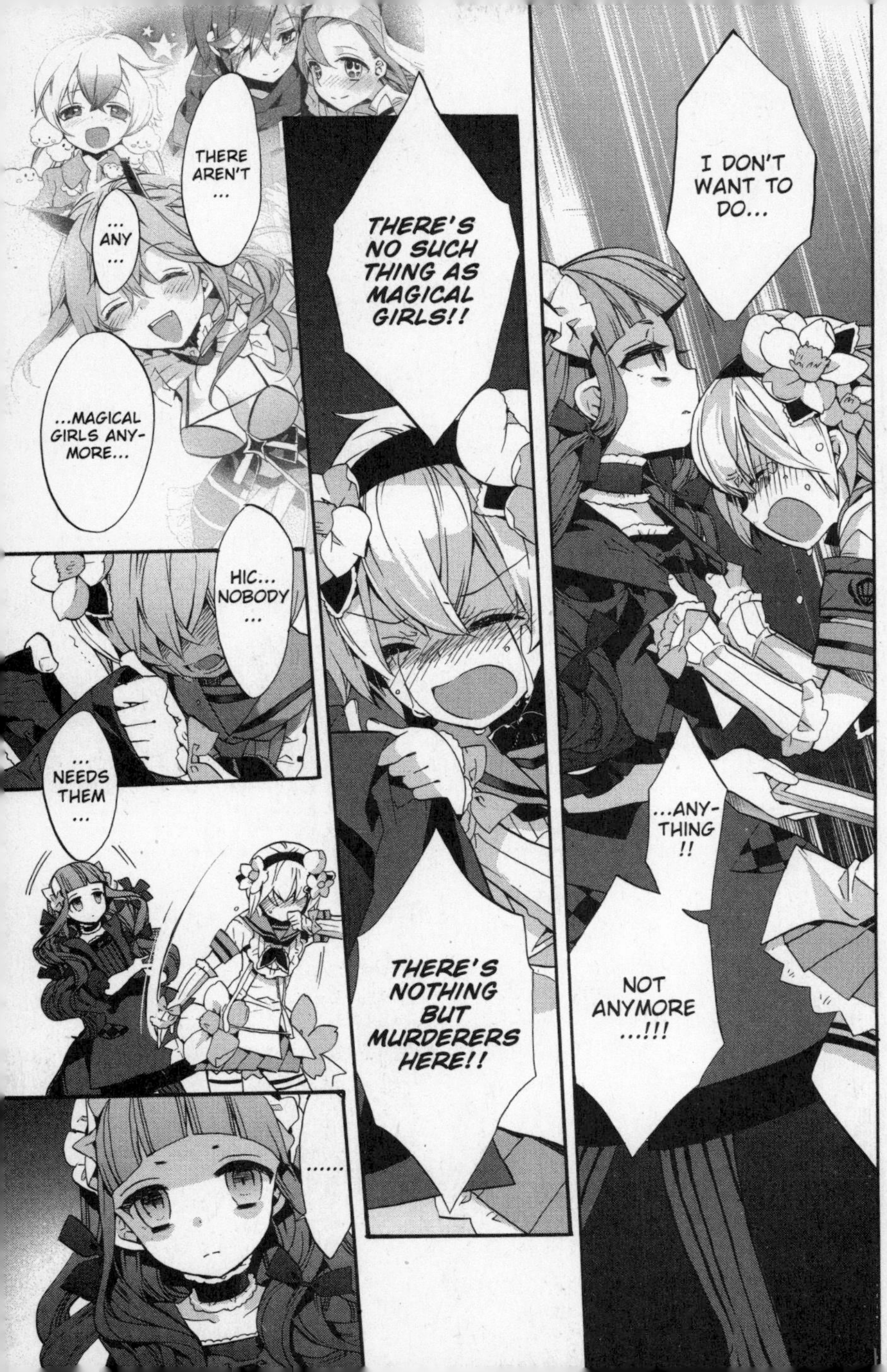
I DON'T WANT TO DO...
...ANYTHING!!
NOT ANYMORE ...!!!
THERE'S NO SUCH THING AS MAGICAL GIRLS!!
THERE'S NOTHING BUT MURDERERS HERE!!
THERE AREN'T ...
... ANY ...
...MAGICAL GIRLS ANYMORE...
HIC... NOBODY ...
... NEEDS THEM ...
......

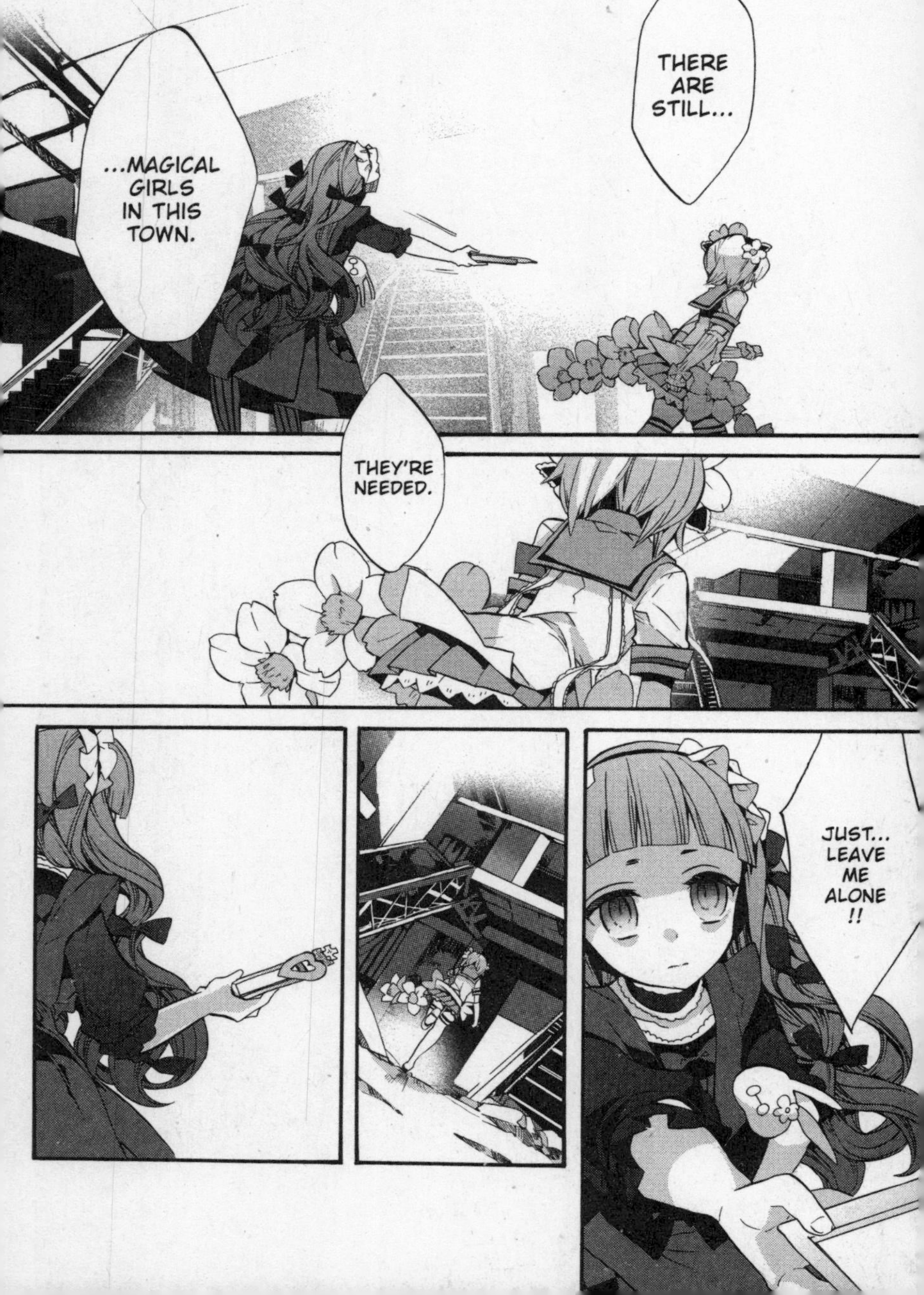
THERE ARE STILL...
...MAGICAL GIRLS IN THIS TOWN.
THEY'RE NEEDED.
JUST... LEAVE ME ALONE !!

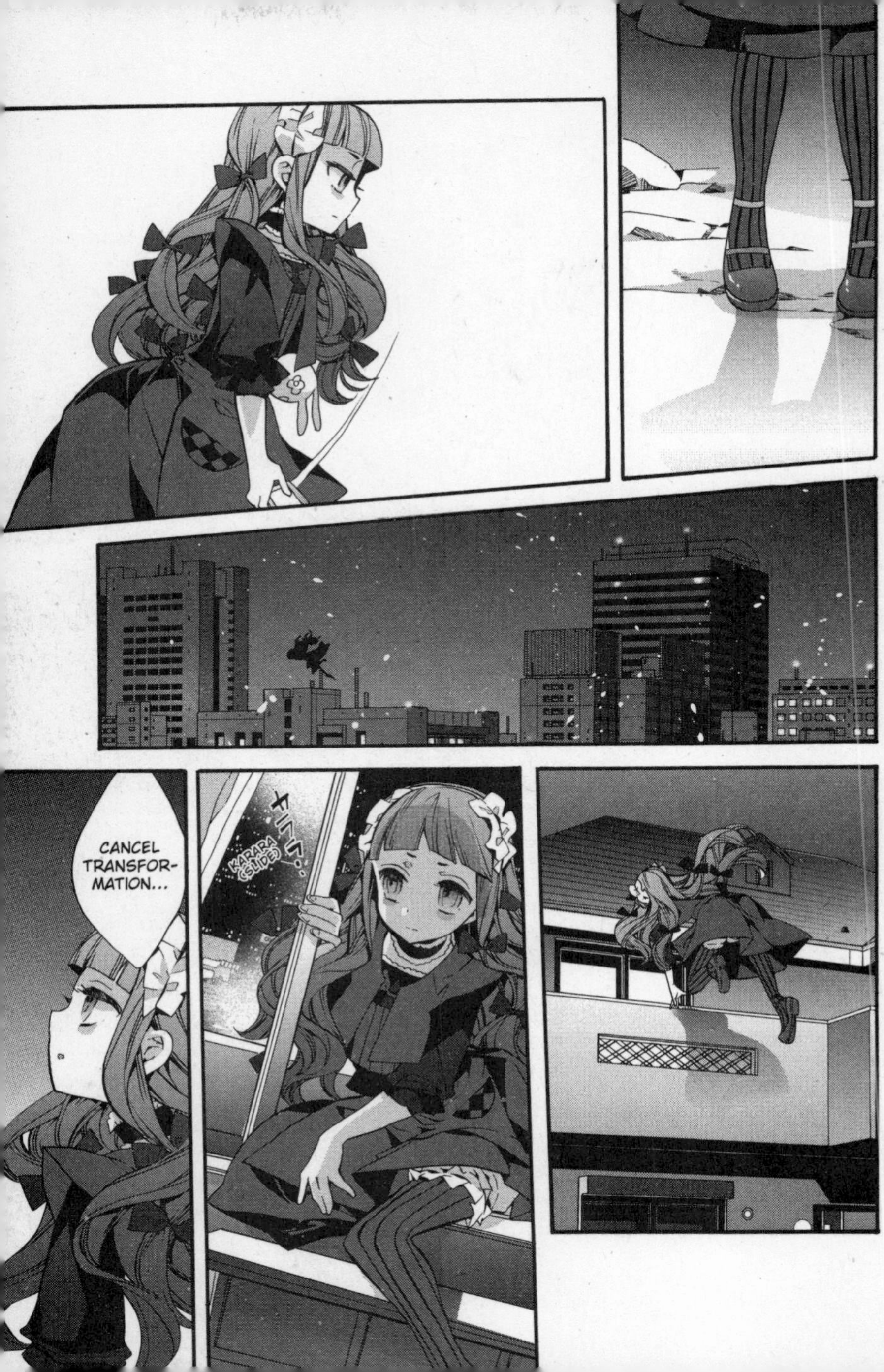
KARARA (SLIDE)
CANCEL TRANSFORMATION...

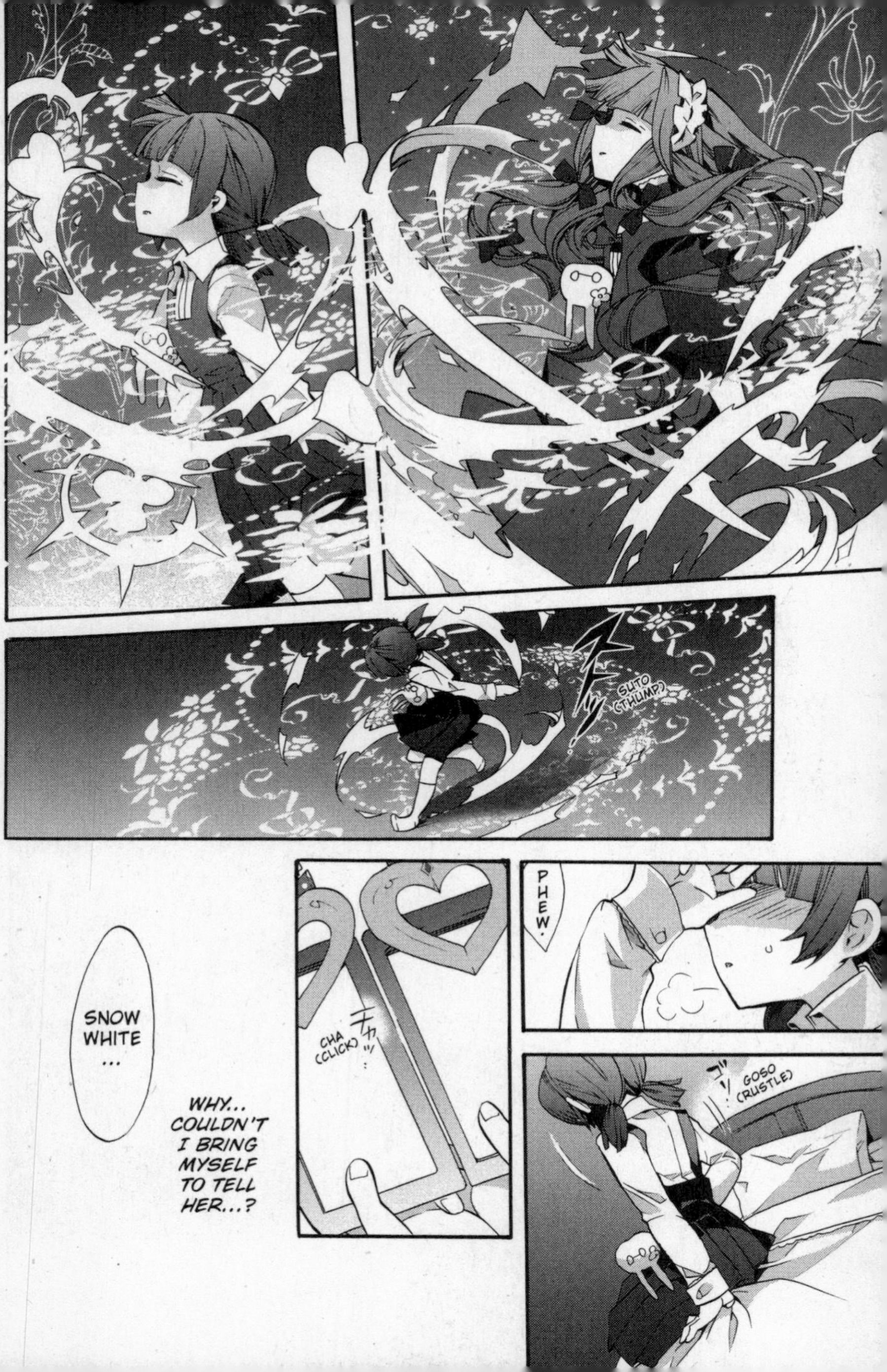
SUTO (THUMP)
PHEW.
GOSO (RUSTLE)
CHA (CLICK)
SNOW WHITE...
WHY... COULDN'T I BRING MYSELF TO TELL HER...?

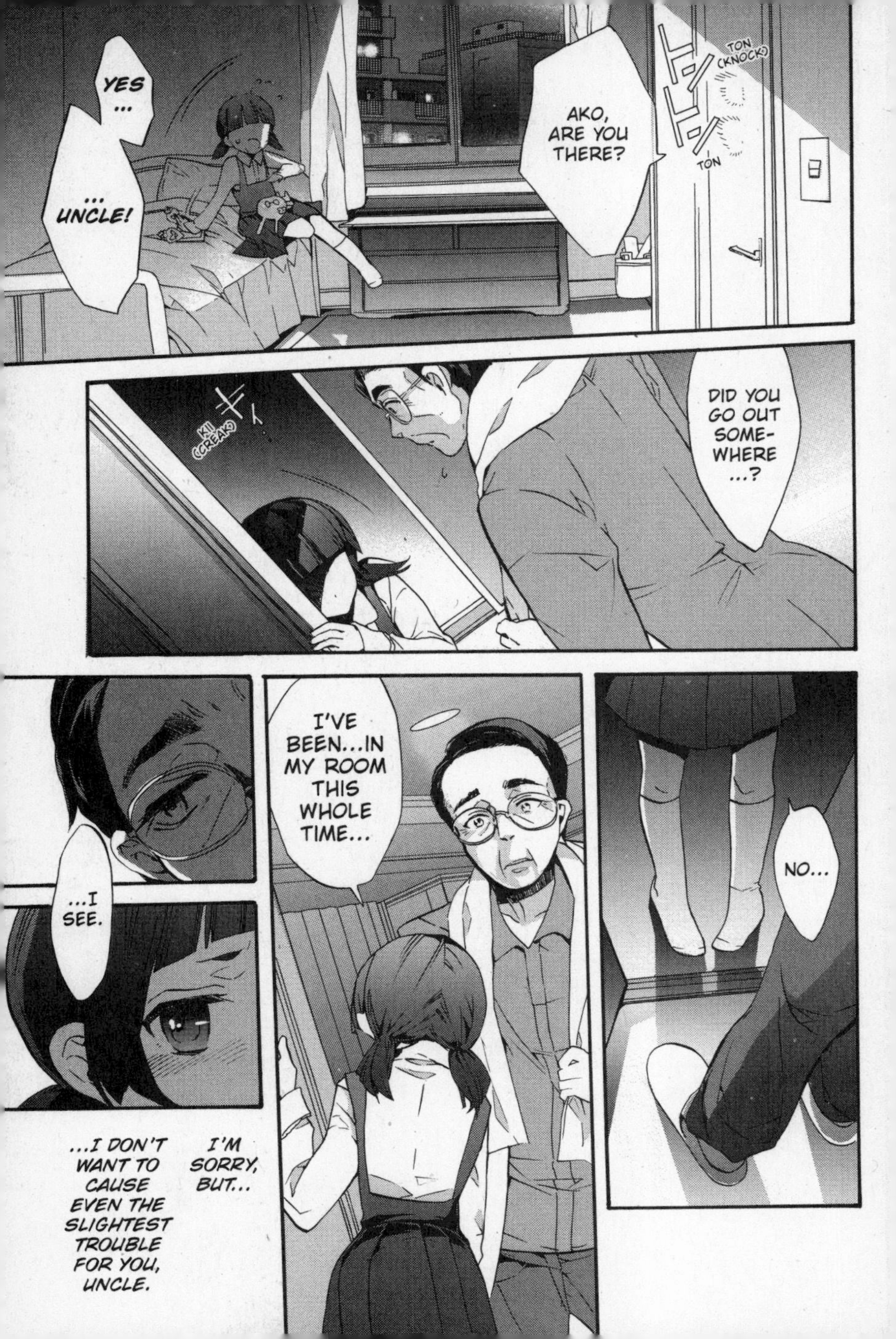
TON (KNOCK)
TON
AKO, ARE YOU THERE?
YES ... ... UNCLE!
DID YOU GO OUT SOME-WHERE ...?
KI! (CREAK)
NO...
I'VE BEEN...IN MY ROOM THIS WHOLE TIME...
...I SEE.
I'M SORRY, BUT...
...I DON'T WANT TO CAUSE EVEN THE SLIGHTEST TROUBLE FOR YOU, UNCLE.

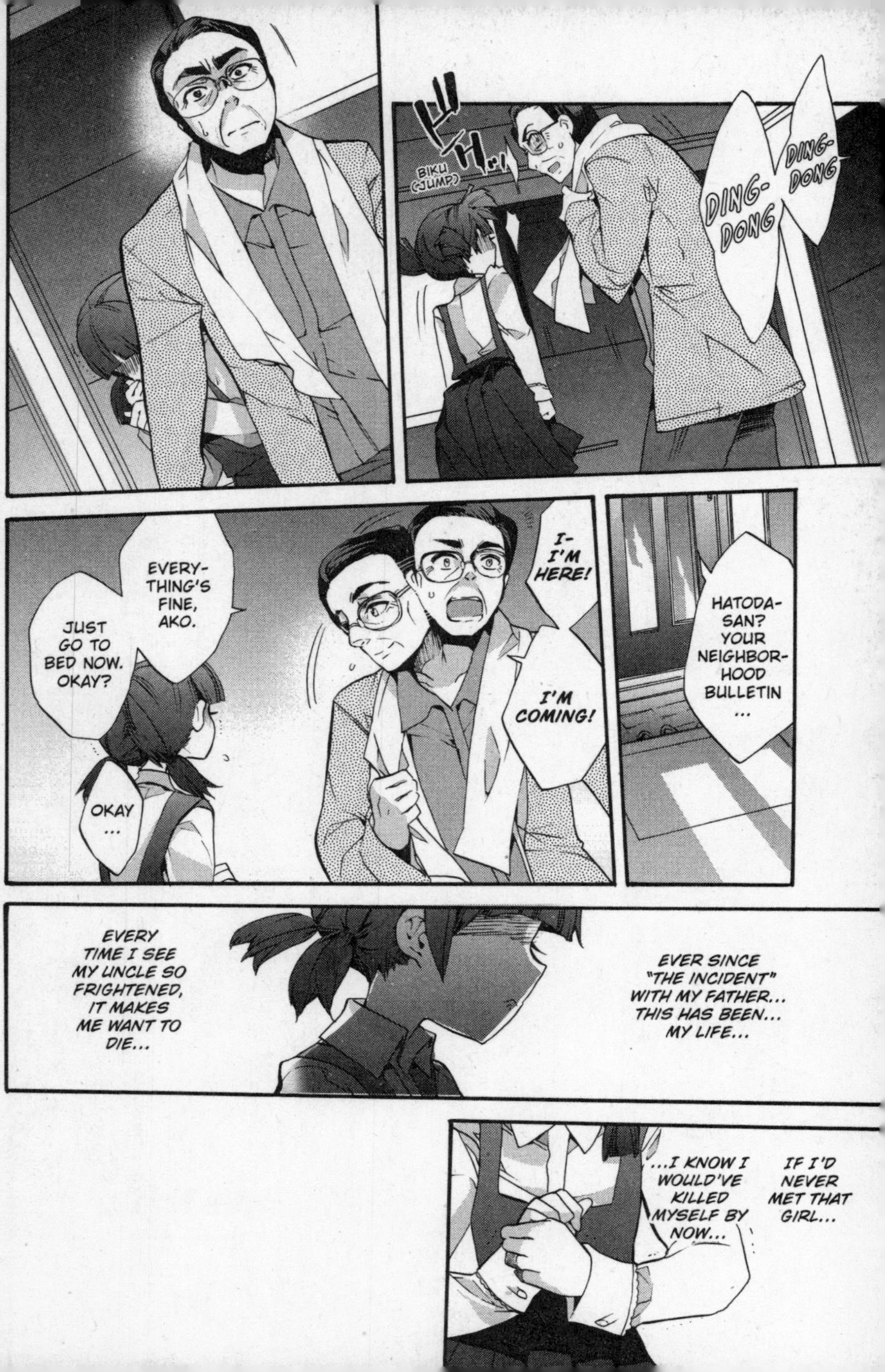
DING-DONG
DING-DONG
BIKU (JUMP)
HATODA-SAN? YOUR NEIGHBOR-HOOD BULLETIN ...
I- I'M HERE!
I'M COMING!
EVERY-THING'S FINE, AKO.
JUST GO TO BED NOW. OKAY?
OKAY ...
EVER SINCE "THE INCIDENT" WITH MY FATHER... THIS HAS BEEN... MY LIFE...
EVERY TIME I SEE MY UNCLE SO FRIGHTENED, IT MAKES ME WANT TO DIE...
IF I'D NEVER MET THAT GIRL...
...I KNOW I WOULD'VE KILLED MYSELF BY NOW...

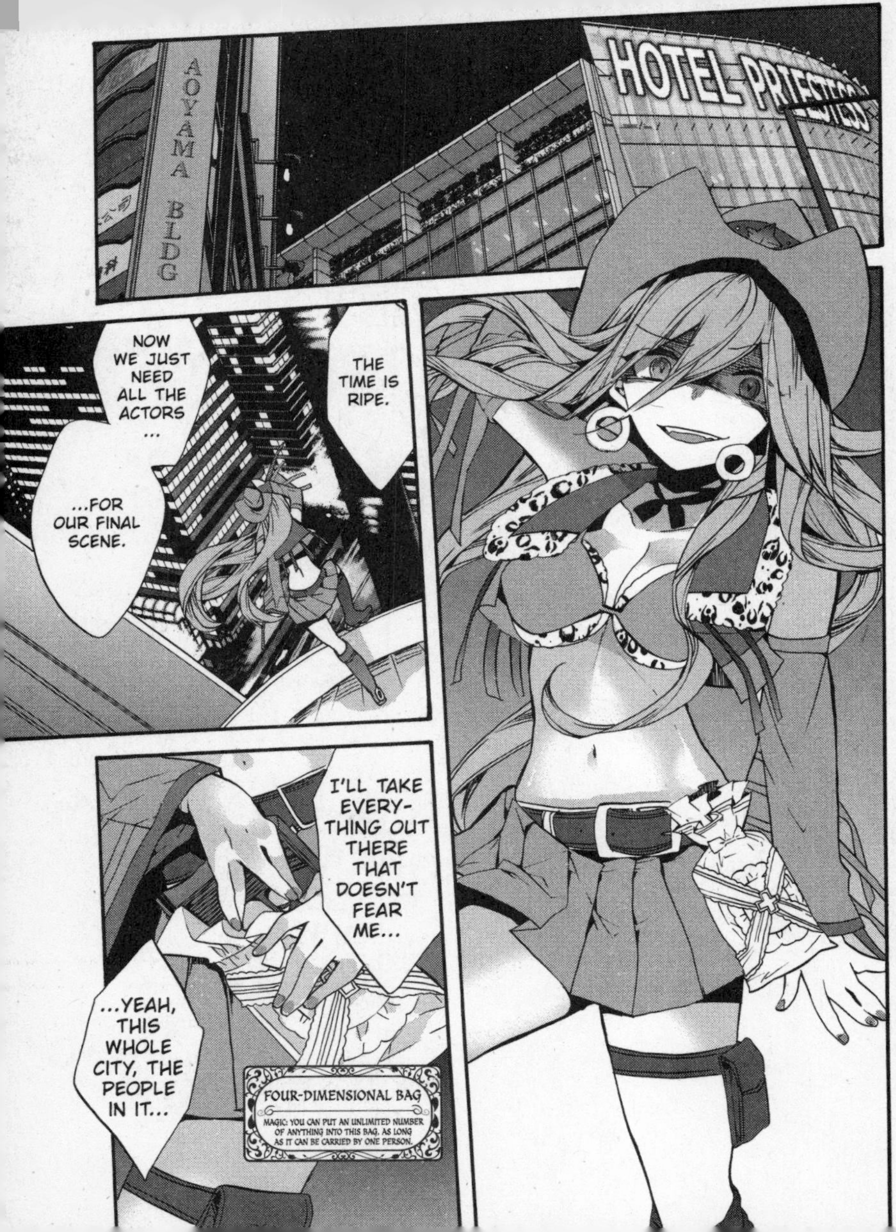
HOTEL PRIESTESS
AOYAMA BLDG
THE TIME IS RIPE.
NOW WE JUST NEED ALL THE ACTORS...
...FOR OUR FINAL SCENE.
I'LL TAKE EVERY-THING OUT THERE THAT DOESN'T FEAR ME...
...YEAH, THIS WHOLE CITY, THE PEOPLE IN IT...
FOUR-DIMENSIONAL BAG
MAGIC: YOU CAN PUT AN UNLIMITED NUMBER OF ANYTHING INTO THIS BAG, AS LONG AS IT CAN BE CARRIED BY ONE PERSON.

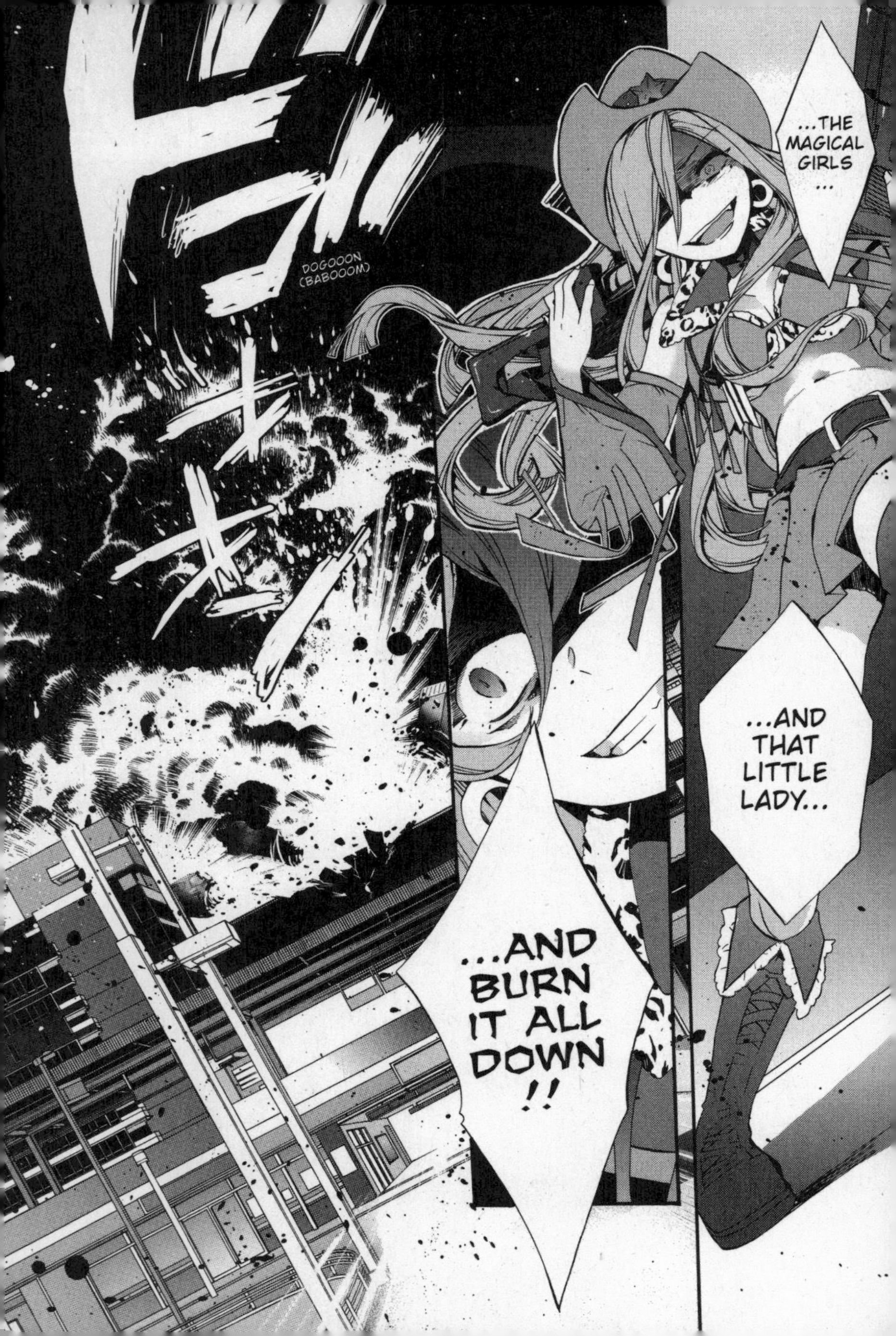
...THE MAGICAL GIRLS ...
...AND THAT LITTLE LADY...
...AND BURN IT ALL DOWN !!
DOGOOON (BABOOOM)

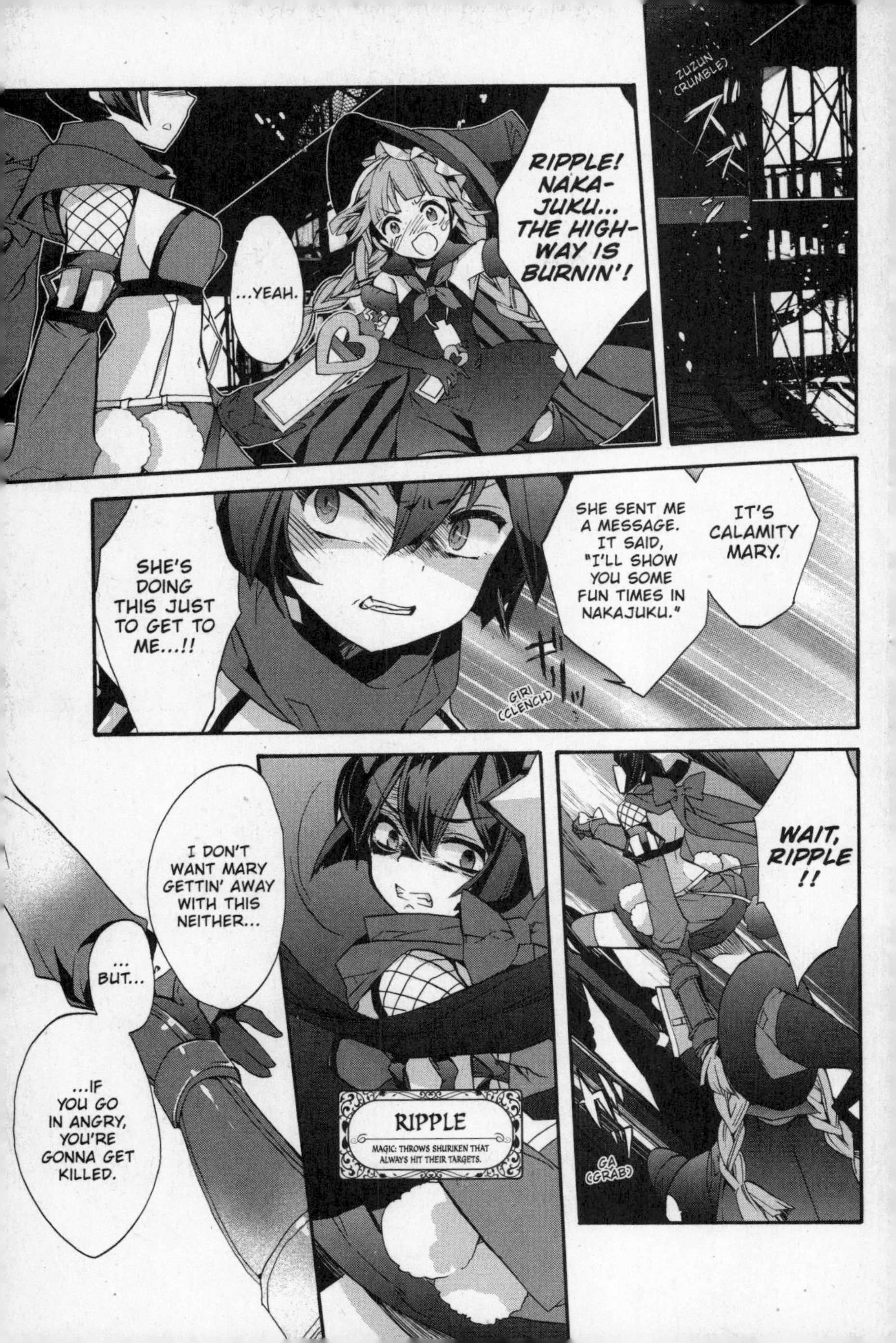
ZUZUN (RUMBLE)
RIPPLE! NAKAJUKU... THE HIGHWAY IS BURNIN'!
...YEAH.
IT'S CALAMITY MARY.
SHE SENT ME A MESSAGE. IT SAID, "I'LL SHOW YOU SOME FUN TIMES IN NAKAJUKU."
GIRI (CLENCH)
SHE'S DOING THIS JUST TO GET TO ME...!!
WAIT, RIPPLE!!
GA (GRAB)
I DON'T WANT MARY GETTIN' AWAY WITH THIS NEITHER...
...BUT...
...IF YOU GO IN ANGRY, YOU'RE GONNA GET KILLED.
RIPPLE
MAGIC: THROWS SHURIKEN THAT ALWAYS HIT THEIR TARGETS.

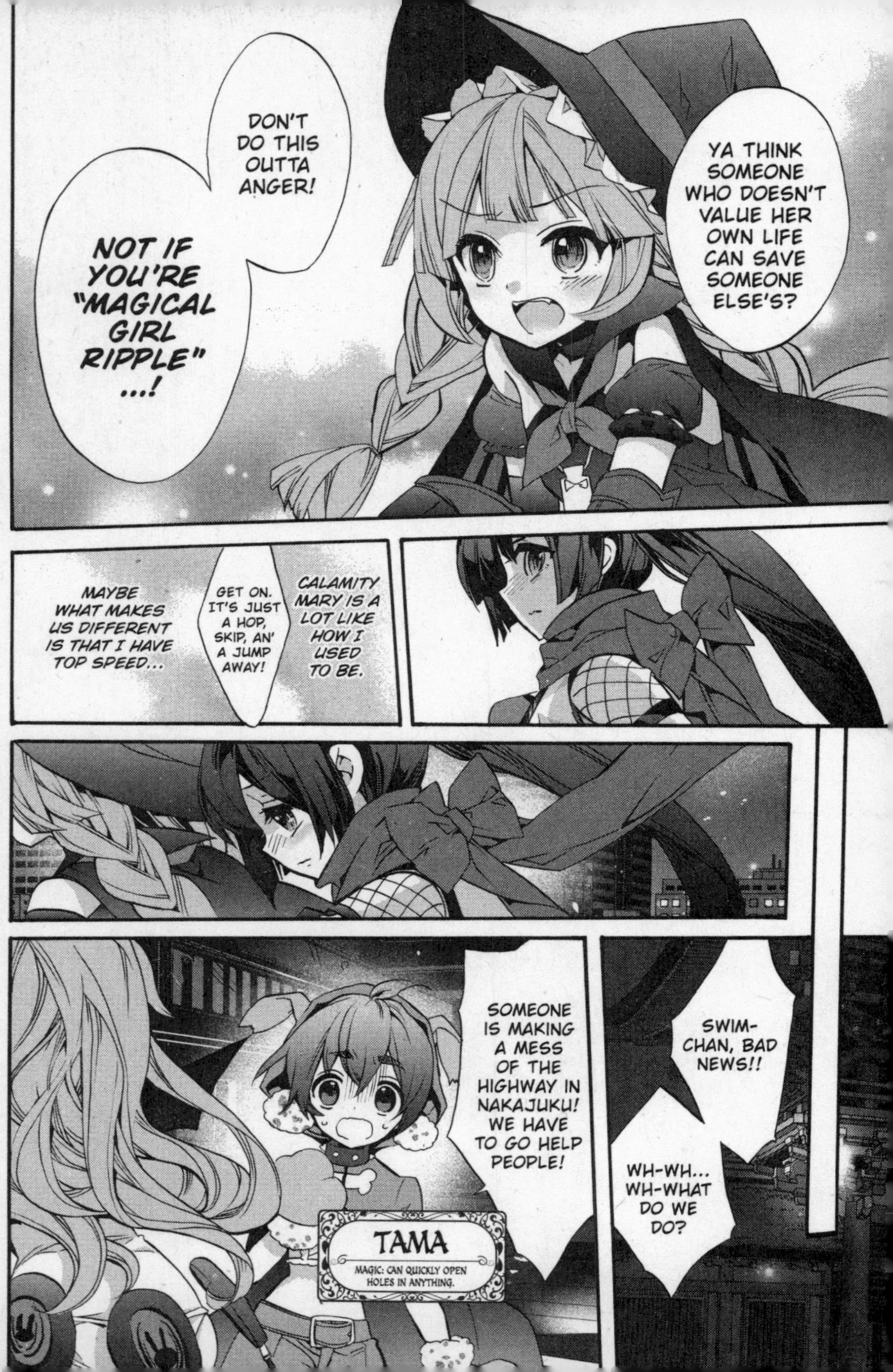
YA THINK SOMEONE WHO DOESN'T VALUE HER OWN LIFE CAN SAVE SOMEONE ELSE'S?
DON'T DO THIS OUTTA ANGER!
NOT IF YOU'RE "MAGICAL GIRL RIPPLE" ...!
CALAMITY MARY IS A LOT LIKE HOW I USED TO BE.
GET ON. IT'S JUST A HOP, SKIP, AN' A JUMP AWAY!
MAYBE WHAT MAKES US DIFFERENT IS THAT I HAVE TOP SPEED...
SWIM-CHAN, BAD NEWS!!
WH-WH... WH-WHAT DO WE DO?
SOMEONE IS MAKING A MESS OF THE HIGHWAY IN NAKAJUKU! WE HAVE TO GO HELP PEOPLE!
TAMA
MAGIC: CAN QUICKLY OPEN HOLES IN ANYTHING.

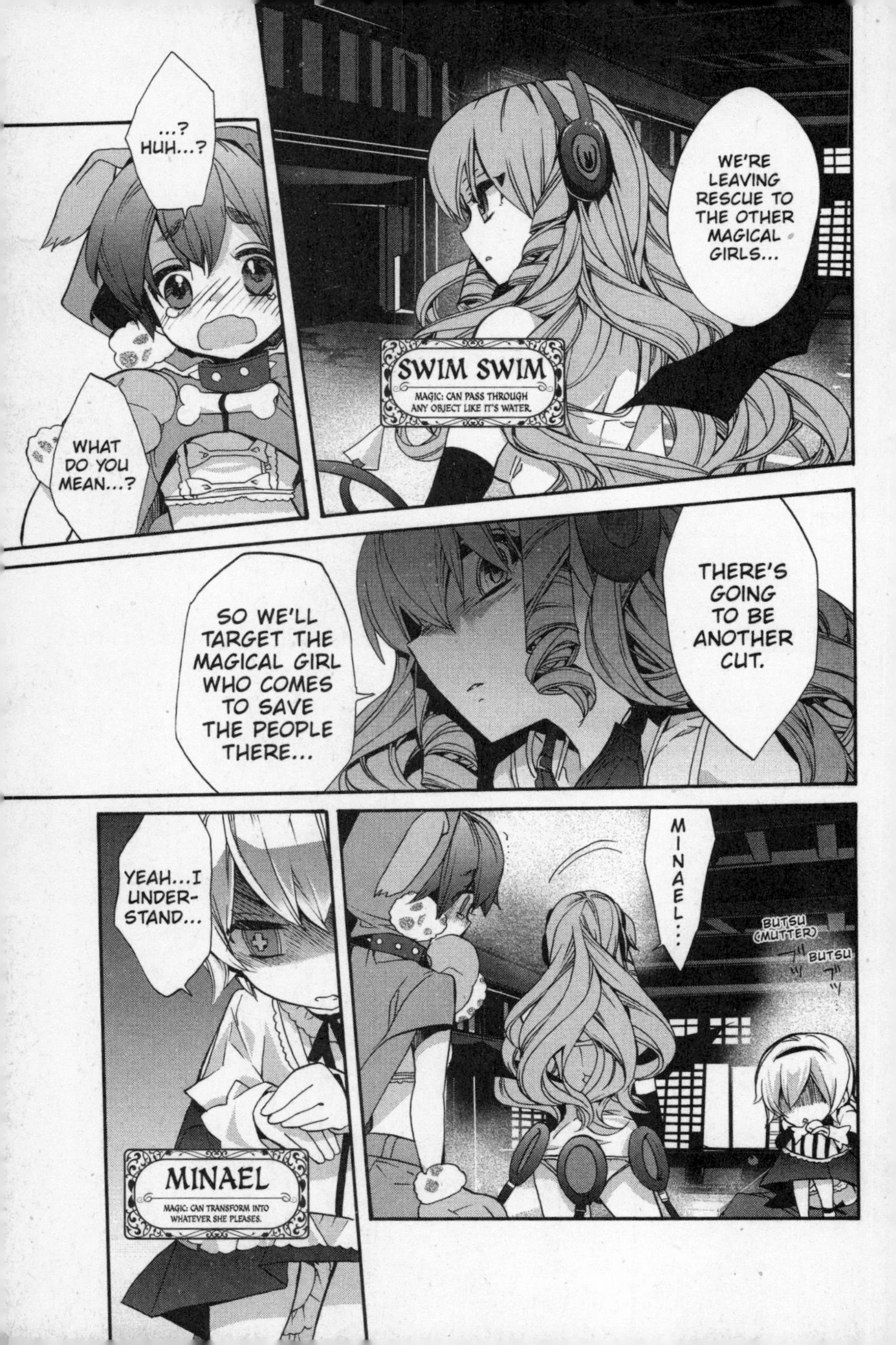
WE'RE LEAVING RESCUE TO THE OTHER MAGICAL GIRLS...
SWIM SWIM
MAGIC: CAN PASS THROUGH ANY OBJECT LIKE IT'S WATER.
...? HUH...?
WHAT DO YOU MEAN...?
THERE'S GOING TO BE ANOTHER CUT.
SO WE'LL TARGET THE MAGICAL GIRL WHO COMES TO SAVE THE PEOPLE THERE...
MINAEL...
BUTSU (MUTTER)
BUTSU
YEAH...I UNDER-STAND...
MINAEL
MAGIC: CAN TRANSFORM INTO WHATEVER SHE PLEASES.

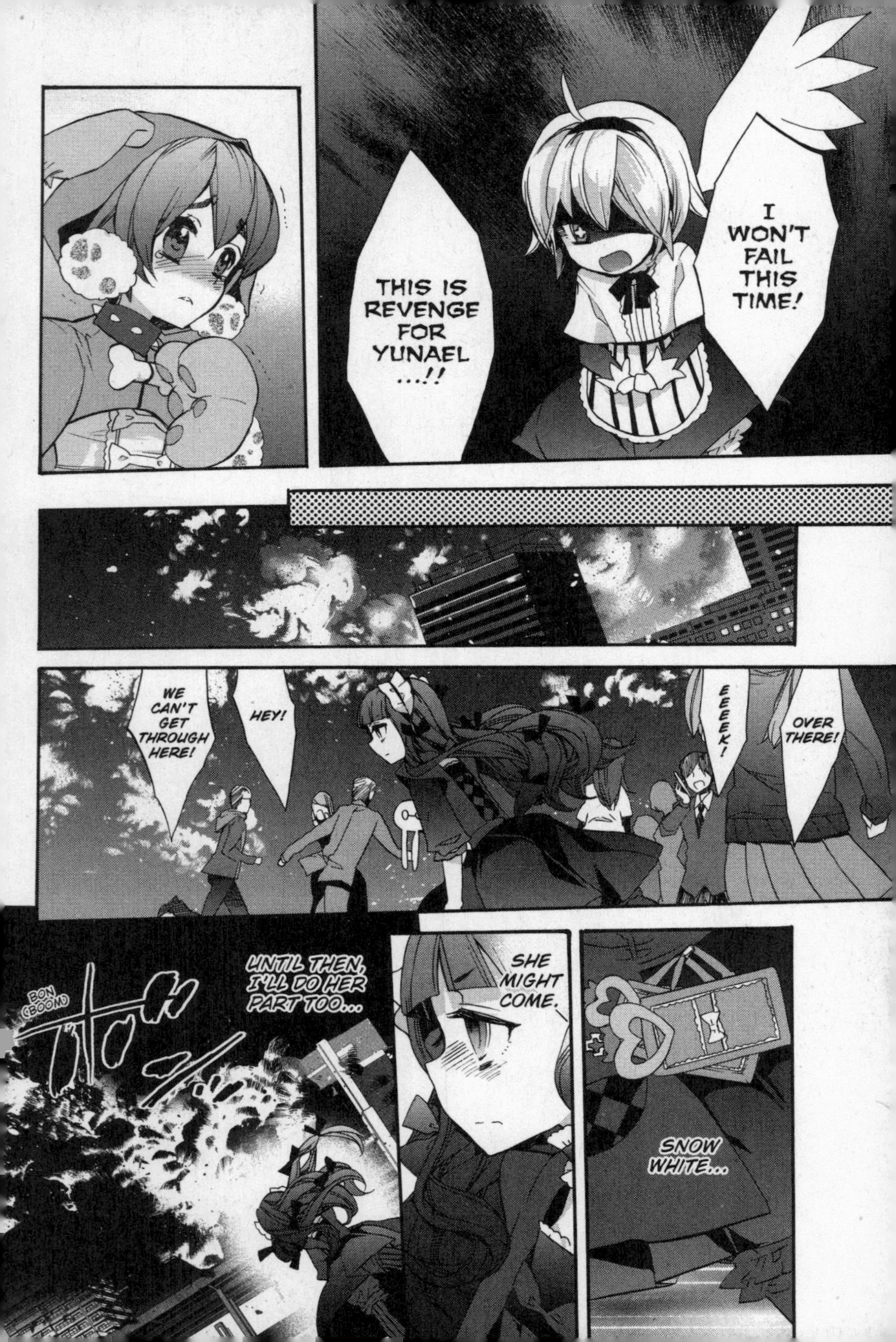
I WON'T FAIL THIS TIME!
THIS IS REVENGE FOR YUNAEL ...!!
OVER THERE!
EEEEK!
HEY!
WE CAN'T GET THROUGH HERE!
SNOW WHITE...
SHE MIGHT COME.
UNTIL THEN, I'LL DO HER PART TOO...
BON (BOOM)

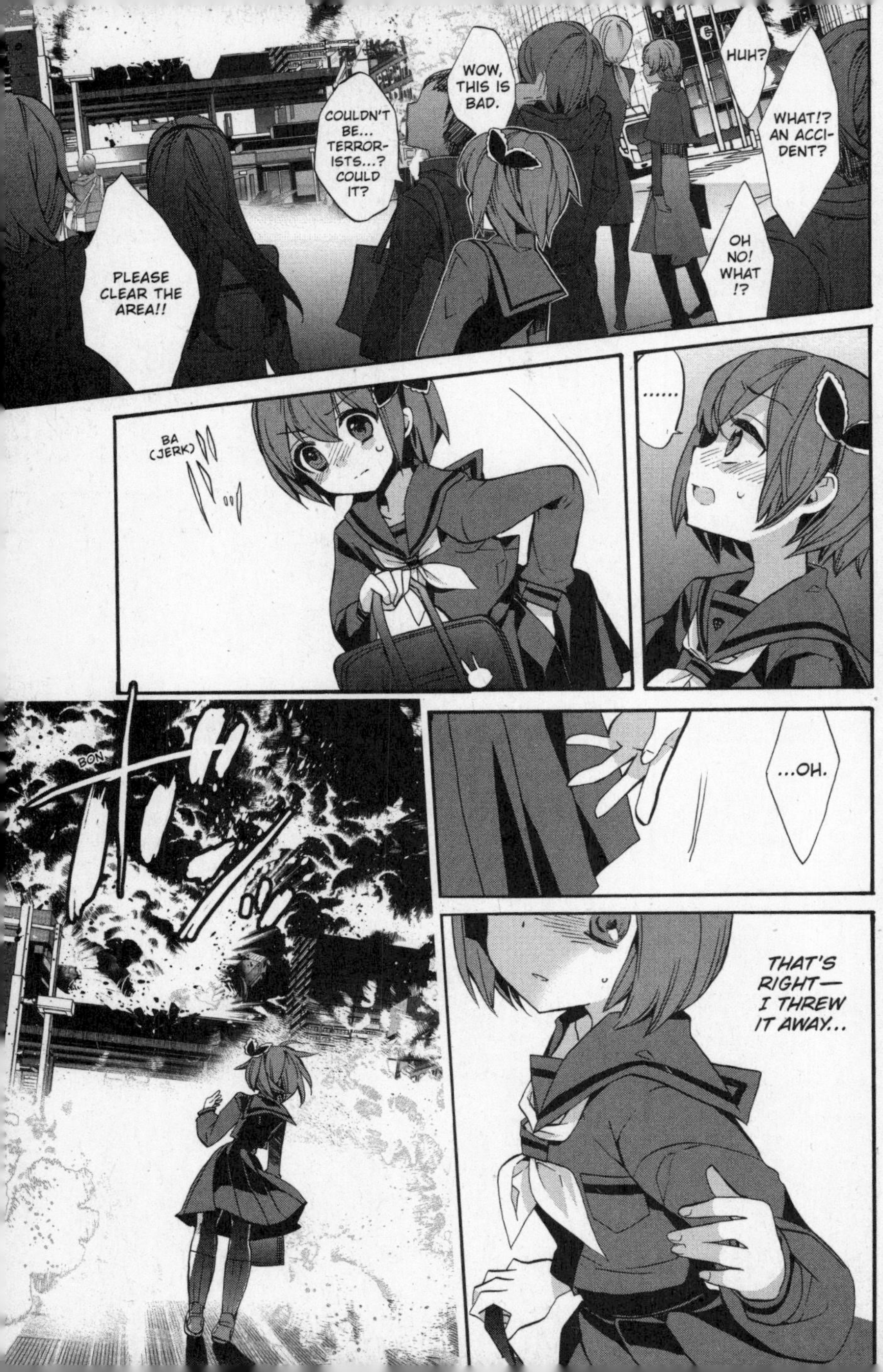
WHAT!? AN ACCI-DENT?
HUH?
OH NO! WHAT!?
WOW, THIS IS BAD.
COULDN'T BE... TERROR-ISTS...? COULD IT?
PLEASE CLEAR THE AREA!!
......
BA (JERK)
...OH.
THAT'S RIGHT— I THREW IT AWAY...
BON

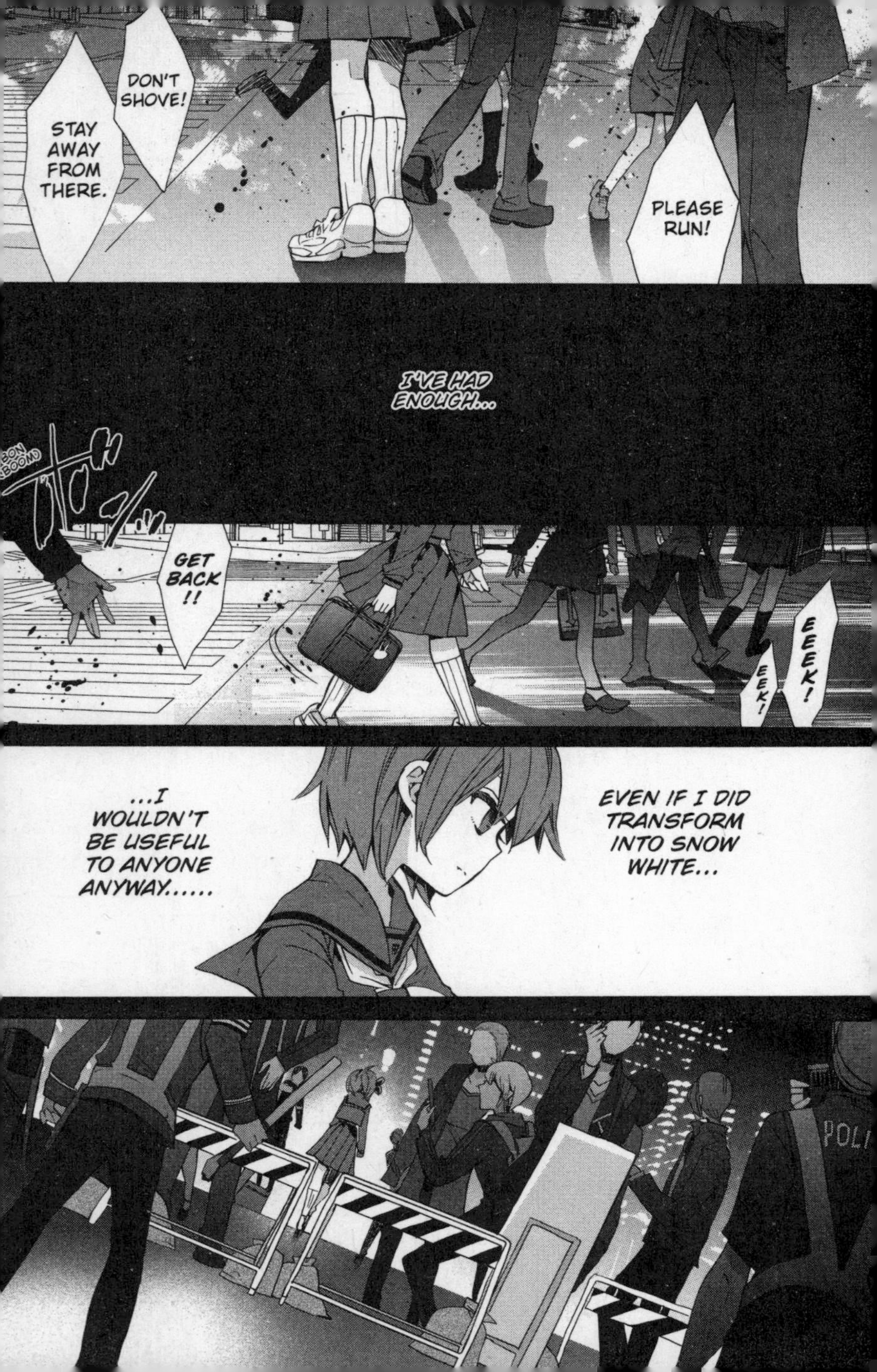
PLEASE RUN!
DON'T SHOVE!
STAY AWAY FROM THERE.
I'VE HAD ENOUGH...
EEEK!
EEEK!
GET BACK!!
EVEN IF I DID TRANSFORM INTO SNOW WHITE...
...I WOULDN'T BE USEFUL TO ANYONE ANYWAY......
POLI

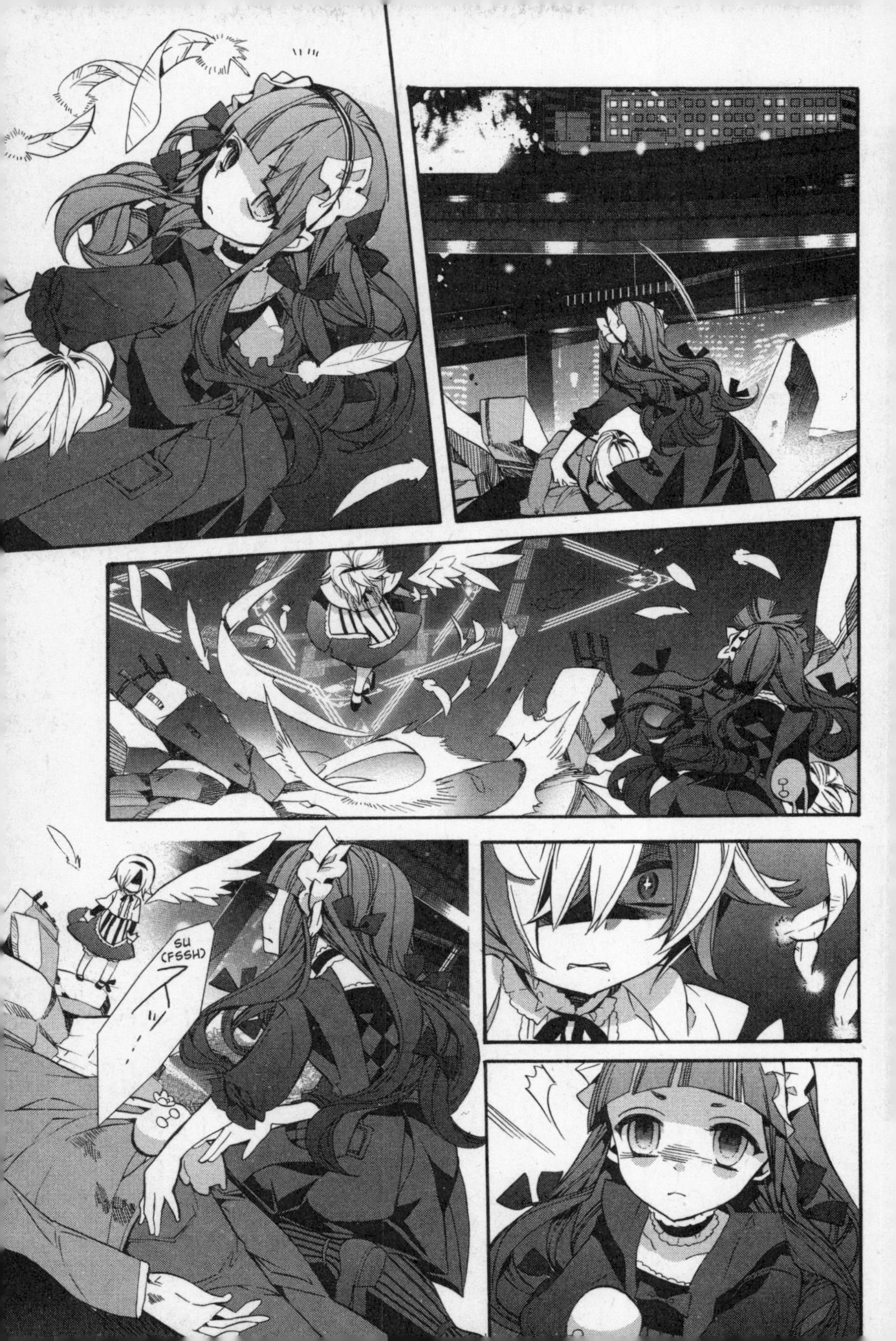
SU
(FSSH)

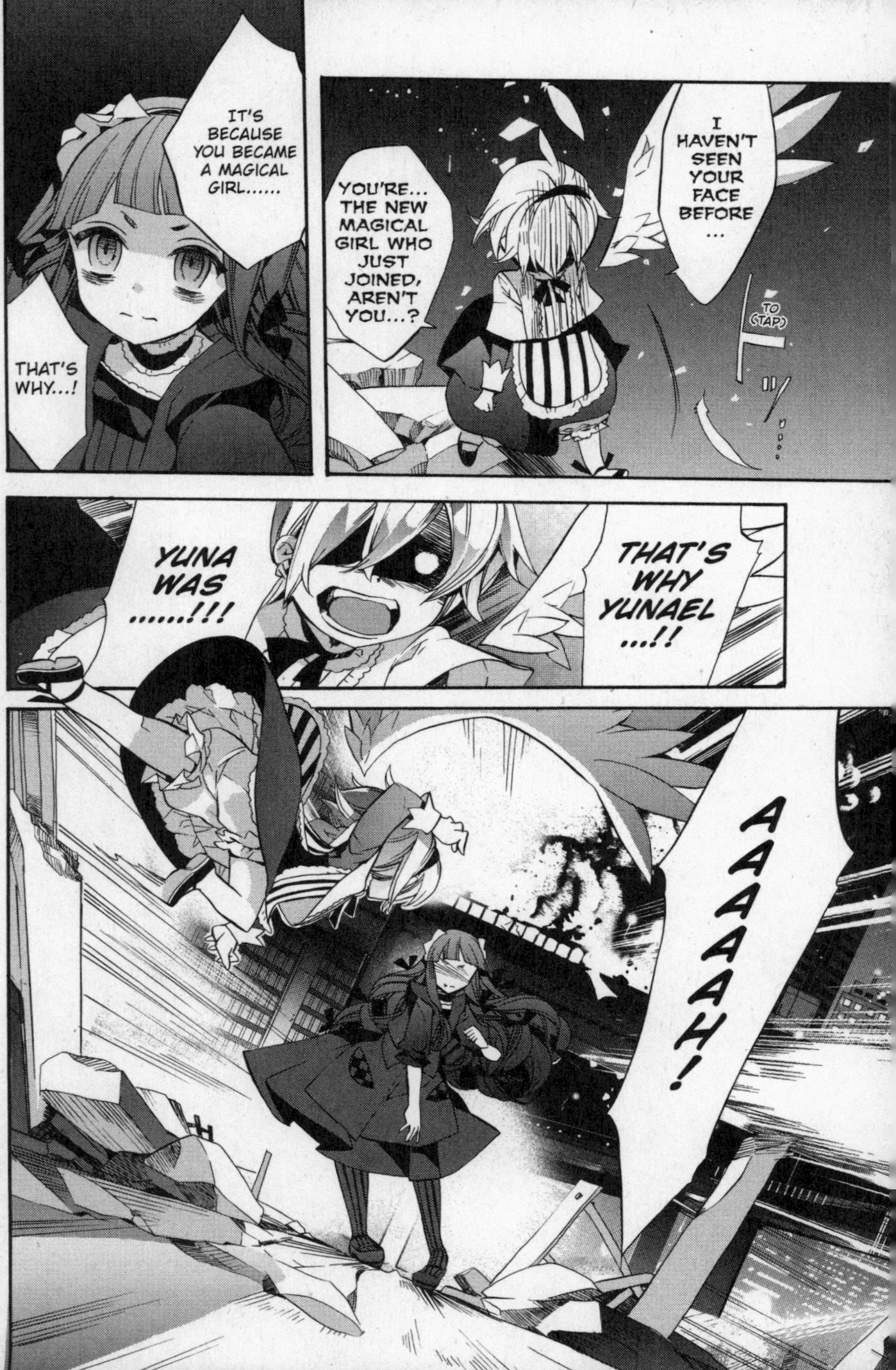
I HAVEN'T SEEN YOUR FACE BEFORE ...
TO (TAP)
YOU'RE... THE NEW MAGICAL GIRL WHO JUST JOINED, AREN'T YOU...?
IT'S BECAUSE YOU BECAME A MAGICAL GIRL......
THAT'S WHY...!
THAT'S WHY YUNAEL ...!!
YUNA WAS ......!!!
AAAAAAH!

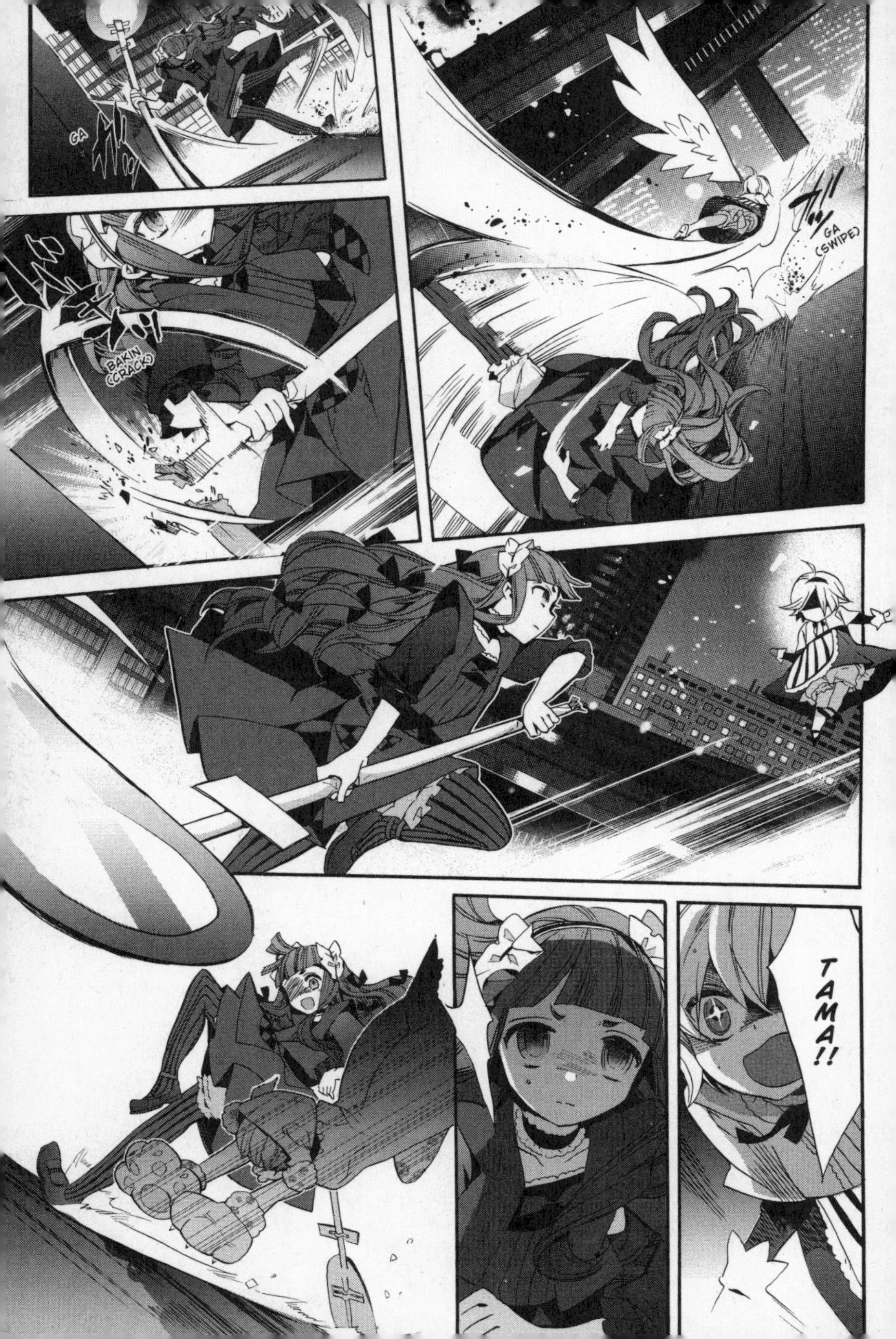
GA
GA (SWIPE)
BAKIN (CRACK)
TAMA!!

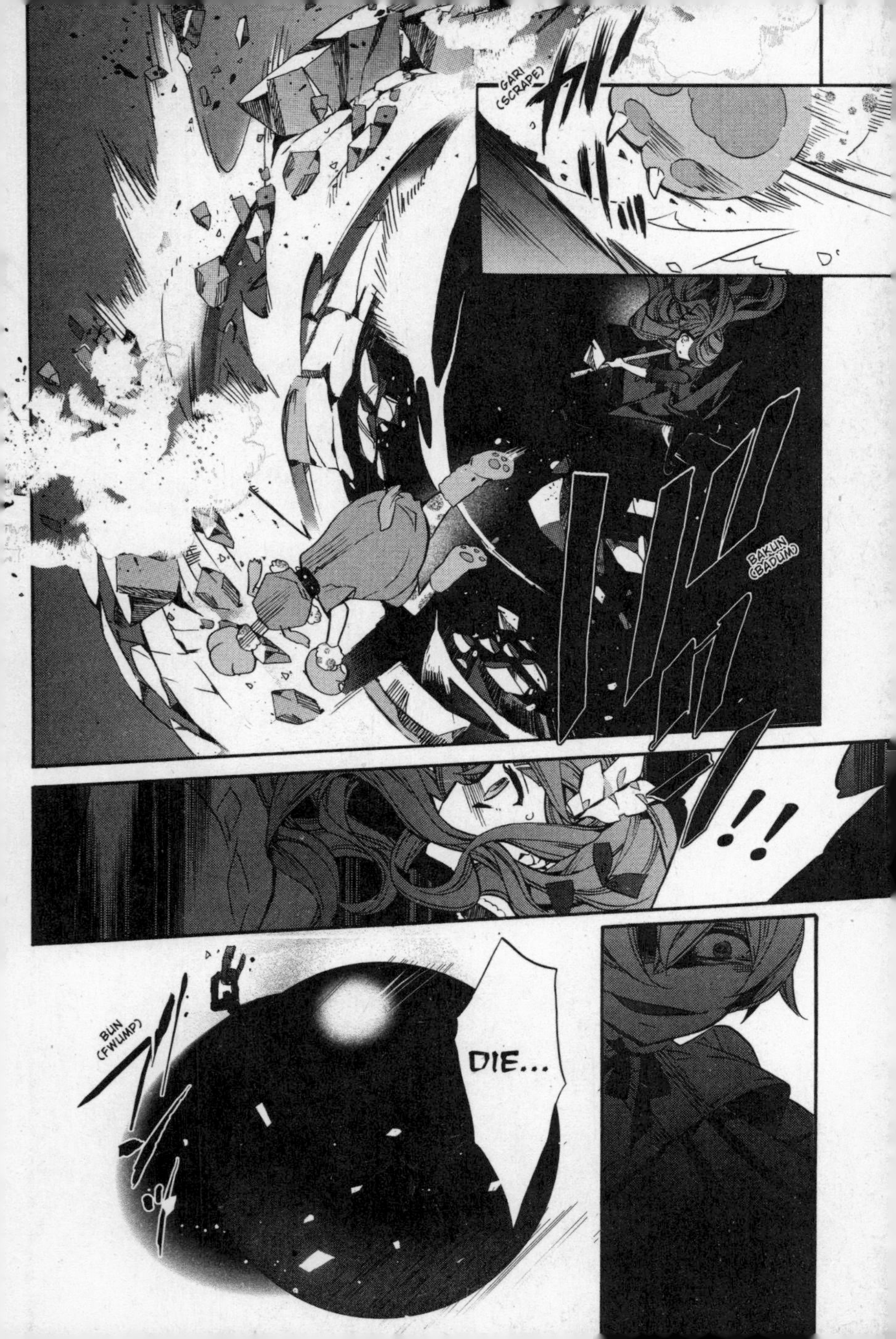
GARI (SCRAPE)
BAKUN (BADUM)
!!
DIE...
BUN (FWUMP)

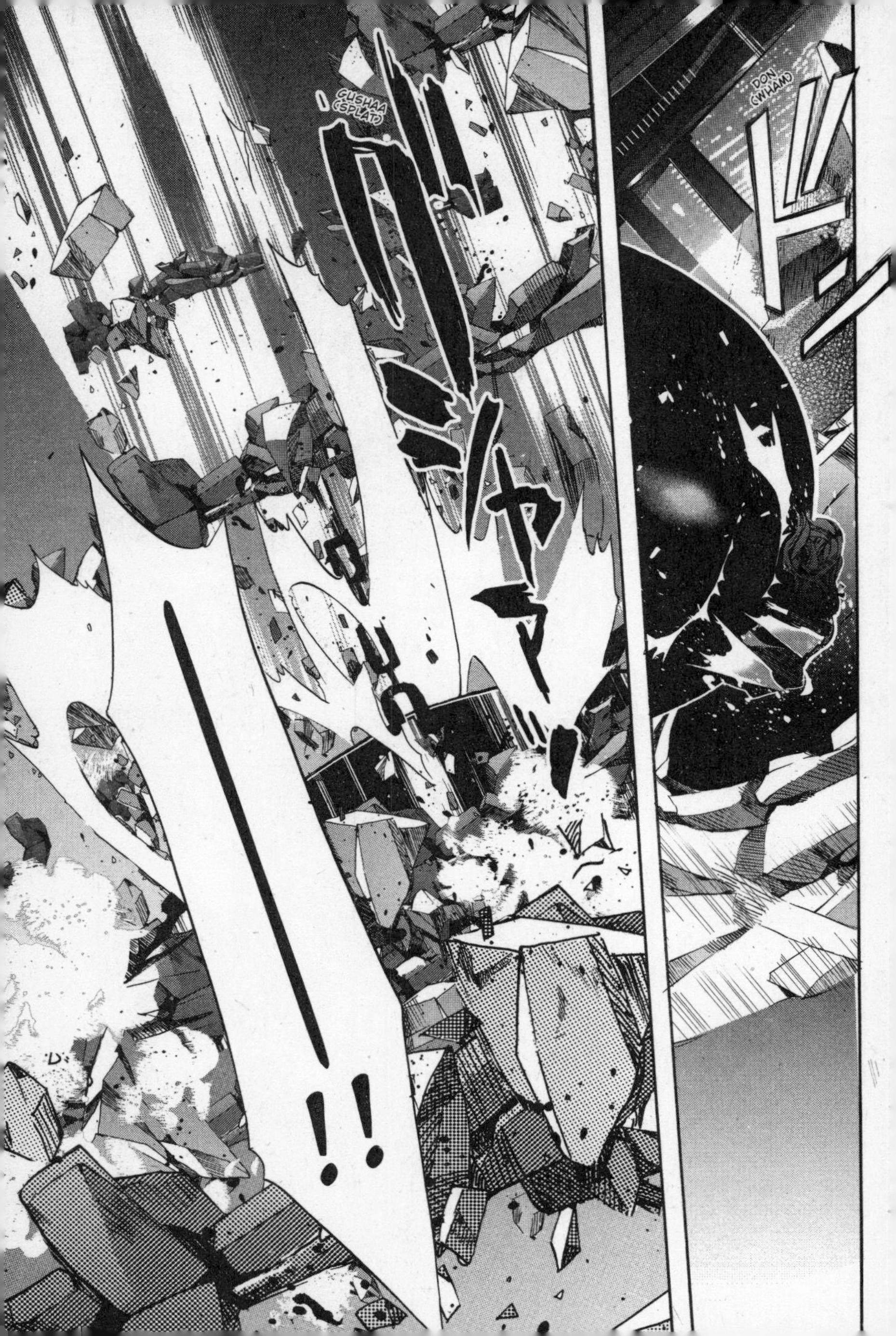
DON (WHAM)
GUSHAA (SPLAT)
―――!!

...I
DID IT.

ゾ
ゾ
ッ
!
ZO
(SHIVER)

．．．．

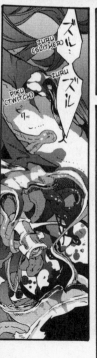

ズ
ル
ッ
!
ZURU
(SLITHER)

ZURU
ズ
ル

PIKU
(TWITCH)

AH
...

I DID IT,
YUNAEL!!

AH
HA
HA
HA!

WAIT,
MINA-
CHAN!!

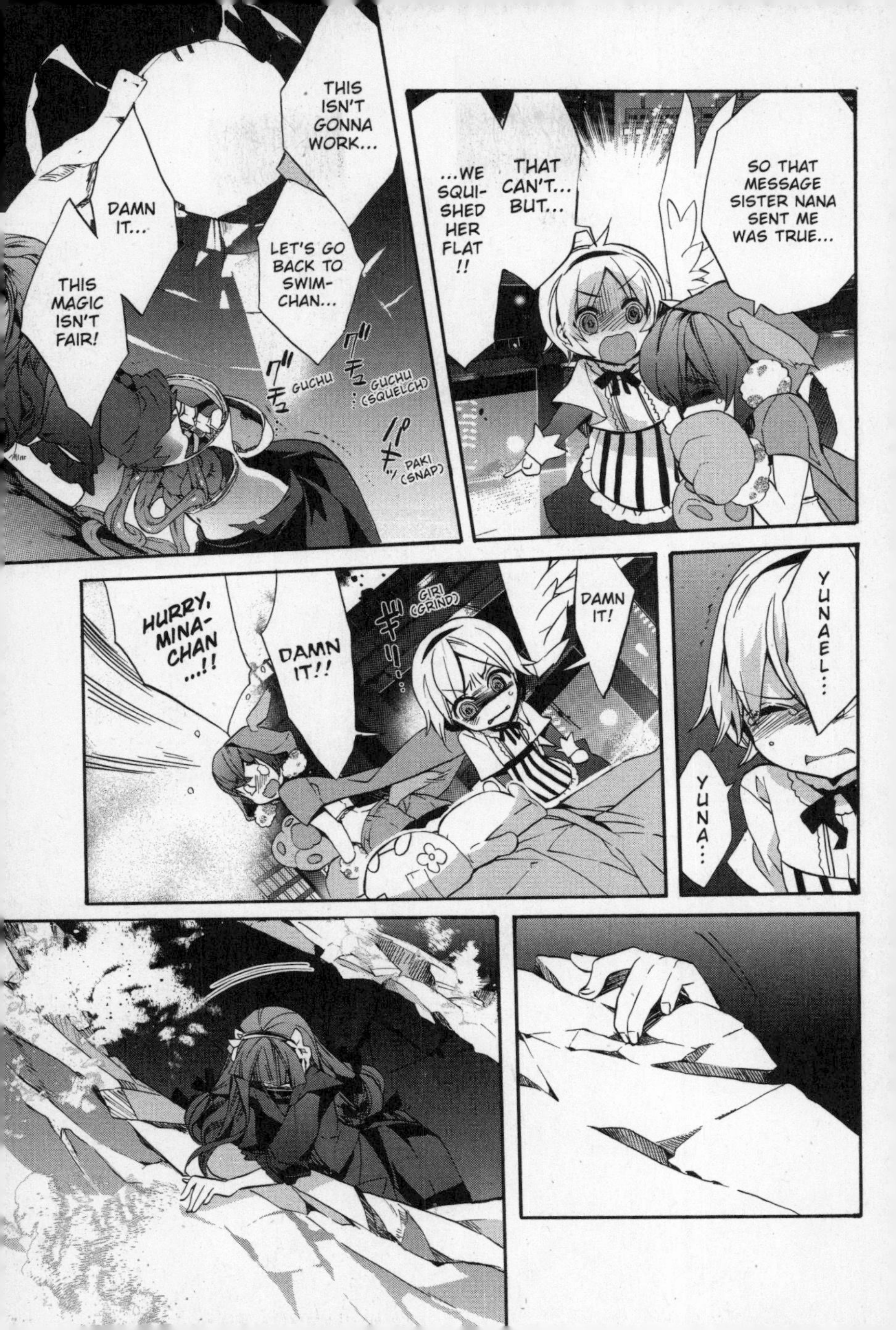
SO THAT MESSAGE SISTER NANA SENT ME WAS TRUE...
THAT CAN'T... BUT...
...WE SQUISHED HER FLAT!!
THIS ISN'T GONNA WORK...
LET'S GO BACK TO SWIM-CHAN...
GUCHU (SQUELCH)
GUCHU
PAKI (SNAP)
DAMN IT...
THIS MAGIC ISN'T FAIR!
YUNAEL...
YUNA...
DAMN IT!
GIRI (GRIND)
DAMN IT!!
HURRY, MINA-CHAN...!!

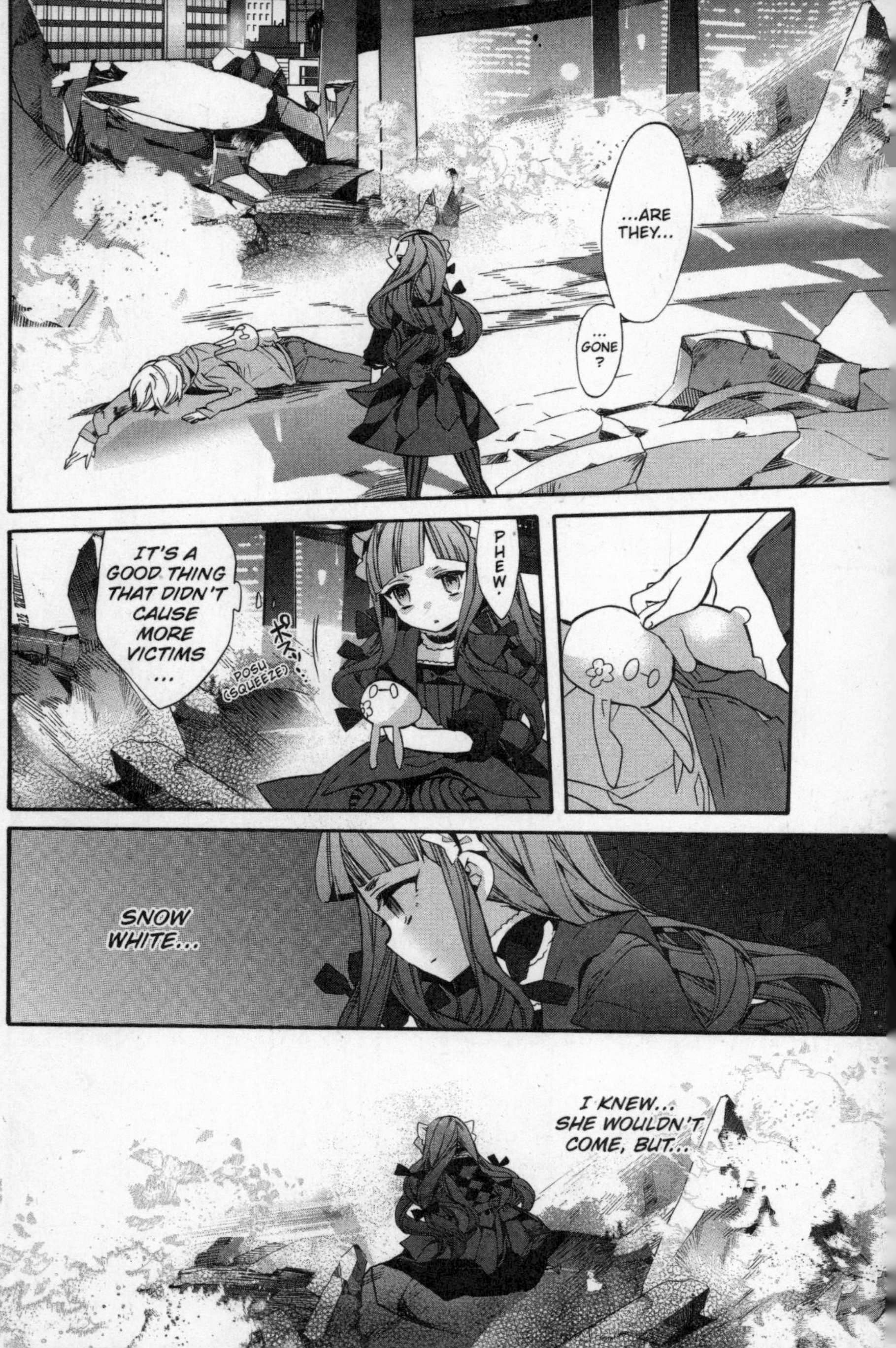
...ARE THEY...
...GONE?
PHEW.
IT'S A GOOD THING THAT DIDN'T CAUSE MORE VICTIMS...
POSU (SQUEEZE)
SNOW WHITE...
I KNEW... SHE WOULDN'T COME, BUT...

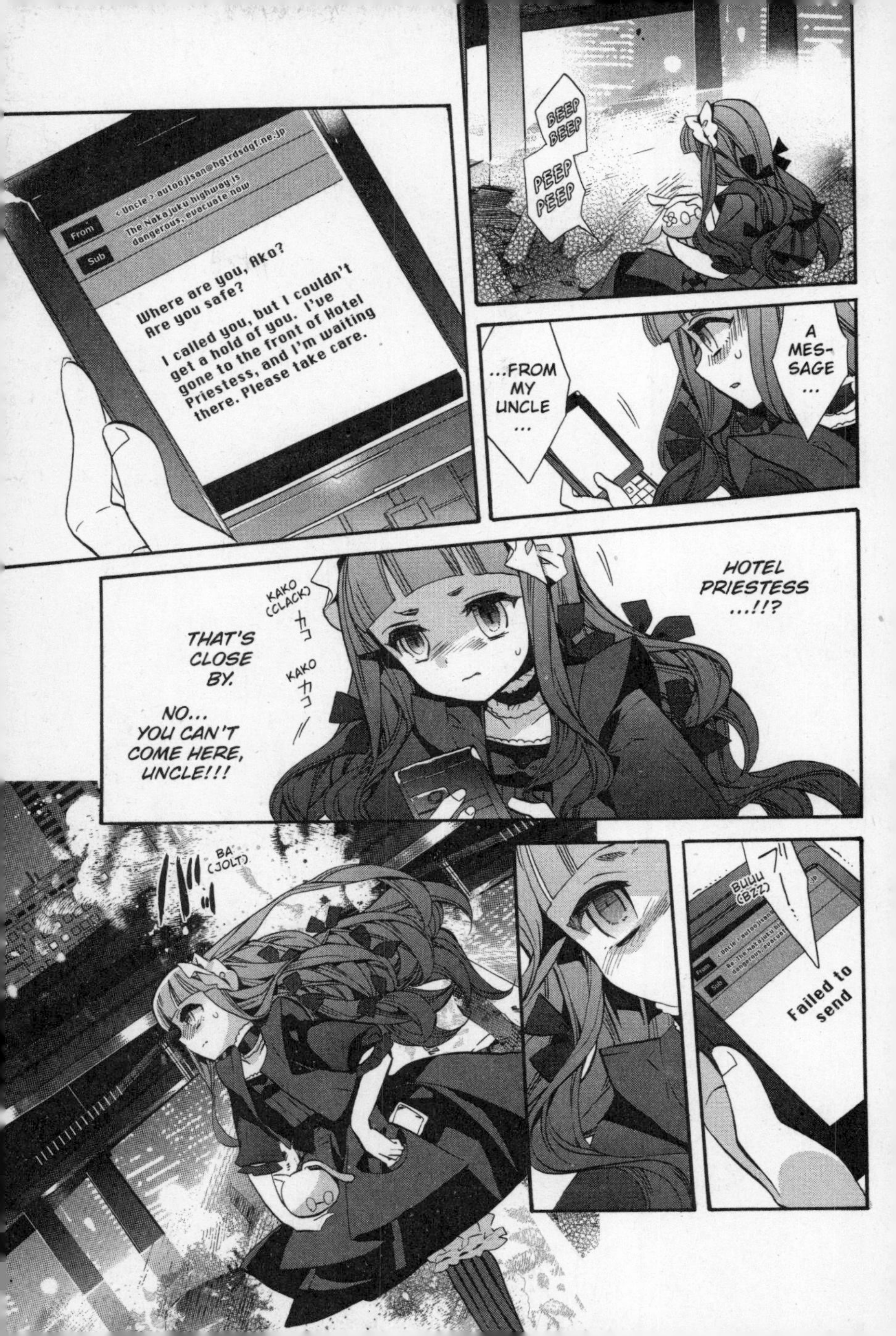

BEEP BEEP
PEEP PEEP
A MES-SAGE...
...FROM MY UNCLE...
From
< Uncle > autoojisan@hgtrdsdgf.ne.jp
Sub
The Nakajuku highway is dangerous, evacuate now
Where are you, Ako? Are you safe?
I called you, but I couldn't get a hold of you. I've gone to the front of Hotel Priestess, and I'm waiting there. Please take care.
HOTEL PRIESTESS ...!!?
KAKO (CLACK)
カコ
THAT'S CLOSE BY.
KAKO
カコ
NO... YOU CAN'T COME HERE, UNCLE!!!
Buuu (BZZ)
ブー
Failed to send
BA (JOLT)

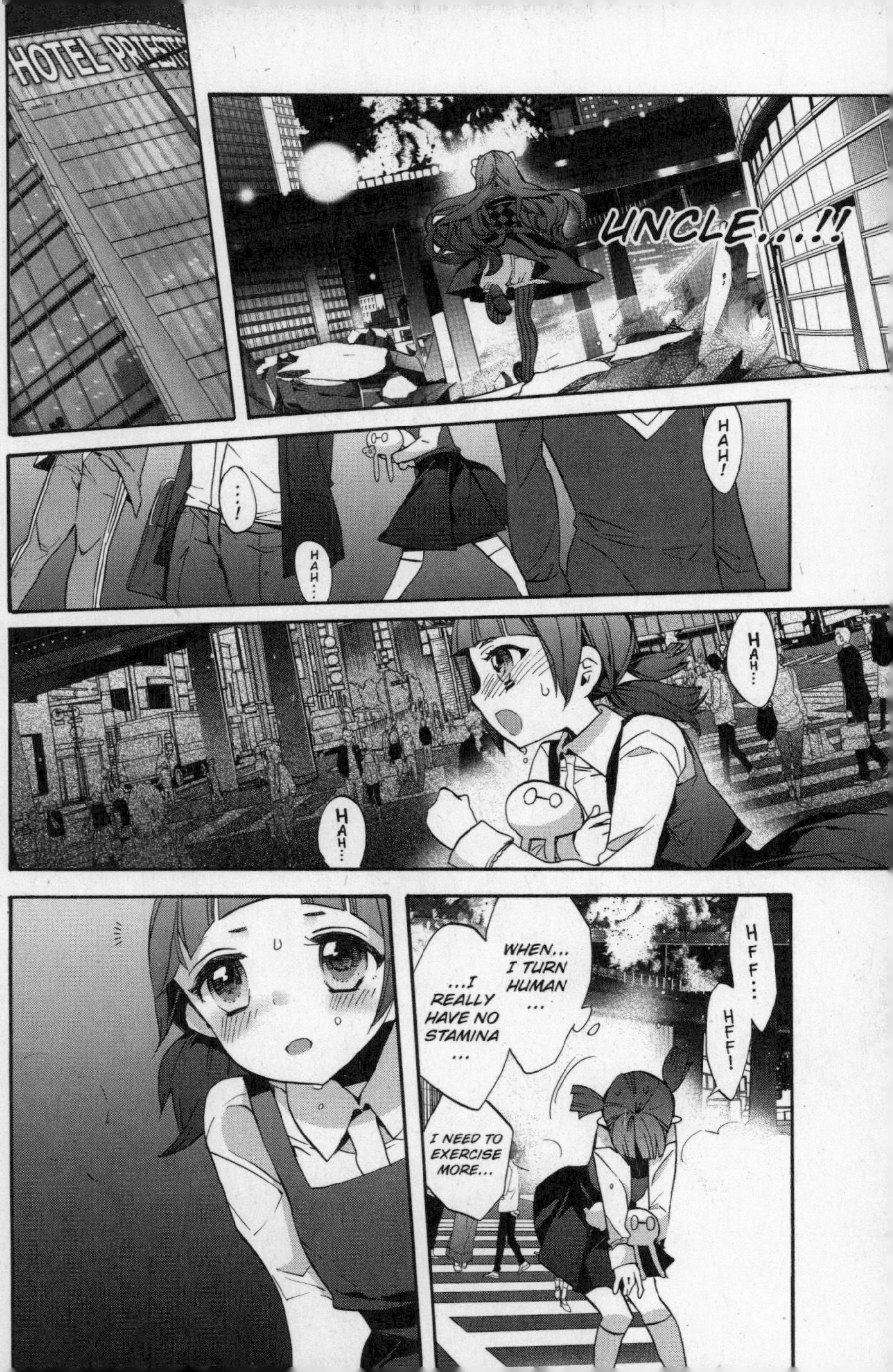
UNCLE...!!
HOTEL
HAH!
...!
HAH...
HAH...
HAH...
HFF... HFF!
WHEN... I TURN HUMAN ...
...I REALLY HAVE NO STAMINA ...
I NEED TO EXERCISE MORE...

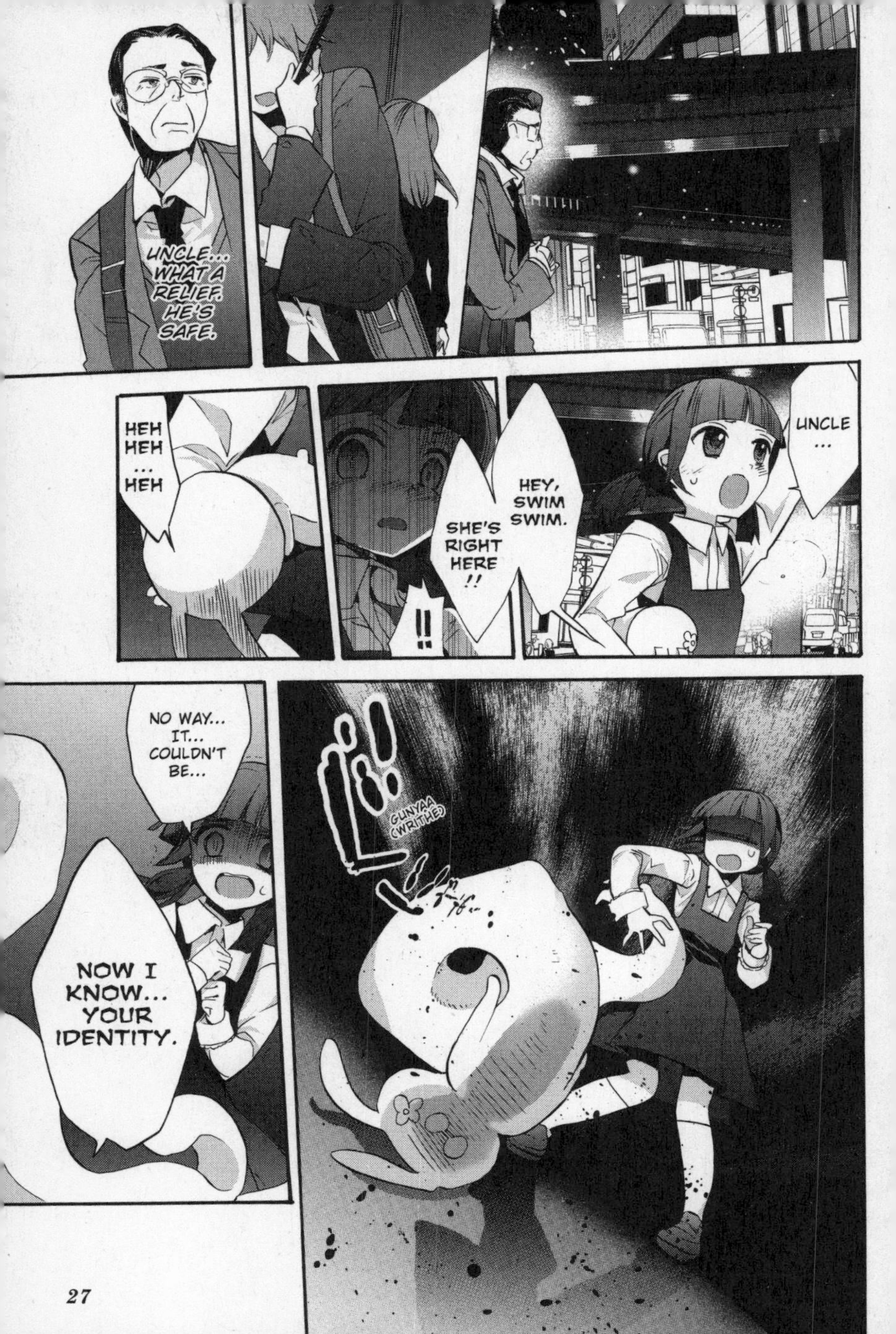
UNCLE... WHAT A RELIEF. HE'S SAFE.
UNCLE ...
HEY, SWIM SWIM.
SHE'S RIGHT HERE !!
!!
HEH HEH ... HEH
GUNYAA (WRITHE)
NO WAY... IT... COULDN'T BE...
NOW I KNOW... YOUR IDENTITY.

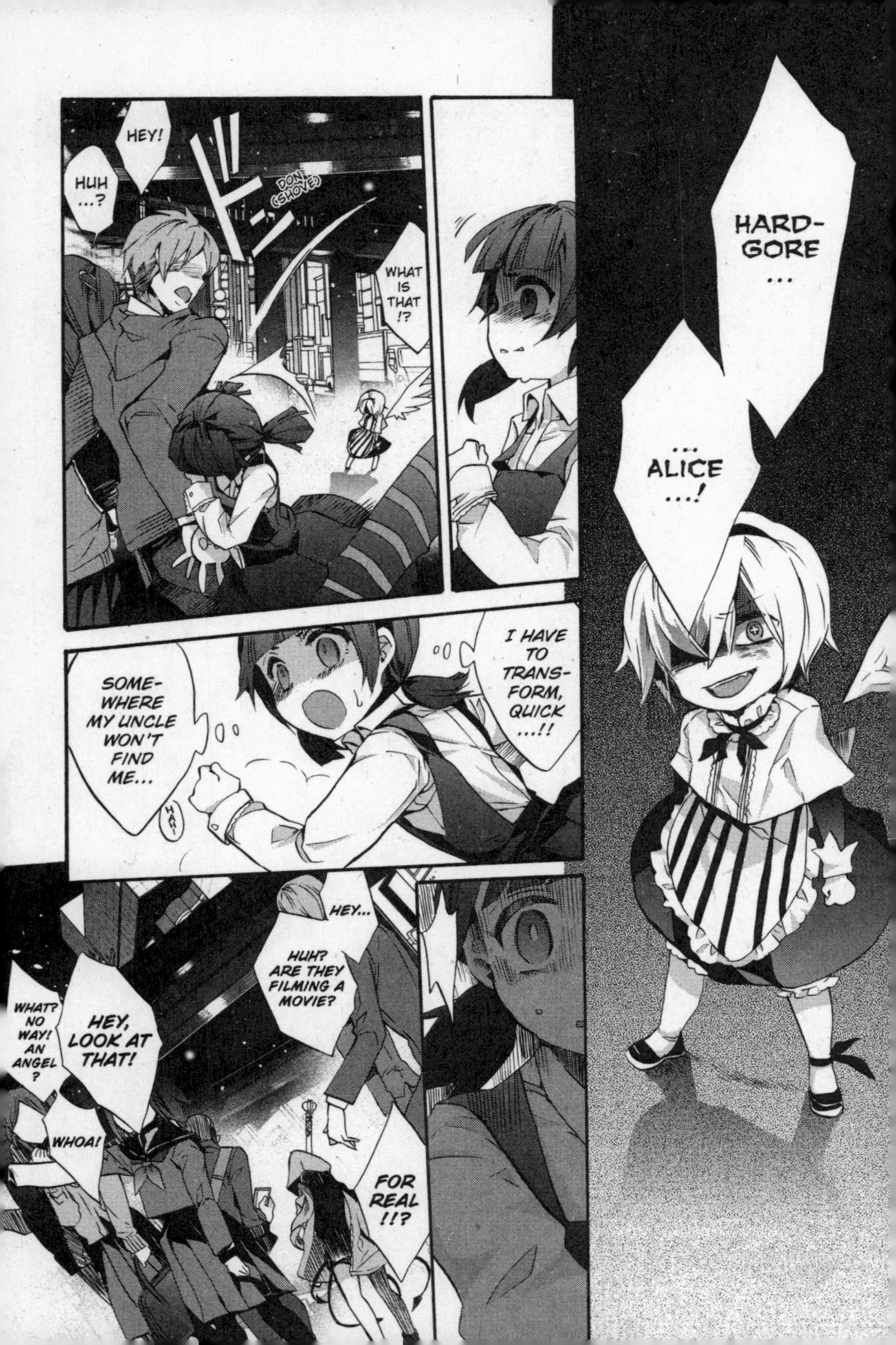
HARD-GORE ...
... ALICE ...!
HEY!
DON (SHOVE)
WHAT IS THAT !?
HUH ...?
I HAVE TO TRANS-FORM, QUICK ...!!
SOME-WHERE MY UNCLE WON'T FIND ME...
HAH!
HEY...
HUH? ARE THEY FILMING A MOVIE?
FOR REAL !!?
HEY, LOOK AT THAT!
WHAT? NO WAY! AN ANGEL ?
WHOA!

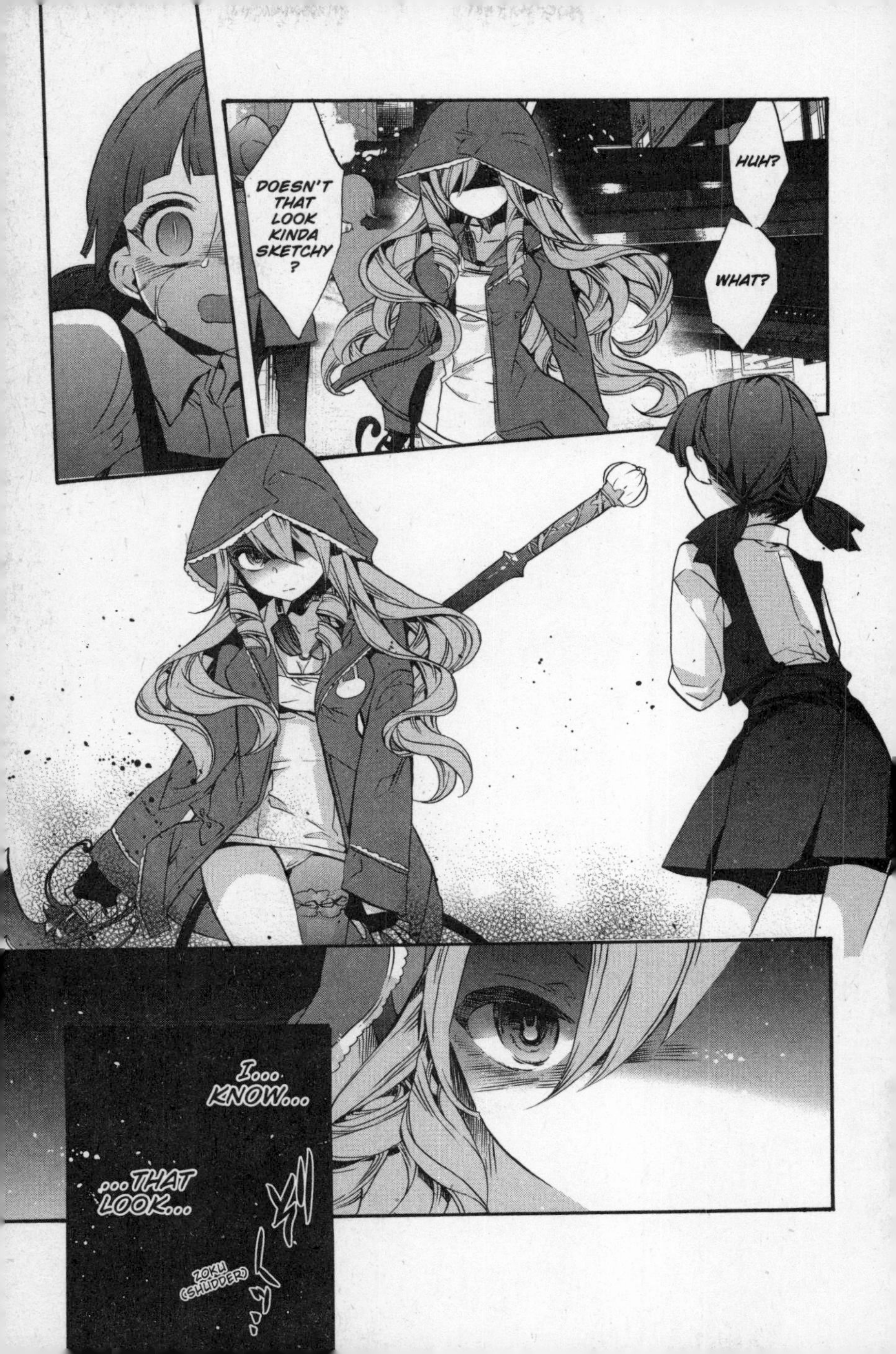
HUH?
WHAT?
DOESN'T THAT LOOK KINDA SKETCHY?
I... KNOW...
...THAT LOOK...
ZOKU (SHUDDER)

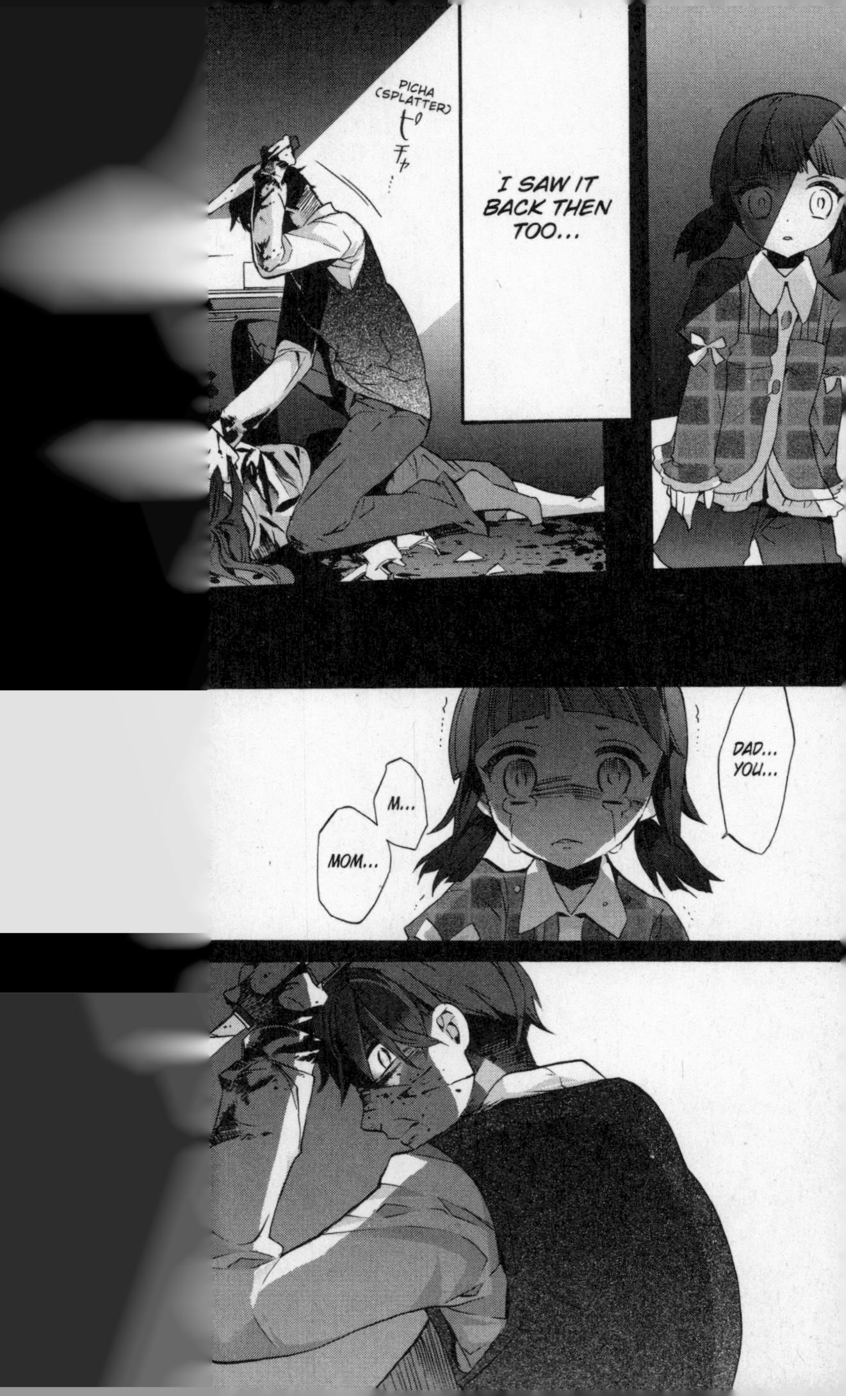
I SAW IT BACK THEN TOO...
PICHA (SPLATTER)
ピチャ…
DAD... YOU...
M...
MOM...

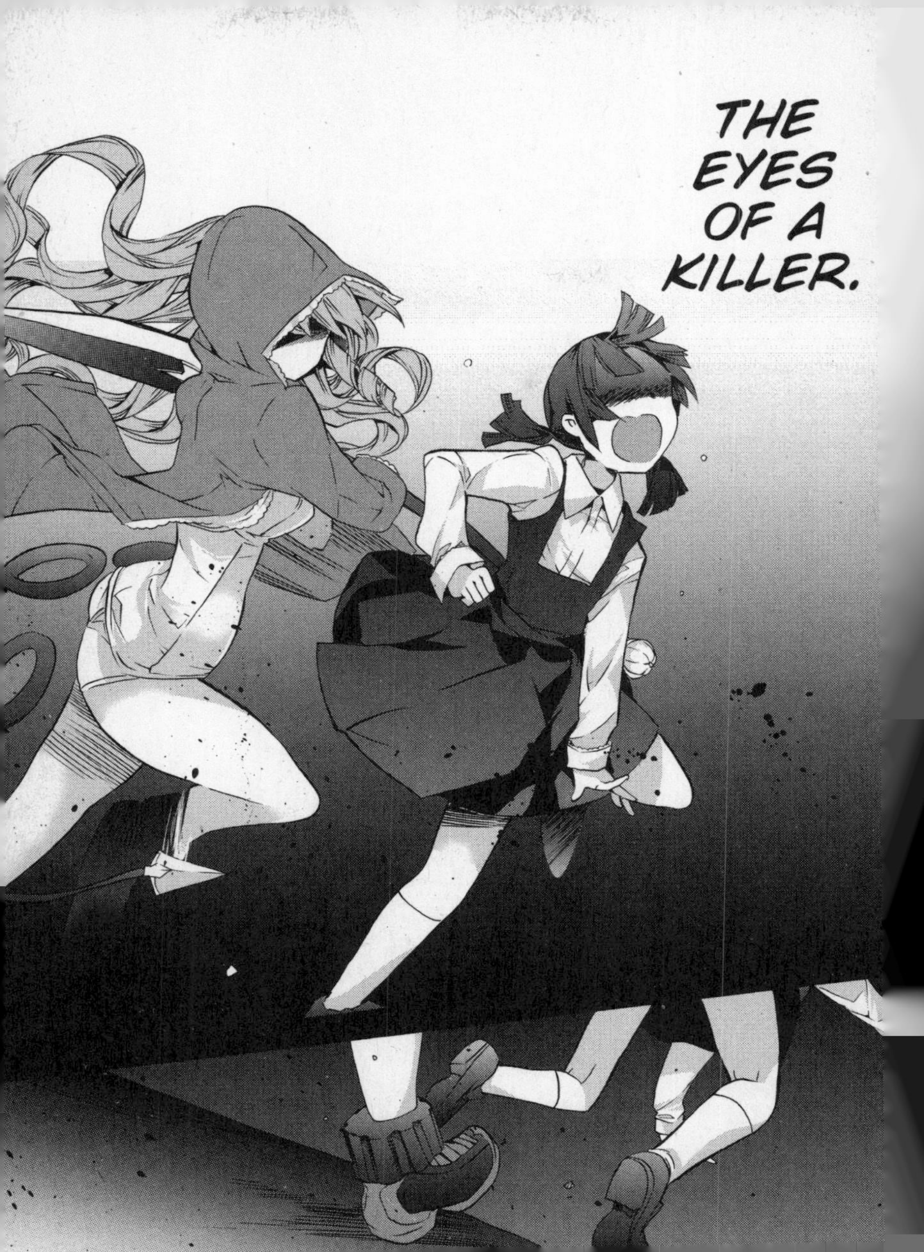
THE EYES OF A KILLER.

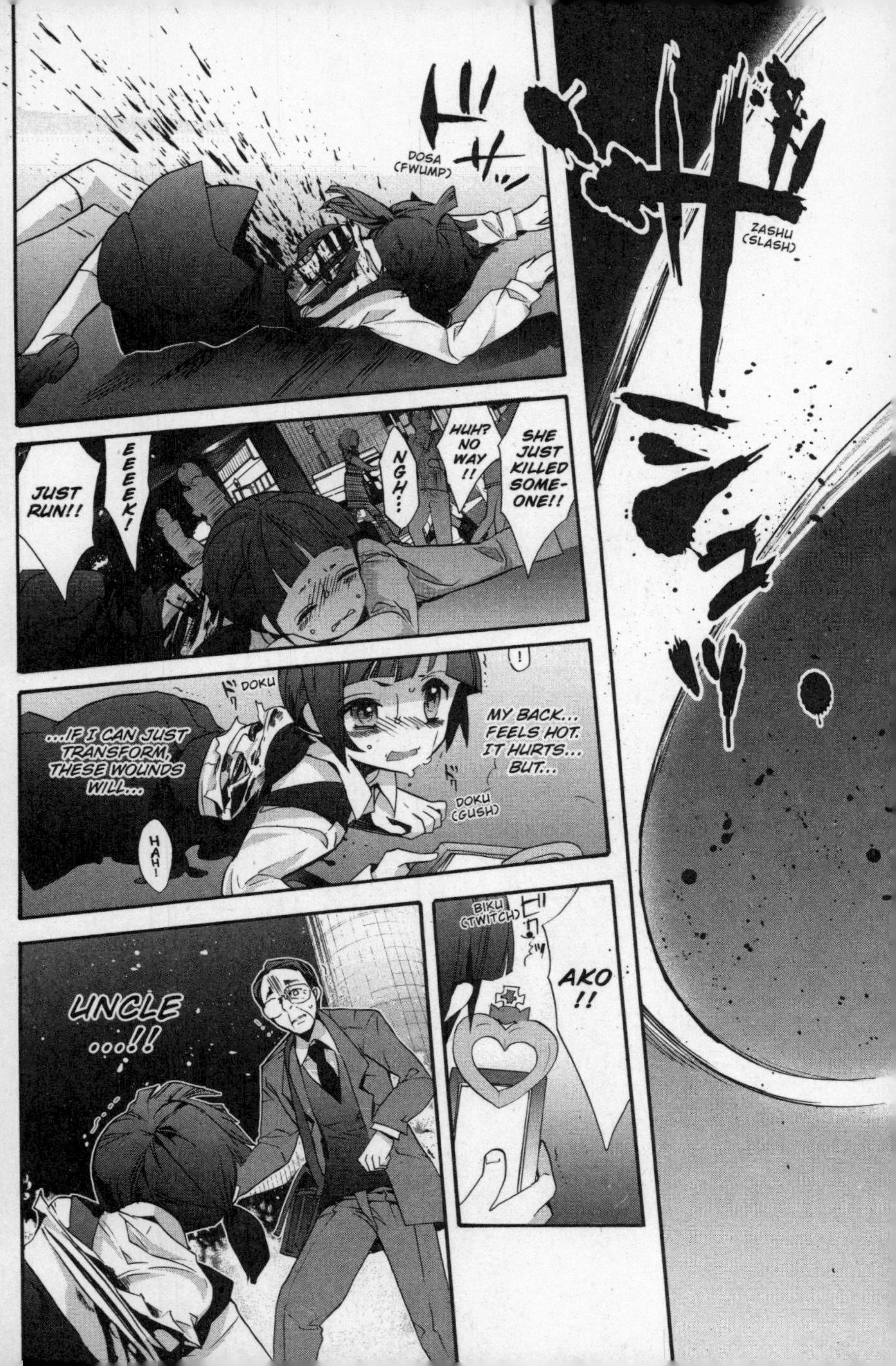
ZASHU (SLASH)
DOSA (FWUMP)
SHE JUST KILLED SOMEONE!!
HUH? NO WAY!!
NGH...
EEEEEK!
JUST RUN!!
!
DOKU
MY BACK... FEELS HOT. IT HURTS... BUT...
DOKU (GUSH)
...IF I CAN JUST TRANSFORM, THESE WOUNDS WILL...
HAH!
BIKU (TWITCH)
AKO!!
UNCLE...!!

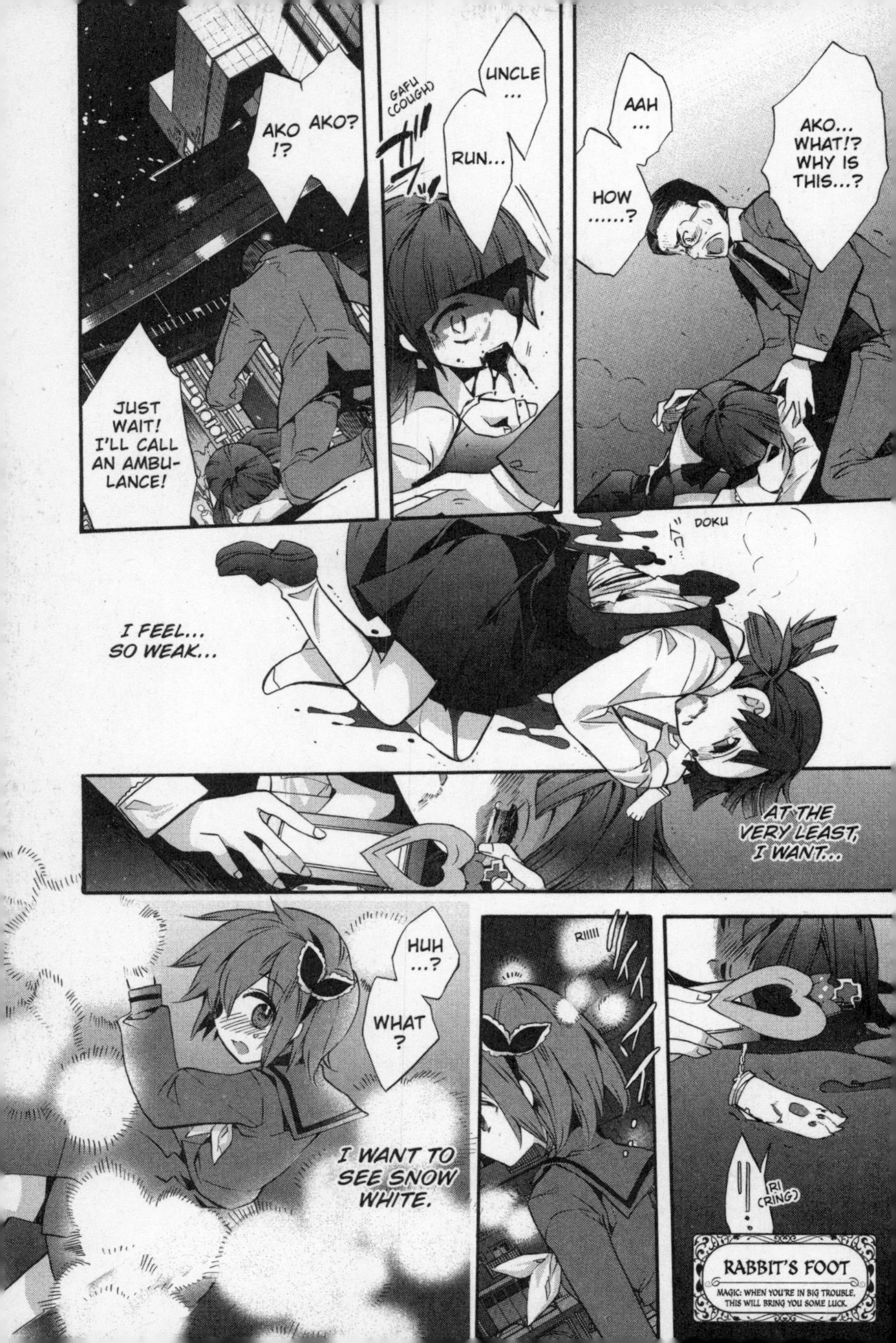
AKO... WHAT!? WHY IS THIS...?
AAH...
HOW......?
GAFU (COUGH)
UNCLE...
RUN...
AKO?
AKO!?
JUST WAIT! I'LL CALL AN AMBULANCE!
DOKU
I FEEL... SO WEAK...
AT THE VERY LEAST, I WANT...
RI (RING)
!
RABBIT'S FOOT
MAGIC: WHEN YOU'RE IN BIG TROUBLE, THIS WILL BRING YOU SOME LUCK.
RIIIII
HUH...?
WHAT?
I WANT TO SEE SNOW WHITE.

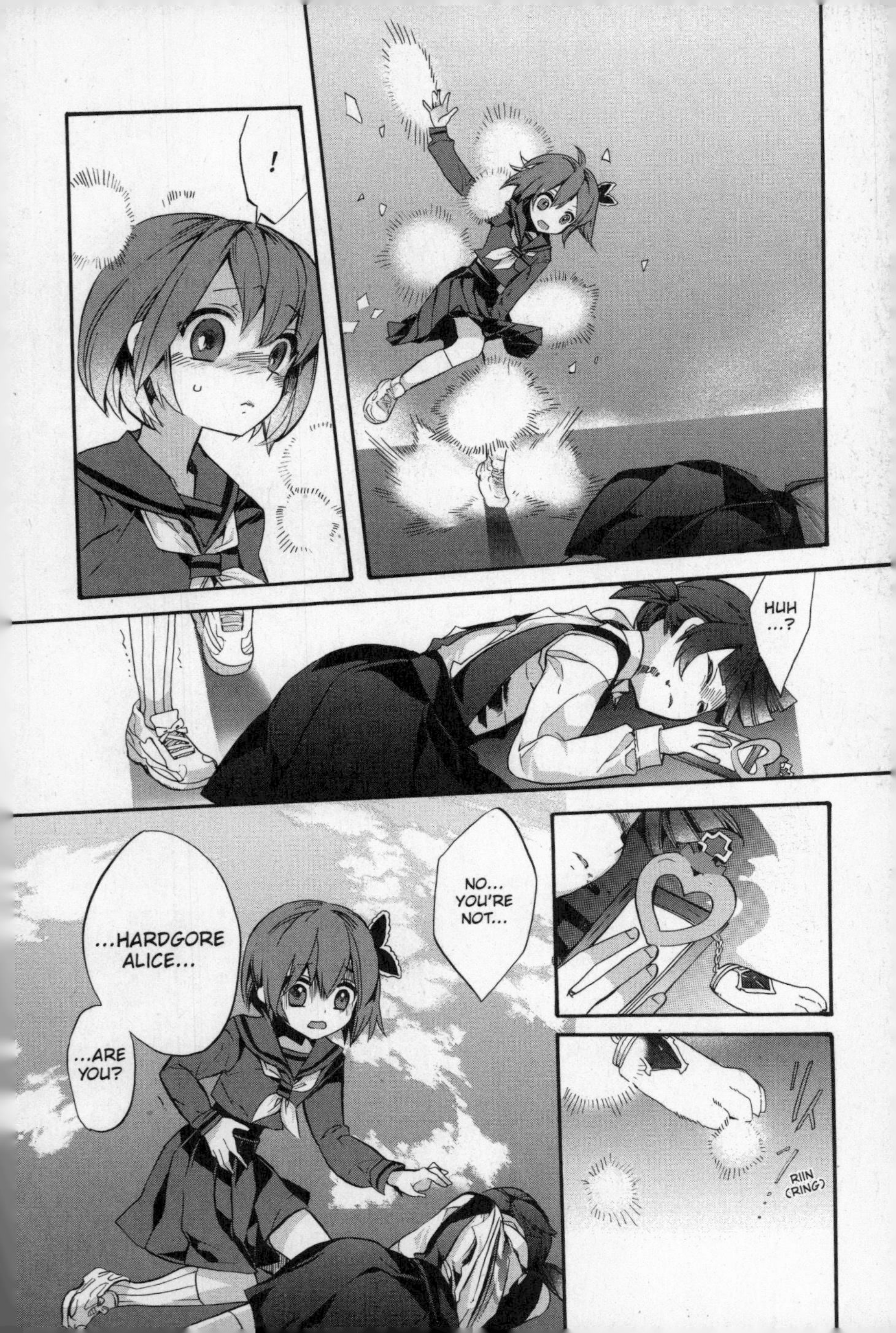
!
HUH
...?
NO...
YOU'RE
NOT...
...HARDGORE
ALICE...
...ARE
YOU?
RIIN
(RING)

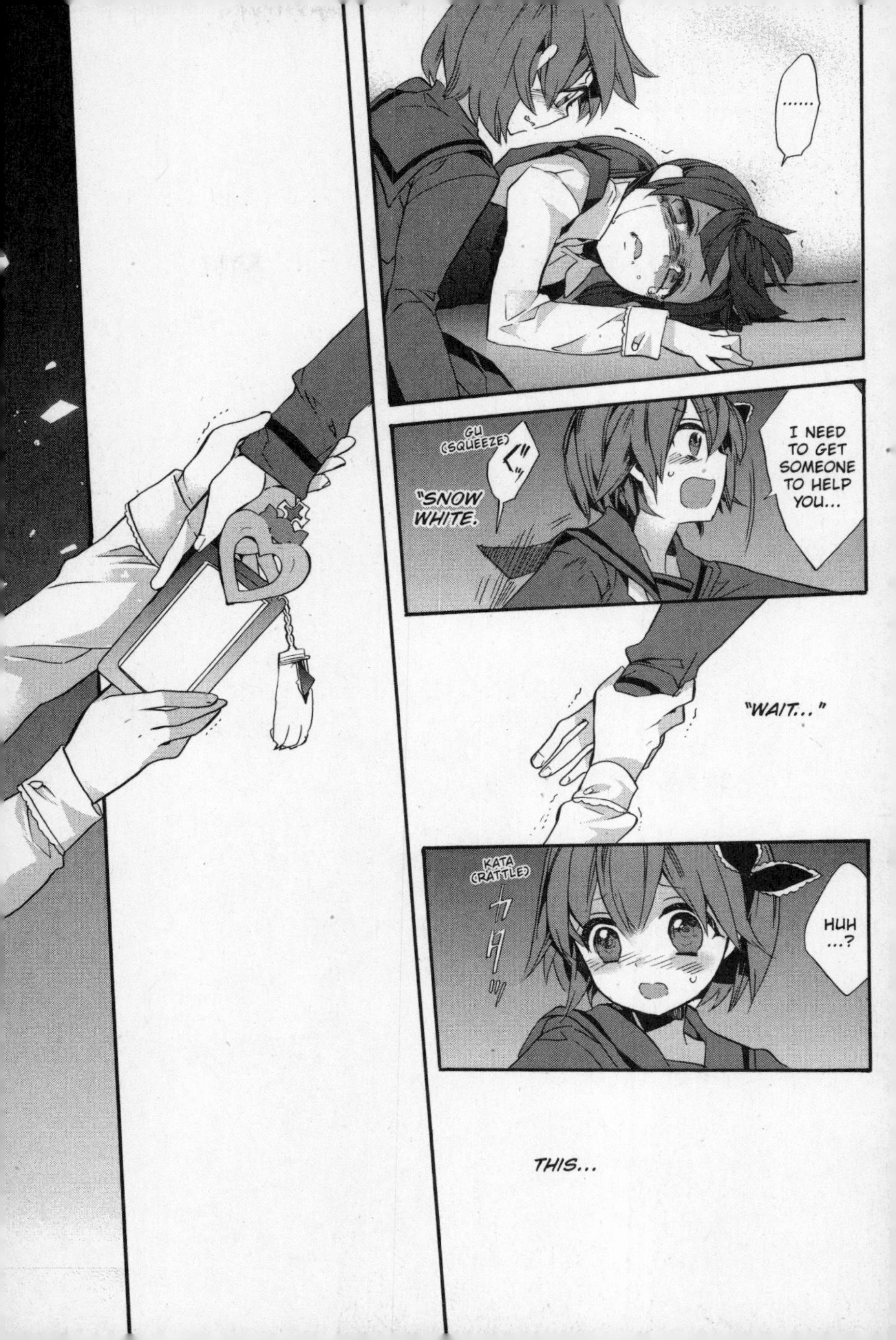
......
I NEED TO GET SOMEONE TO HELP YOU...
GU (SQUEEZE)
"SNOW WHITE.
"WAIT..."
HUH ...?
KATA (RATTLE)
THIS...

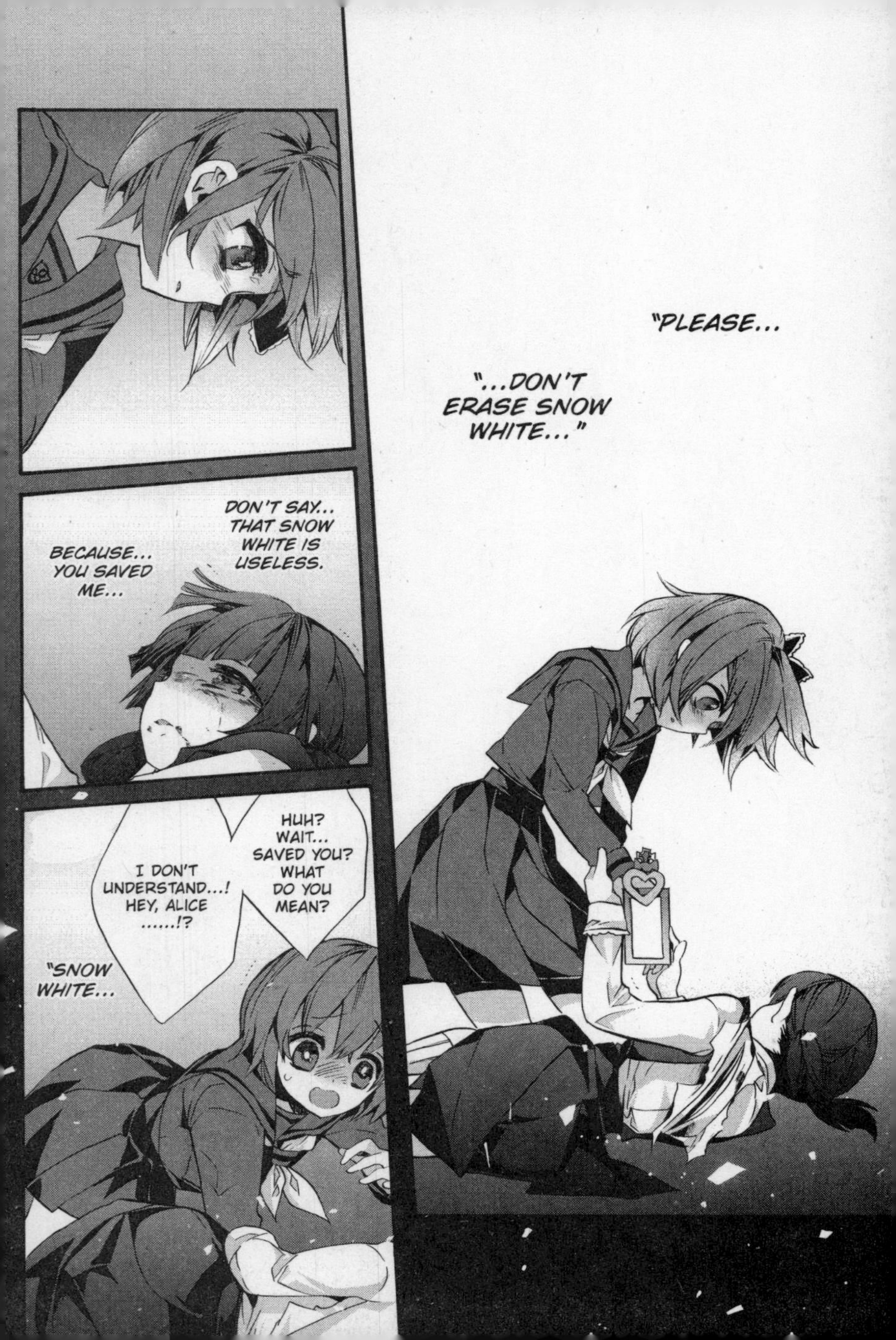
DON'T SAY... THAT SNOW WHITE IS USELESS.
BECAUSE... YOU SAVED ME...
HUH? WAIT... SAVED YOU? WHAT DO YOU MEAN?
I DON'T UNDERSTAND...! HEY, ALICE ......!?
"SNOW WHITE...
"PLEASE...
"...DON'T ERASE SNOW WHITE..."

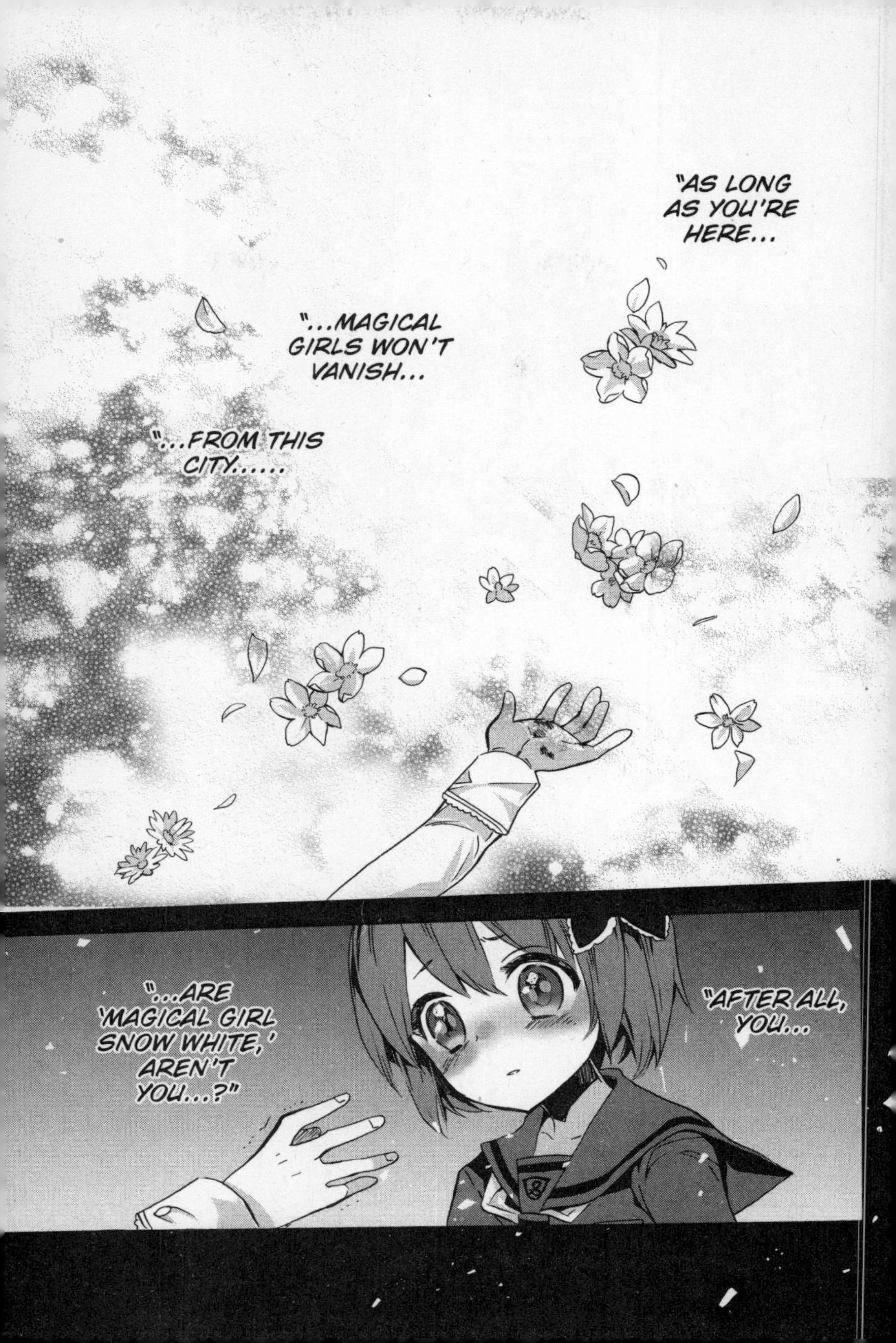
"AS LONG AS YOU'RE HERE...
"...MAGICAL GIRLS WON'T VANISH...
"...FROM THIS CITY......
"AFTER ALL, YOU...
"...ARE 'MAGICAL GIRL SNOW WHITE,' AREN'T YOU...?"

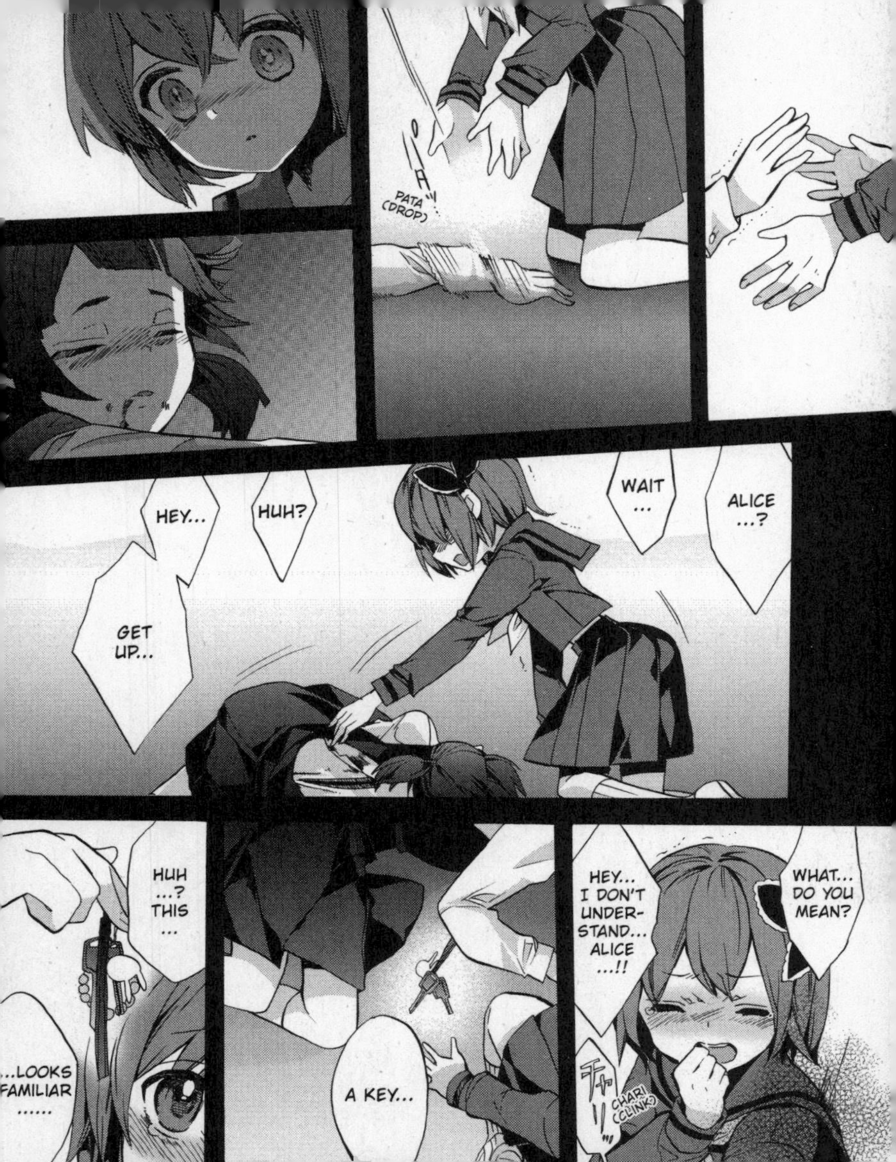
PATA (DROP)
ALICE ...?
WAIT ...
HUH?
HEY...
GET UP...
WHAT... DO YOU MEAN?
HEY... I DON'T UNDER-STAND... ALICE ...!!
CHARI (CLINK)
A KEY...
HUH ...? THIS ...
...LOOKS FAMILIAR ......

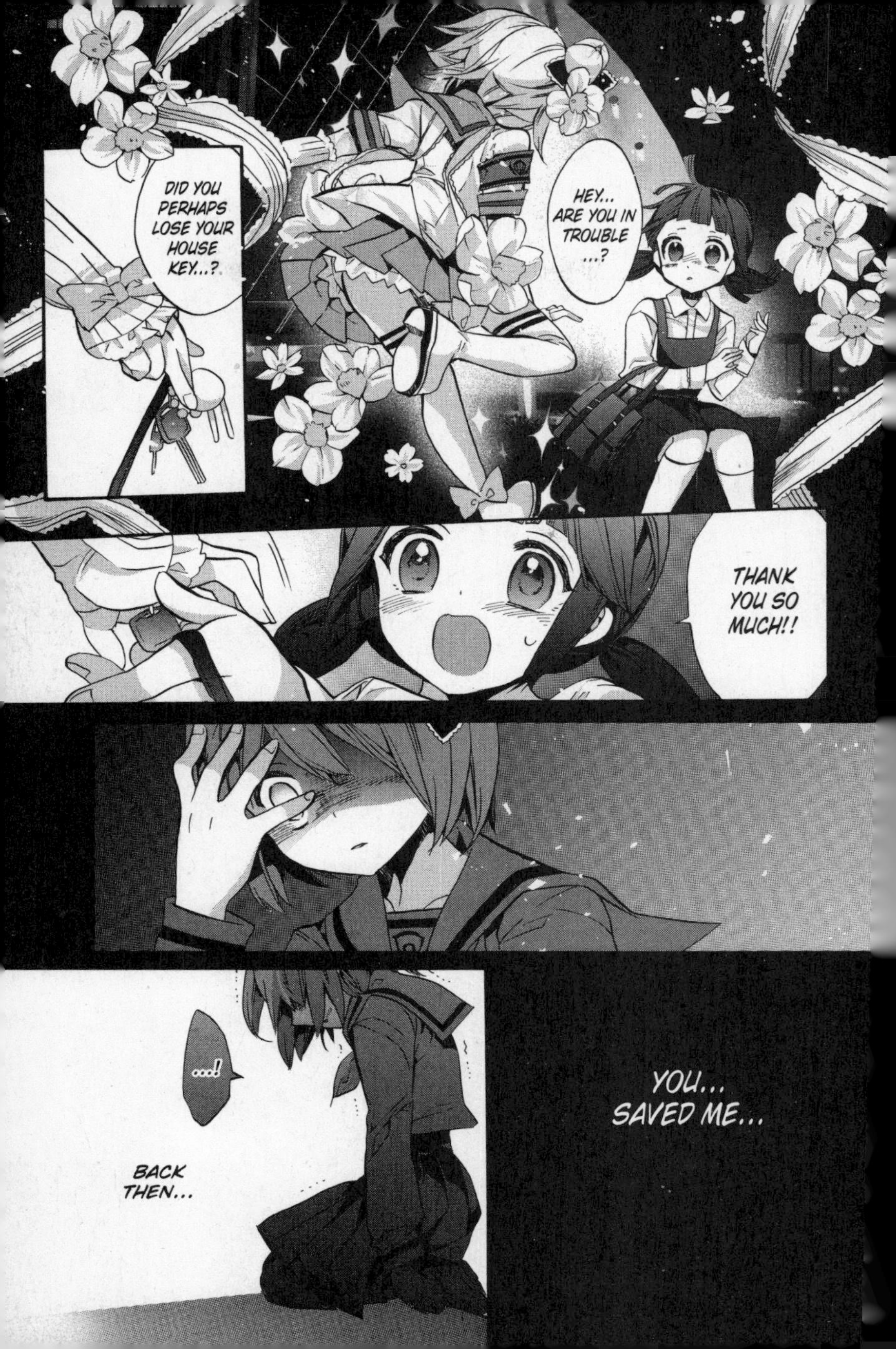
HEY... ARE YOU IN TROUBLE ...?
DID YOU PERHAPS LOSE YOUR HOUSE KEY...?
THANK YOU SO MUCH!!
YOU... SAVED ME...
...!
BACK THEN...

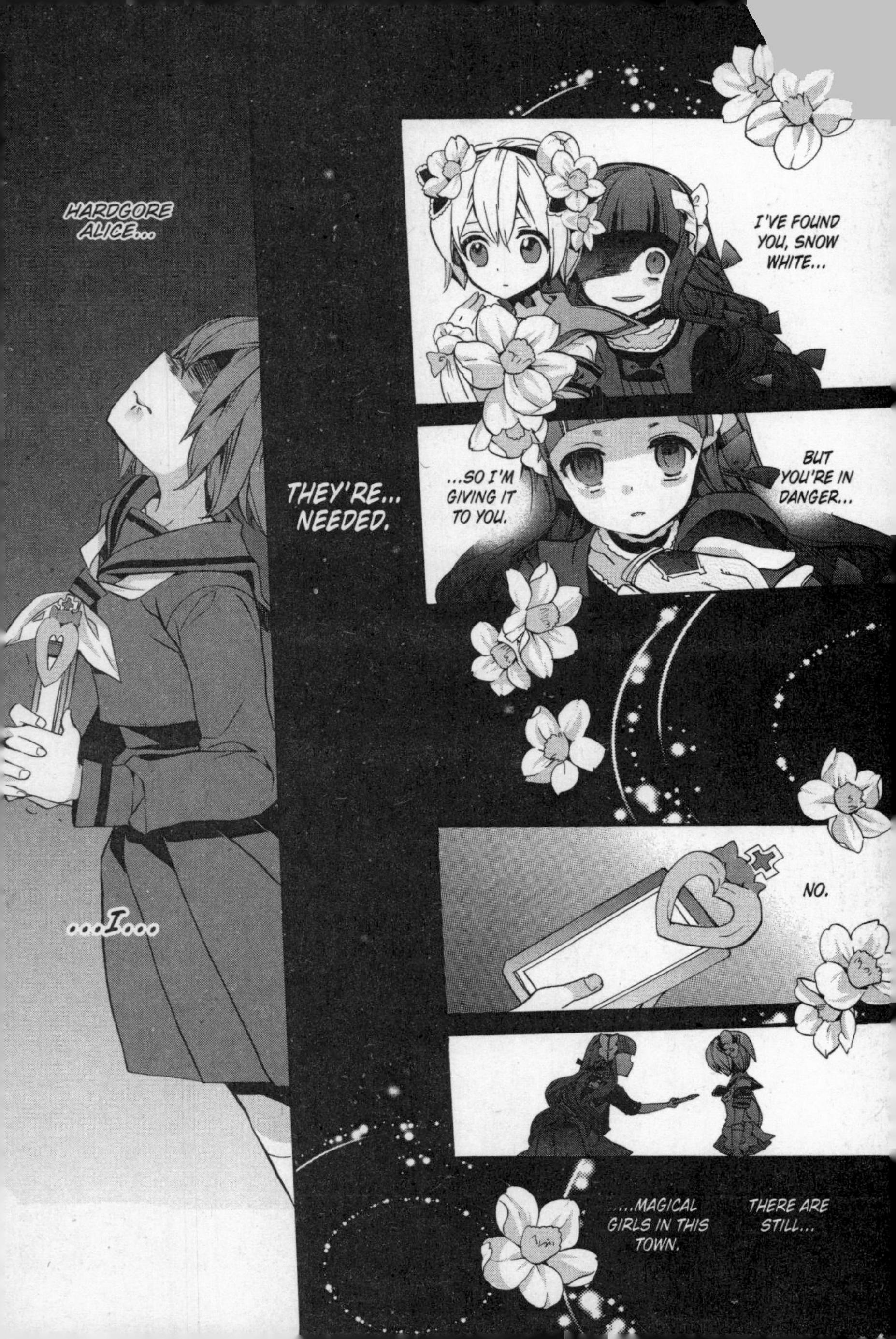

I'VE FOUND YOU, SNOW WHITE...
BUT YOU'RE IN DANGER...
...SO I'M GIVING IT TO YOU.
THEY'RE... NEEDED.
NO.
THERE ARE STILL...
...MAGICAL GIRLS IN THIS TOWN.
HARDGORE ALICE...
...I...

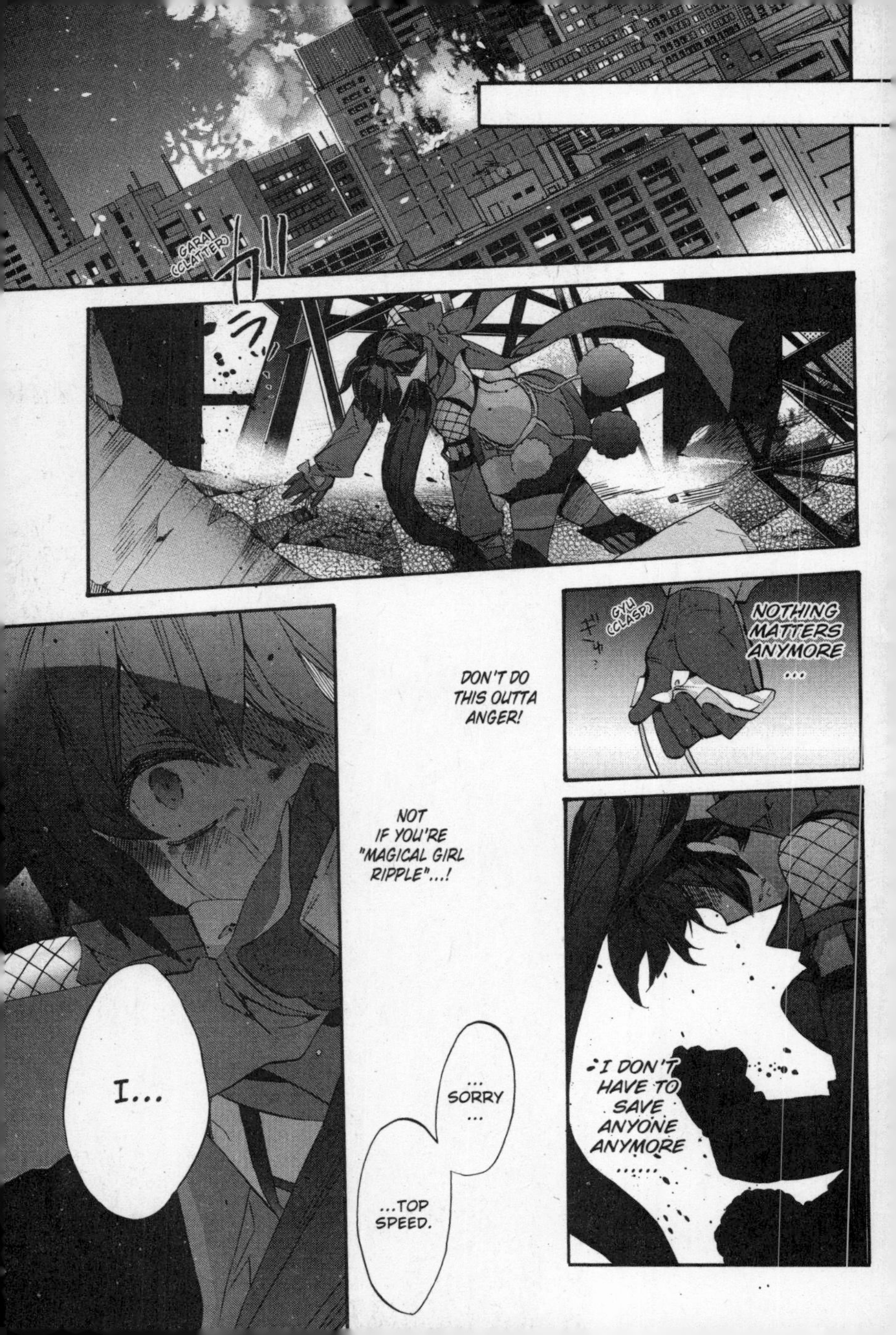
GARA (CLATTER)
GYU (CLASP)
NOTHING MATTERS ANYMORE ...
I DON'T HAVE TO SAVE ANYONE ANYMORE ......
DON'T DO THIS OUTTA ANGER!
NOT IF YOU'RE "MAGICAL GIRL RIPPLE"...!
I...
...SORRY...
...TOP SPEED.

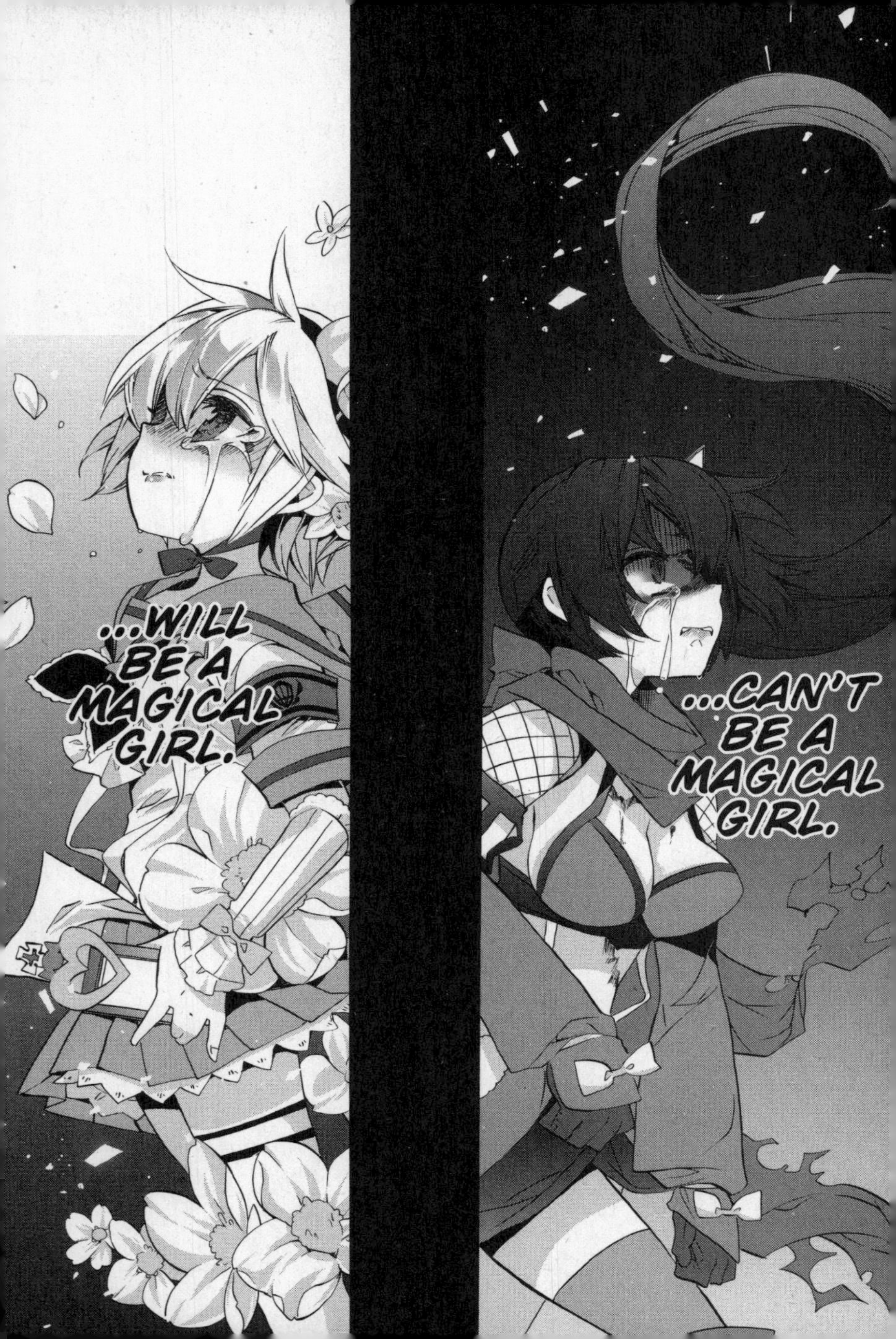
...CAN'T BE A MAGICAL GIRL.
...WILL BE A MAGICAL GIRL.

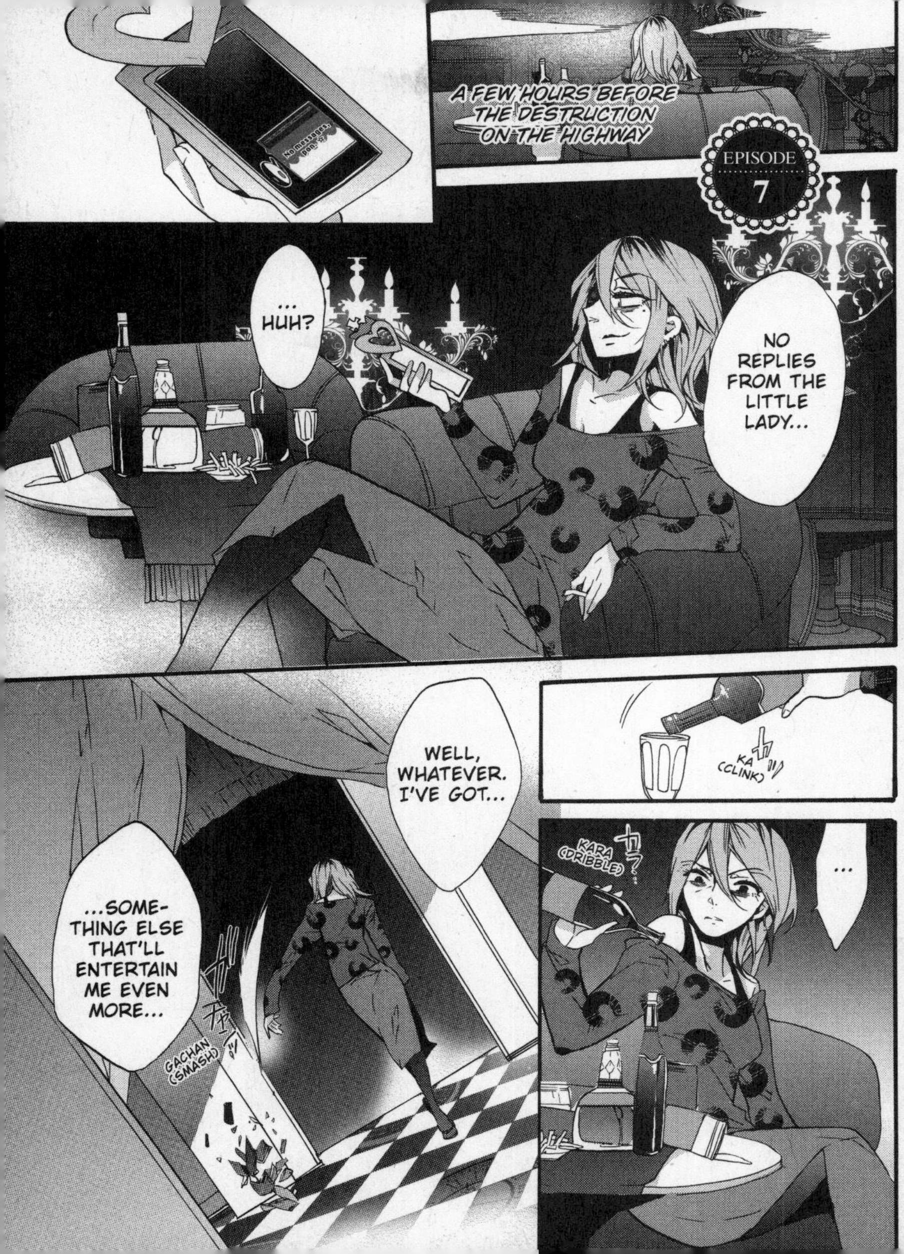

A FEW HOURS BEFORE THE DESTRUCTION ON THE HIGHWAY
EPISODE 7
No messages, pon. ☆
NO REPLIES FROM THE LITTLE LADY...
...HUH?
KA (CLINK)
...
KARA (DRIBBLE)
WELL, WHATEVER. I'VE GOT...
...SOME-THING ELSE THAT'LL ENTERTAIN ME EVEN MORE...
GACHAN (SMASH)

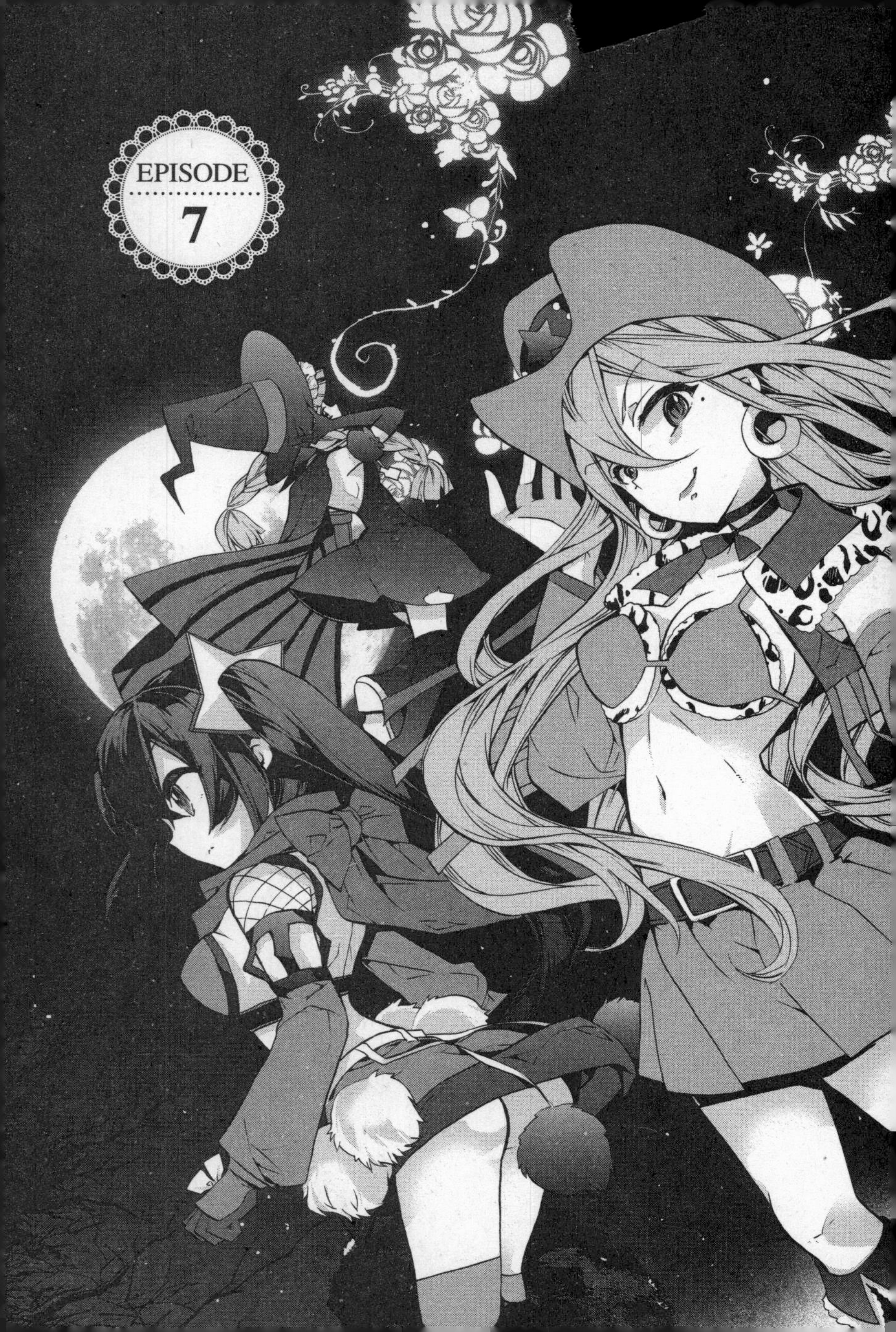
EPISODE
7

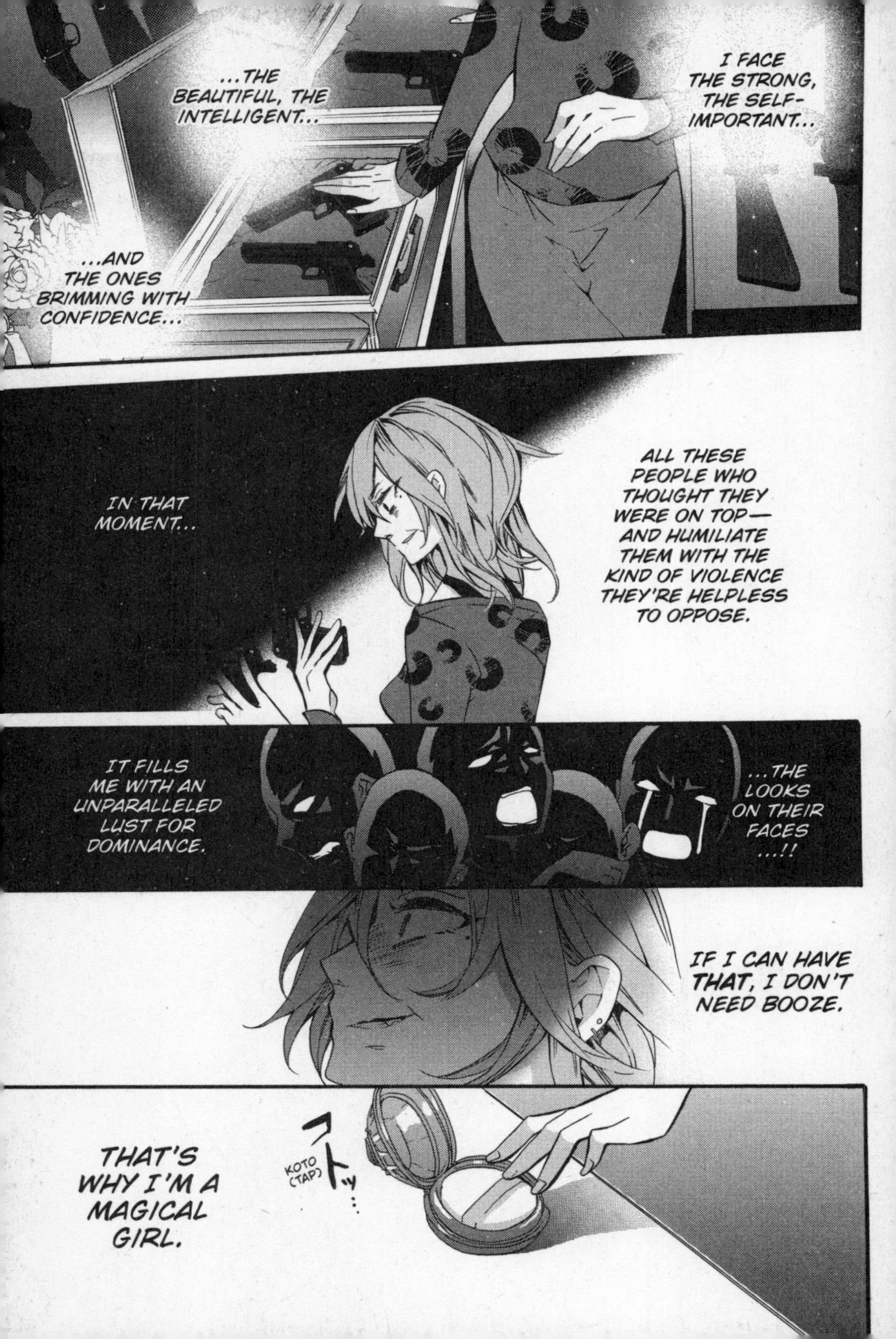
I FACE THE STRONG, THE SELF-IMPORTANT...
...THE BEAUTIFUL, THE INTELLIGENT...
...AND THE ONES BRIMMING WITH CONFIDENCE...
ALL THESE PEOPLE WHO THOUGHT THEY WERE ON TOP— AND HUMILIATE THEM WITH THE KIND OF VIOLENCE THEY'RE HELPLESS TO OPPOSE.
IN THAT MOMENT...
...THE LOOKS ON THEIR FACES ...!!
IT FILLS ME WITH AN UNPARALLELED LUST FOR DOMINANCE.
IF I CAN HAVE THAT, I DON'T NEED BOOZE.
KOTO (TAP)
THAT'S WHY I'M A MAGICAL GIRL.

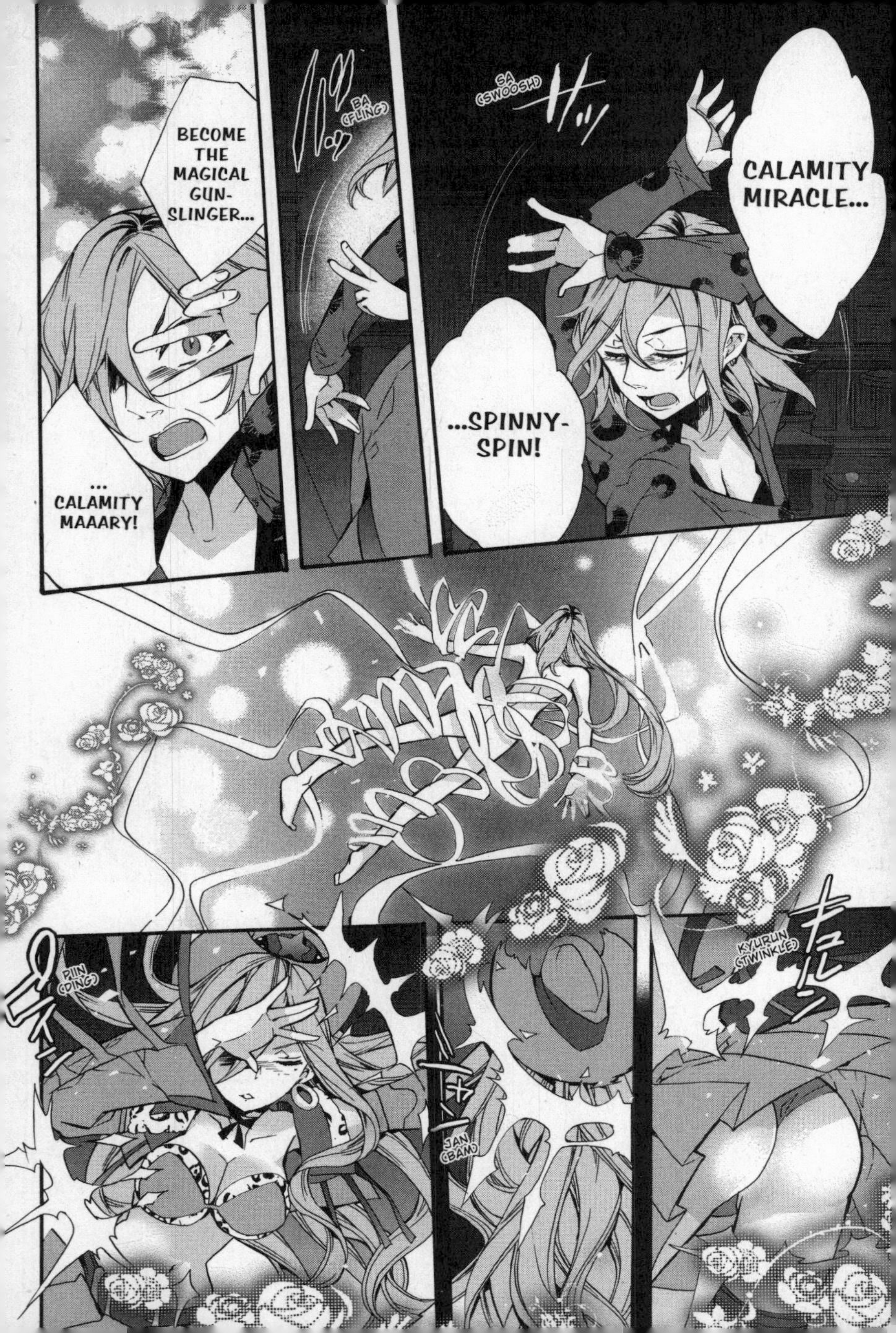
SA (SWOOSH)
CALAMITY MIRACLE...
...SPINNY-SPIN!
BA (FLING)
BECOME THE MAGICAL GUN-SLINGER...
... CALAMITY MAAARY!
KYURUN (TWINKLE)
JAN (BAM)
PIIN (DING)

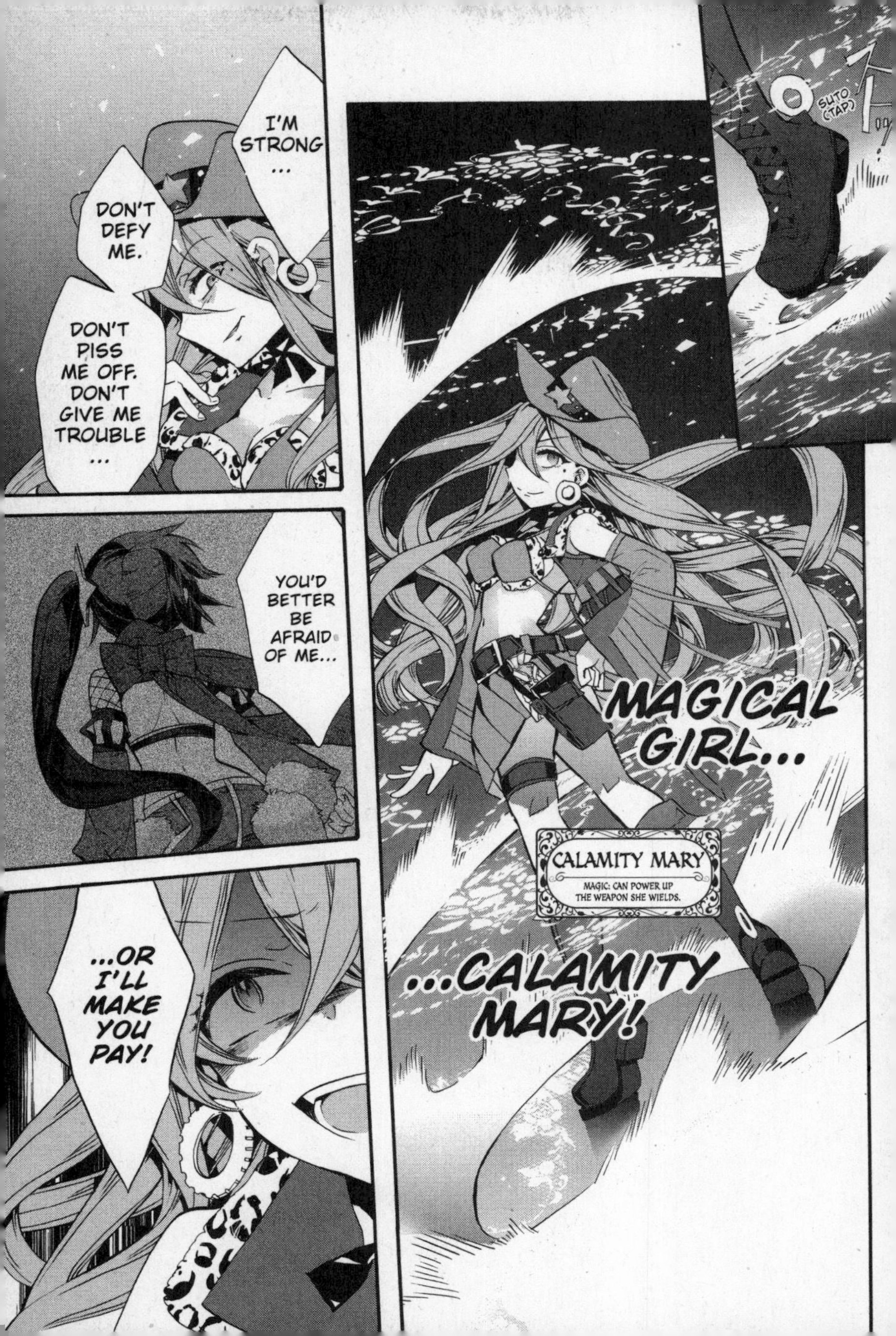
SUTO (TAP)
MAGICAL GIRL...
CALAMITY MARY
MAGIC: CAN POWER UP THE WEAPON SHE WIELDS.
...CALAMITY MARY!
I'M STRONG...
DON'T DEFY ME.
DON'T PISS ME OFF. DON'T GIVE ME TROUBLE...
YOU'D BETTER BE AFRAID OF ME...
...OR I'LL MAKE YOU PAY!

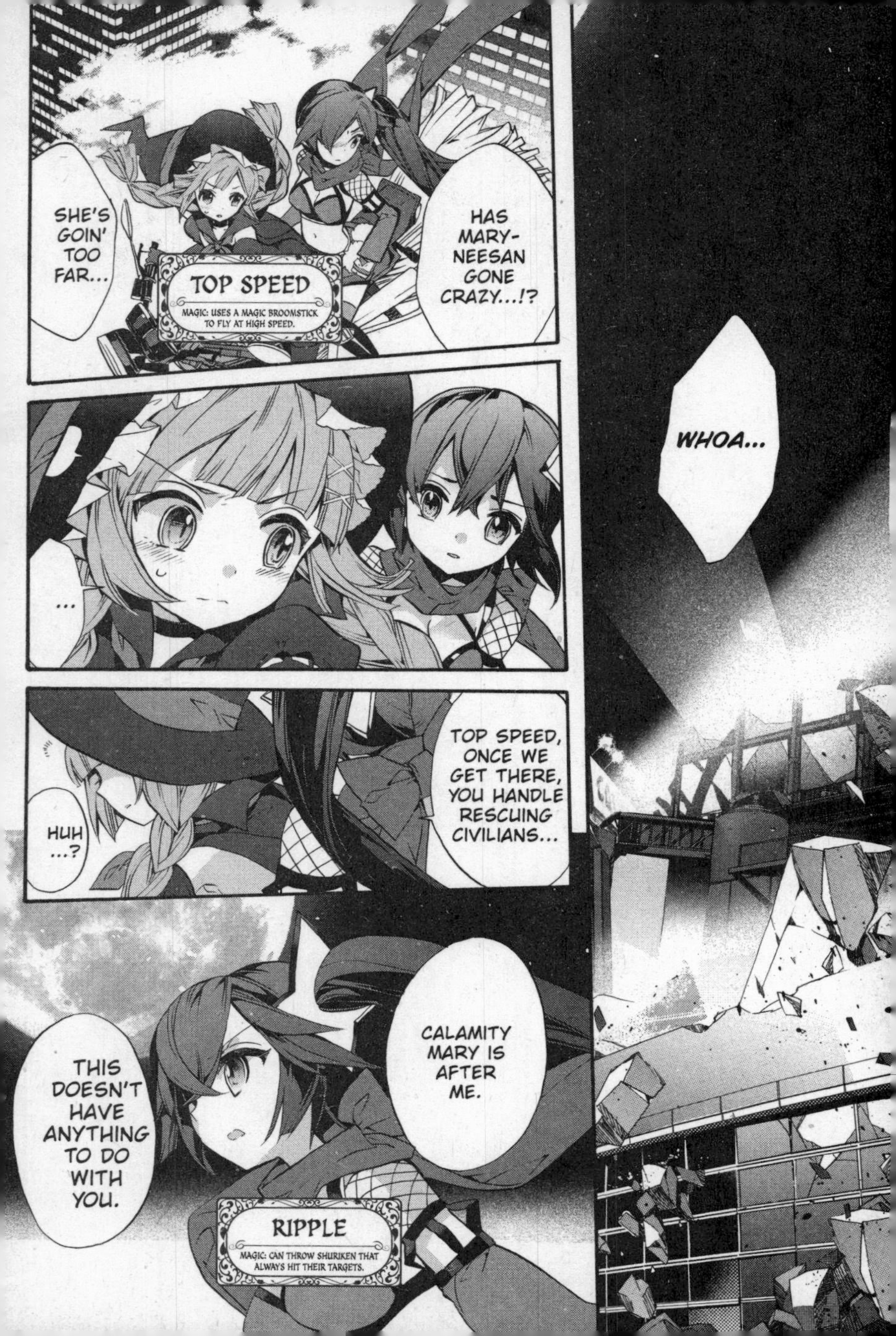
WHOA...
HAS MARY-NEESAN GONE CRAZY...!?
TOP SPEED
MAGIC: USES A MAGIC BROOMSTICK TO FLY AT HIGH SPEED.
SHE'S GOIN' TOO FAR...
...
TOP SPEED, ONCE WE GET THERE, YOU HANDLE RESCUING CIVILIANS...
HUH ...?
CALAMITY MARY IS AFTER ME.
THIS DOESN'T HAVE ANYTHING TO DO WITH YOU.
RIPPLE
MAGIC: CAN THROW SHURIKEN THAT ALWAYS HIT THEIR TARGETS.

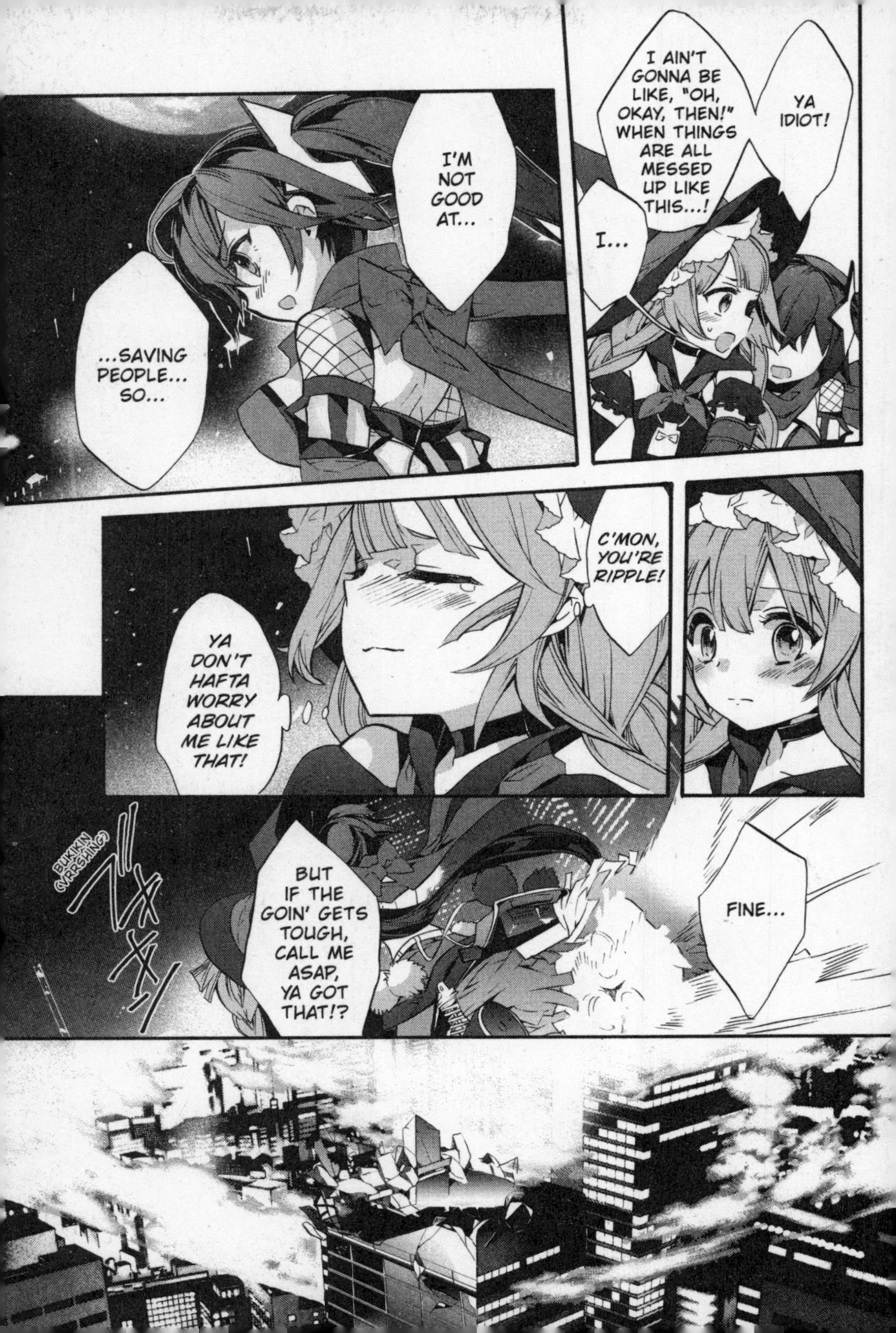
I AIN'T GONNA BE LIKE, "OH, OKAY, THEN!" WHEN THINGS ARE ALL MESSED UP LIKE THIS...!
YA IDIOT!
I...
I'M NOT GOOD AT...
...SAVING PEOPLE... SO...
C'MON, YOU'RE RIPPLE!
YA DON'T HAFTA WORRY ABOUT ME LIKE THAT!
FINE...
BUT IF THE GOIN' GETS TOUGH, CALL ME ASAP, YA GOT THAT!?
BUKIKIN (VRRSHING)

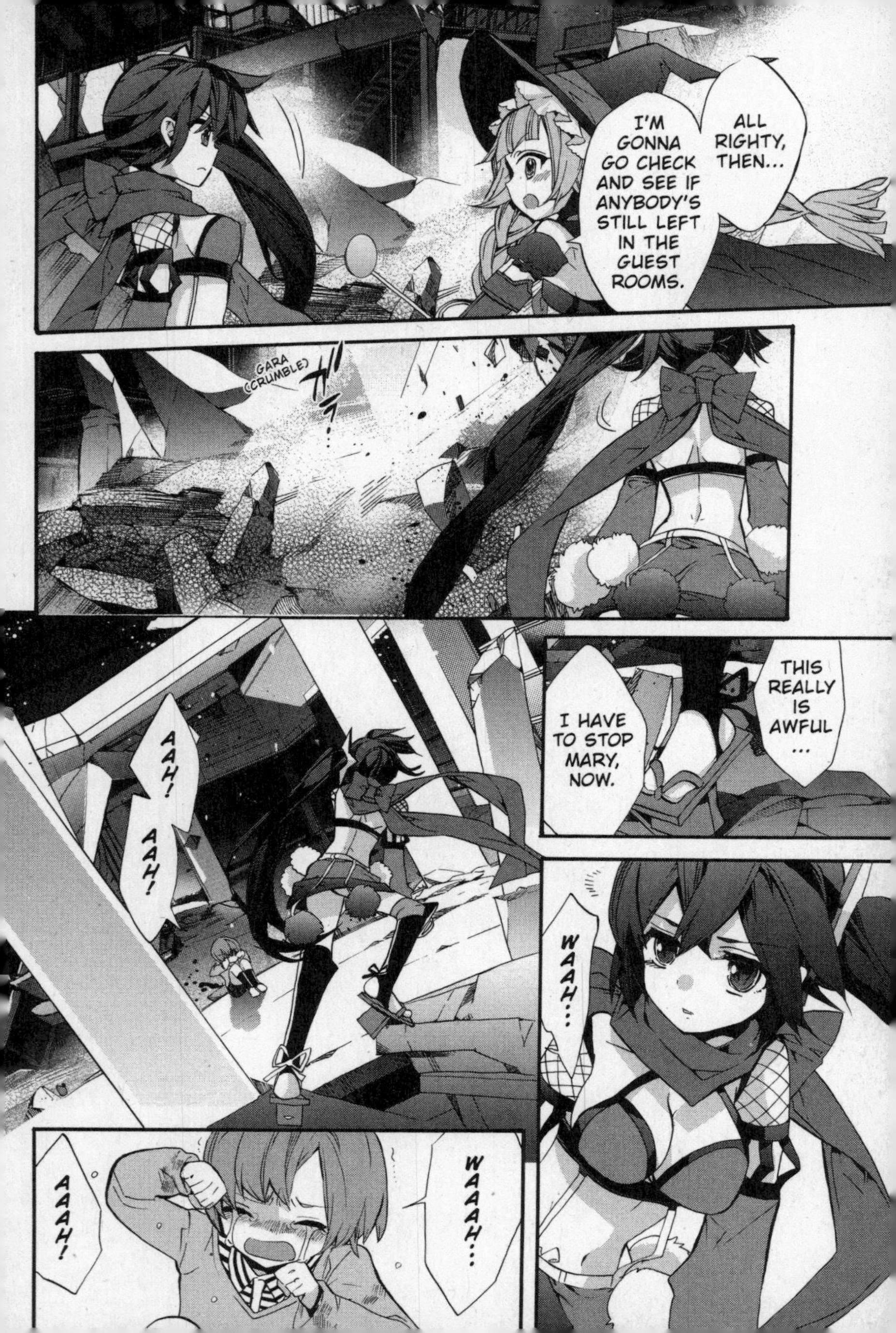
ALL RIGHTY, THEN...
I'M GONNA GO CHECK AND SEE IF ANYBODY'S STILL LEFT IN THE GUEST ROOMS.
GARA (CRUMBLE)
THIS REALLY IS AWFUL...
I HAVE TO STOP MARY, NOW.
WAAAH...
AAH! AAH!
WAAAAH...
AAAAH!

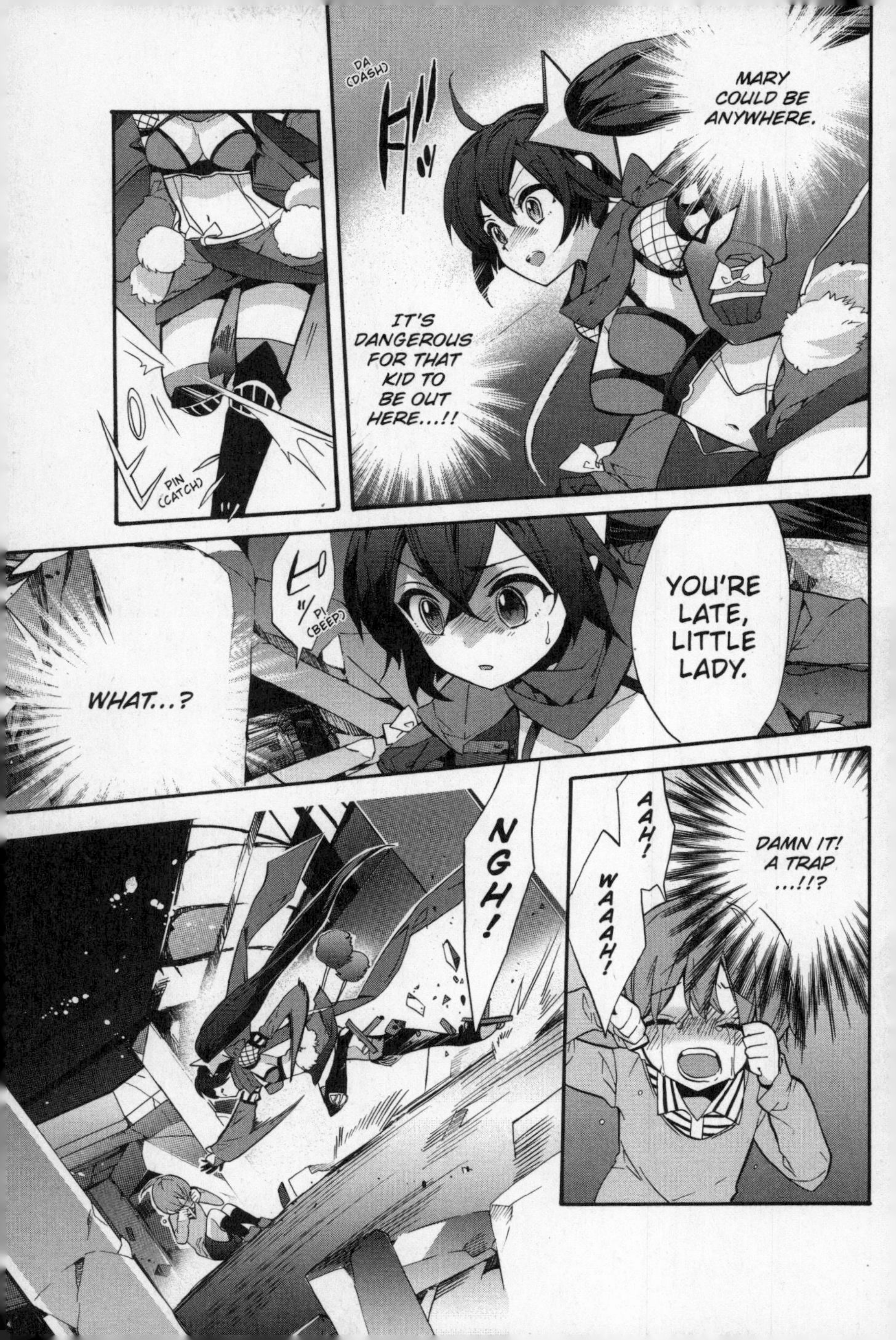
MARY COULD BE ANYWHERE.
DA (DASH)
IT'S DANGEROUS FOR THAT KID TO BE OUT HERE...!!
PIN (CATCH)
YOU'RE LATE, LITTLE LADY.
PI (BEEP)
WHAT...?
DAMN IT! A TRAP ...!!?
AAH! WAAAAH!
NGH!

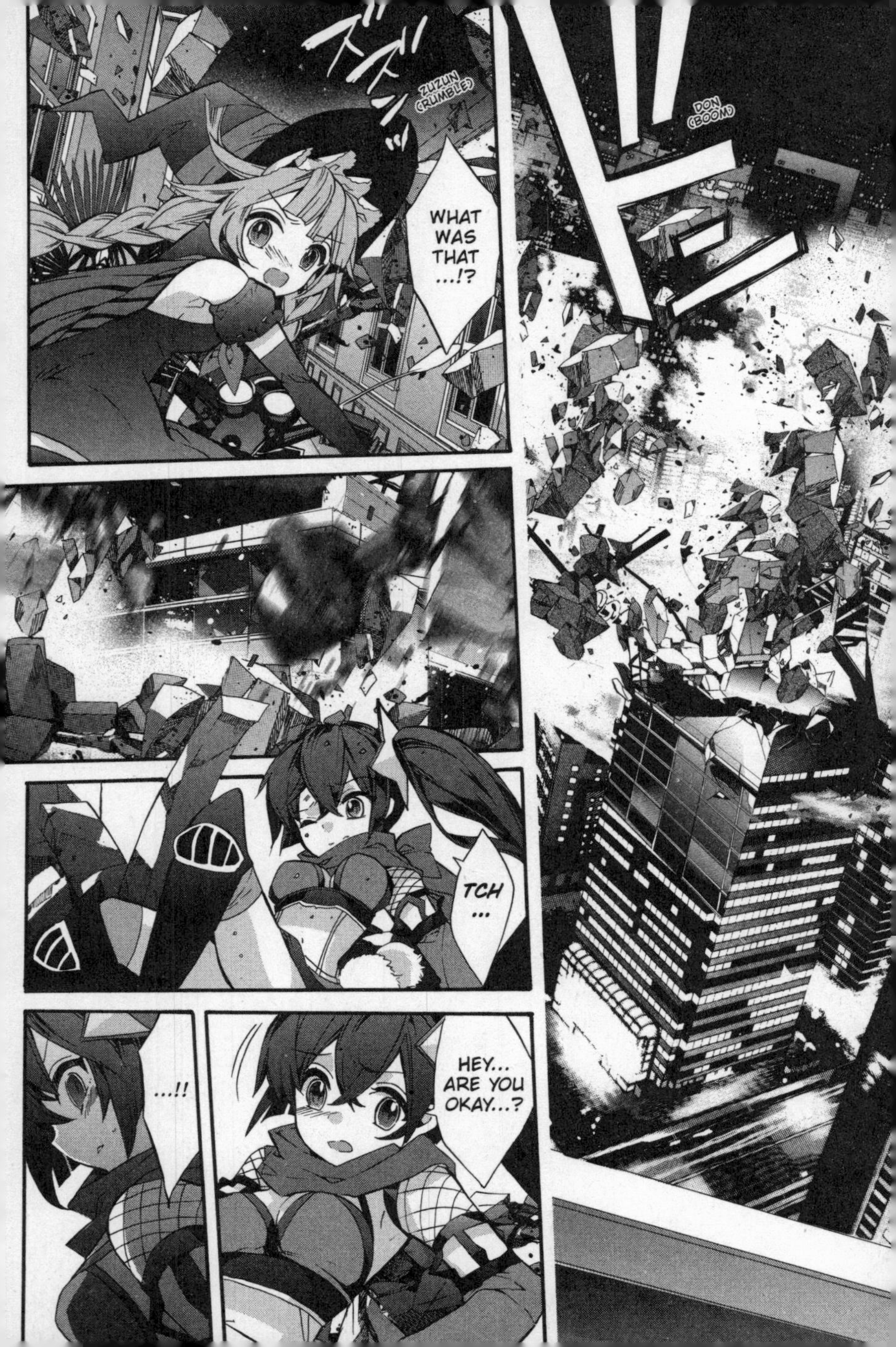
DON (BOOM)
ZUZUN (RUMBLE)
WHAT WAS THAT ...!?
TCH ...
HEY... ARE YOU OKAY...?
...!!

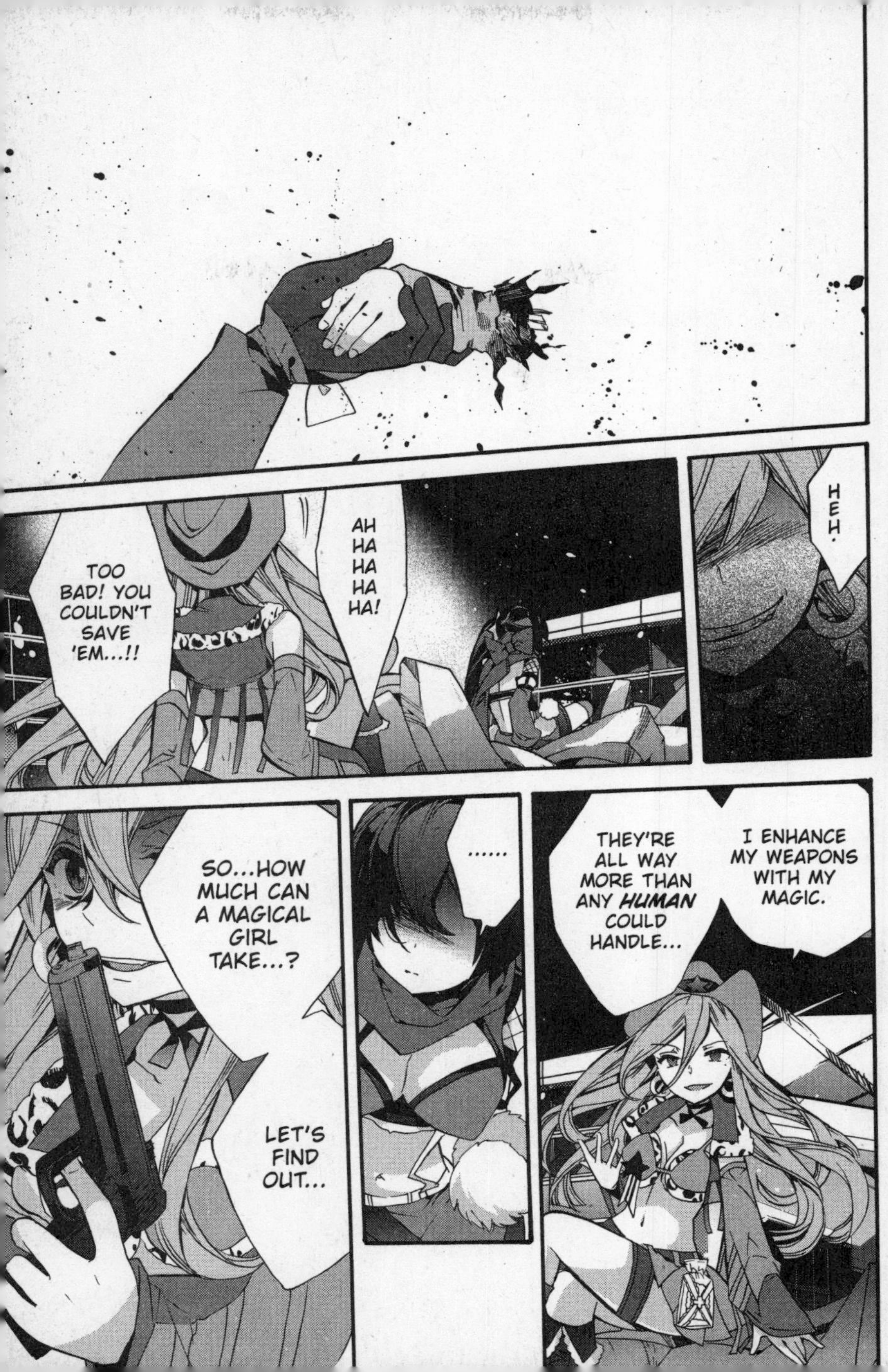
HEH.
AH HA HA HA HA!
TOO BAD! YOU COULDN'T SAVE 'EM...!!
I ENHANCE MY WEAPONS WITH MY MAGIC.
THEY'RE ALL WAY MORE THAN ANY *HUMAN* COULD HANDLE...
......
SO...HOW MUCH CAN A MAGICAL GIRL TAKE...?
LET'S FIND OUT...

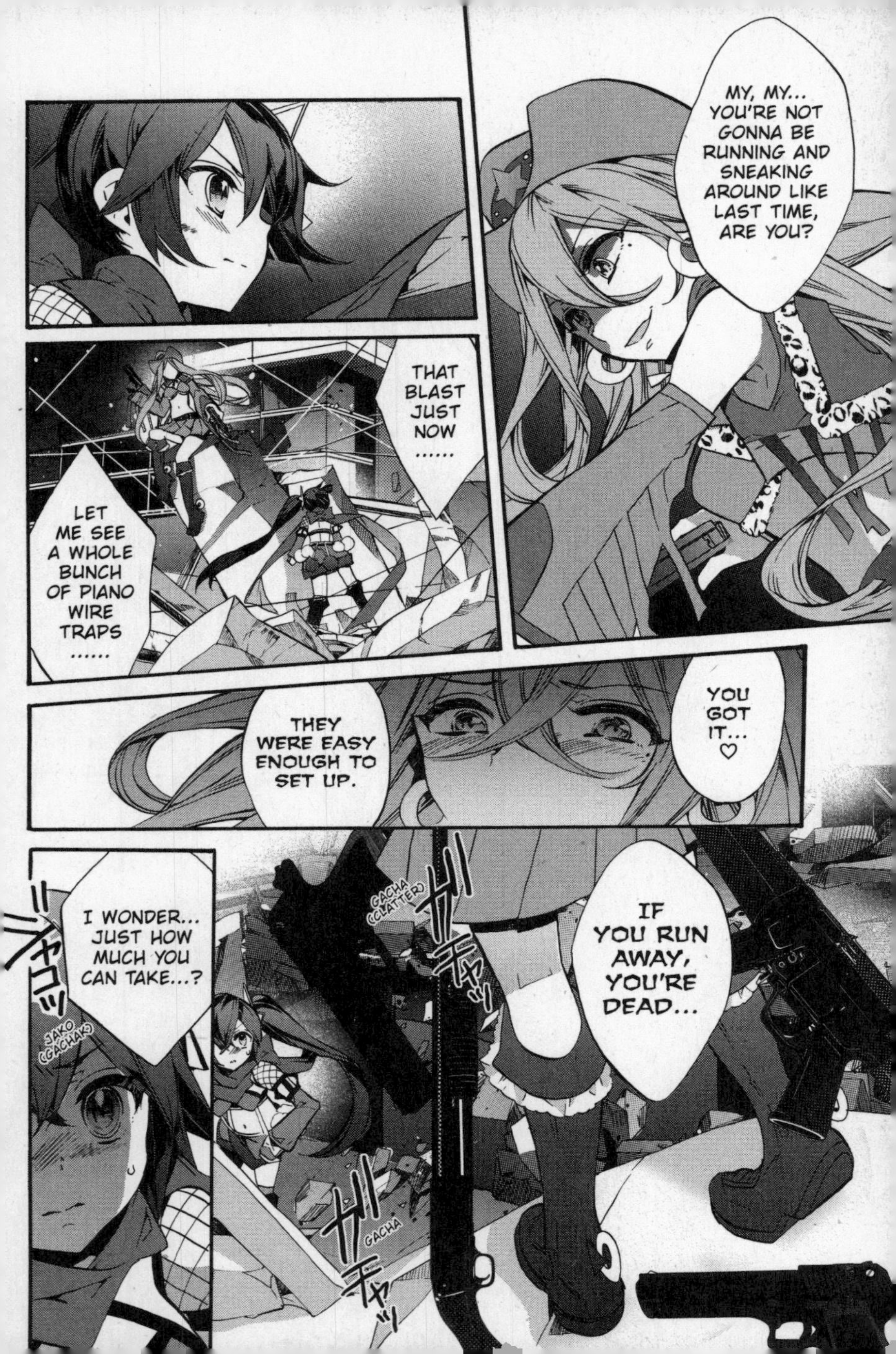
MY, MY... YOU'RE NOT GONNA BE RUNNING AND SNEAKING AROUND LIKE LAST TIME, ARE YOU?
THAT BLAST JUST NOW ......
LET ME SEE A WHOLE BUNCH OF PIANO WIRE TRAPS ......
YOU GOT IT...♡
THEY WERE EASY ENOUGH TO SET UP.
IF YOU RUN AWAY, YOU'RE DEAD...
GACHA (CLATTER)
GACHA
I WONDER... JUST HOW MUCH YOU CAN TAKE...?
JAKO (GACHAK)

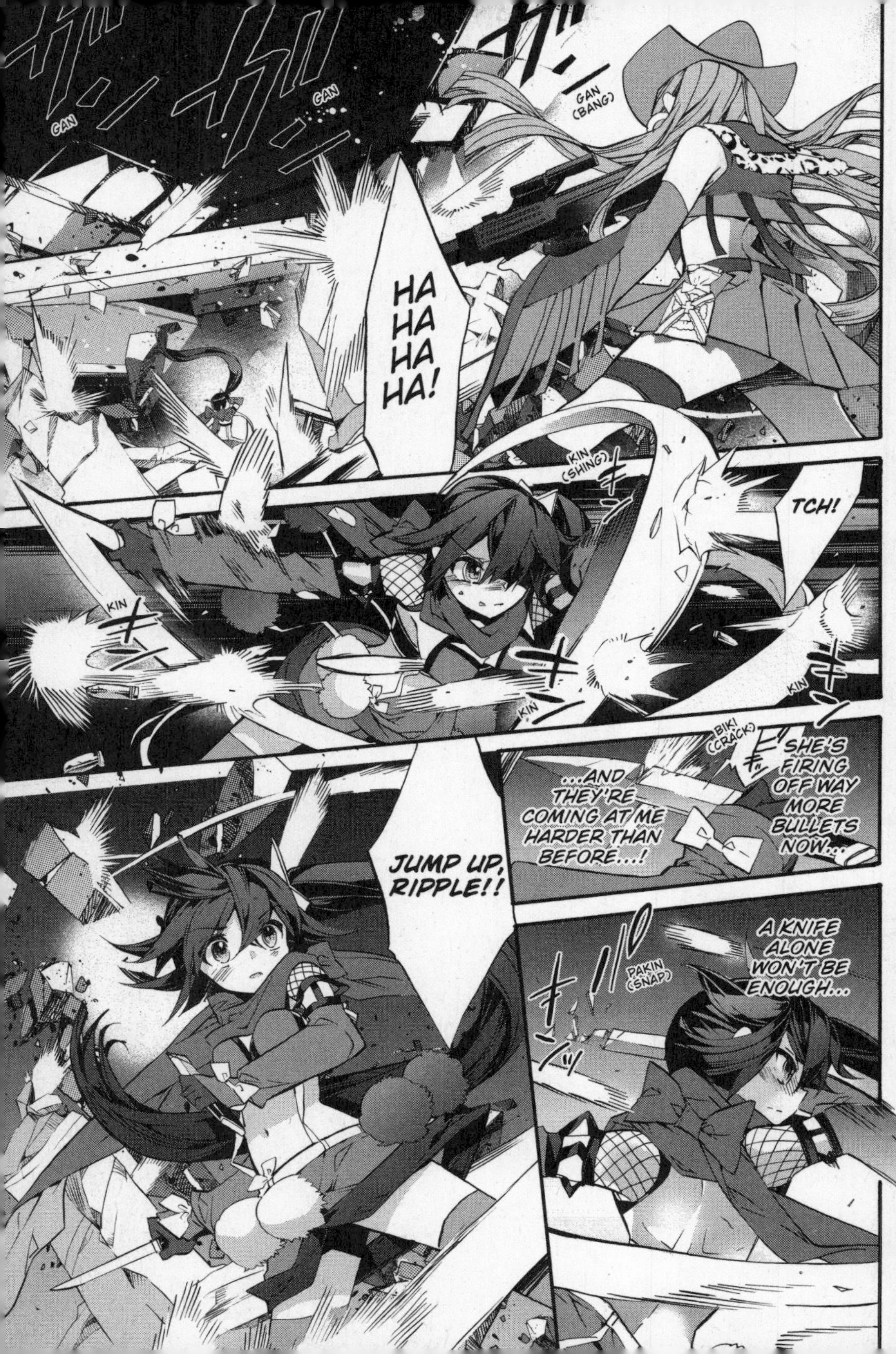
GAN (BANG)
GAN
GAN
HA HA HA HA!
TCH!
KIN (SHING)
KIN
KIN
KIN
SHE'S FIRING OFF WAY MORE BULLETS NOW...
BIKI (CRACK)
...AND THEY'RE COMING AT ME HARDER THAN BEFORE...!
JUMP UP, RIPPLE!!
A KNIFE ALONE WON'T BE ENOUGH...
PAKIN (SNAP)

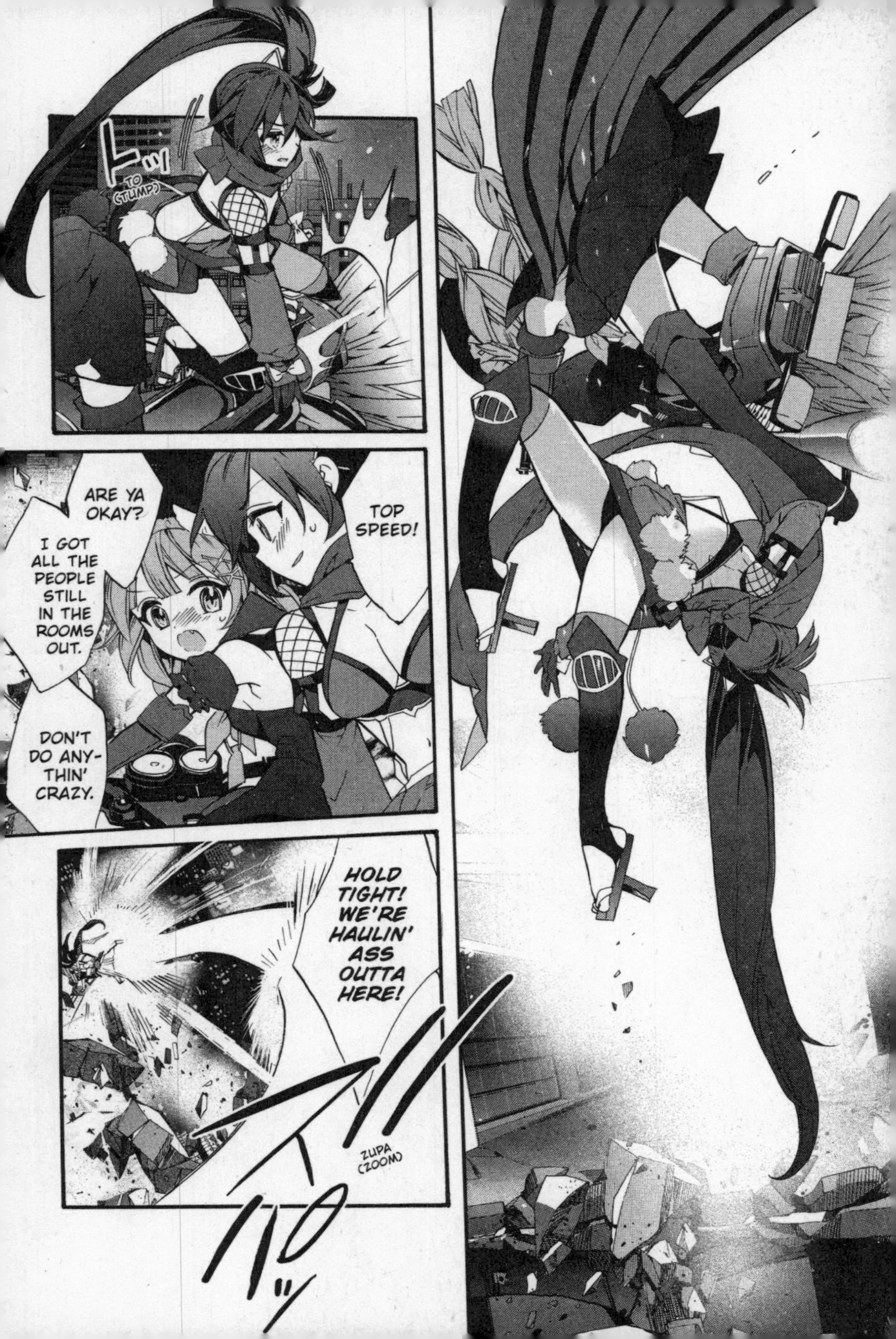
TO
(TUMP)
TOP SPEED!
ARE YA OKAY?
I GOT ALL THE PEOPLE STILL IN THE ROOMS OUT.
DON'T DO ANY-THIN' CRAZY.
HOLD TIGHT! WE'RE HAULIN' ASS OUTTA HERE!
ZUPA
(ZOOM)

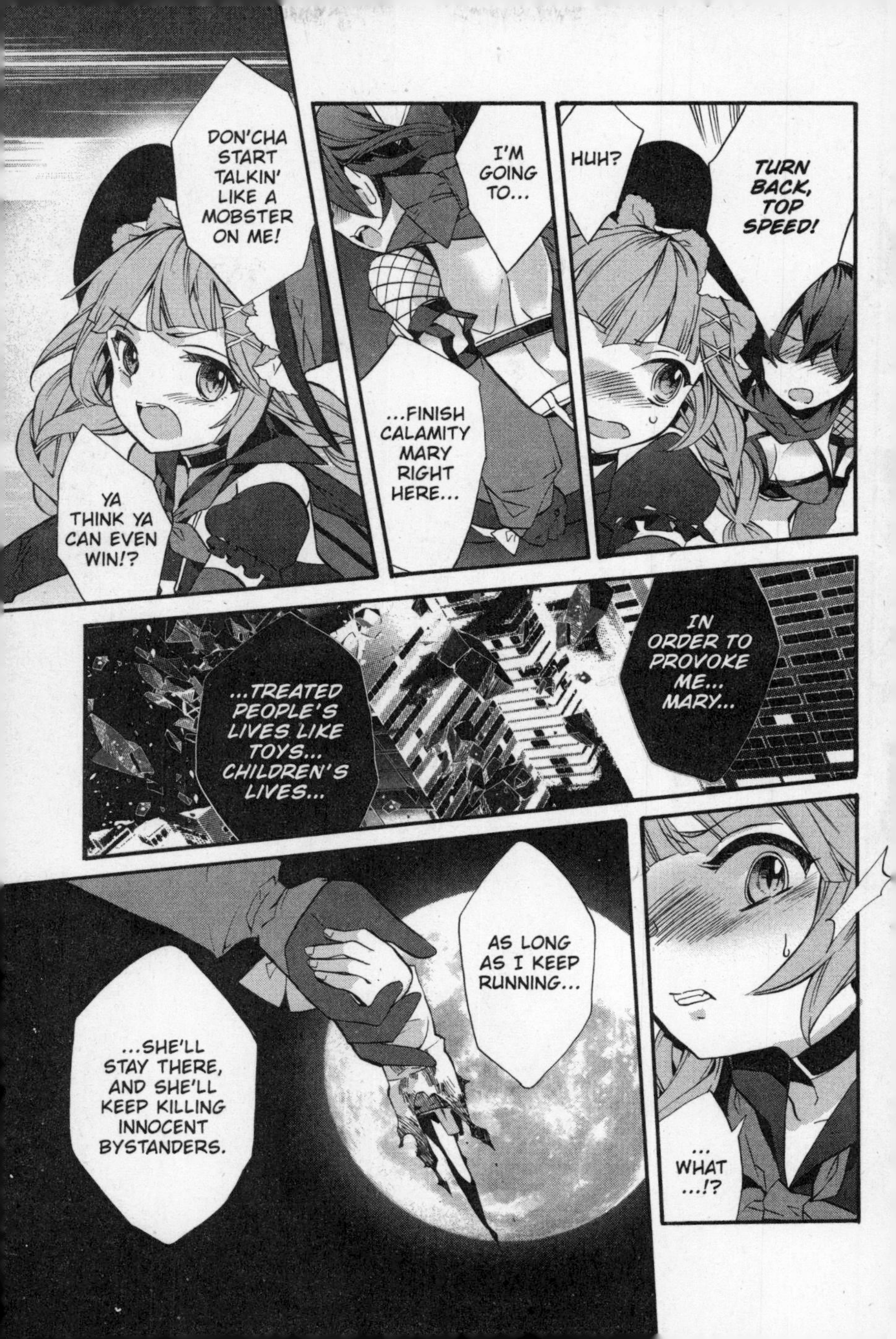
TURN BACK, TOP SPEED!
HUH?
I'M GOING TO...
...FINISH CALAMITY MARY RIGHT HERE...
DON'CHA START TALKIN' LIKE A MOBSTER ON ME!
YA THINK YA CAN EVEN WIN!?
IN ORDER TO PROVOKE ME... MARY...
...TREATED PEOPLE'S LIVES LIKE TOYS... CHILDREN'S LIVES...
... WHAT ...!?
AS LONG AS I KEEP RUNNING...
...SHE'LL STAY THERE, AND SHE'LL KEEP KILLING INNOCENT BYSTANDERS.

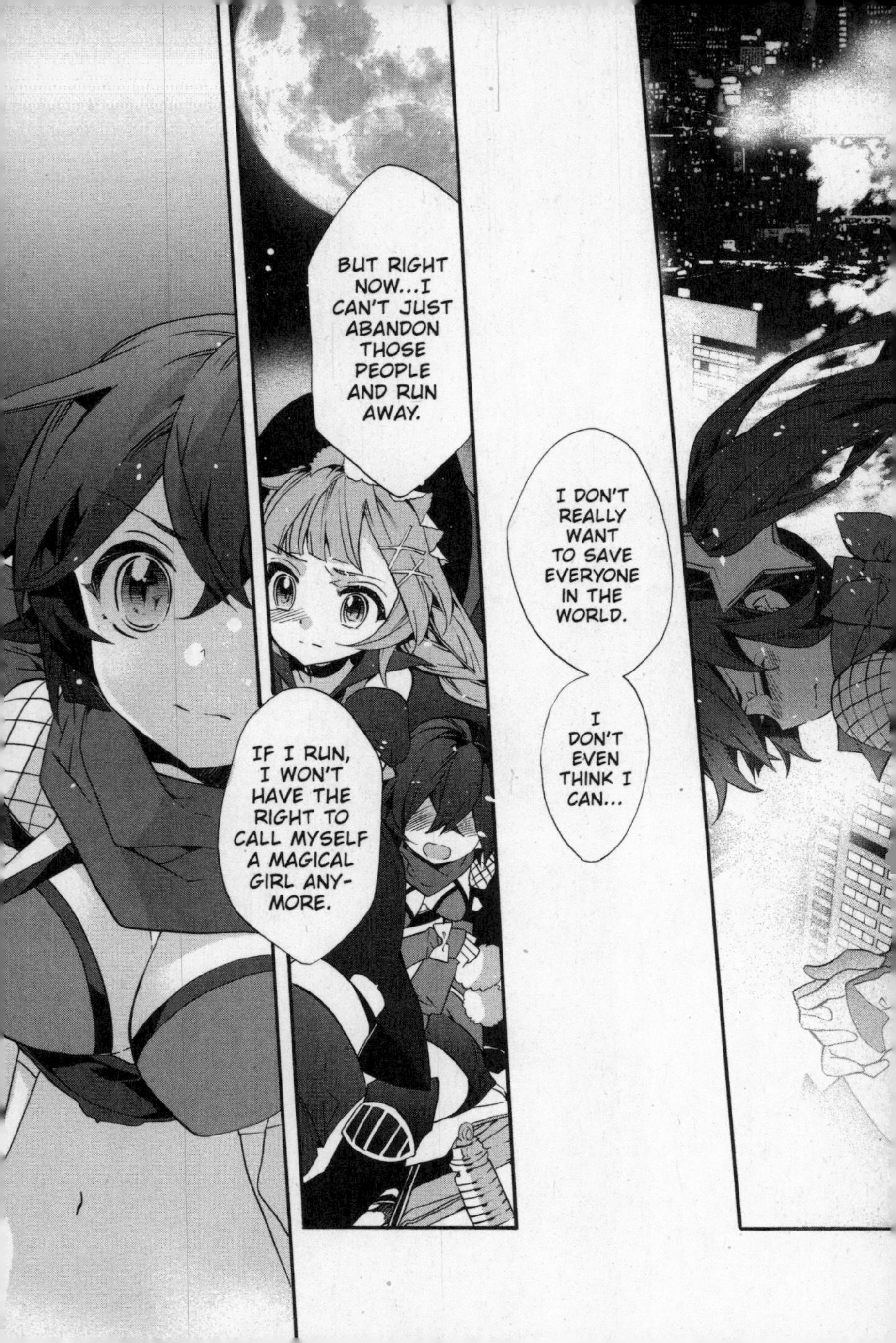
I DON'T REALLY WANT TO SAVE EVERYONE IN THE WORLD.
I DON'T EVEN THINK I CAN...
BUT RIGHT NOW...I CAN'T JUST ABANDON THOSE PEOPLE AND RUN AWAY.
IF I RUN, I WON'T HAVE THE RIGHT TO CALL MYSELF A MAGICAL GIRL ANY-MORE.

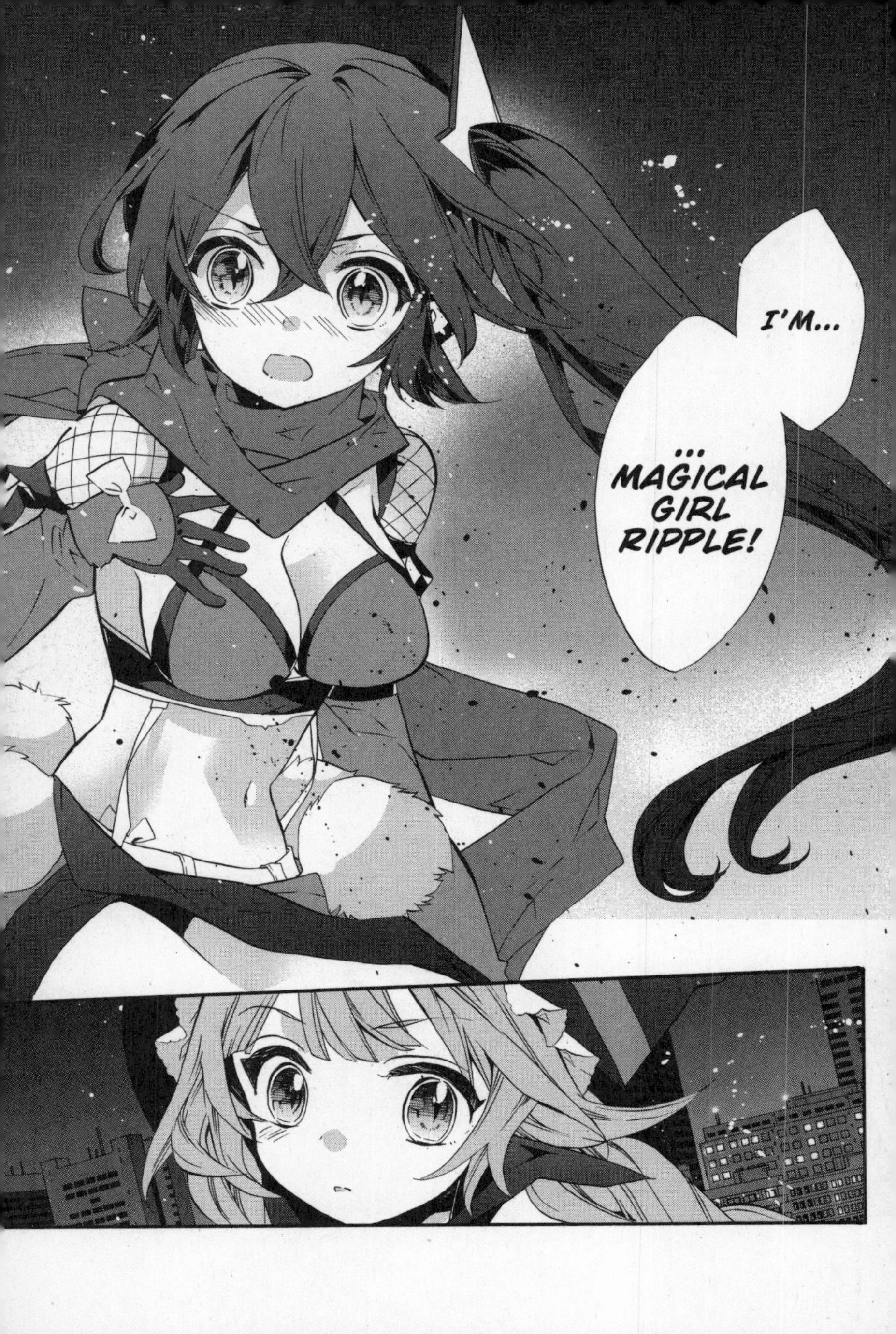
I'M...
...MAGICAL GIRL RIPPLE!

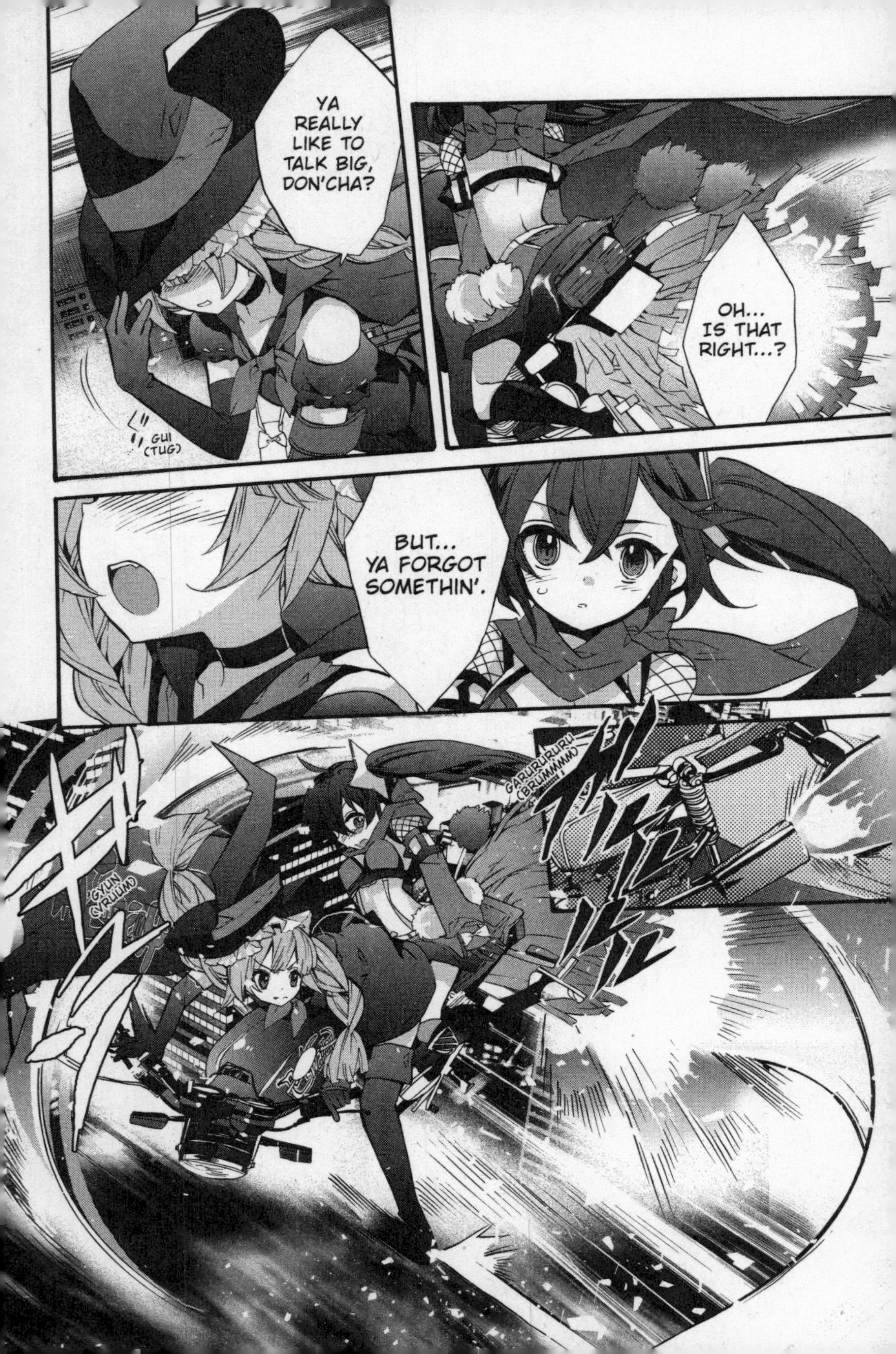
OH... IS THAT RIGHT...?
YA REALLY LIKE TO TALK BIG, DON'CHA?
GUI (TUG)
BUT... YA FORGOT SOMETHIN'.
GARURURURU (BRUMMMM)
GYUN (VRUUM)

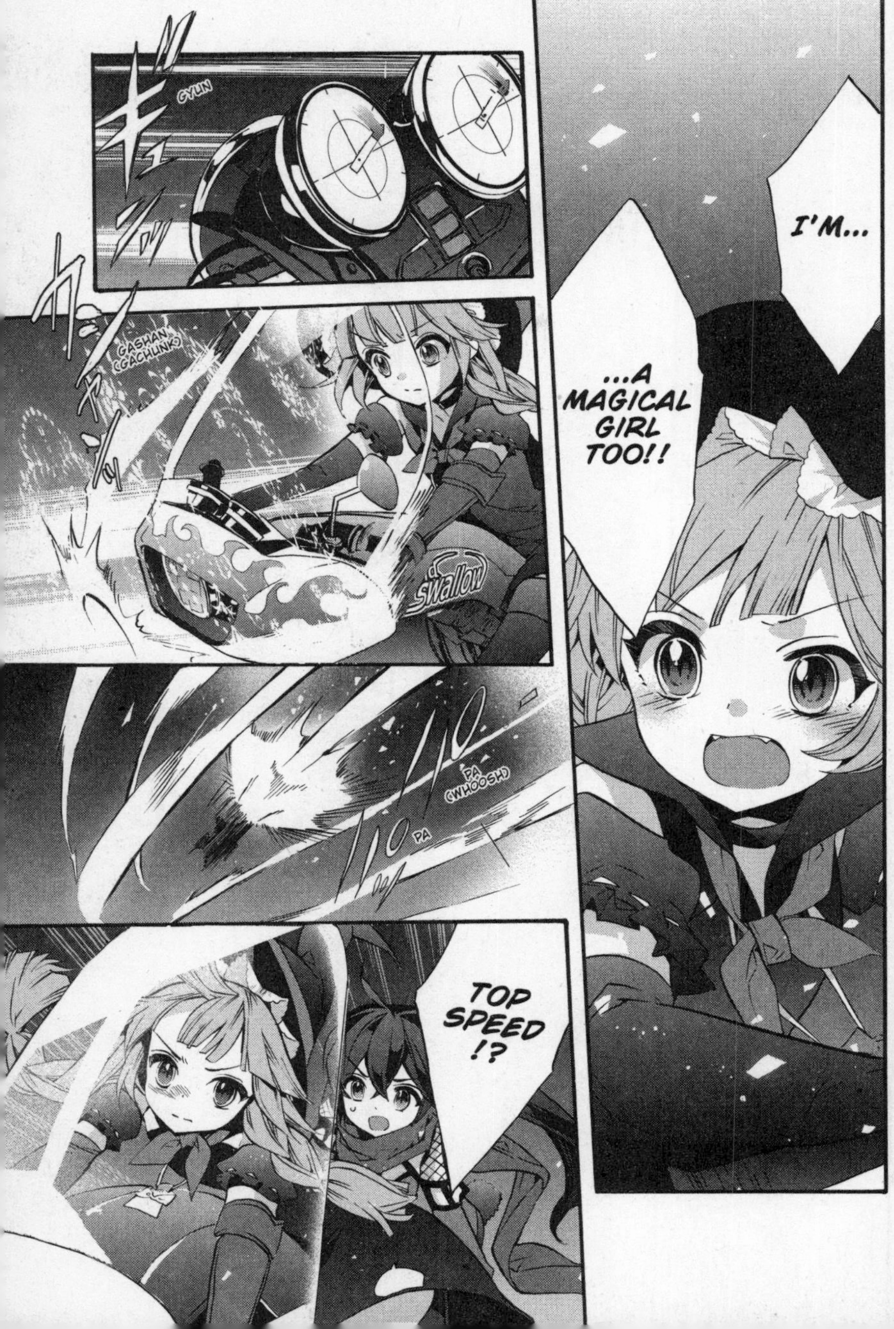
I'M...
...A MAGICAL GIRL TOO!!
GYUN
GASHAN (GACHUNK)
PA (WHOOSH)
PA
TOP SPEED!?

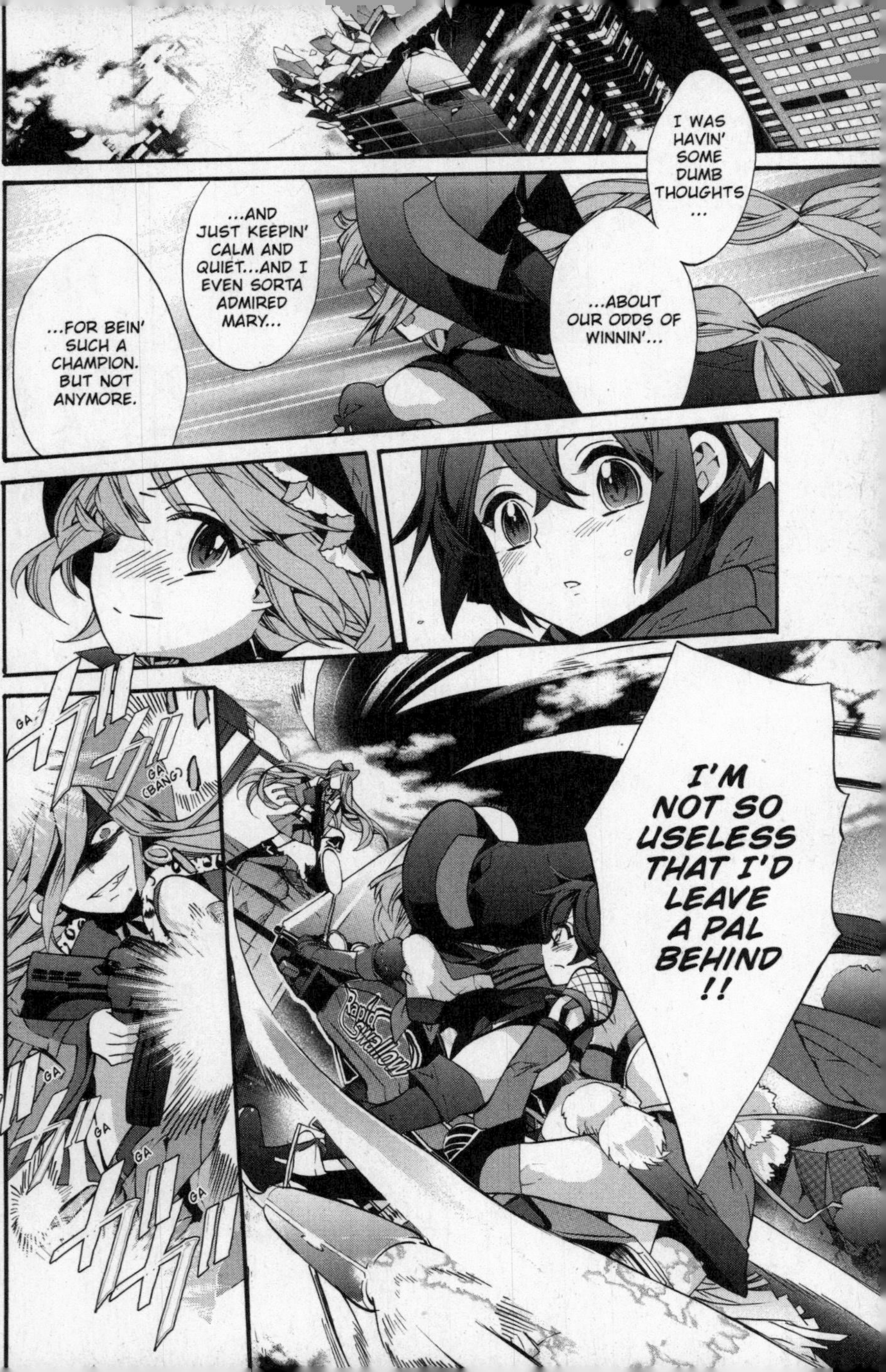
I WAS HAVIN' SOME DUMB THOUGHTS...
...ABOUT OUR ODDS OF WINNIN'...
...AND JUST KEEPIN' CALM AND QUIET...AND I EVEN SORTA ADMIRED MARY...
...FOR BEIN' SUCH A CHAMPION. BUT NOT ANYMORE.
I'M NOT SO USELESS THAT I'D LEAVE A PAL BEHIND!!
Rapid Swallow
GA
GA (BANG)
GA
GA
GA

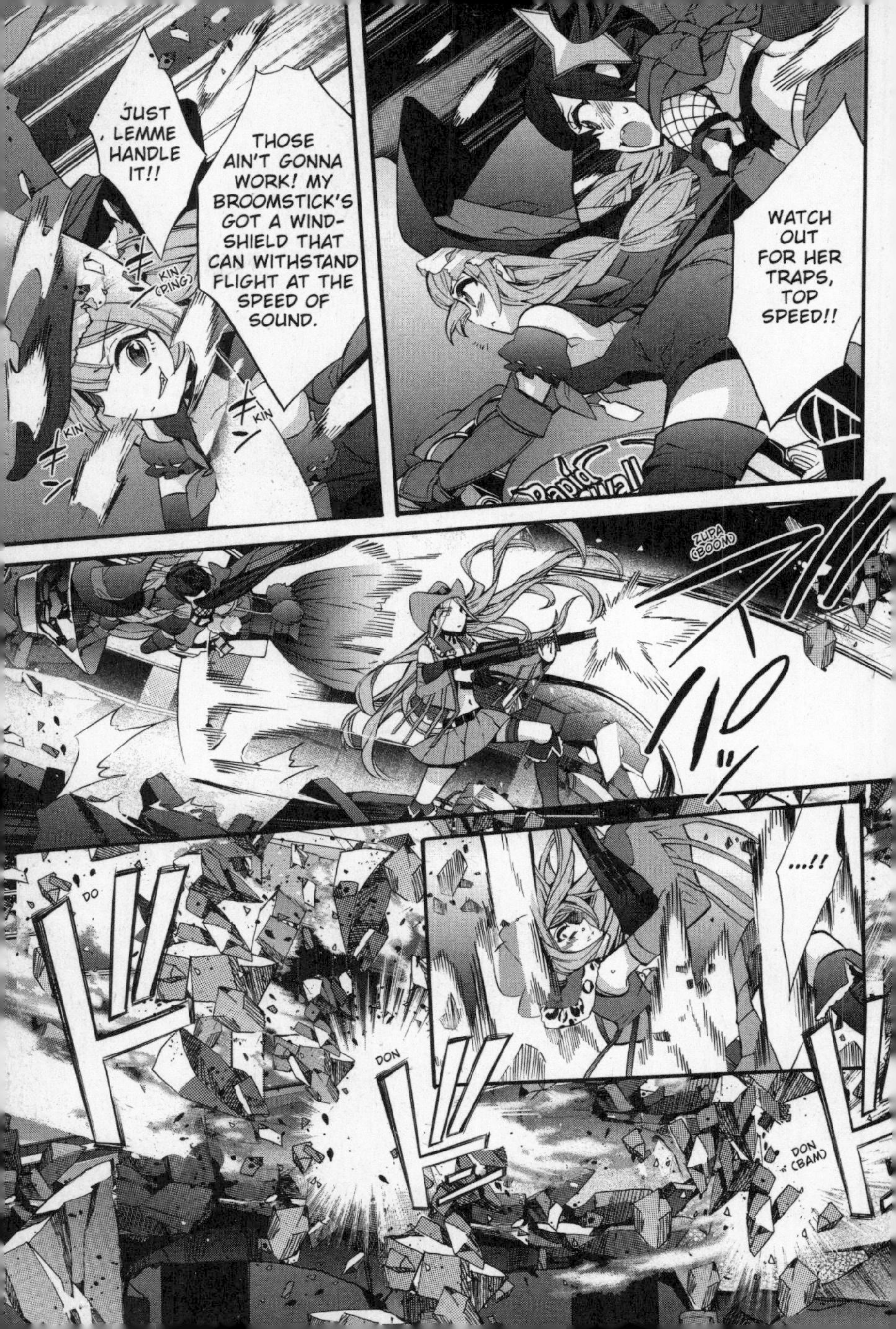
WATCH OUT FOR HER TRAPS, TOP SPEED!!
THOSE AIN'T GONNA WORK! MY BROOMSTICK'S GOT A WIND-SHIELD THAT CAN WITHSTAND FLIGHT AT THE SPEED OF SOUND.
JUST LEMME HANDLE IT!!
KIN (PING)
KIN
KIN
ZUPA (BOOM)
...!!
DON (BAM)
DON
DO

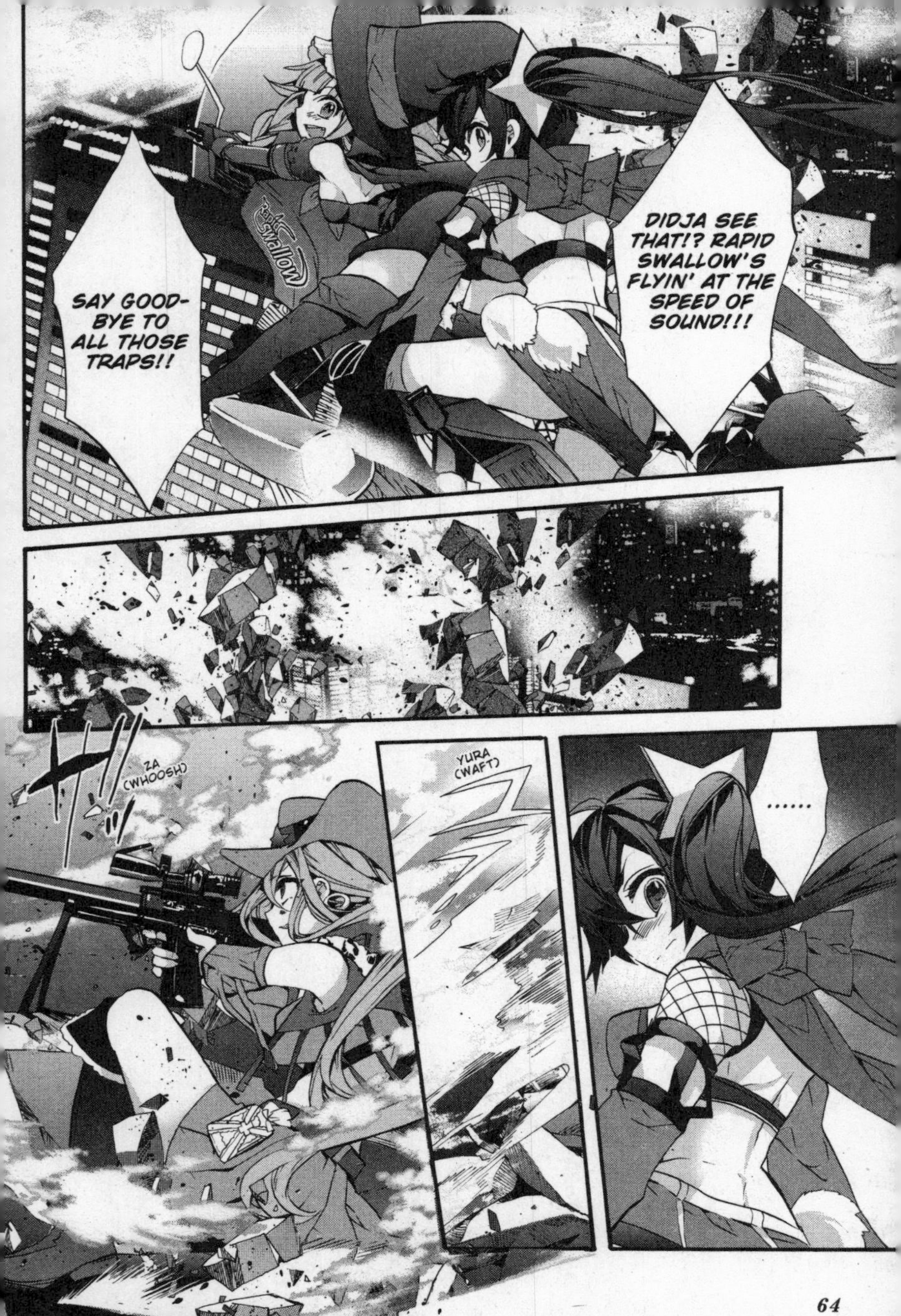
DIDJA SEE THAT!? RAPID SWALLOW'S FLYIN' AT THE SPEED OF SOUND!!!
SAY GOOD-BYE TO ALL THOSE TRAPS!!
......
YURA (WAFT)
ZA (WHOOSH)

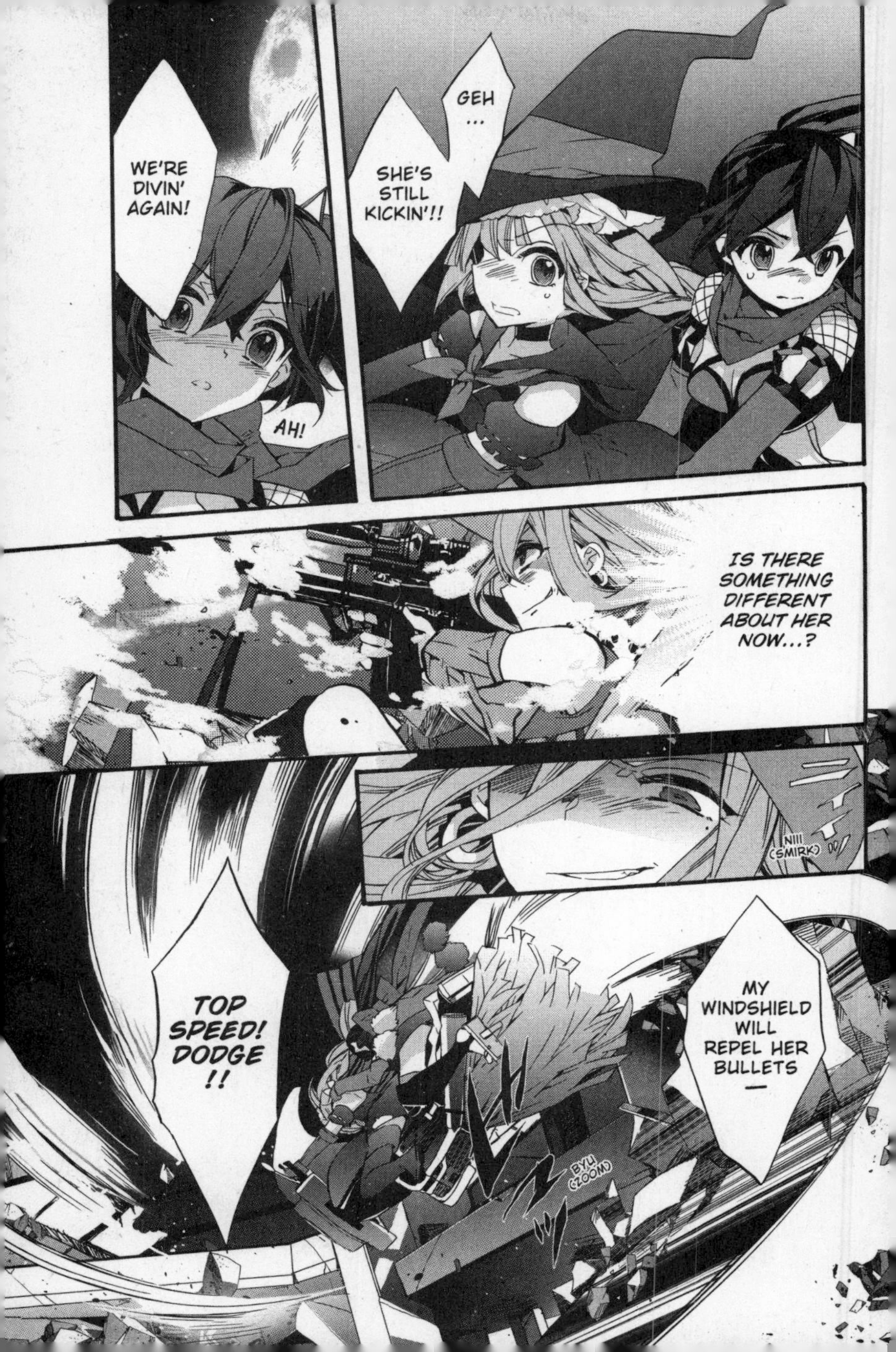
GEH...
SHE'S STILL KICKIN'!!
WE'RE DIVIN' AGAIN!
AH!
IS THERE SOMETHING DIFFERENT ABOUT HER NOW...?
NIII (SMIRK)
MY WINDSHIELD WILL REPEL HER BULLETS—
TOP SPEED! DODGE!!
BYU (ZOOM)

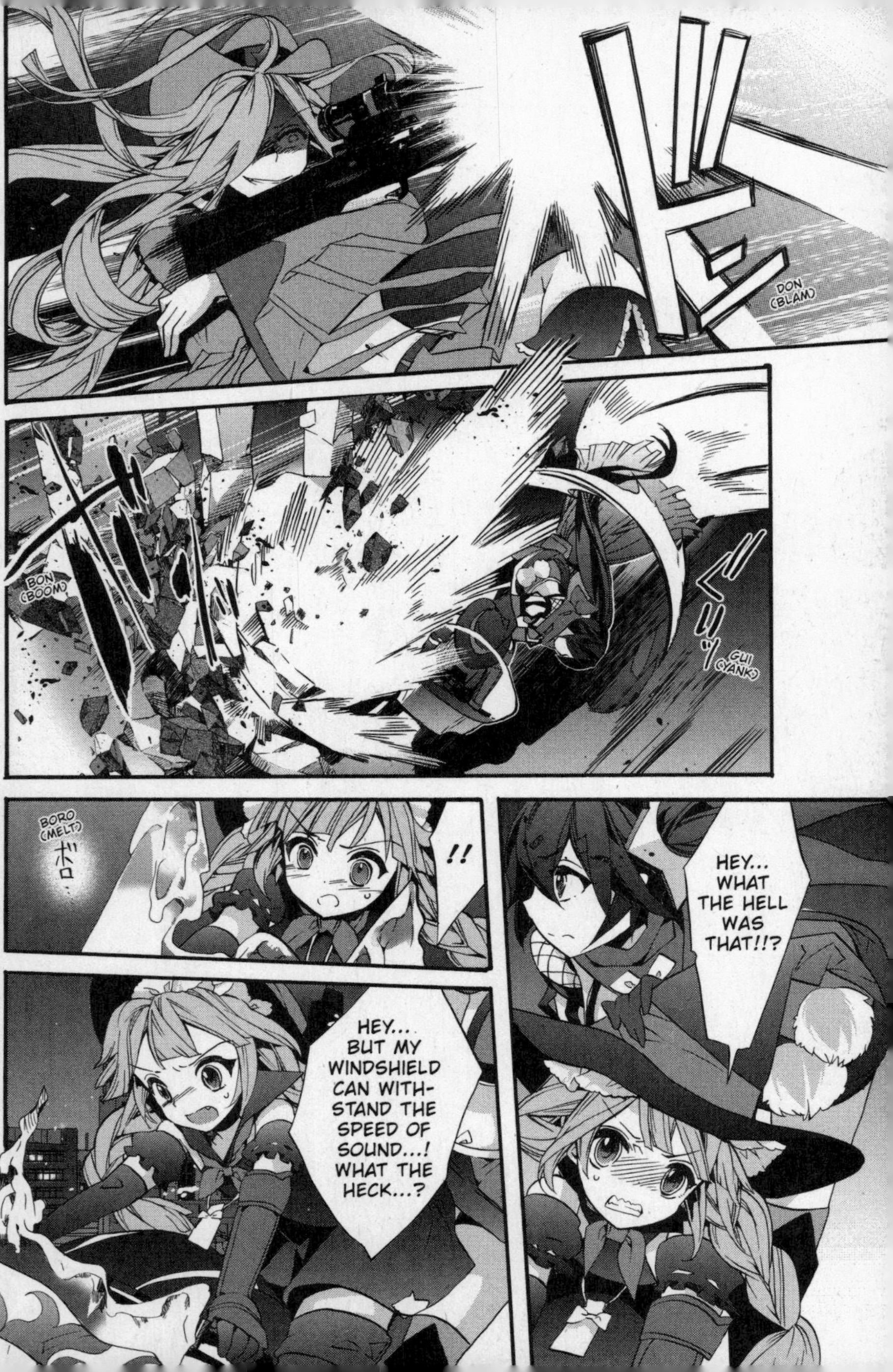
DON (BLAM)
GUI (YANK)
BON (BOOM)
HEY... WHAT THE HELL WAS THAT!!?
BORO (MELT)
ボロ
!!
HEY... BUT MY WINDSHIELD CAN WITH-STAND THE SPEED OF SOUND...! WHAT THE HECK...?

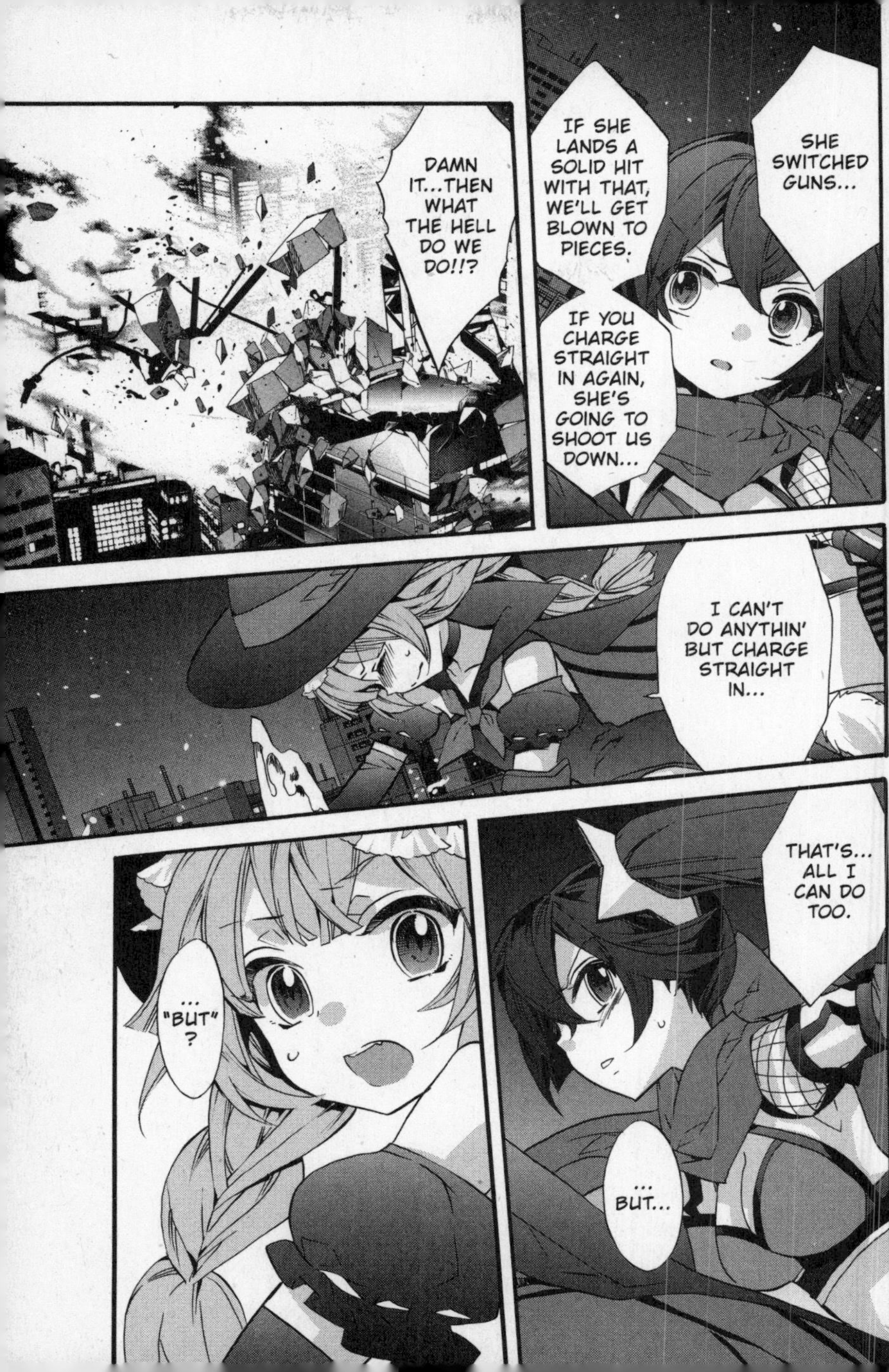
SHE SWITCHED GUNS...
IF SHE LANDS A SOLID HIT WITH THAT, WE'LL GET BLOWN TO PIECES.
IF YOU CHARGE STRAIGHT IN AGAIN, SHE'S GOING TO SHOOT US DOWN...
DAMN IT...THEN WHAT THE HELL DO WE DO!!?
I CAN'T DO ANYTHIN' BUT CHARGE STRAIGHT IN...
THAT'S... ALL I CAN DO TOO.
... BUT...
... "BUT" ?

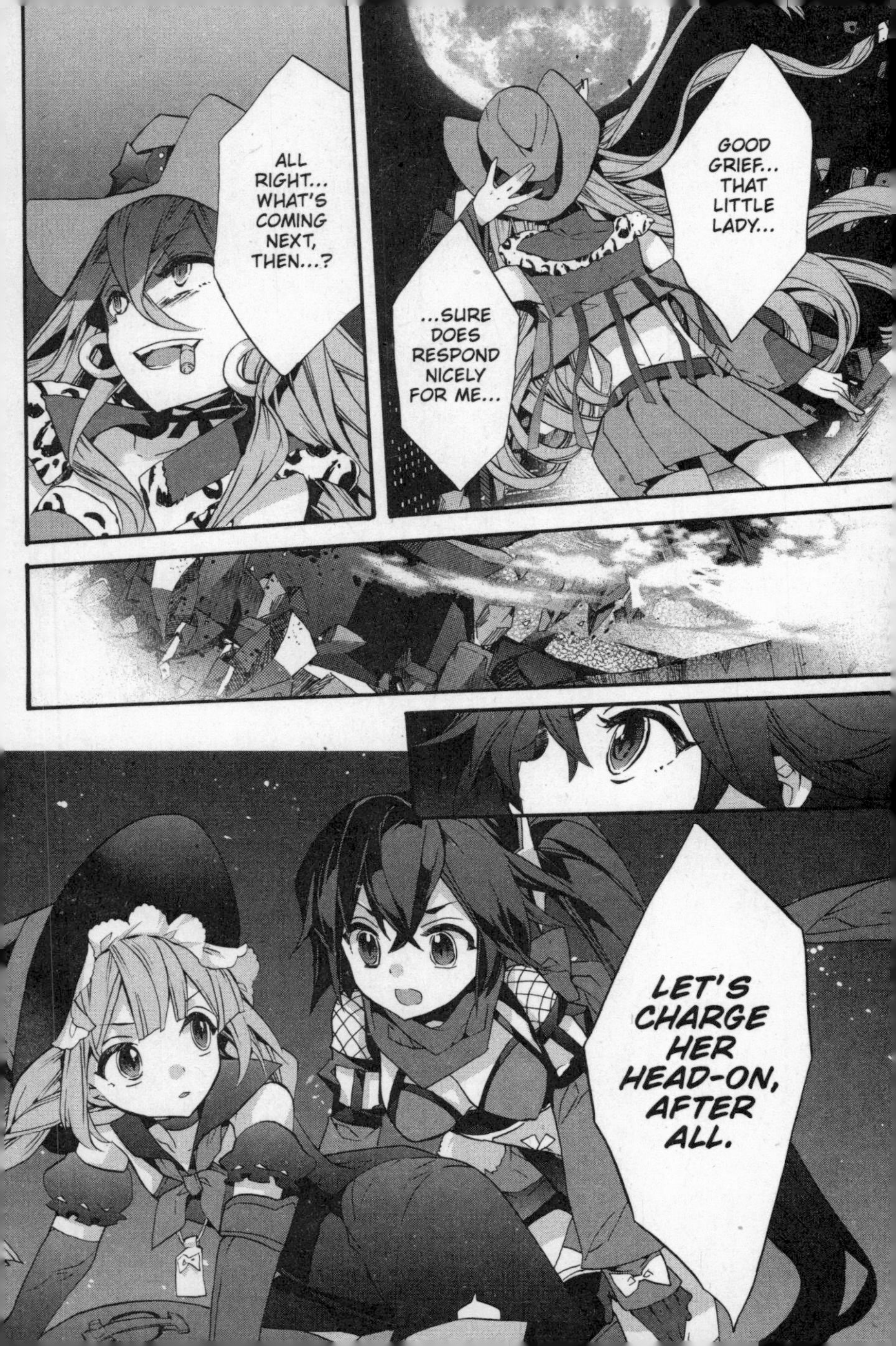
GOOD GRIEF... THAT LITTLE LADY...
...SURE DOES RESPOND NICELY FOR ME...
ALL RIGHT... WHAT'S COMING NEXT, THEN...?
LET'S CHARGE HER HEAD-ON, AFTER ALL.

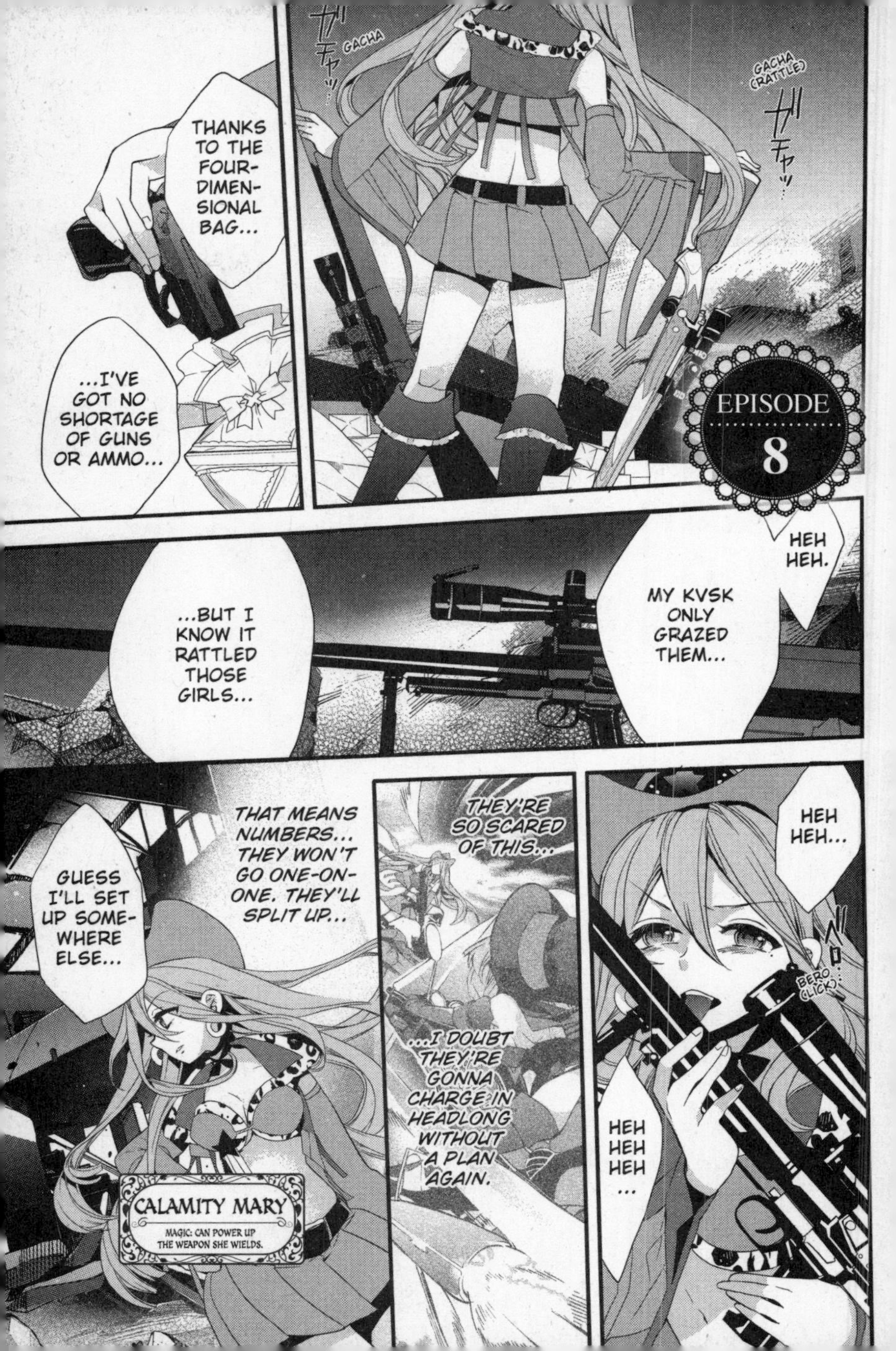
GACHA
GACHA (RATTLE)
EPISODE 8
THANKS TO THE FOUR-DIMENSIONAL BAG...
...I'VE GOT NO SHORTAGE OF GUNS OR AMMO...
HEH HEH.
MY KVSK ONLY GRAZED THEM...
...BUT I KNOW IT RATTLED THOSE GIRLS...
HEH HEH...
BERO (LICK)
HEH HEH HEH...
THEY'RE SO SCARED OF THIS...
...I DOUBT THEY'RE GONNA CHARGE IN HEADLONG WITHOUT A PLAN AGAIN.
THAT MEANS NUMBERS... THEY WON'T GO ONE-ON-ONE. THEY'LL SPLIT UP...
GUESS I'LL SET UP SOMEWHERE ELSE...
CALAMITY MARY
MAGIC: CAN POWER UP THE WEAPON SHE WIELDS.

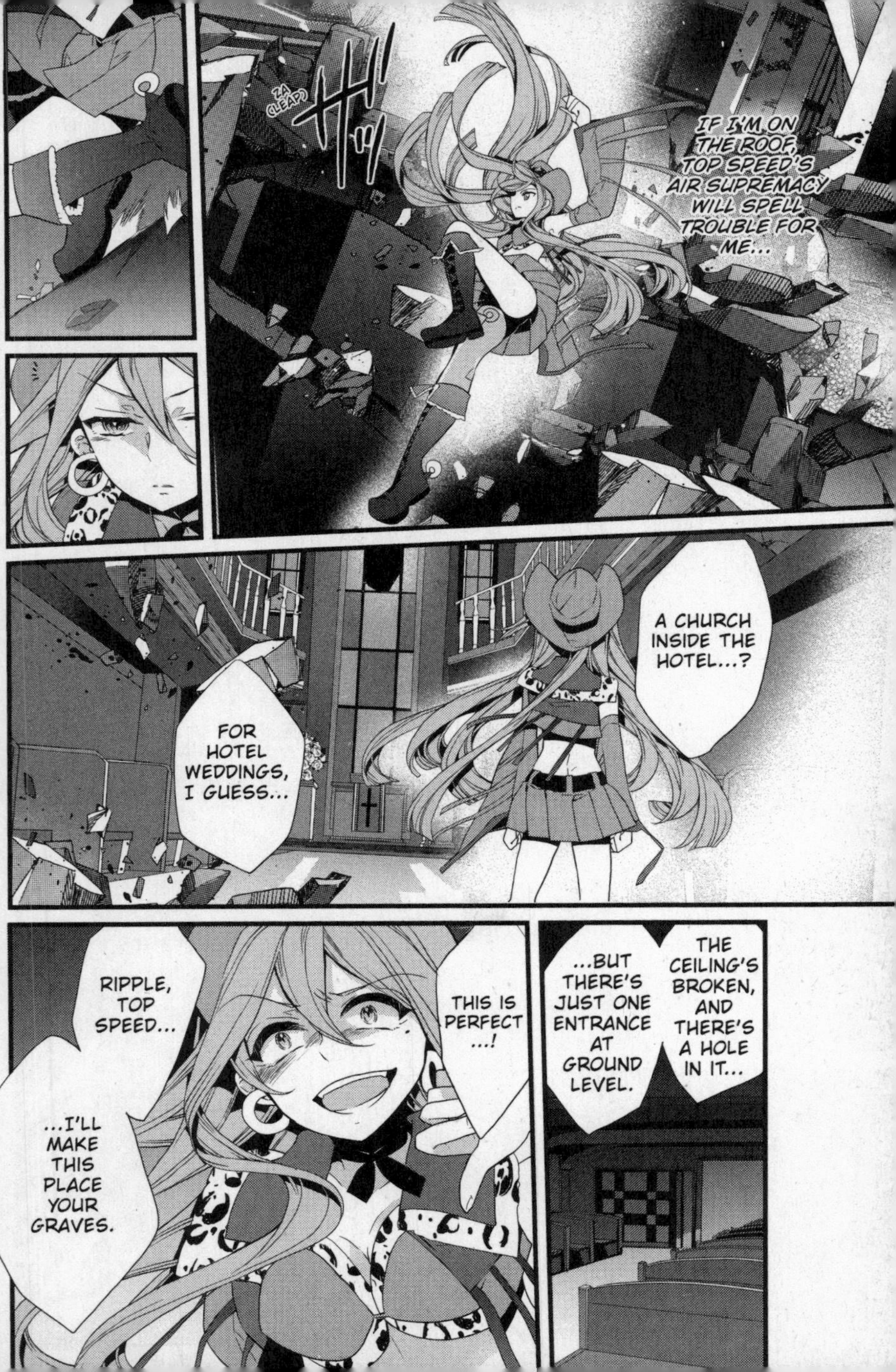
ZA (LEAP)
IF I'M ON THE ROOF, TOP SPEED'S AIR SUPREMACY WILL SPELL TROUBLE FOR ME...
A CHURCH INSIDE THE HOTEL...?
FOR HOTEL WEDDINGS, I GUESS...
THE CEILING'S BROKEN, AND THERE'S A HOLE IN IT...
...BUT THERE'S JUST ONE ENTRANCE AT GROUND LEVEL.
THIS IS PERFECT...!
RIPPLE, TOP SPEED...
...I'LL MAKE THIS PLACE YOUR GRAVES.

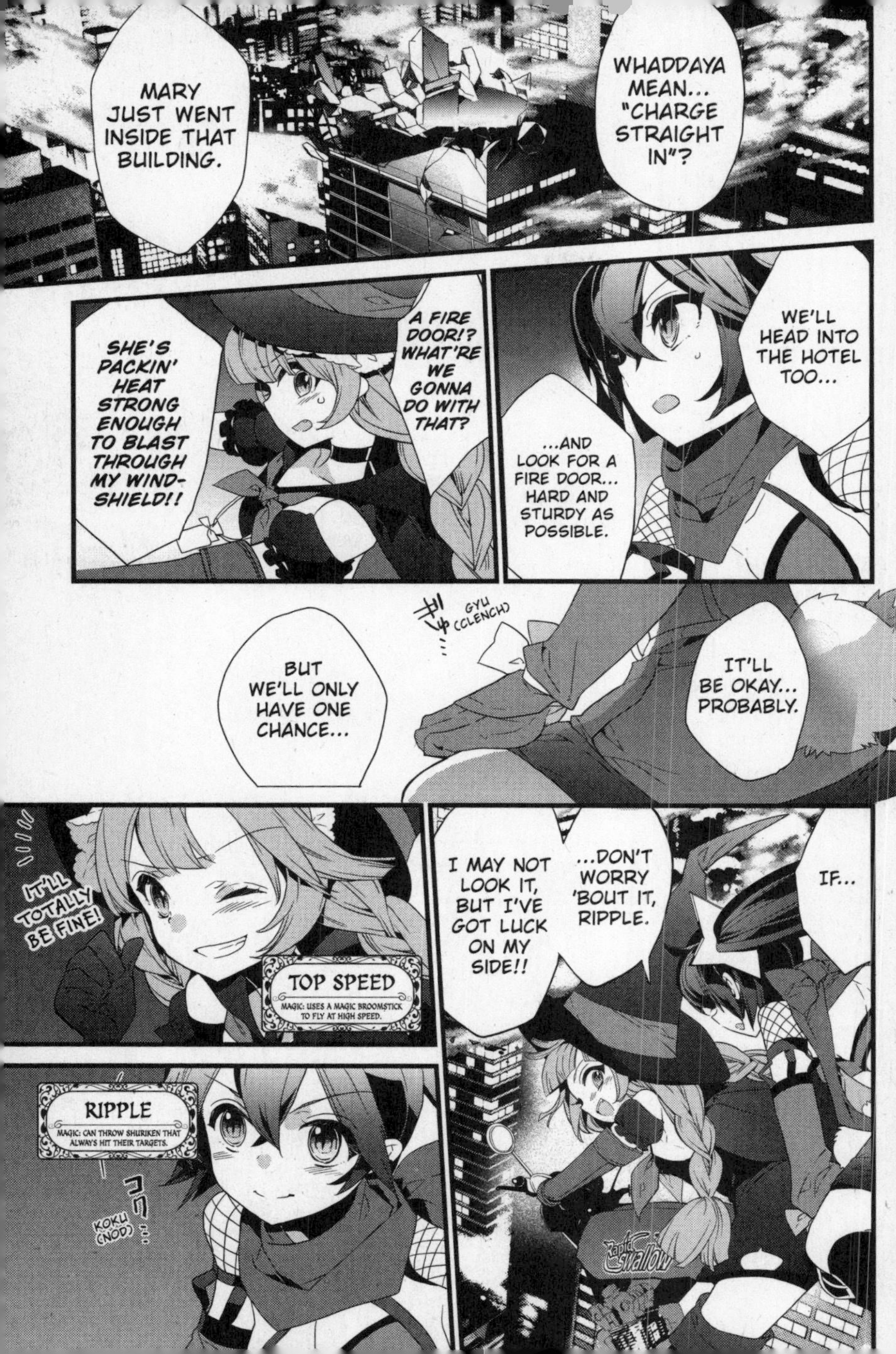
WHADDAYA MEAN... "CHARGE STRAIGHT IN"?
MARY JUST WENT INSIDE THAT BUILDING.
WE'LL HEAD INTO THE HOTEL TOO...
...AND LOOK FOR A FIRE DOOR... HARD AND STURDY AS POSSIBLE.
A FIRE DOOR!? WHAT'RE WE GONNA DO WITH THAT?
SHE'S PACKIN' HEAT STRONG ENOUGH TO BLAST THROUGH MY WIND-SHIELD!!
IT'LL BE OKAY... PROBABLY.
GYU (CLENCH)
BUT WE'LL ONLY HAVE ONE CHANCE...
IF...
...DON'T WORRY 'BOUT IT, RIPPLE.
I MAY NOT LOOK IT, BUT I'VE GOT LUCK ON MY SIDE!!
Rapid Swallow
IT'LL TOTALLY BE FINE!
TOP SPEED
MAGIC: USES A MAGIC BROOMSTICK TO FLY AT HIGH SPEED.
RIPPLE
MAGIC: CAN THROW SHURIKEN THAT ALWAYS HIT THEIR TARGETS.
KOKU (NOD)

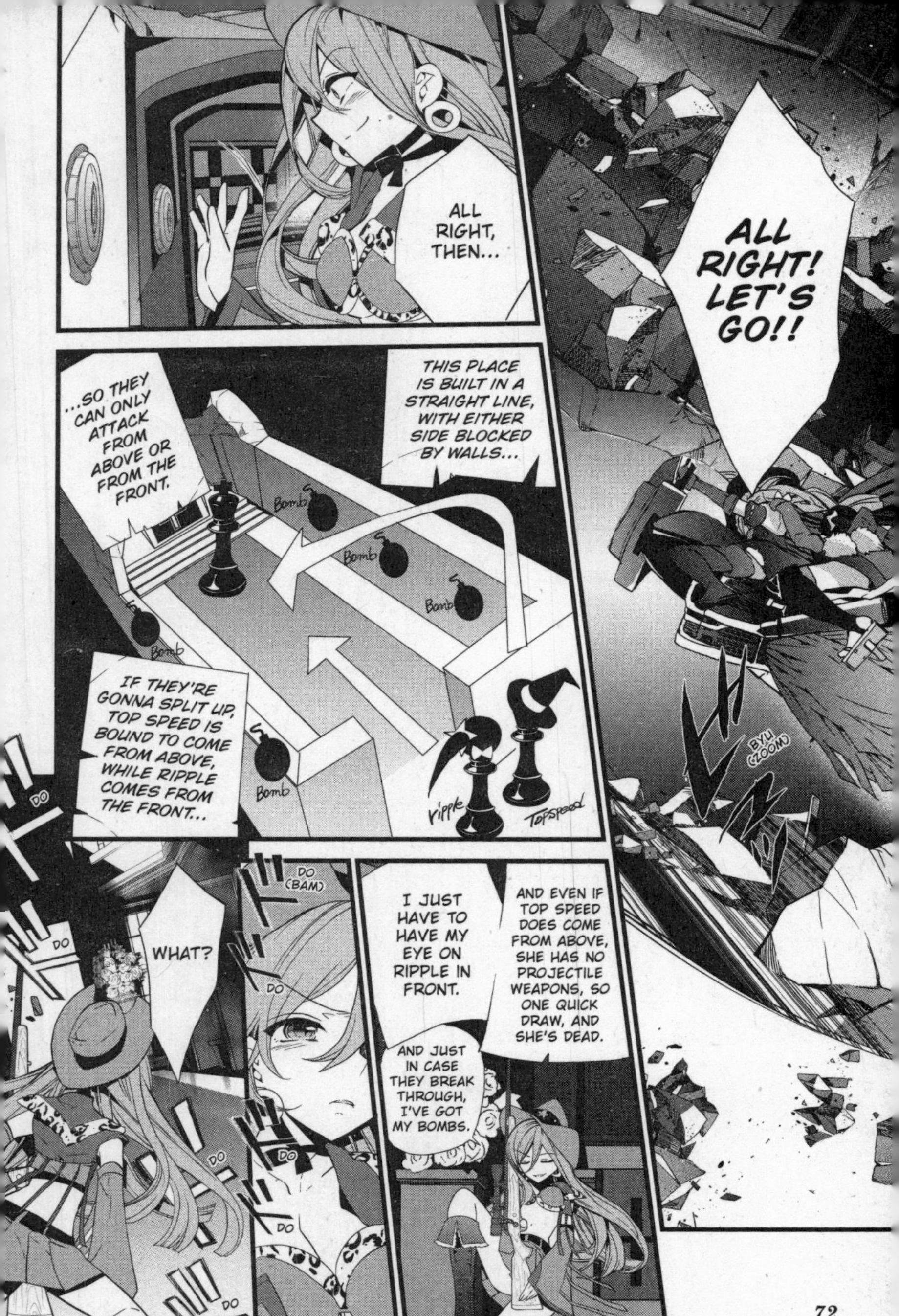
ALL RIGHT! LET'S GO!!
BYU (ZOOM)
ALL RIGHT, THEN...
THIS PLACE IS BUILT IN A STRAIGHT LINE, WITH EITHER SIDE BLOCKED BY WALLS...
...SO THEY CAN ONLY ATTACK FROM ABOVE OR FROM THE FRONT.
Bomb
Bomb
Bomb
Bomb
Bomb
IF THEY'RE GONNA SPLIT UP, TOP SPEED IS BOUND TO COME FROM ABOVE, WHILE RIPPLE COMES FROM THE FRONT...
Topspeed
ripple
AND EVEN IF TOP SPEED DOES COME FROM ABOVE, SHE HAS NO PROJECTILE WEAPONS, SO ONE QUICK DRAW, AND SHE'S DEAD.
I JUST HAVE TO HAVE MY EYE ON RIPPLE IN FRONT.
AND JUST IN CASE THEY BREAK THROUGH, I'VE GOT MY BOMBS.
DO (BAM)
WHAT?
DO
DO
DO
DO
DO
DO
DO

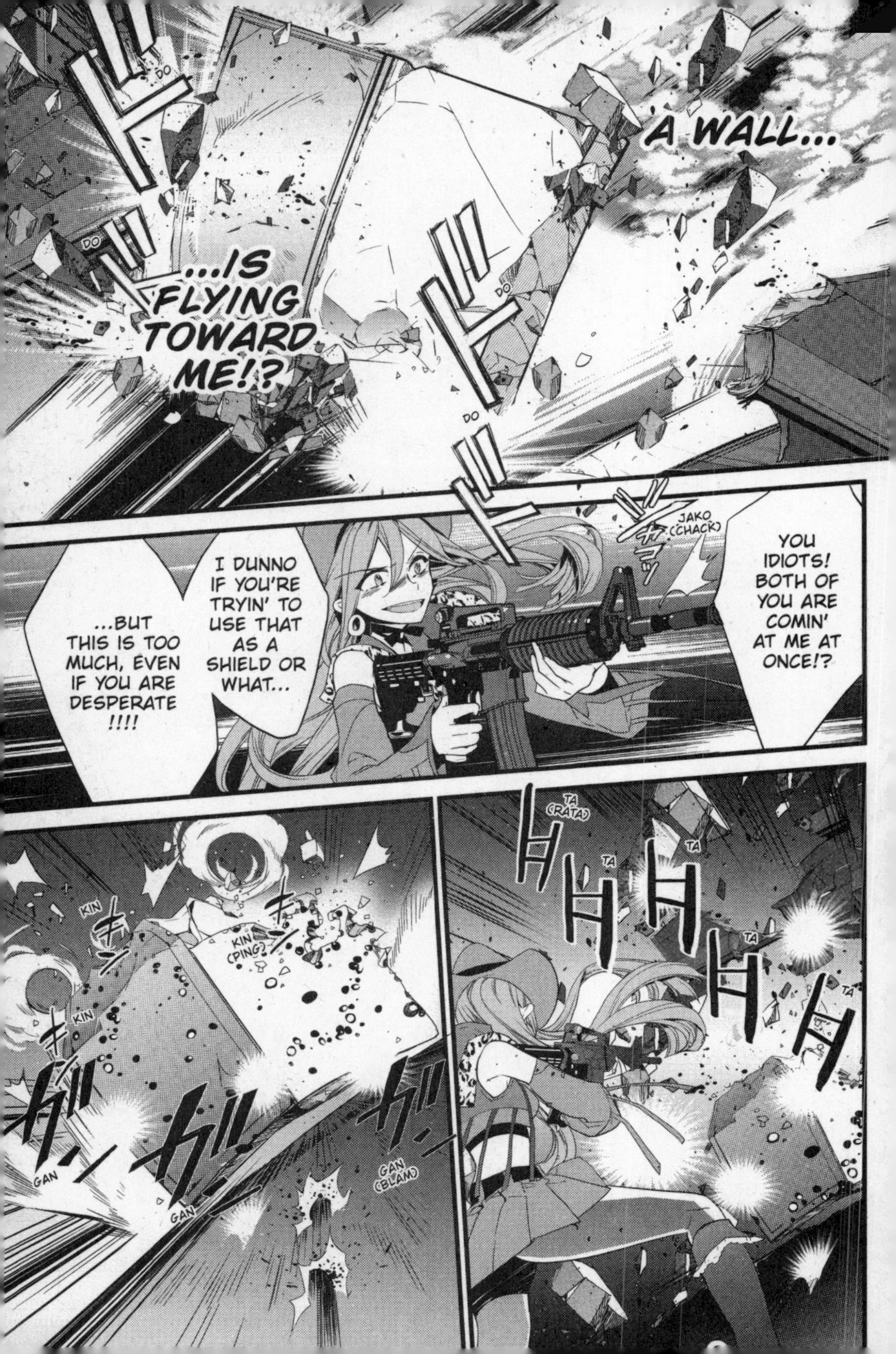
A WALL...
...IS FLYING TOWARD ME!?
DO
DO
DO
DO
JAKO (CHACK)
YOU IDIOTS! BOTH OF YOU ARE COMIN' AT ME AT ONCE!?
I DUNNO IF YOU'RE TRYIN' TO USE THAT AS A SHIELD OR WHAT...
...BUT THIS IS TOO MUCH, EVEN IF YOU ARE DESPERATE!!!!
TA (RATA)
TA
TA
TA
TA
KIN
KIN (PING)
KIN
GAN (BLAM)
GAN
GAN

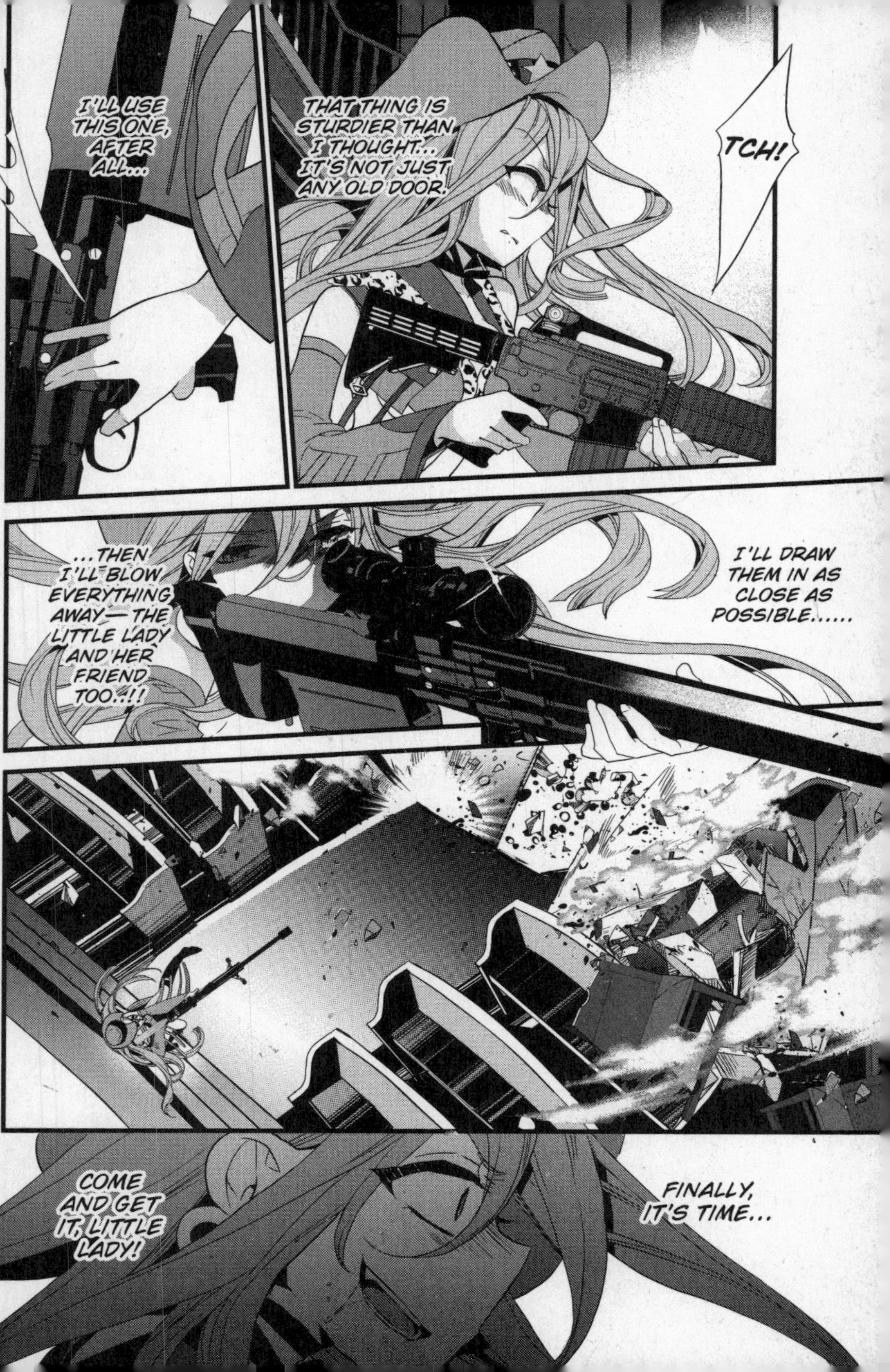
TCH!
THAT THING IS STURDIER THAN I THOUGHT... IT'S NOT JUST ANY OLD DOOR.
I'LL USE THIS ONE, AFTER ALL...
I'LL DRAW THEM IN AS CLOSE AS POSSIBLE......
...THEN I'LL BLOW EVERYTHING AWAY—THE LITTLE LADY AND HER FRIEND TOO..!!
FINALLY, IT'S TIME...
COME AND GET IT, LITTLE LADY!

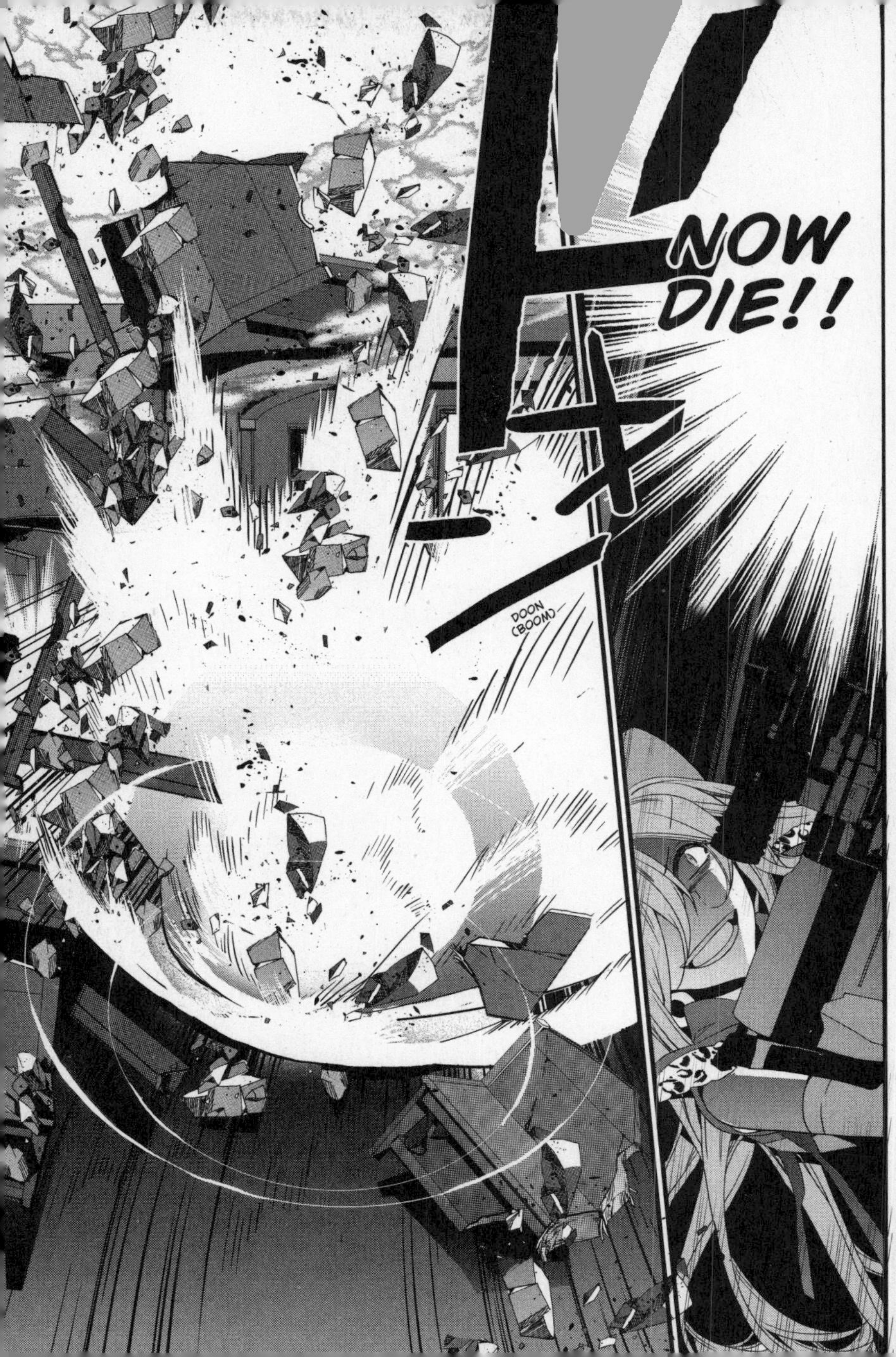
NOW DIE!!
DOON (BOOM)

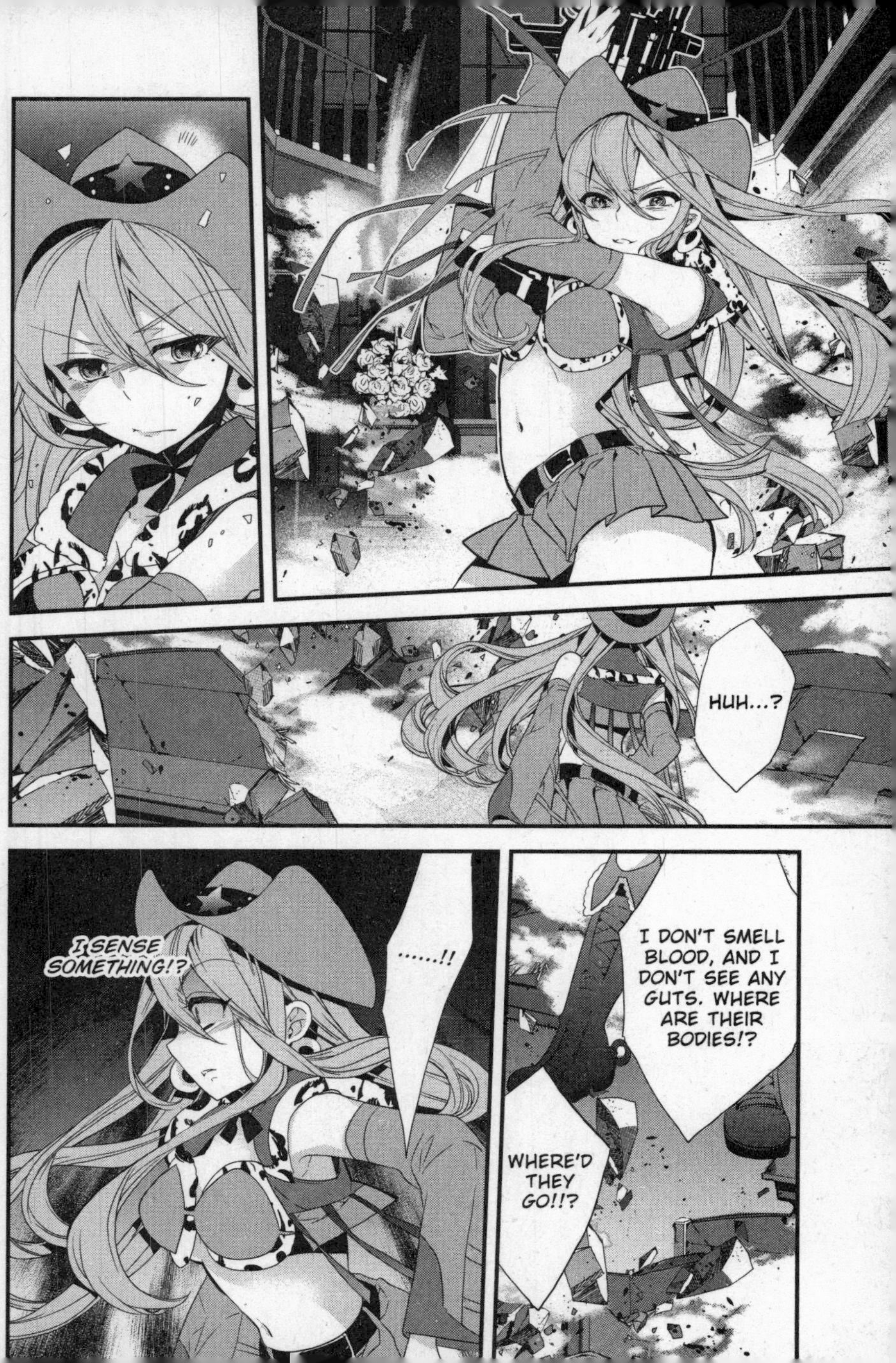
HUH...?
I DON'T SMELL BLOOD, AND I DON'T SEE ANY GUTS. WHERE ARE THEIR BODIES!?
WHERE'D THEY GO!!?
......!!
I SENSE SOMETHING!?

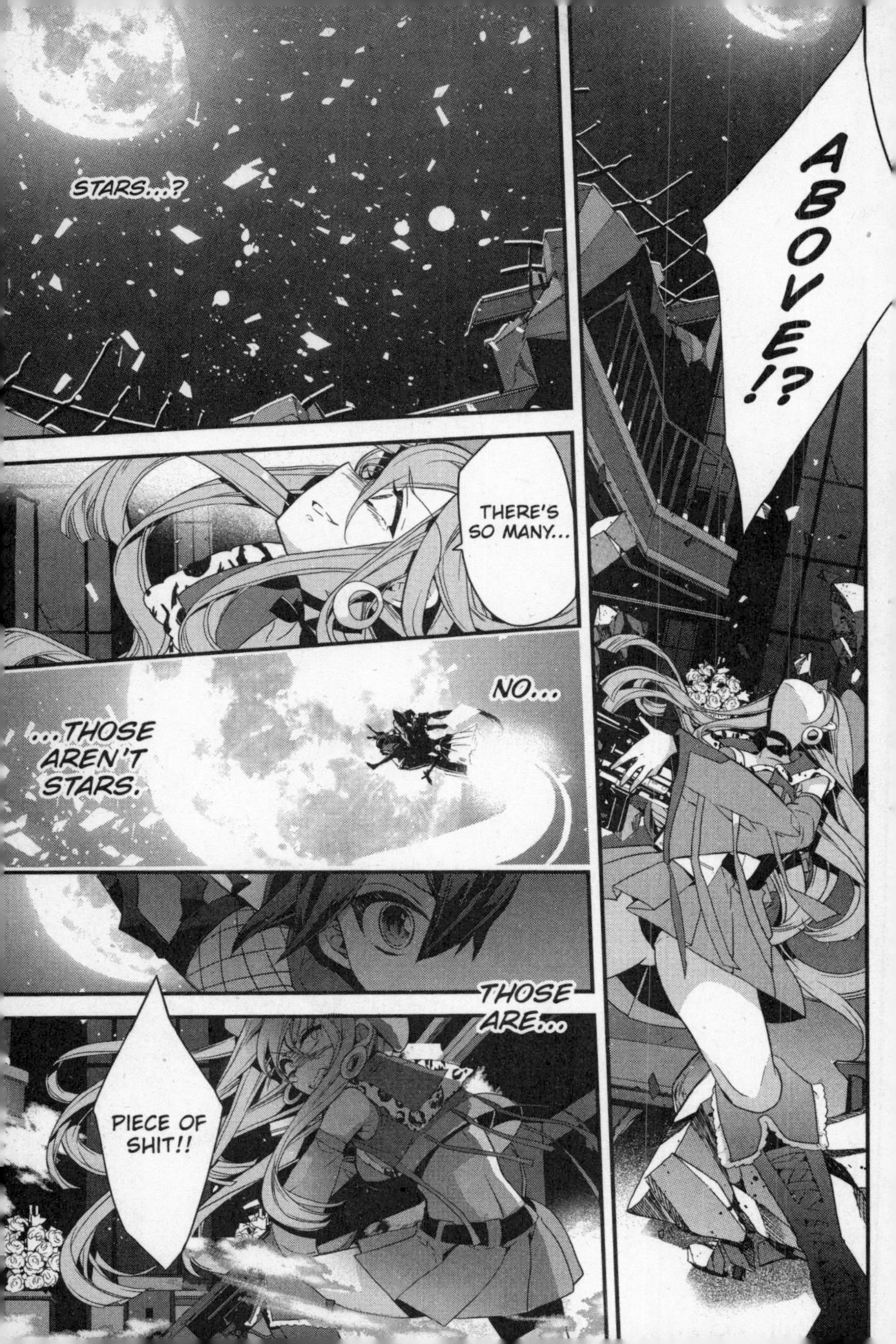
ABOVE!?
STARS...?
THERE'S SO MANY...
NO...
...THOSE AREN'T STARS.
THOSE ARE...
PIECE OF SHIT!!

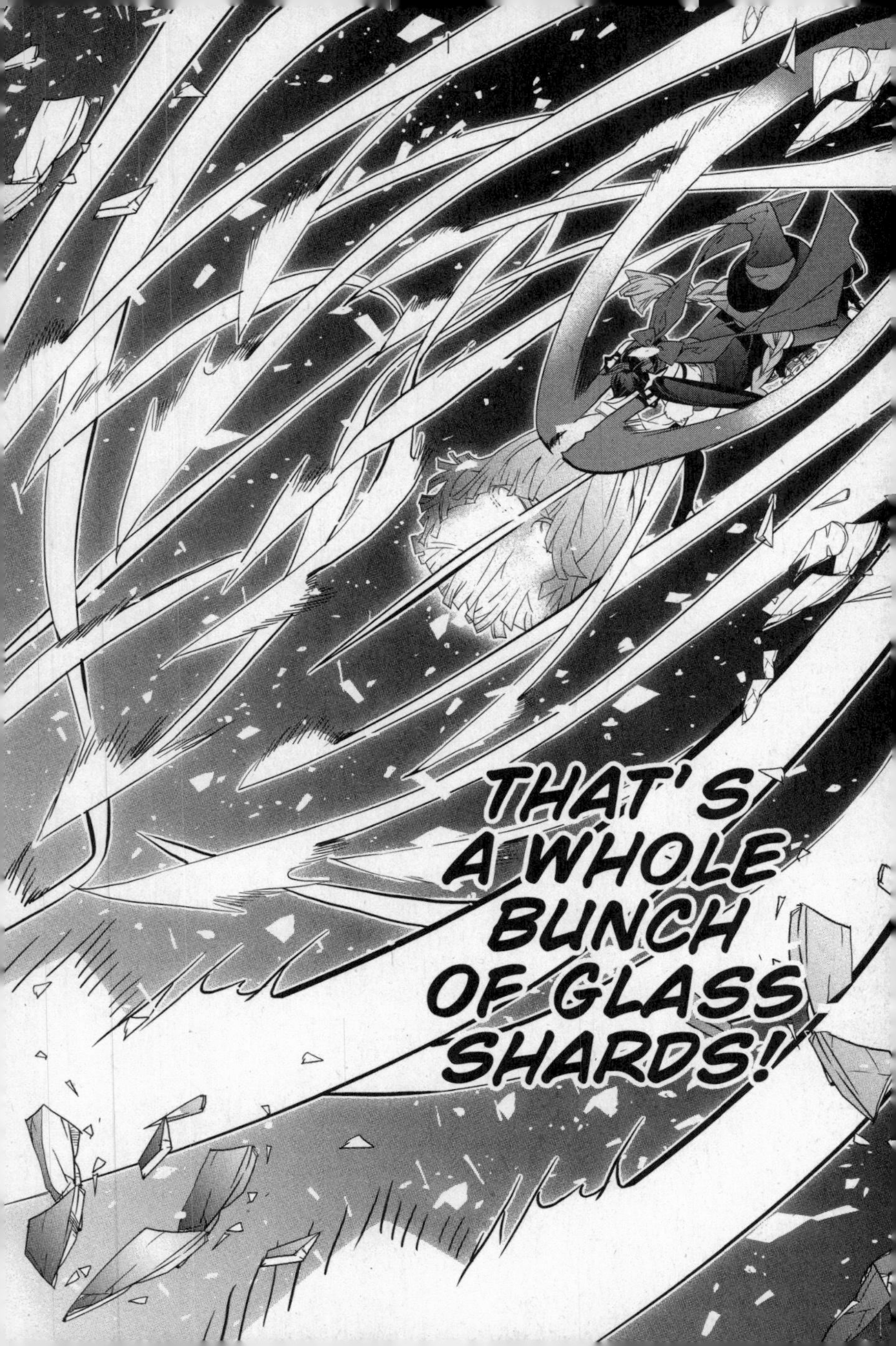
THAT'S A WHOLE BUNCH OF GLASS SHARDS!

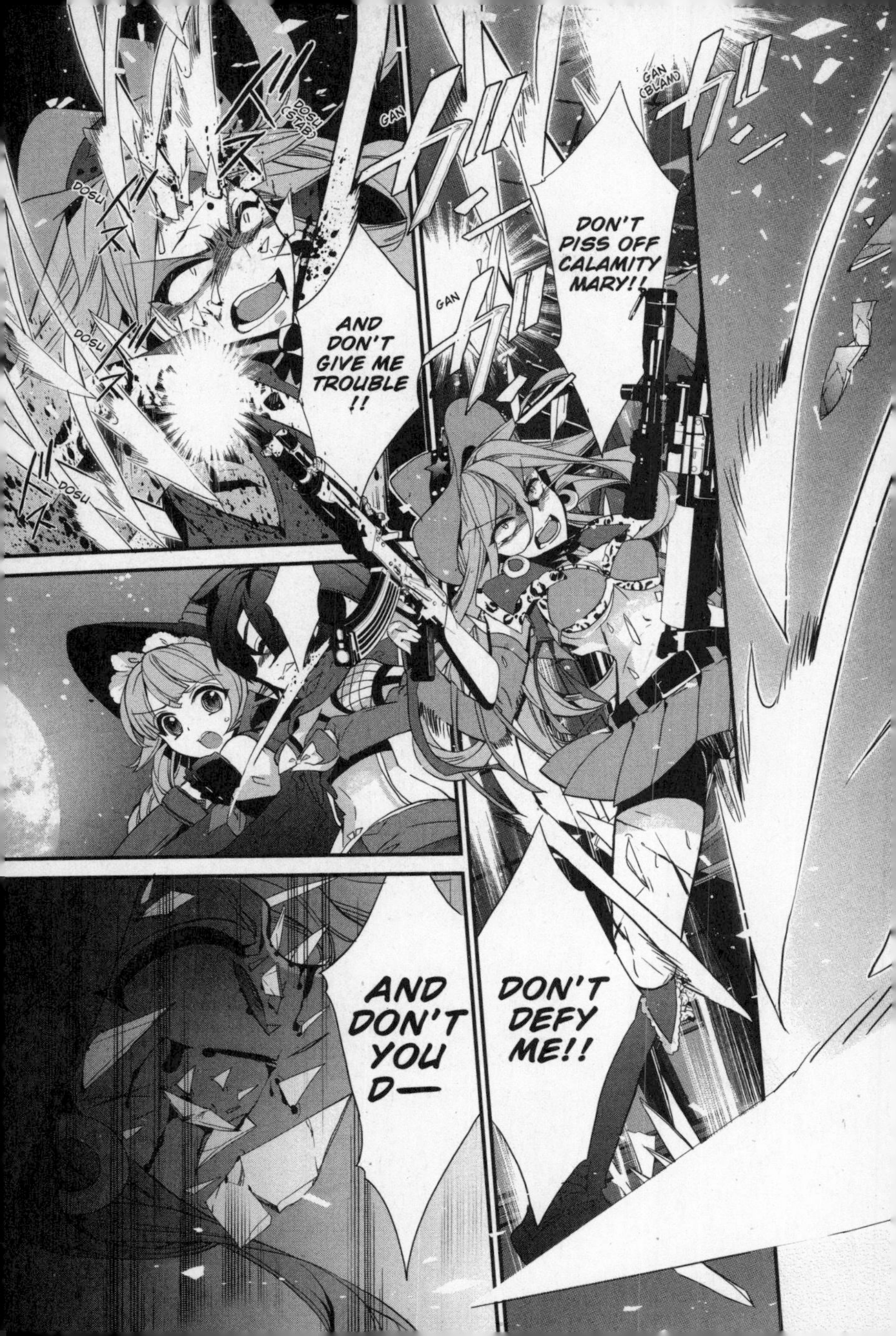
GAN (BLAM)
DON'T PISS OFF CALAMITY MARY!!
GAN
GAN
AND DON'T GIVE ME TROUBLE!!
DON'T DEFY ME!!
AND DON'T YOU D—
DOSU (STAB)
DOSU
DOSU
DOSU

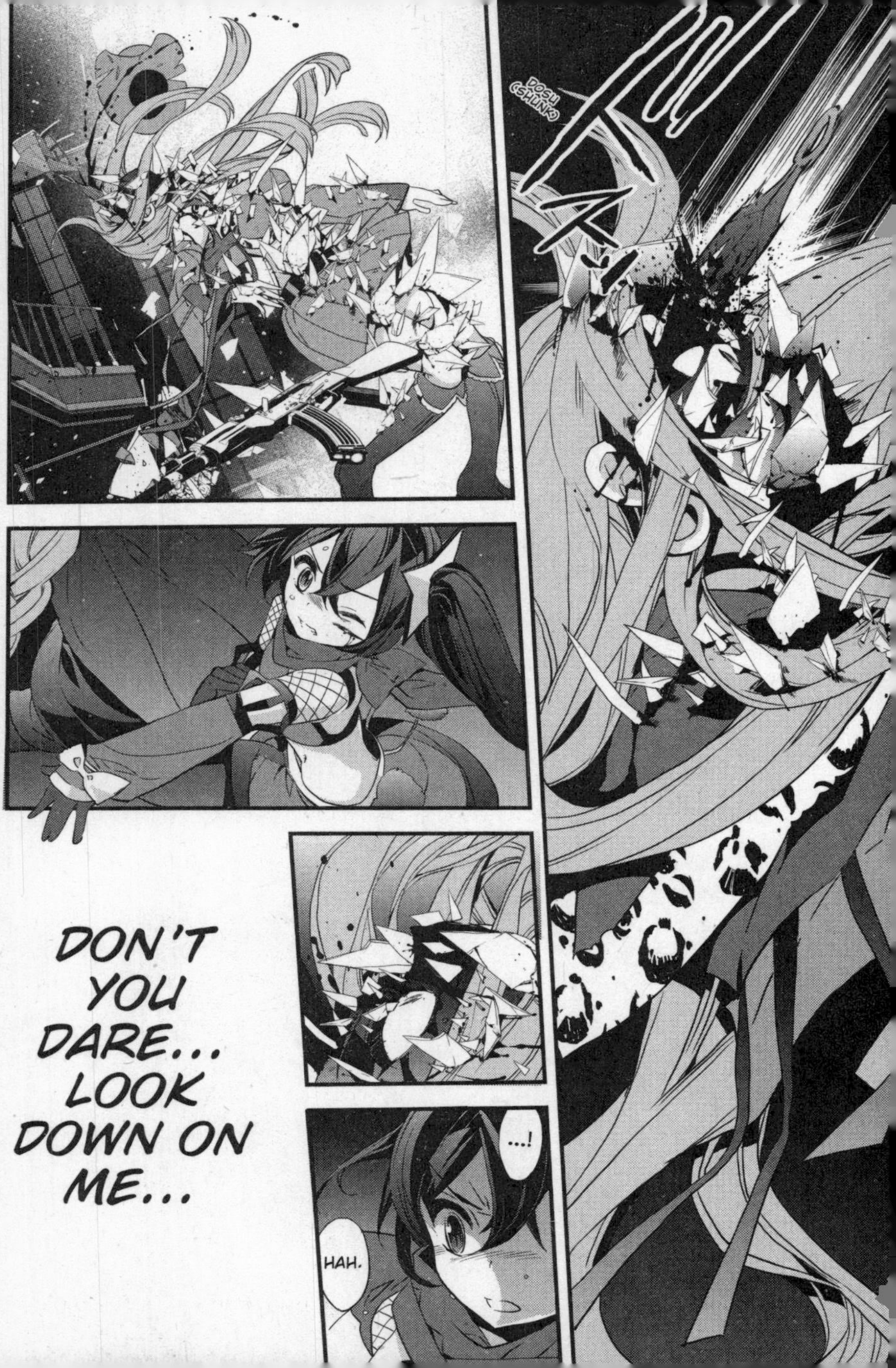
DOSU (SHLNK)
DON'T YOU DARE... LOOK DOWN ON ME...
...!
HAH.

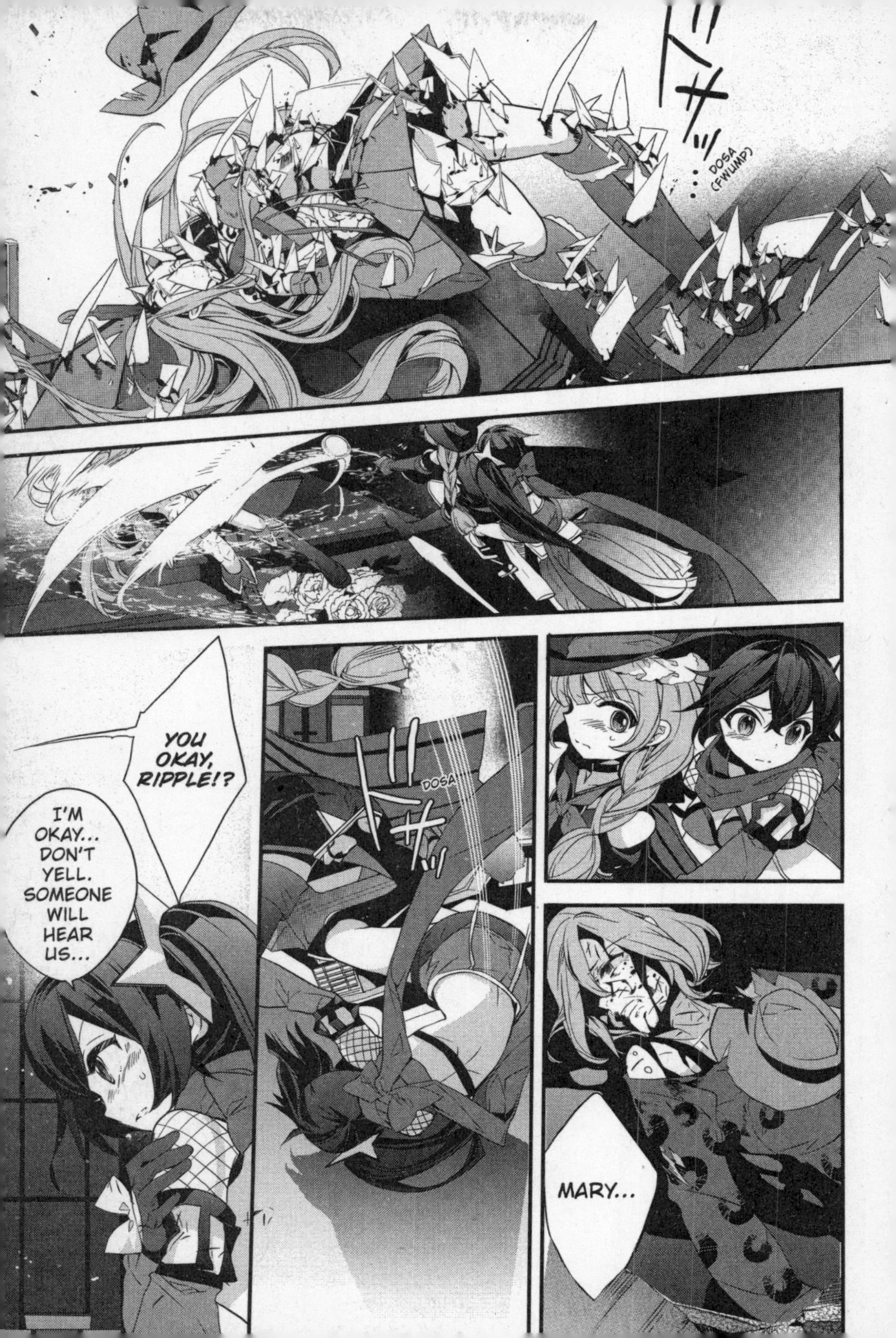
ドサッ
DOSA (FWUMP)
MARY...
ドサッ
DOSA
YOU OKAY, RIPPLE!?
I'M OKAY... DON'T YELL. SOMEONE WILL HEAR US...

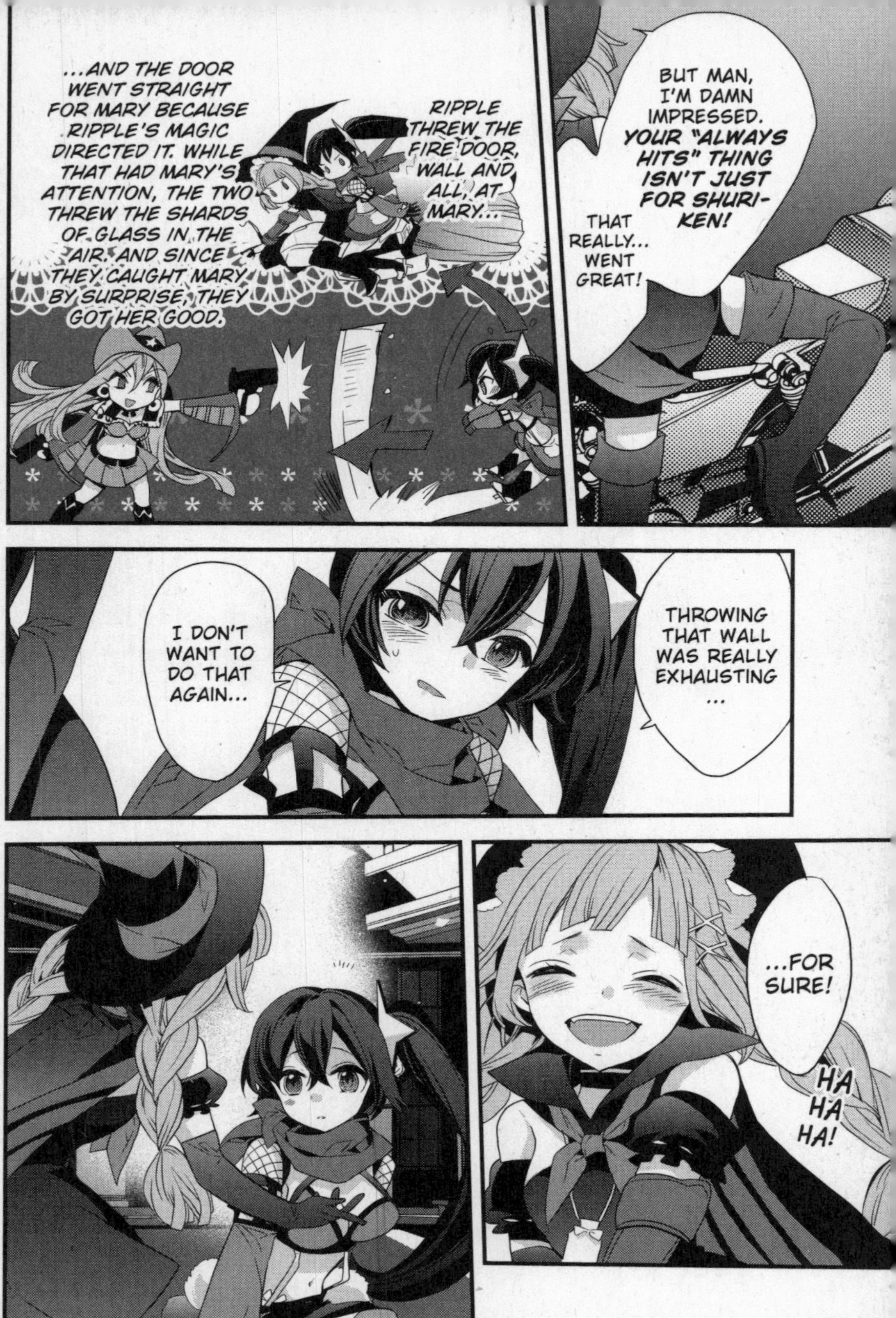
BUT MAN, I'M DAMN IMPRESSED. YOUR "ALWAYS HITS" THING ISN'T JUST FOR SHURIKEN!
THAT REALLY... WENT GREAT!
RIPPLE THREW THE FIRE DOOR, WALL AND ALL, AT MARY...
...AND THE DOOR WENT STRAIGHT FOR MARY BECAUSE RIPPLE'S MAGIC DIRECTED IT. WHILE THAT HAD MARY'S ATTENTION, THE TWO THREW THE SHARDS OF GLASS IN THE AIR. AND SINCE THEY CAUGHT MARY BY SURPRISE, THEY GOT HER GOOD.
THROWING THAT WALL WAS REALLY EXHAUSTING...
I DON'T WANT TO DO THAT AGAIN...
...FOR SURE!
HA HA HA!

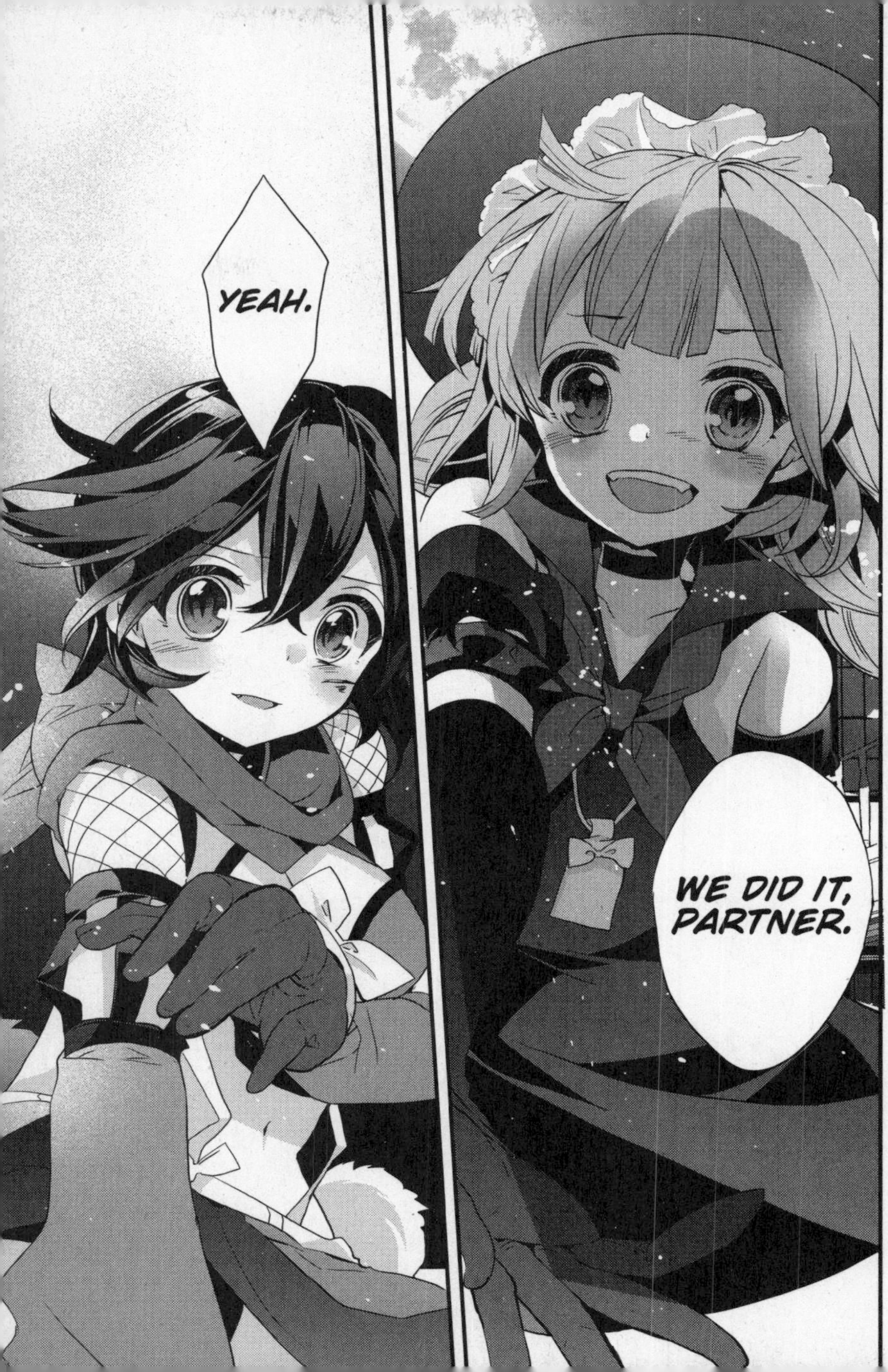
WE DID IT, PARTNER.
YEAH.

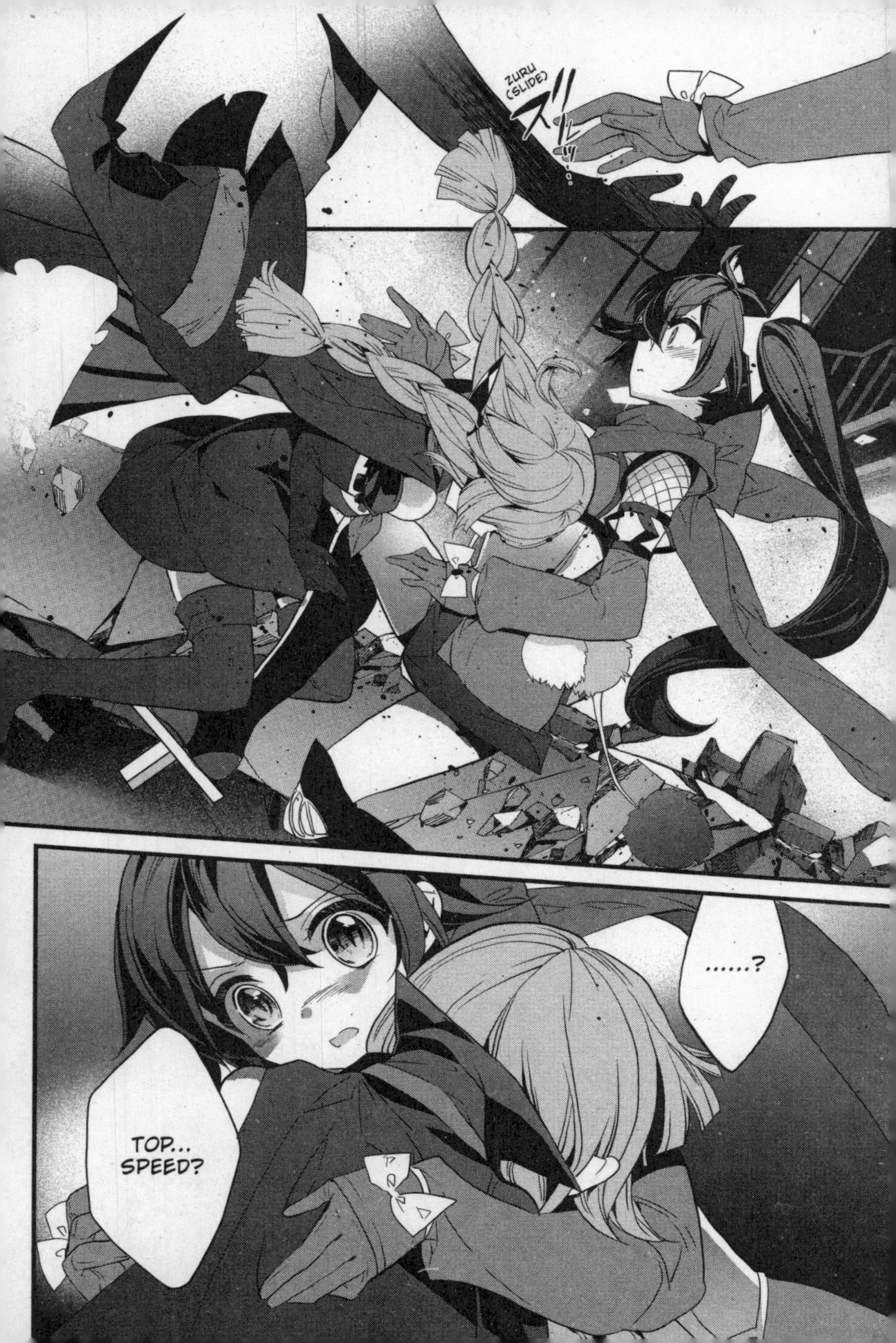
ZURU (SLIDE)
......?
TOP... SPEED?

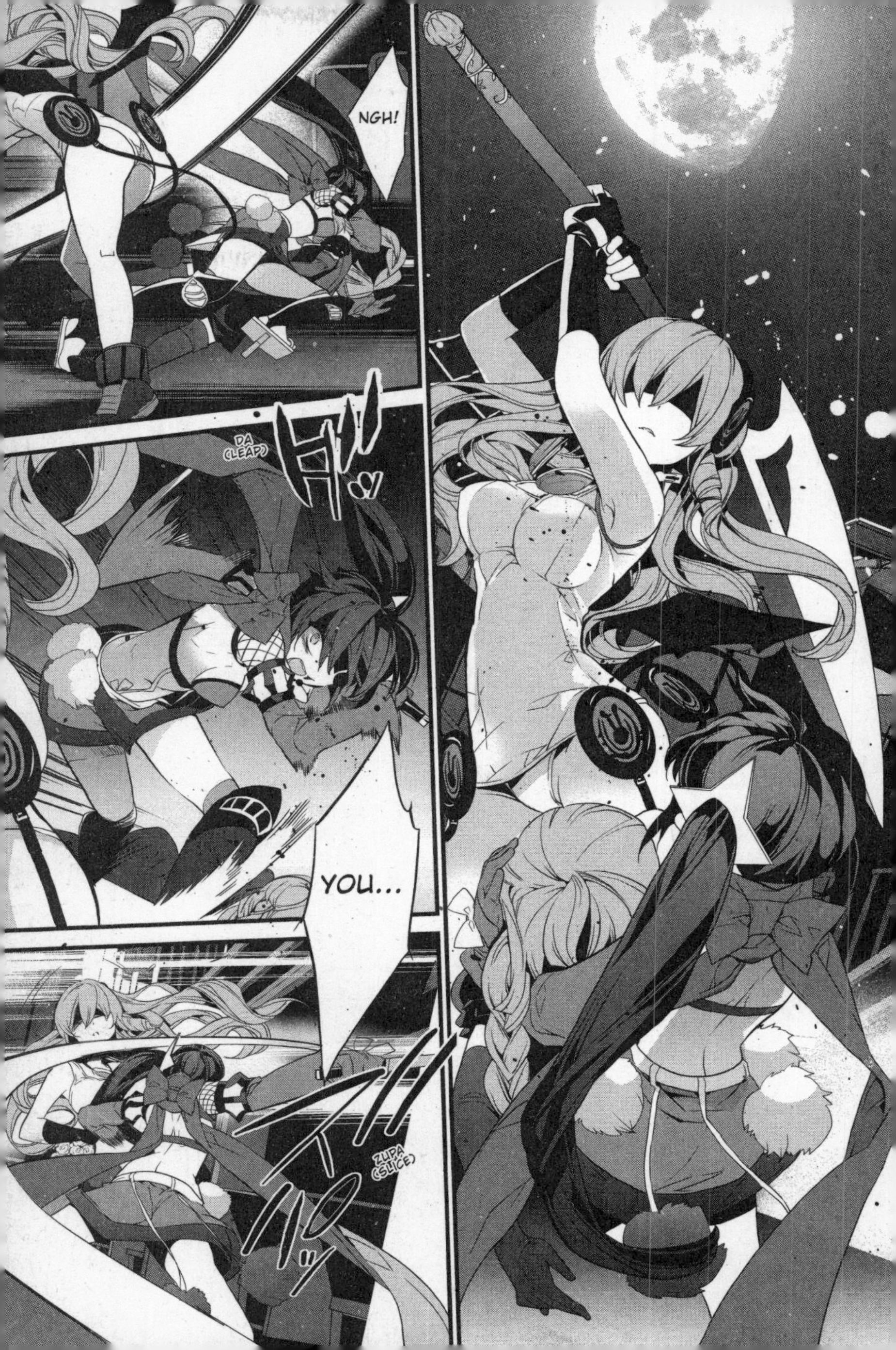
NGH!
DA (LEAP)
YOU...
ZUPA (SLICE)

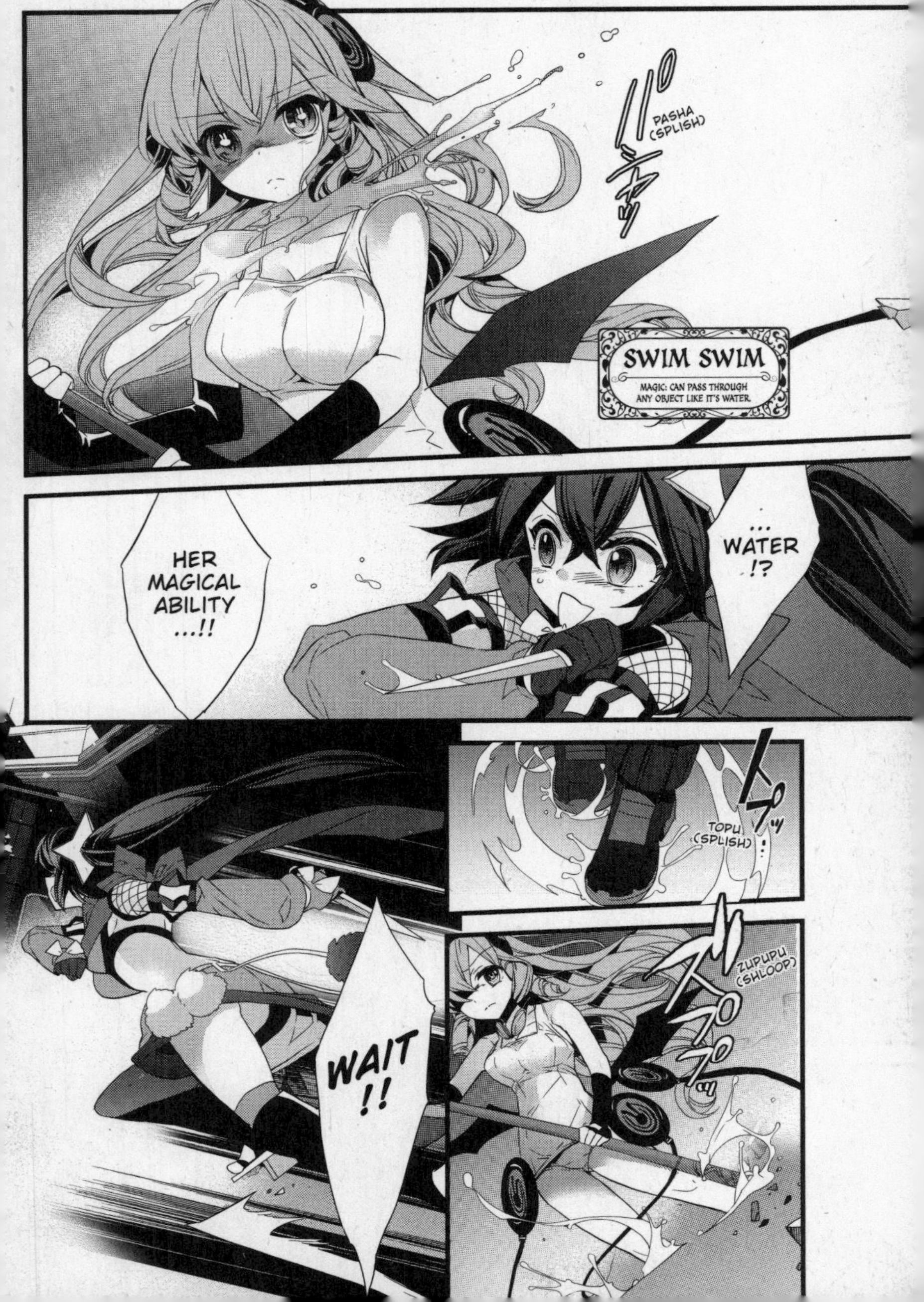

パシャッ
PASHA (SPLISH)
SWIM SWIM
MAGIC: CAN PASS THROUGH ANY OBJECT LIKE IT'S WATER.
...WATER!?
HER MAGICAL ABILITY...!!
トプッ
TOPU (SPLISH)
ZUPUPU (SHLOOP)
WAIT!!

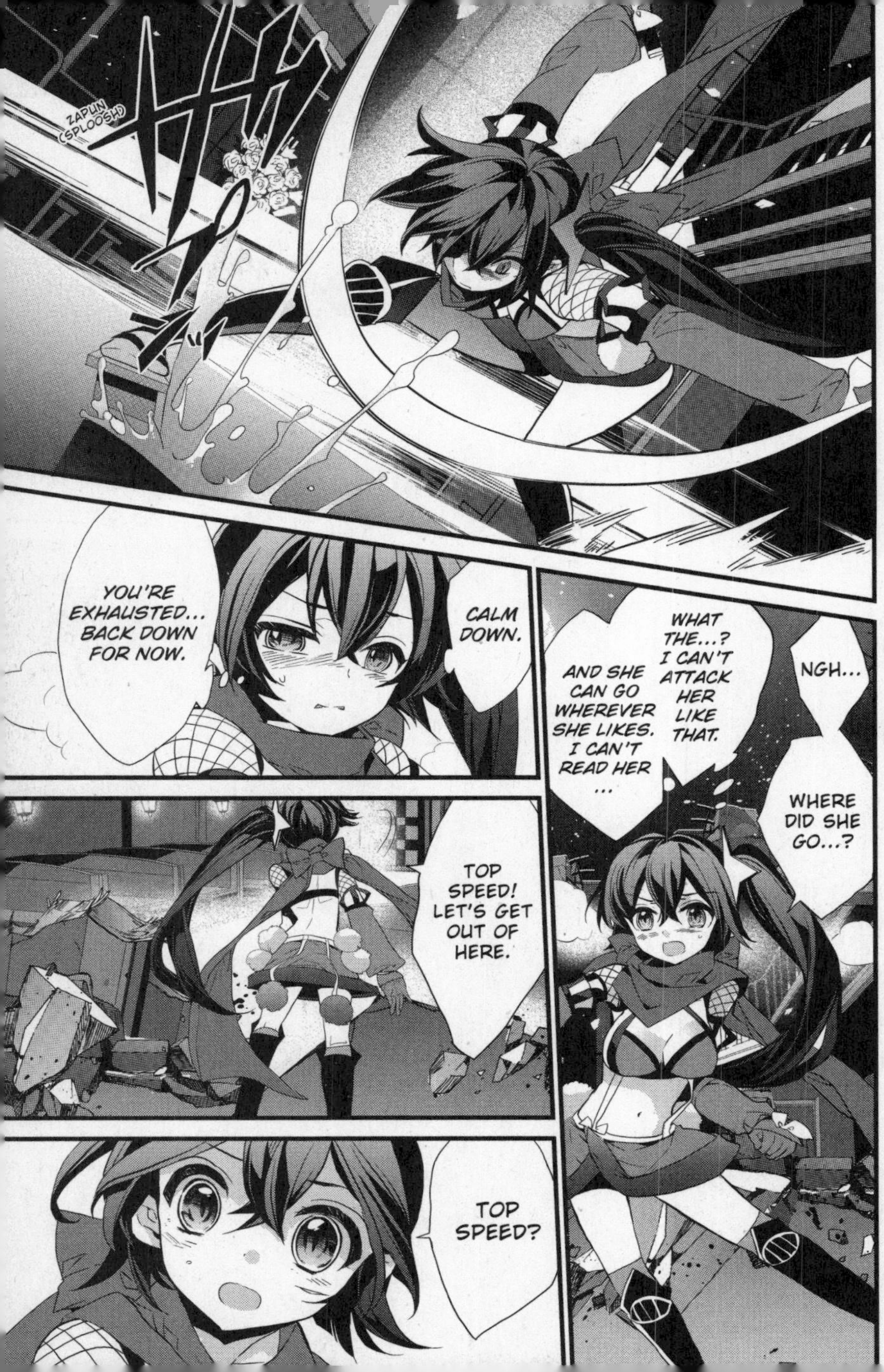
ZAPUN (SPLOOSH)
NGH...
WHAT THE...? I CAN'T ATTACK HER LIKE THAT.
AND SHE CAN GO WHEREVER SHE LIKES. I CAN'T READ HER...
WHERE DID SHE GO...?
CALM DOWN.
YOU'RE EXHAUSTED... BACK DOWN FOR NOW.
TOP SPEED! LET'S GET OUT OF HERE.
TOP SPEED?

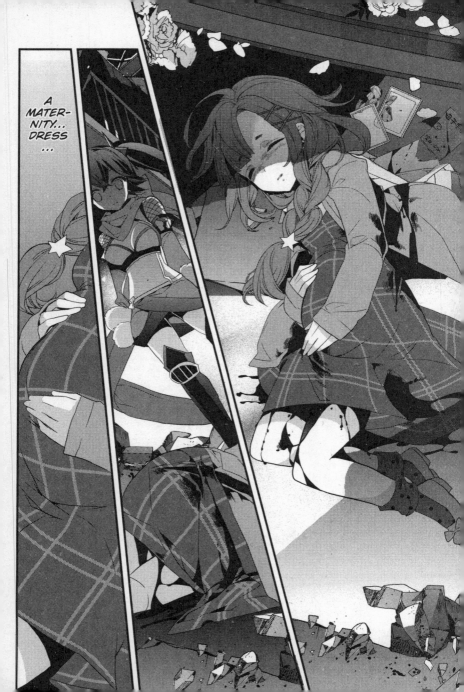

A MATER-
NITY...
DRESS
...

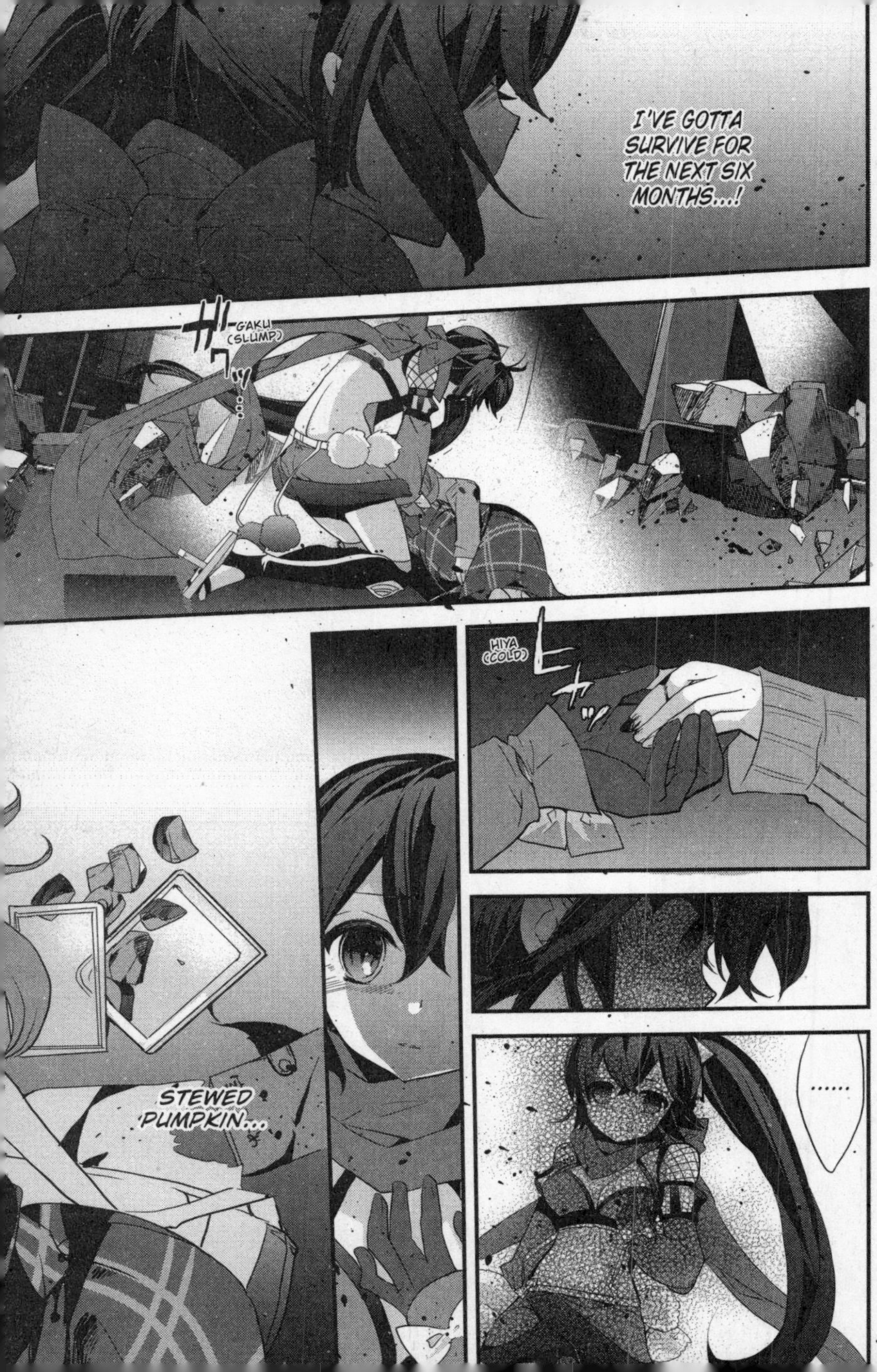
I'VE GOTTA SURVIVE FOR THE NEXT SIX MONTHS...!
GAKU (SLUMP)
HIYA (COLD)
STEWED PUMPKIN...
......

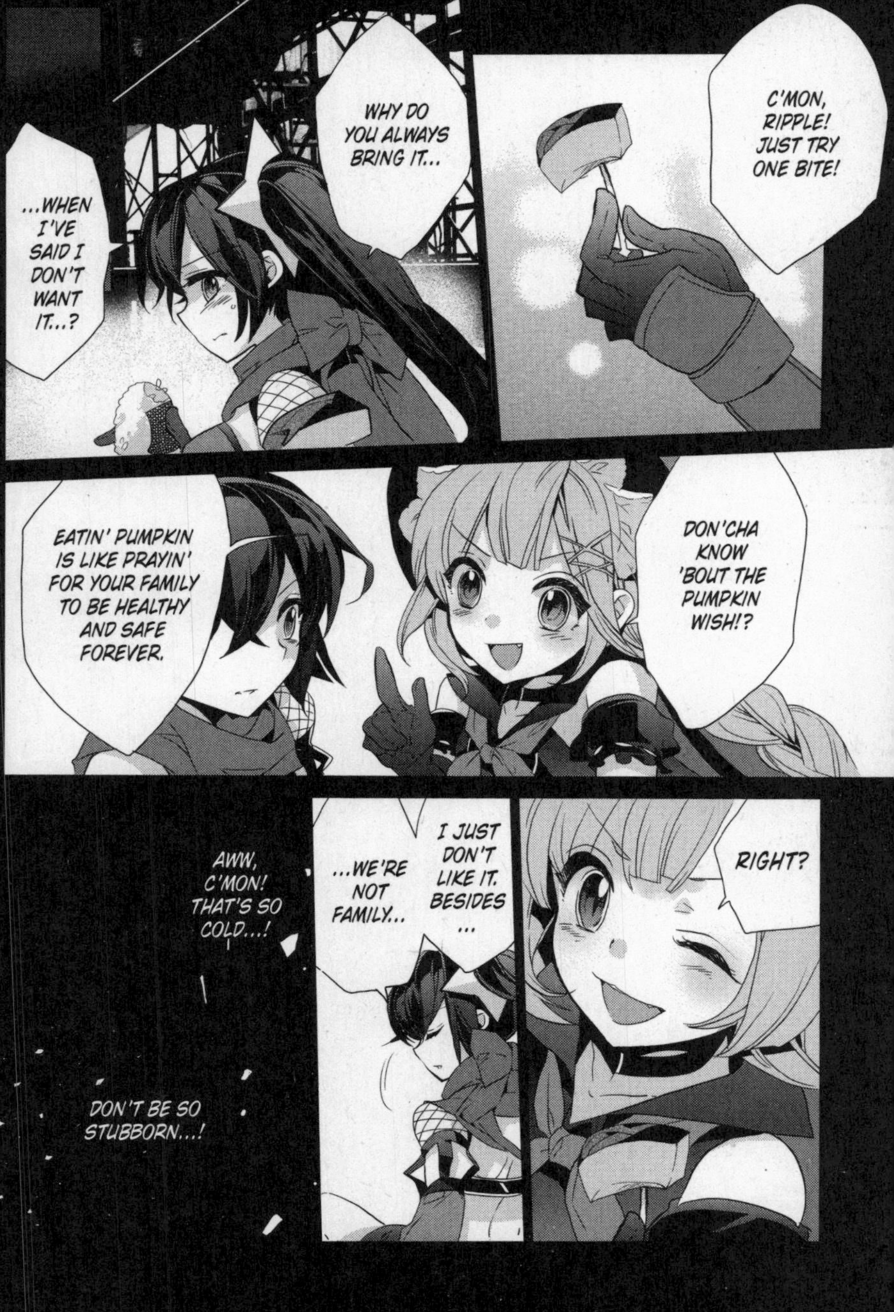
C'MON, RIPPLE! JUST TRY ONE BITE!
WHY DO YOU ALWAYS BRING IT...
...WHEN I'VE SAID I DON'T WANT IT...?
DON'CHA KNOW 'BOUT THE PUMPKIN WISH!?
EATIN' PUMPKIN IS LIKE PRAYIN' FOR YOUR FAMILY TO BE HEALTHY AND SAFE FOREVER.
RIGHT?
I JUST DON'T LIKE IT. BESIDES ...
...WE'RE NOT FAMILY...
AWW, C'MON! THAT'S SO COLD...!
DON'T BE SO STUBBORN...!

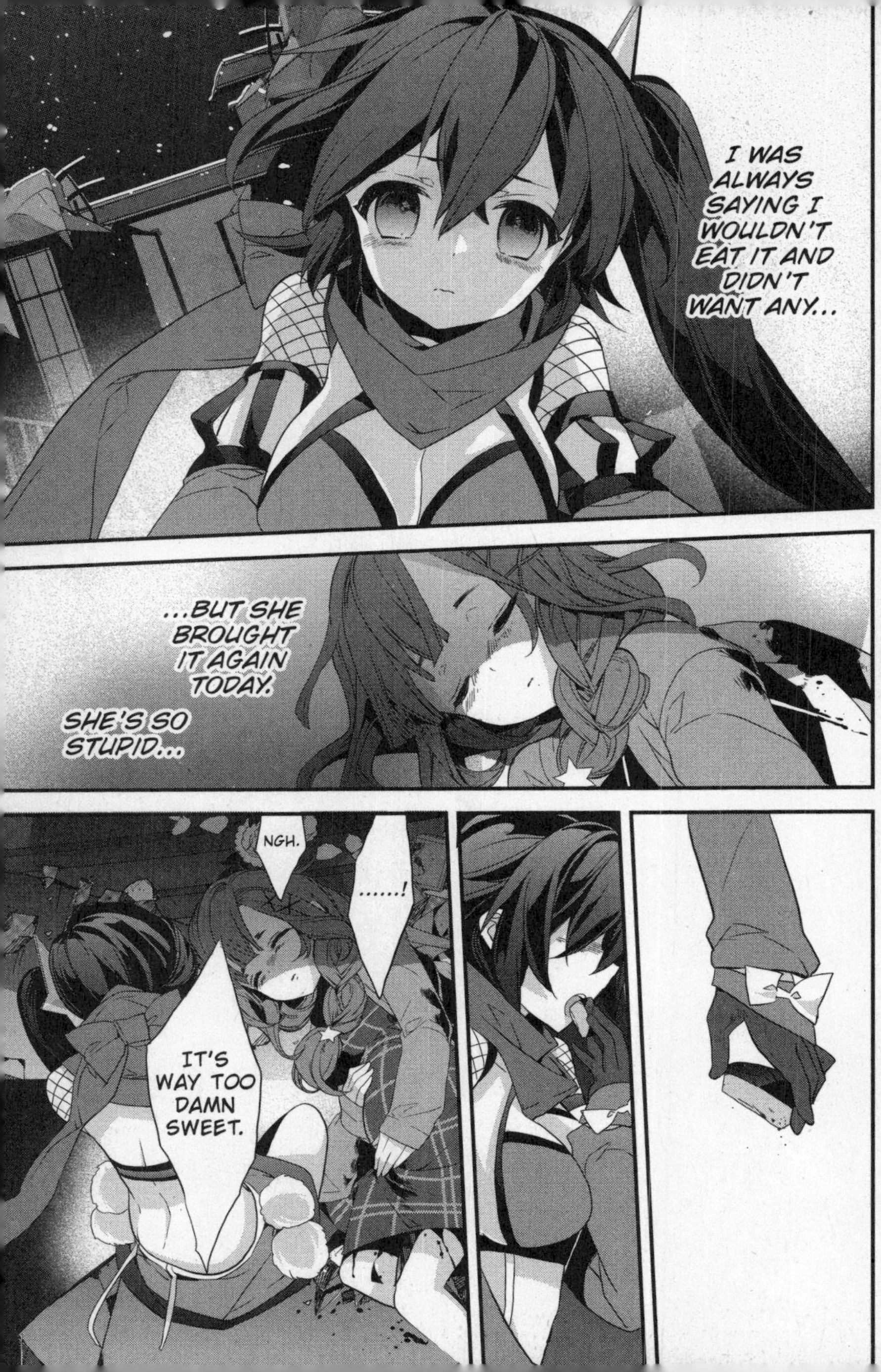
I WAS ALWAYS SAYING I WOULDN'T EAT IT AND DIDN'T WANT ANY...
...BUT SHE BROUGHT IT AGAIN TODAY.
SHE'S SO STUPID...
NGH.
......!
IT'S WAY TOO DAMN SWEET.

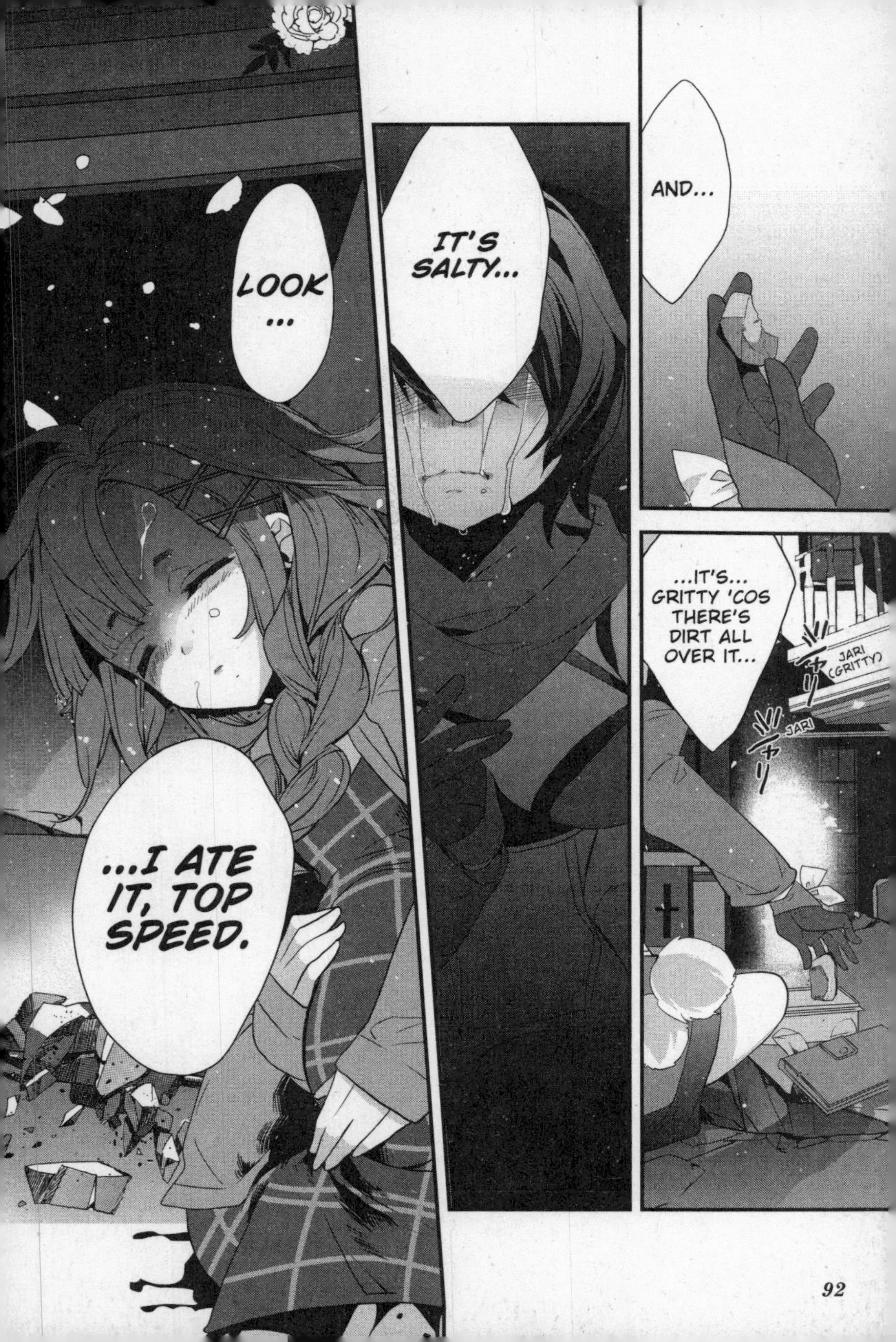
AND...
...IT'S... GRITTY 'COS THERE'S DIRT ALL OVER IT...
JARI (GRITTY)
JARI
IT'S SALTY...
LOOK ...
...I ATE IT, TOP SPEED.

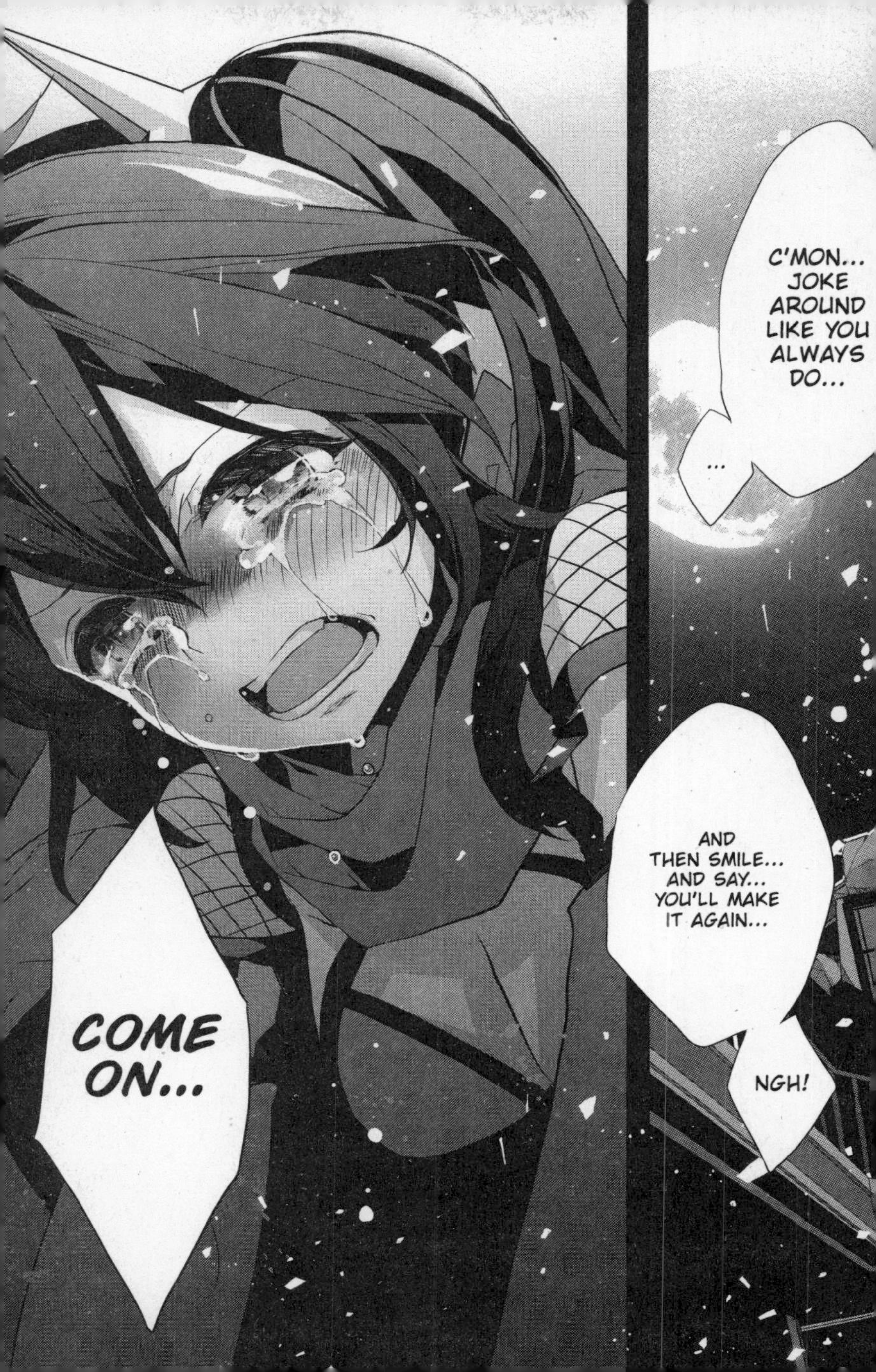
C'MON... JOKE AROUND LIKE YOU ALWAYS DO...
...
AND THEN SMILE... AND SAY... YOU'LL MAKE IT AGAIN...
NGH!
COME ON...

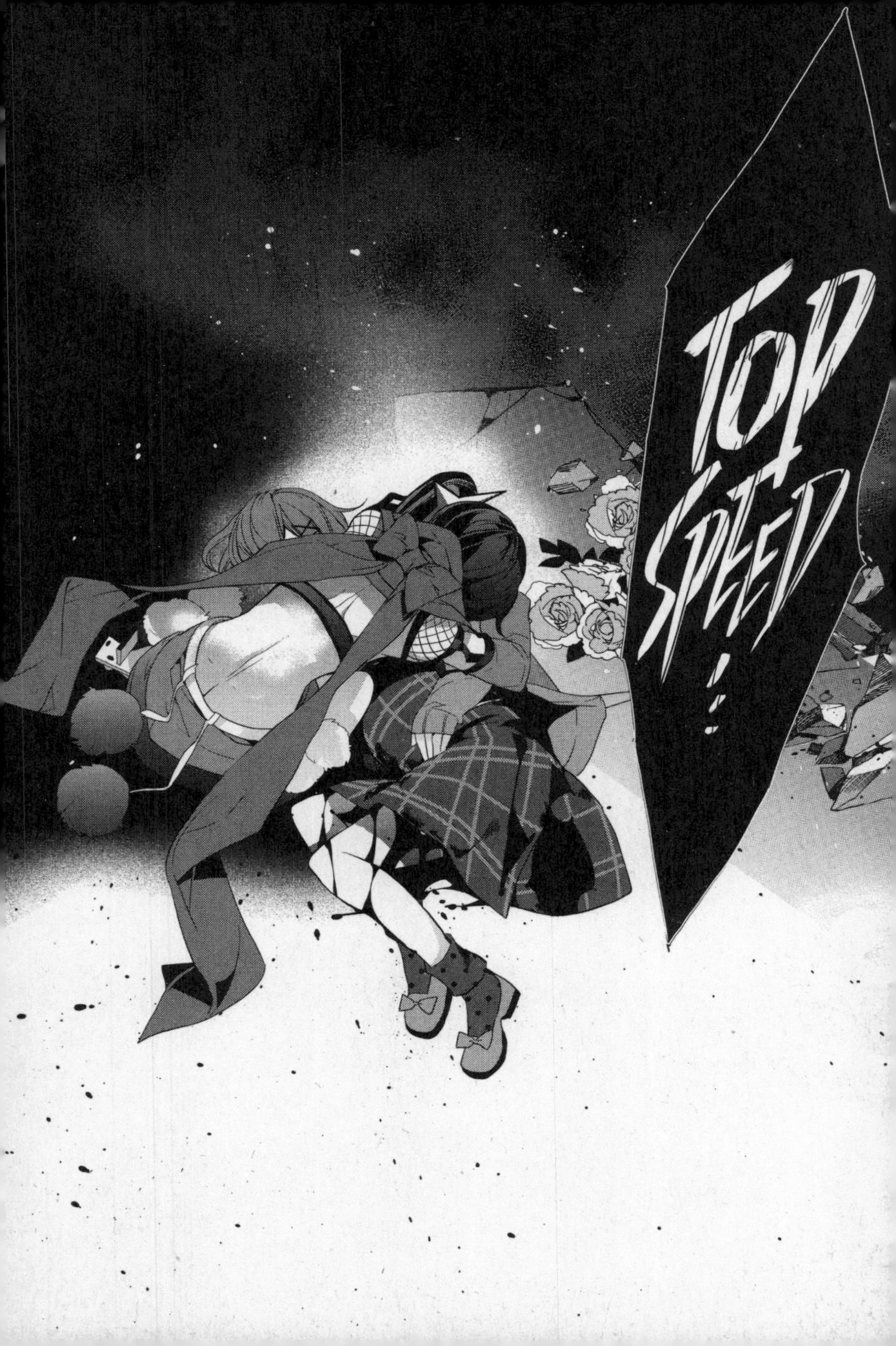
TOP SPEED!!

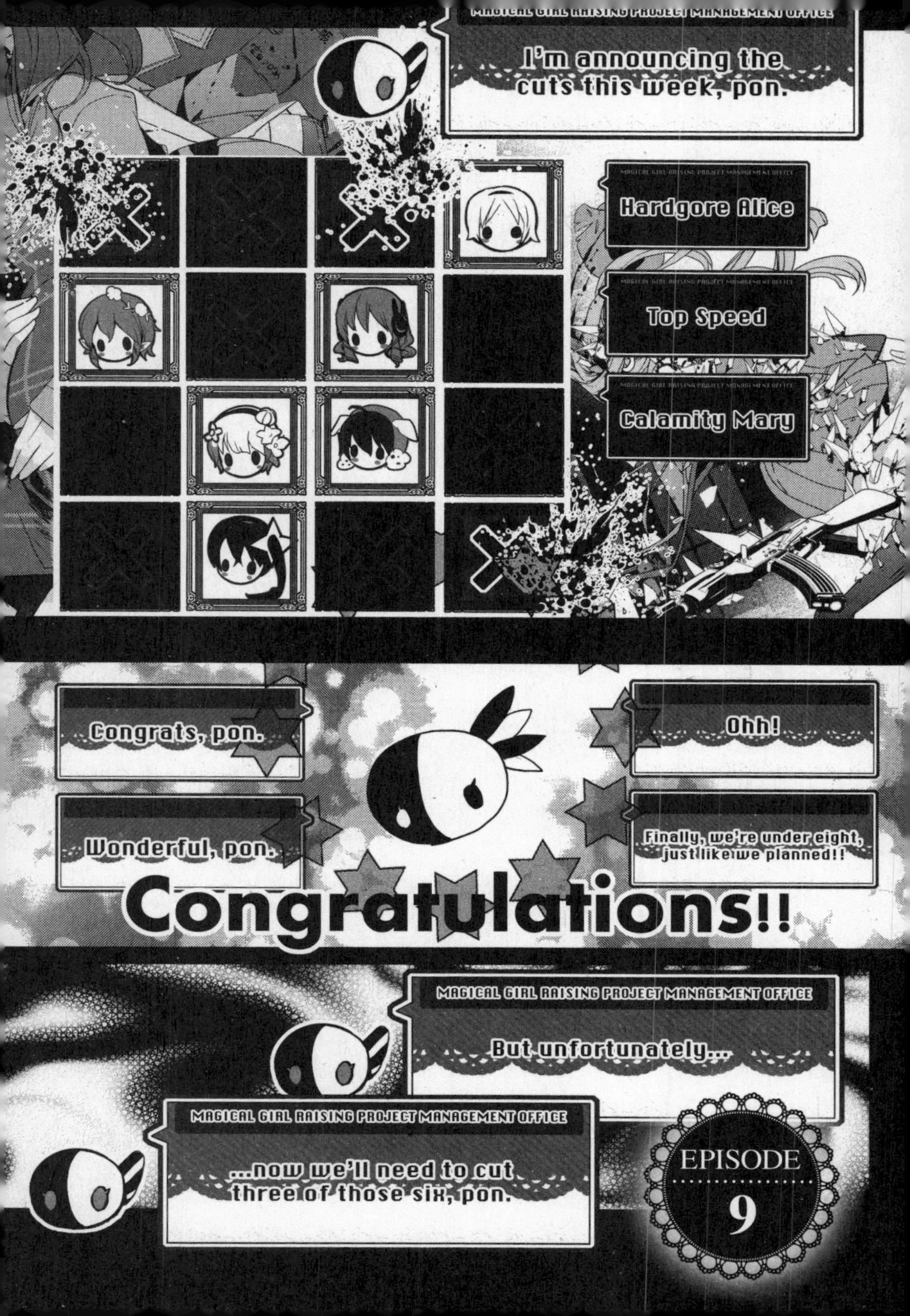
MAGICAL GIRL RAISING PROJECT MANAGEMENT OFFICE
I'm announcing the cuts this week, pon.
MAGICAL GIRL RAISING PROJECT MANAGEMENT OFFICE
Hardgore Alice
MAGICAL GIRL RAISING PROJECT MANAGEMENT OFFICE
Top Speed
MAGICAL GIRL RAISING PROJECT MANAGEMENT OFFICE
Calamity Mary
Ohh!
Congrats, pon.
Finally, we're under eight, just like we planned!!
Wonderful, pon.
Congratulations!!
MAGICAL GIRL RAISING PROJECT MANAGEMENT OFFICE
But unfortunately...
MAGICAL GIRL RAISING PROJECT MANAGEMENT OFFICE
...now we'll need to cut three of those six, pon.
EPISODE 9

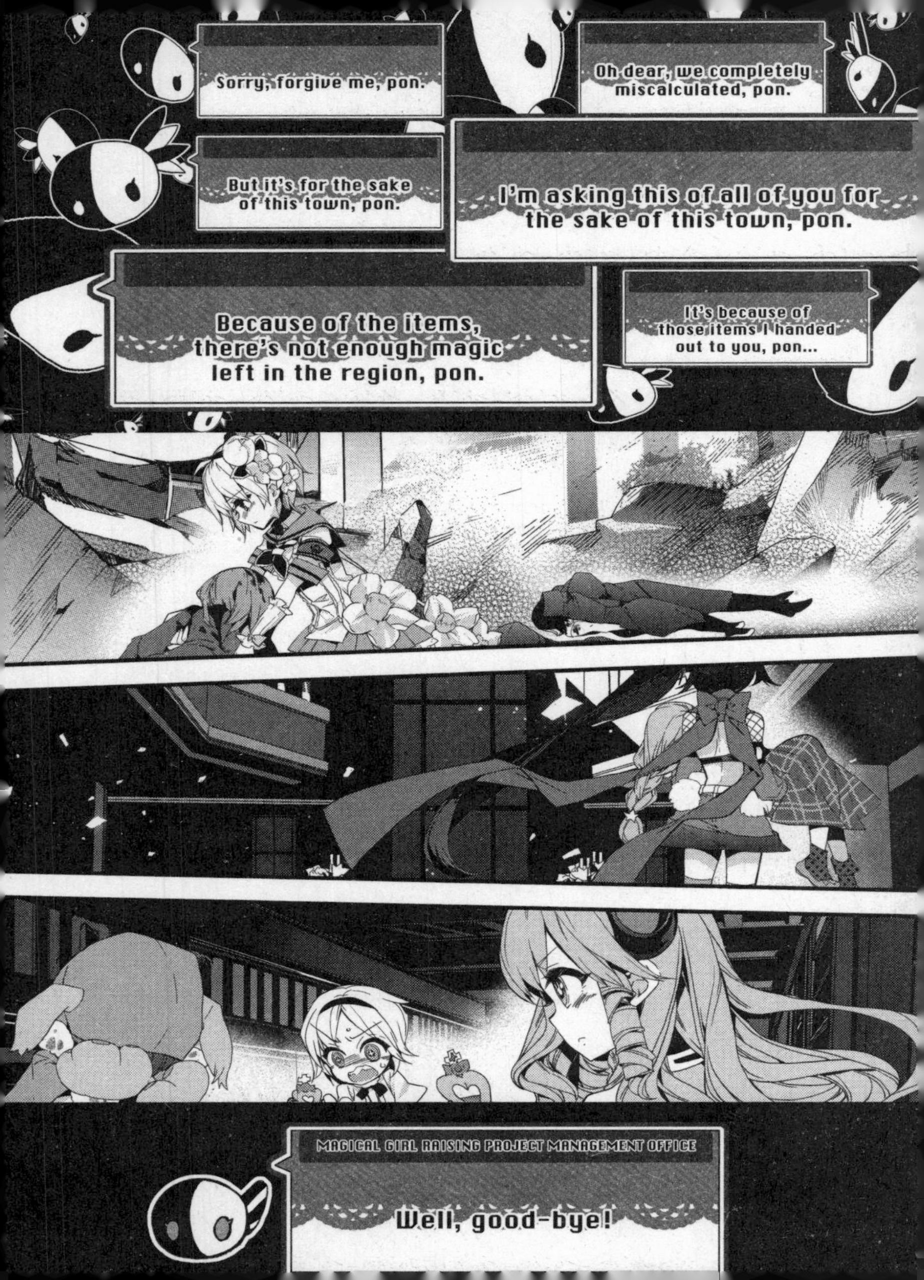
Oh dear, we completely miscalculated, pon.
Sorry, forgive me, pon.
I'm asking this of all of you for the sake of this town, pon.
But it's for the sake of this town, pon.
It's because of those items I handed out to you, pon...
Because of the items, there's not enough magic left in the region, pon.
MAGICAL GIRL RAISING PROJECT MANAGEMENT OFFICE
Well, good-bye!

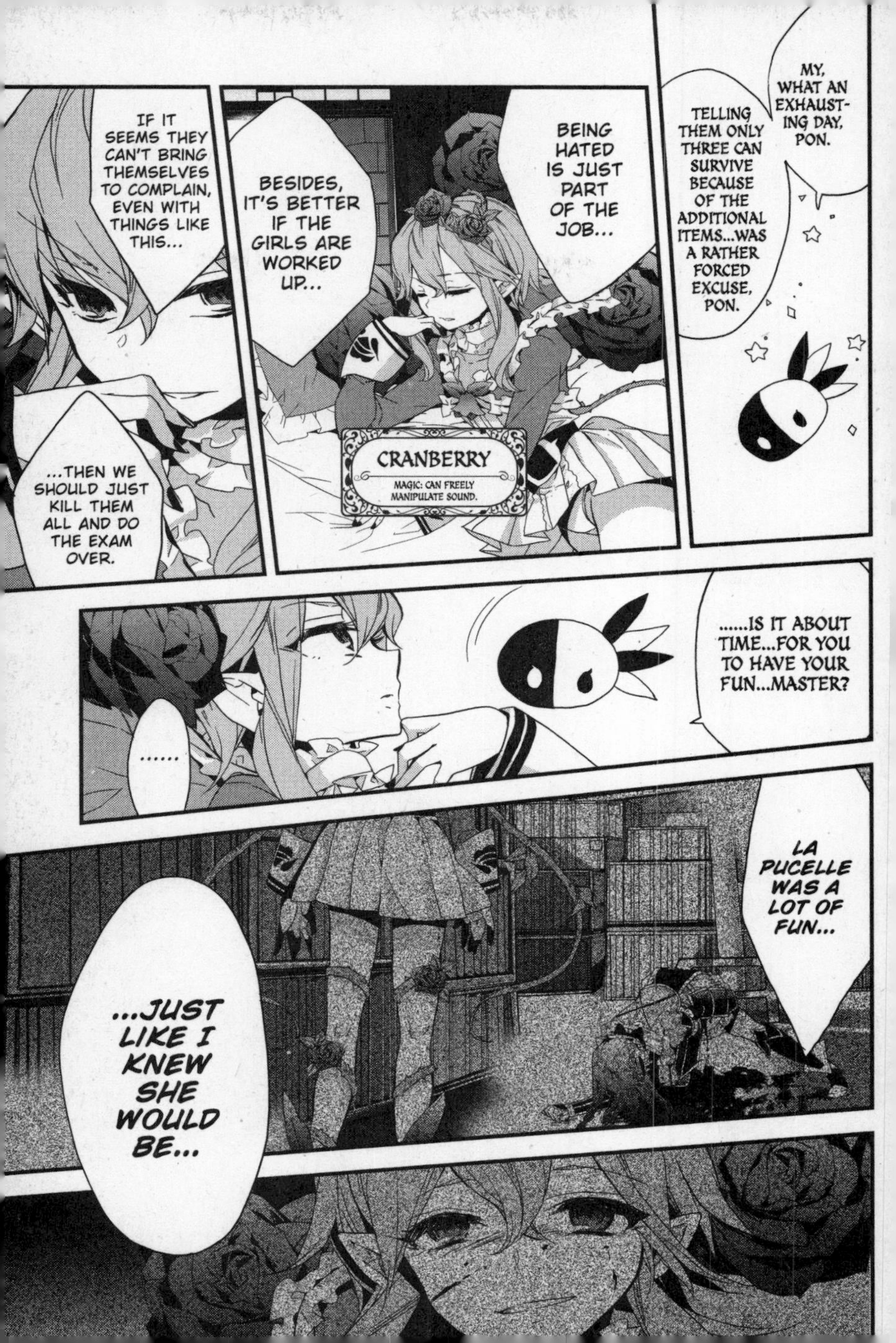
MY, WHAT AN EXHAUST-ING DAY, PON.
TELLING THEM ONLY THREE CAN SURVIVE BECAUSE OF THE ADDITIONAL ITEMS...WAS A RATHER FORCED EXCUSE, PON.
BEING HATED IS JUST PART OF THE JOB...
BESIDES, IT'S BETTER IF THE GIRLS ARE WORKED UP...
CRANBERRY
MAGIC: CAN FREELY MANIPULATE SOUND.
IF IT SEEMS THEY CAN'T BRING THEMSELVES TO COMPLAIN, EVEN WITH THINGS LIKE THIS...
...THEN WE SHOULD JUST KILL THEM ALL AND DO THE EXAM OVER.
......IS IT ABOUT TIME...FOR YOU TO HAVE YOUR FUN...MASTER?
......
LA PUCELLE WAS A LOT OF FUN...
...JUST LIKE I KNEW SHE WOULD BE...

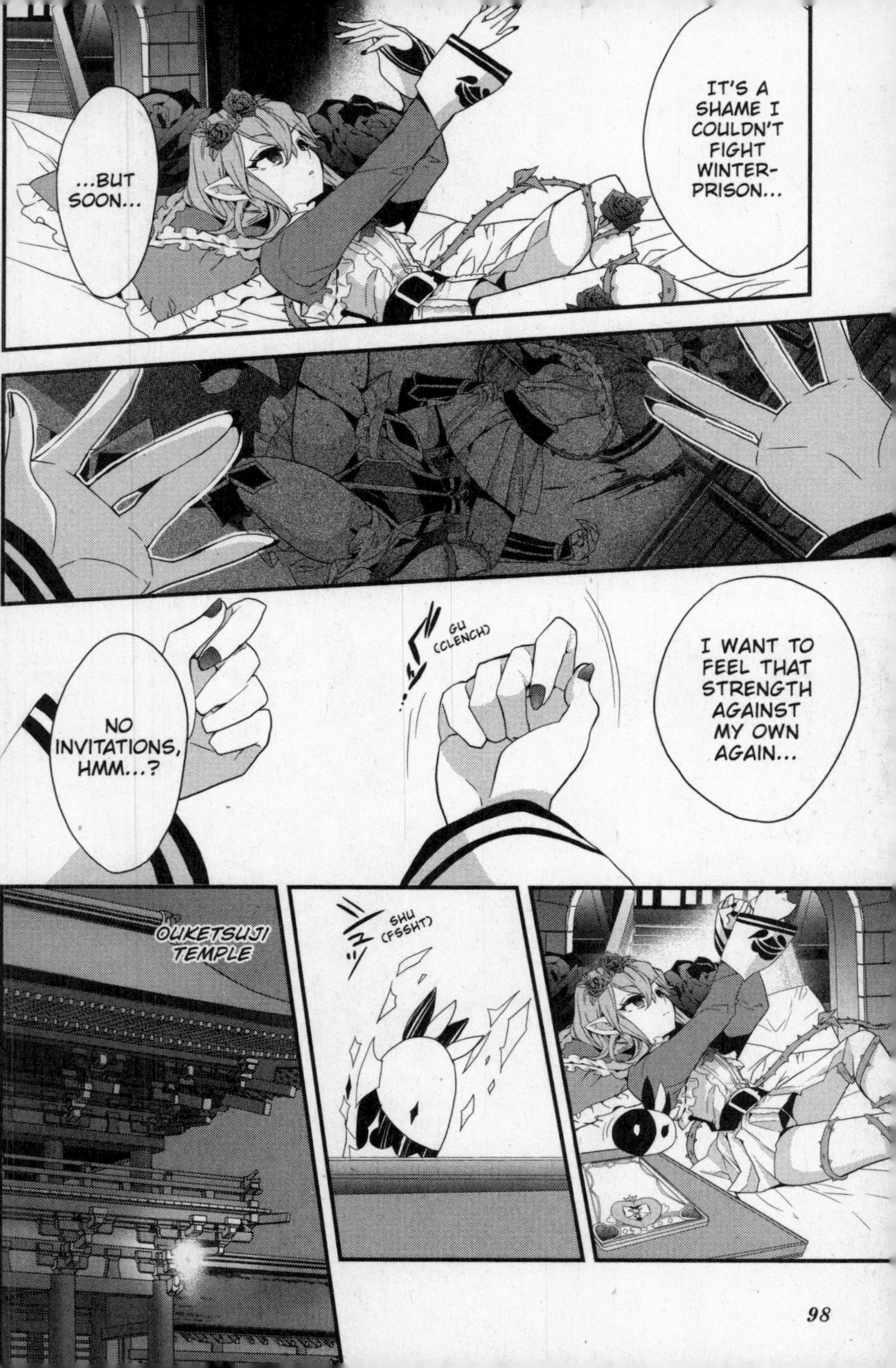
IT'S A SHAME I COULDN'T FIGHT WINTER-PRISON...
...BUT SOON...
I WANT TO FEEL THAT STRENGTH AGAINST MY OWN AGAIN...
GU (CLENCH)
NO INVITATIONS, HMM...?
SHU (FSSHT)
OUKETSUJI TEMPLE

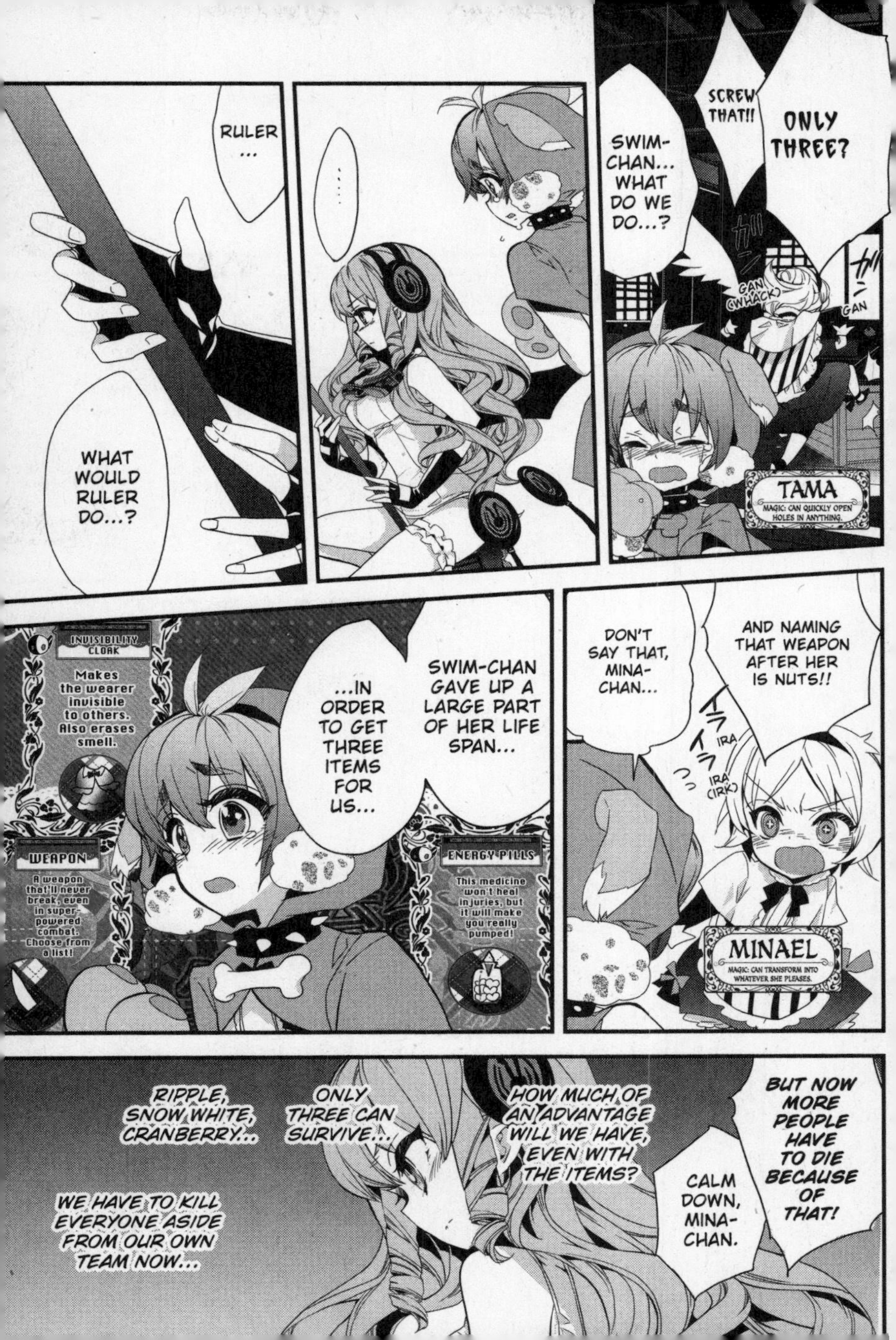
ONLY THREE?
SCREW THAT!!
GAN (WHACK)
GAN
SWIM-CHAN... WHAT DO WE DO...?
TAMA
MAGIC: CAN QUICKLY OPEN HOLES IN ANYTHING.
......
RULER ...
WHAT WOULD RULER DO...?
AND NAMING THAT WEAPON AFTER HER IS NUTS!!
DON'T SAY THAT, MINA-CHAN...
IRA
IRA (IRK)
MINAEL
MAGIC: CAN TRANSFORM INTO WHATEVER SHE PLEASES.
SWIM-CHAN GAVE UP A LARGE PART OF HER LIFE SPAN...
...IN ORDER TO GET THREE ITEMS FOR US...
ENERGY PILLS
This medicine won't heal injuries, but it will make you really pumped!
INVISIBILITY CLOAK
Makes the wearer invisible to others. Also erases smell.
WEAPON
A weapon that'll never break, even in super-powered combat. Choose from a list!
BUT NOW MORE PEOPLE HAVE TO DIE BECAUSE OF THAT!
CALM DOWN, MINA-CHAN.
HOW MUCH OF AN ADVANTAGE WILL WE HAVE, EVEN WITH THE ITEMS?
ONLY THREE CAN SURVIVE...
RIPPLE, SNOW WHITE, CRANBERRY...
WE HAVE TO KILL EVERYONE ASIDE FROM OUR OWN TEAM NOW...

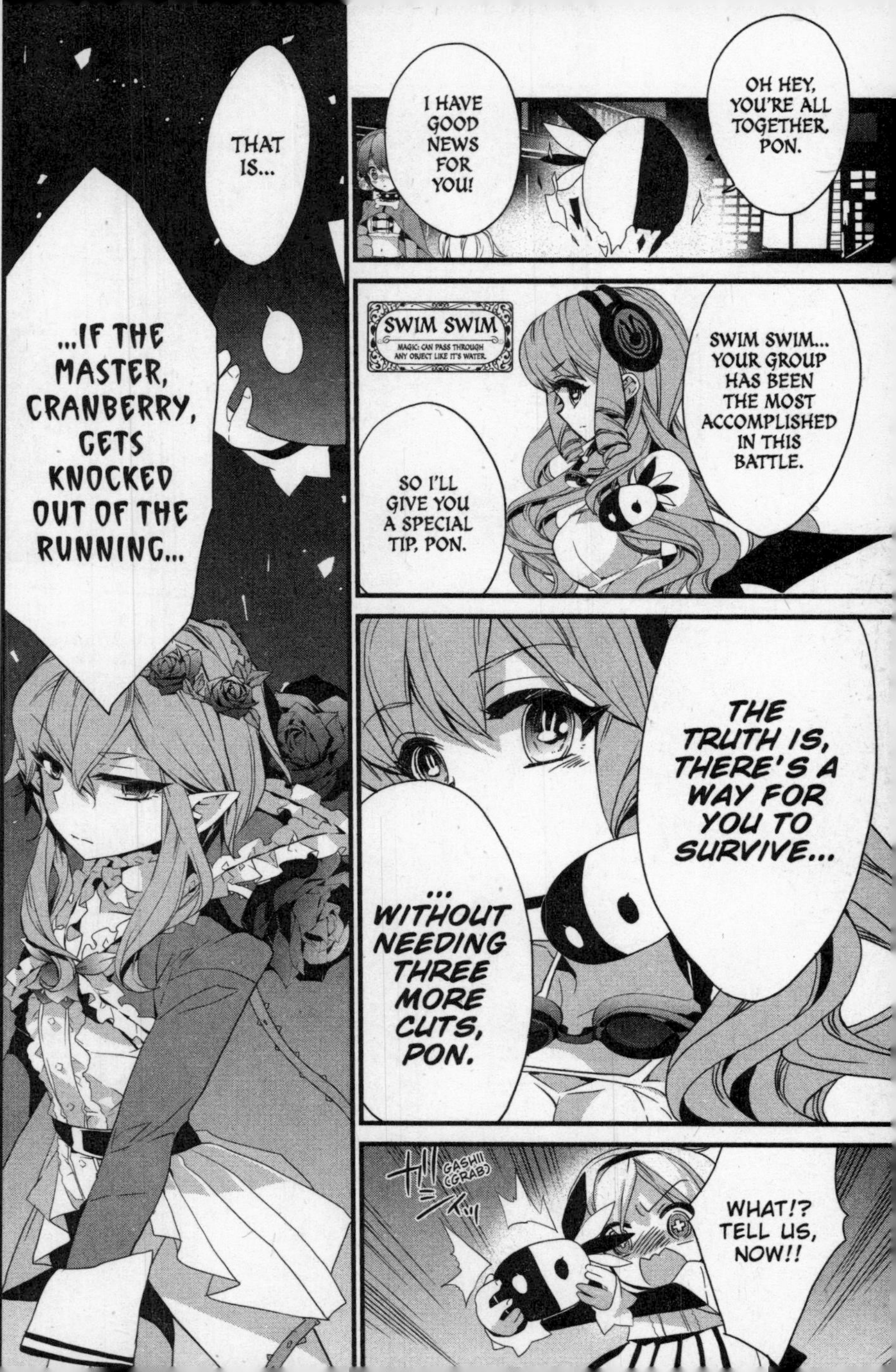
OH HEY, YOU'RE ALL TOGETHER, PON.
I HAVE GOOD NEWS FOR YOU!
SWIM SWIM
MAGIC: CAN PASS THROUGH ANY OBJECT LIKE IT'S WATER.
SWIM SWIM... YOUR GROUP HAS BEEN THE MOST ACCOMPLISHED IN THIS BATTLE.
SO I'LL GIVE YOU A SPECIAL TIP, PON.
THE TRUTH IS, THERE'S A WAY FOR YOU TO SURVIVE...
...WITHOUT NEEDING THREE MORE CUTS, PON.
GASHII (GRAB)
WHAT!? TELL US, NOW!!
THAT IS...
...IF THE MASTER, CRANBERRY, GETS KNOCKED OUT OF THE RUNNING...

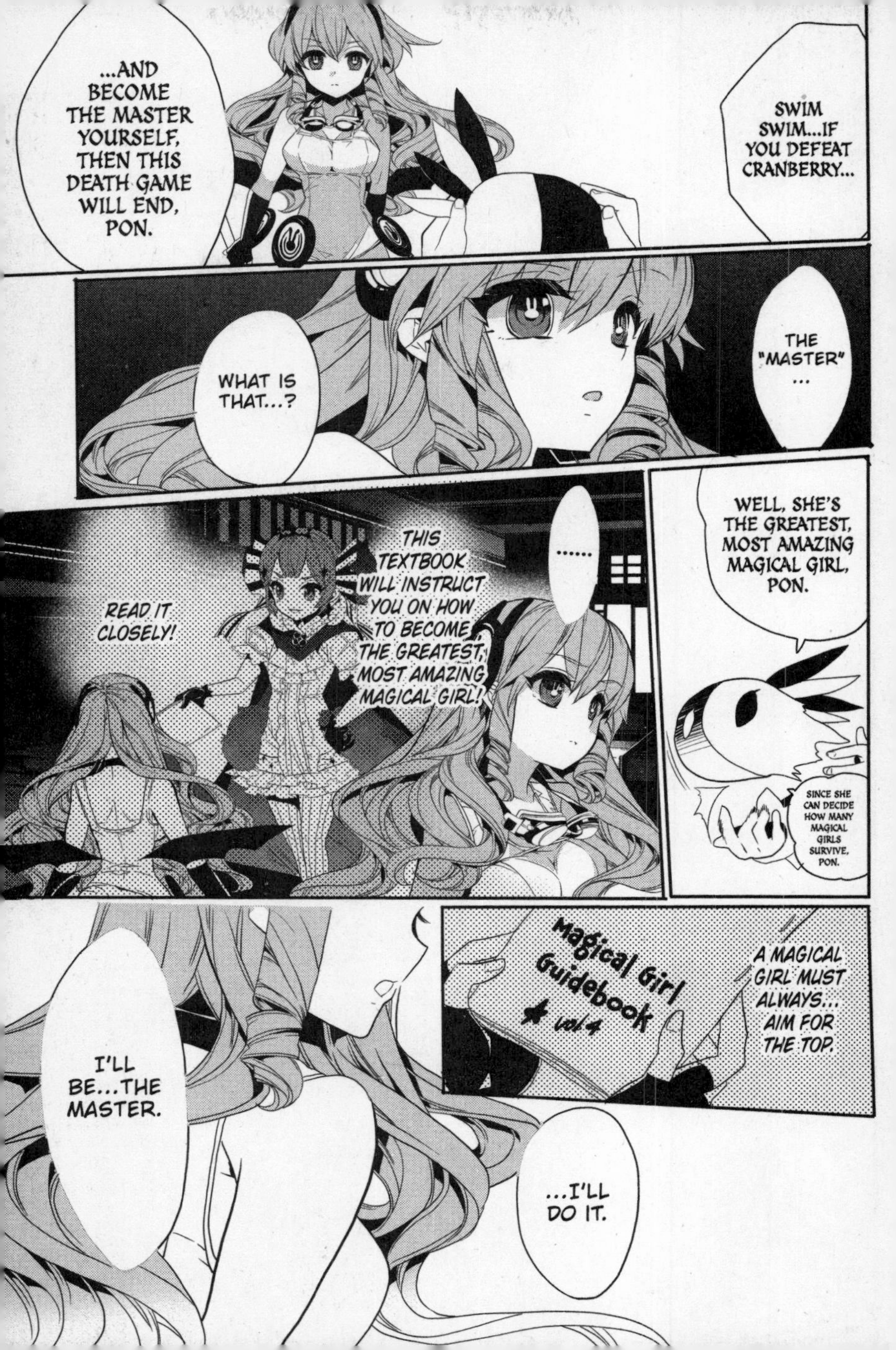
SWIM SWIM...IF YOU DEFEAT CRANBERRY...
...AND BECOME THE MASTER YOURSELF, THEN THIS DEATH GAME WILL END, PON.
THE "MASTER"...
WHAT IS THAT...?
WELL, SHE'S THE GREATEST, MOST AMAZING MAGICAL GIRL, PON.
SINCE SHE CAN DECIDE HOW MANY MAGICAL GIRLS SURVIVE, PON.
......
THIS TEXTBOOK WILL INSTRUCT YOU ON HOW TO BECOME THE GREATEST, MOST AMAZING MAGICAL GIRL!
READ IT CLOSELY!
Magical Girl Guidebook vol.4
A MAGICAL GIRL MUST ALWAYS... AIM FOR THE TOP.
...I'LL DO IT.
I'LL BE...THE MASTER.

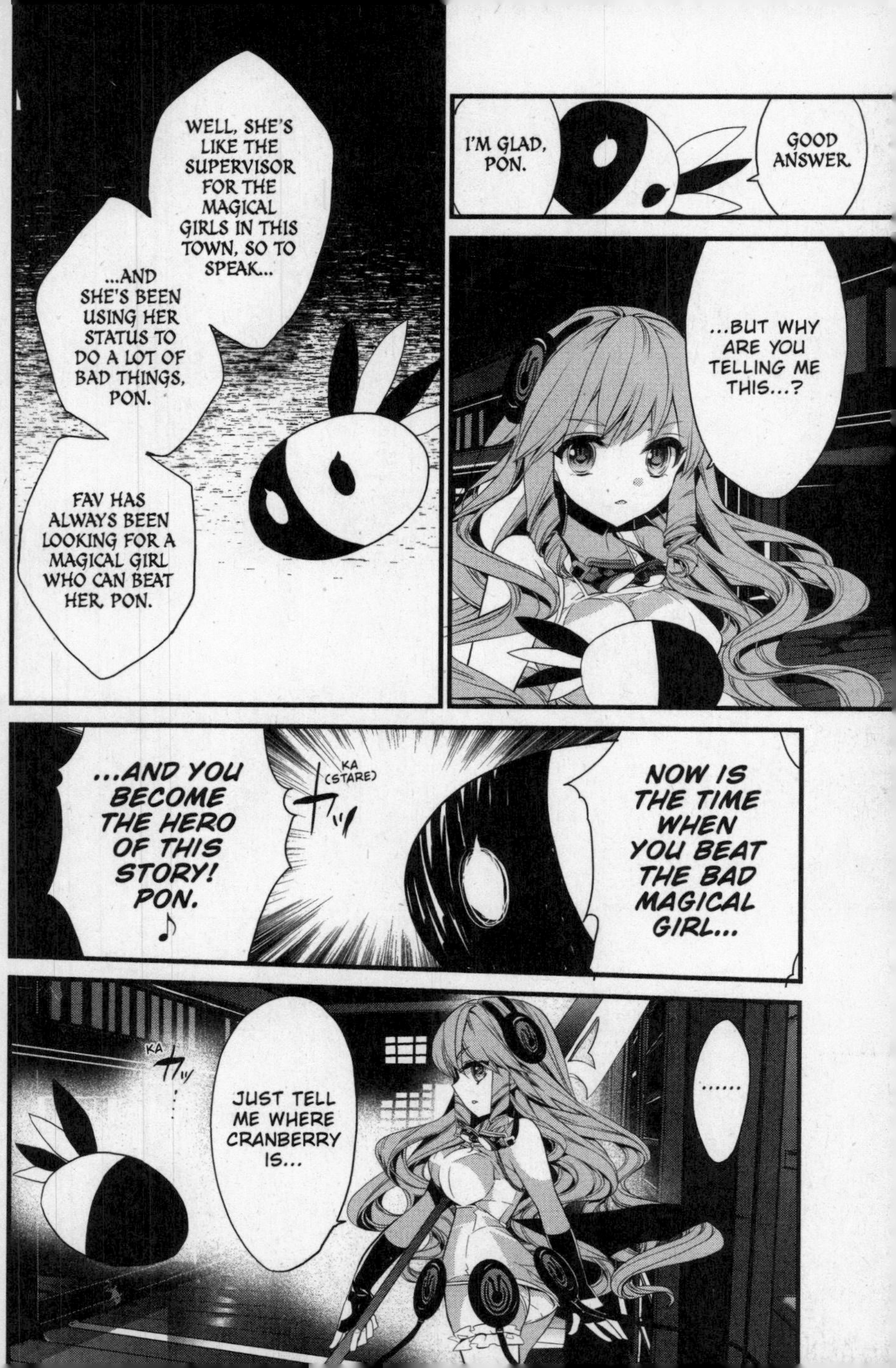
GOOD ANSWER.
I'M GLAD, PON.
...BUT WHY ARE YOU TELLING ME THIS...?
WELL, SHE'S LIKE THE SUPERVISOR FOR THE MAGICAL GIRLS IN THIS TOWN, SO TO SPEAK...
...AND SHE'S BEEN USING HER STATUS TO DO A LOT OF BAD THINGS, PON.
FAV HAS ALWAYS BEEN LOOKING FOR A MAGICAL GIRL WHO CAN BEAT HER, PON.
NOW IS THE TIME WHEN YOU BEAT THE BAD MAGICAL GIRL...
KA (STARE)
...AND YOU BECOME THE HERO OF THIS STORY! PON. ♪
......
JUST TELL ME WHERE CRANBERRY IS...
KA

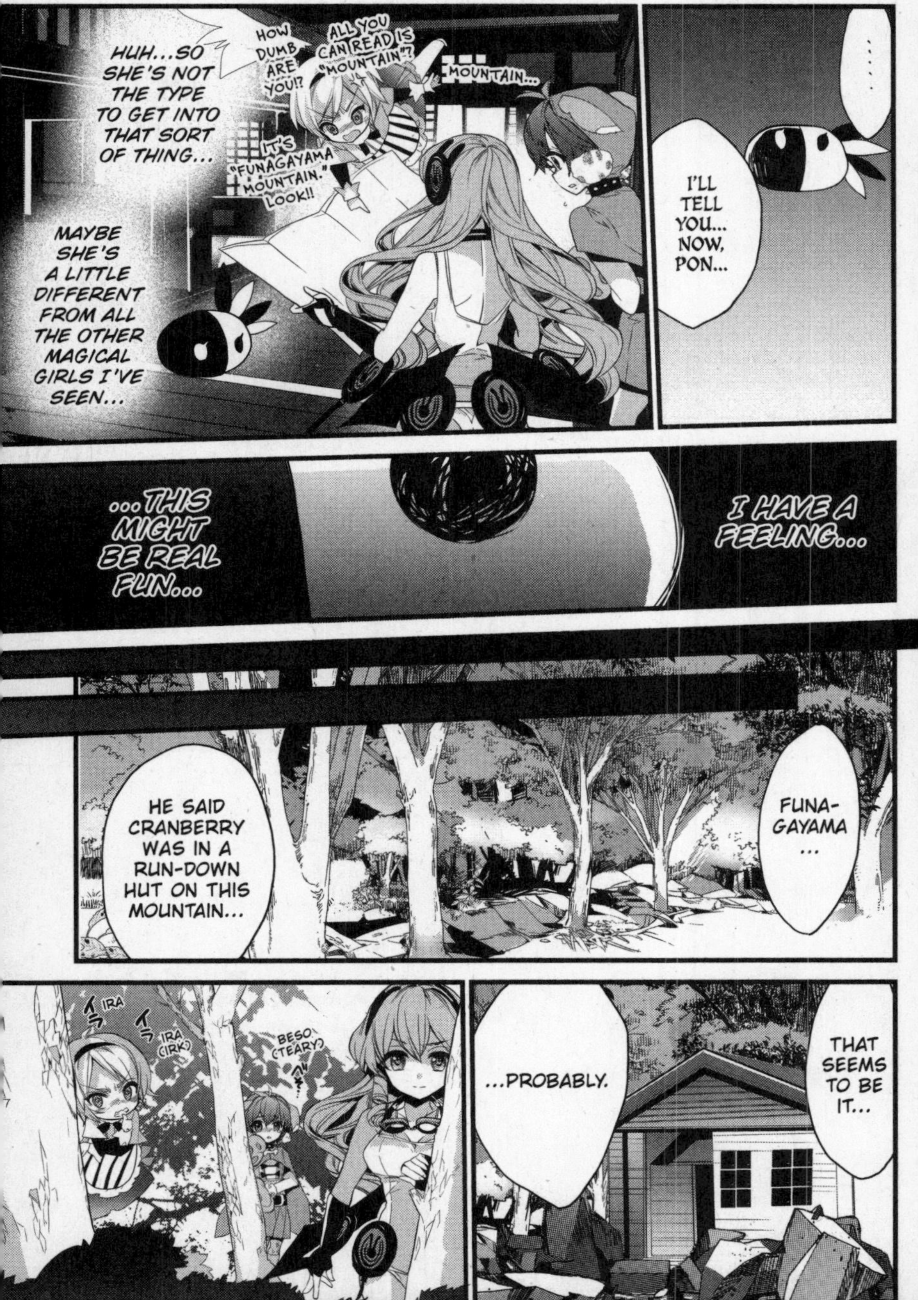
. . . . .
I'LL TELL YOU... NOW, PON...
MOUNTAIN...
ALL YOU CAN READ IS "MOUNTAIN"?
HOW DUMB ARE YOU!?
IT'S "FUNAGAYAMA MOUNTAIN." LOOK!!
HUH...SO SHE'S NOT THE TYPE TO GET INTO THAT SORT OF THING...
MAYBE SHE'S A LITTLE DIFFERENT FROM ALL THE OTHER MAGICAL GIRLS I'VE SEEN...
I HAVE A FEELING...
...THIS MIGHT BE REAL FUN...
FUNA-GAYAMA ...
HE SAID CRANBERRY WAS IN A RUN-DOWN HUT ON THIS MOUNTAIN...
THAT SEEMS TO BE IT...
...PROBABLY.
BESO (TEARY)
IRA IRA (IRK)

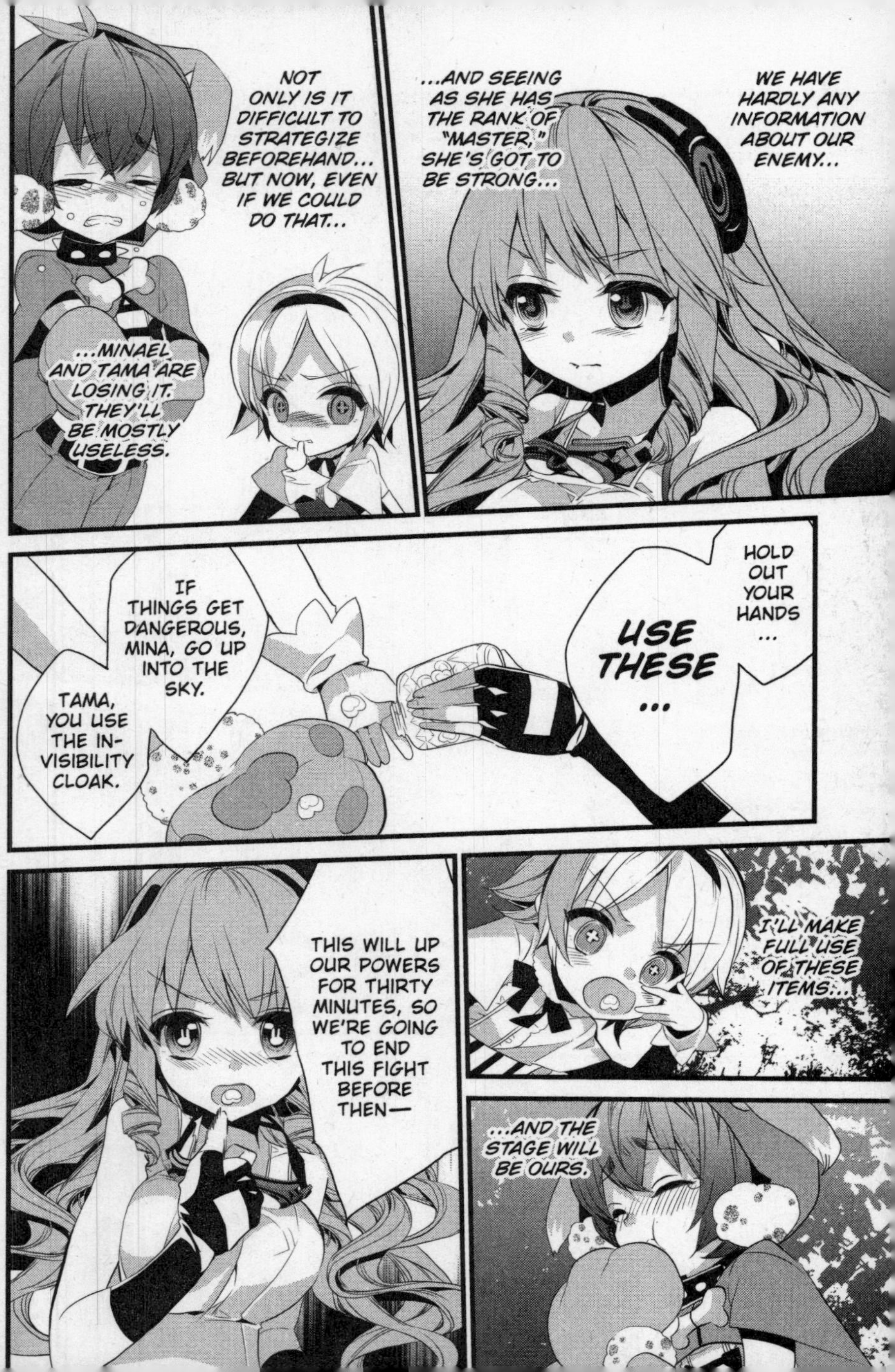

WE HAVE HARDLY ANY INFORMATION ABOUT OUR ENEMY...
...AND SEEING AS SHE HAS THE RANK OF "MASTER," SHE'S GOT TO BE STRONG...
NOT ONLY IS IT DIFFICULT TO STRATEGIZE BEFOREHAND... BUT NOW, EVEN IF WE COULD DO THAT...
...MINAEL AND TAMA ARE LOSING IT. THEY'LL BE MOSTLY USELESS.
HOLD OUT YOUR HANDS ...
USE THESE ...
IF THINGS GET DANGEROUS, MINA, GO UP INTO THE SKY.
TAMA, YOU USE THE IN-VISIBILITY CLOAK.
I'LL MAKE FULL USE OF THESE ITEMS...
...AND THE STAGE WILL BE OURS.
THIS WILL UP OUR POWERS FOR THIRTY MINUTES, SO WE'RE GOING TO END THIS FIGHT BEFORE THEN—

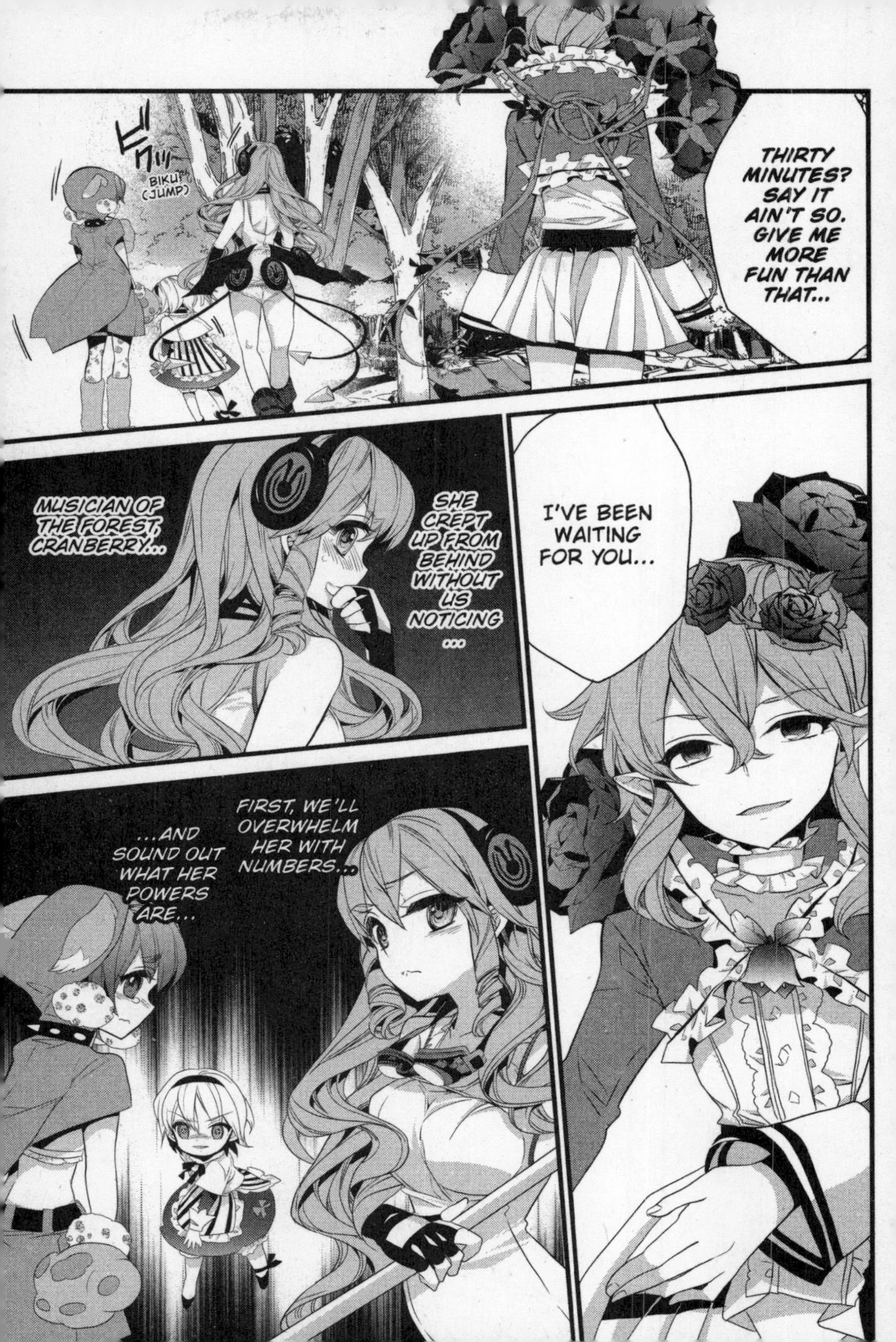
THIRTY MINUTES? SAY IT AIN'T SO. GIVE ME MORE FUN THAN THAT...
BIKU! (JUMP)
I'VE BEEN WAITING FOR YOU...
SHE CREPT UP FROM BEHIND WITHOUT US NOTICING...
MUSICIAN OF THE FOREST, CRANBERRY...
FIRST, WE'LL OVERWHELM HER WITH NUMBERS...
...AND SOUND OUT WHAT HER POWERS ARE...

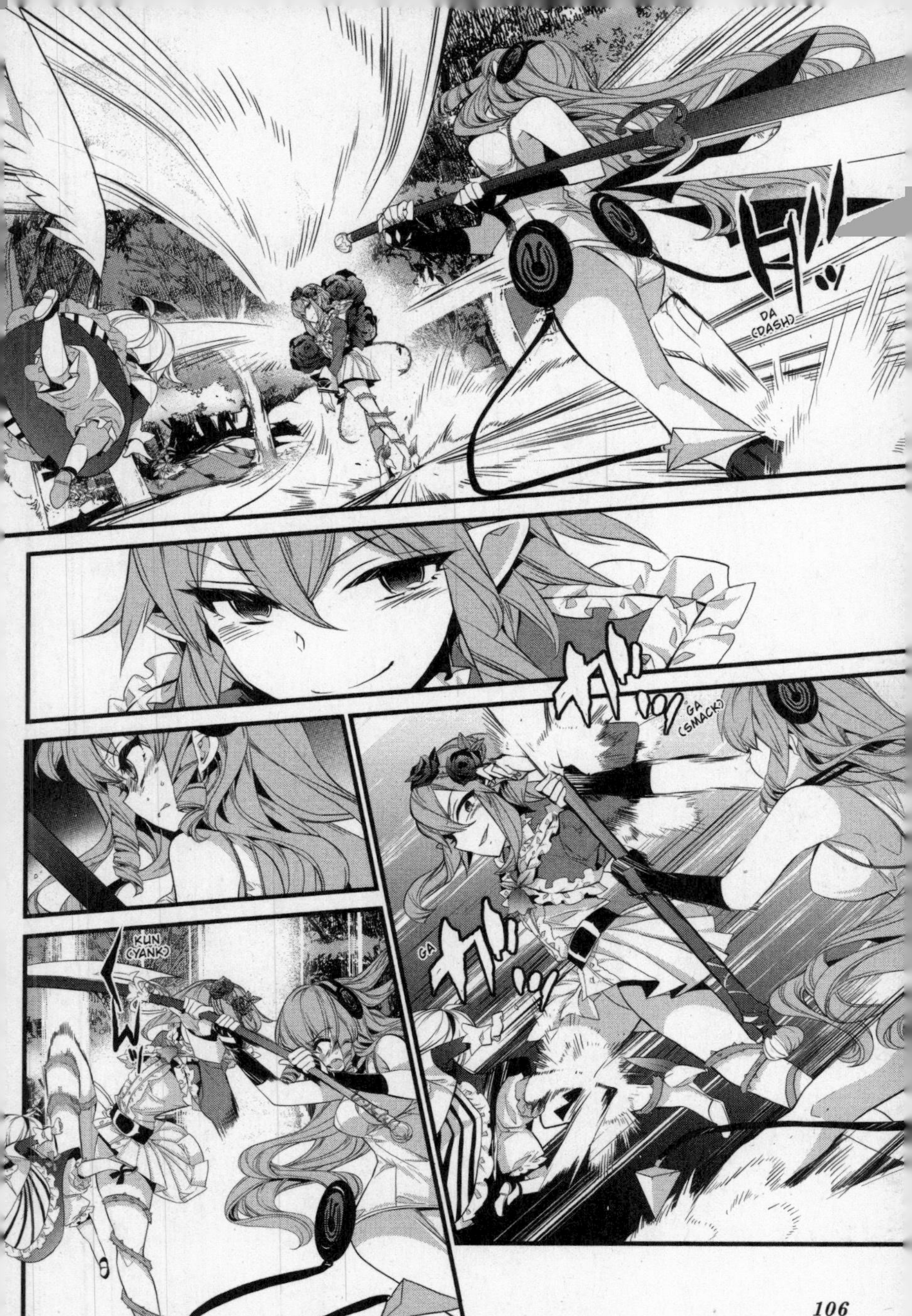
DA (DASH)
GA (SMACK)
GA
KUN (YANK)

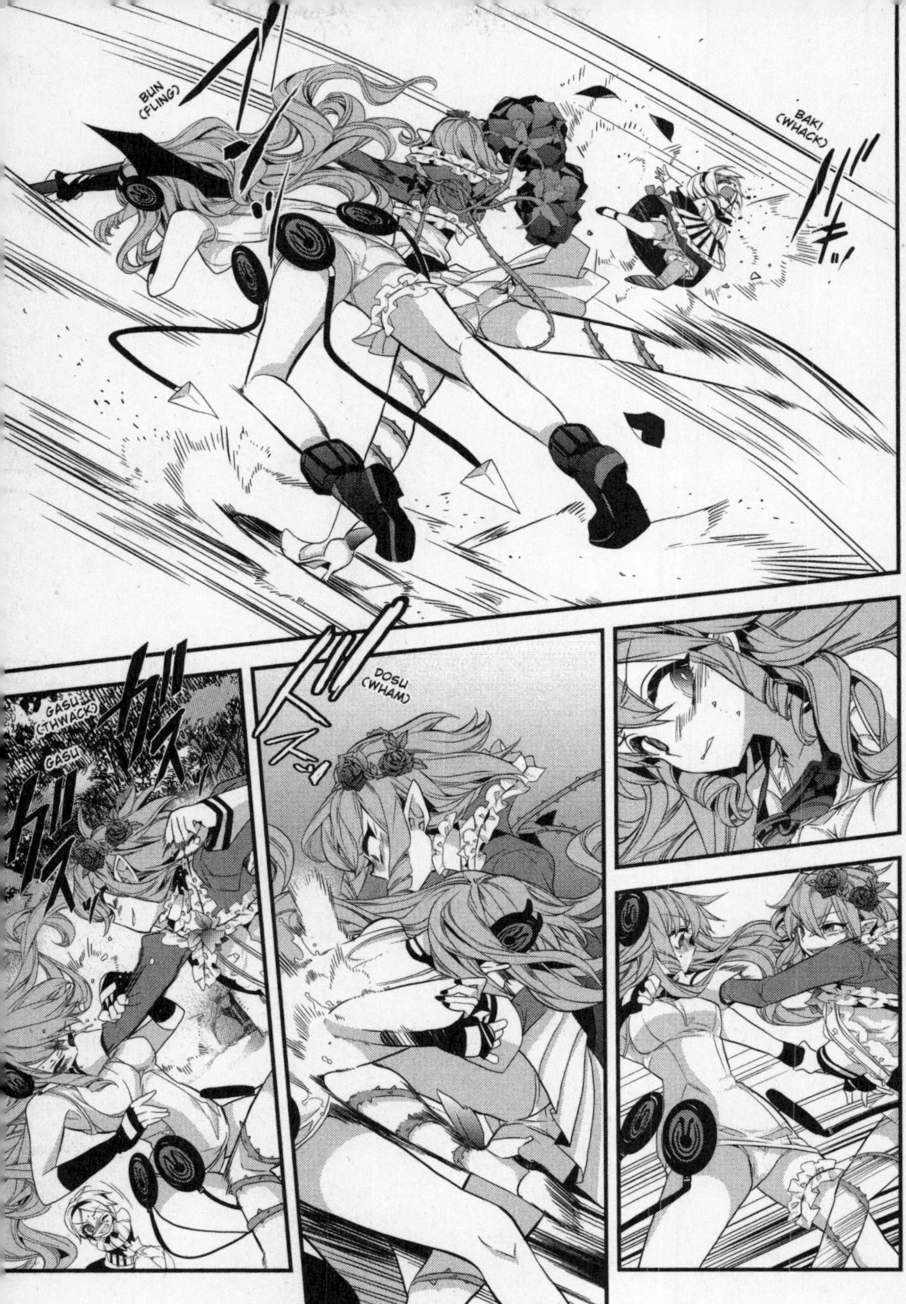
BAKI (WHACK)
BUN (FLING)
DOSU (WHAM)
GASU (THWACK)
GASU

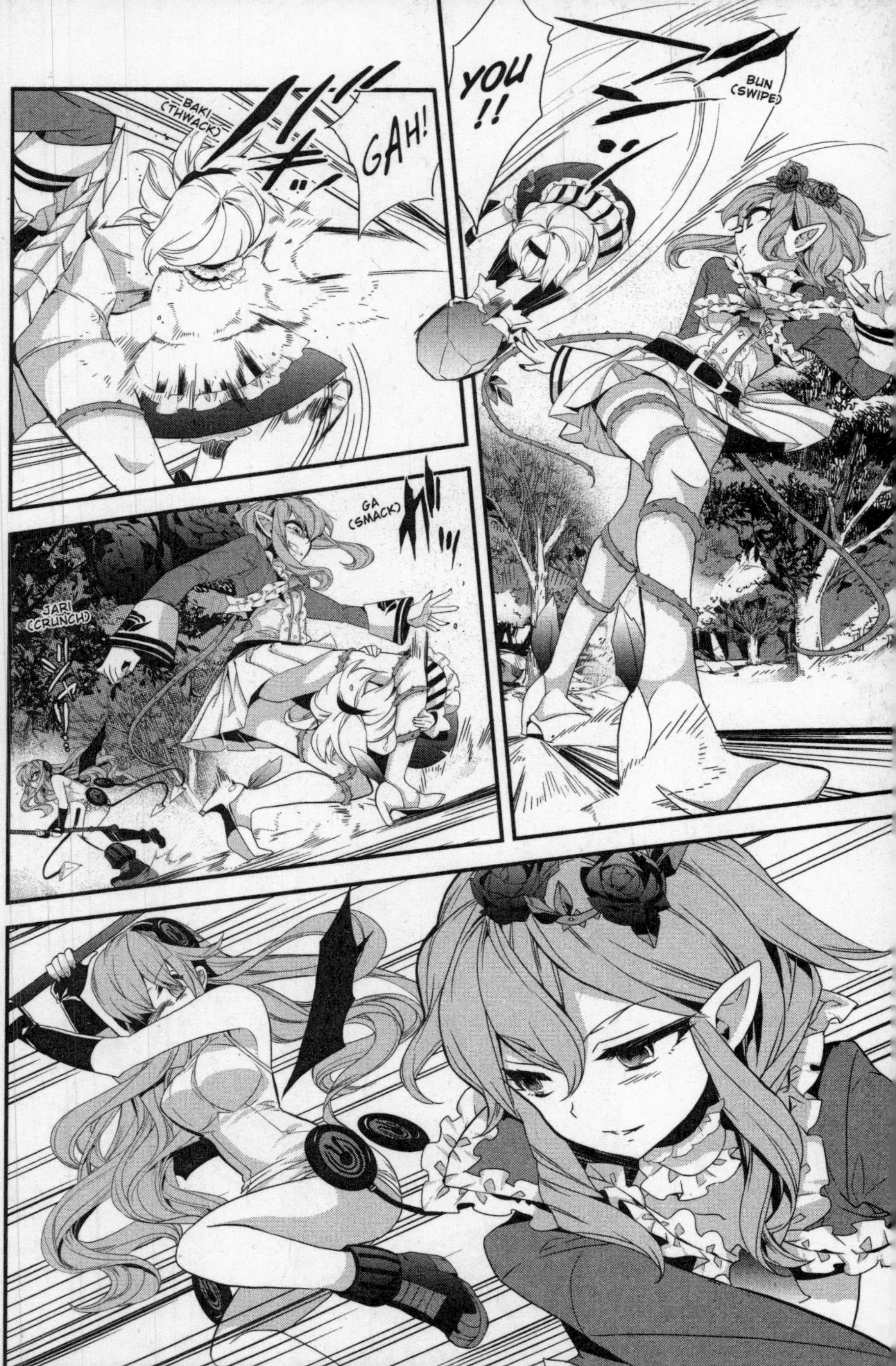
BUN (SWIPE)
YOU !!
GAH!
BAKI (THWACK)
GA (SMACK)
JARI (CRUNCH)

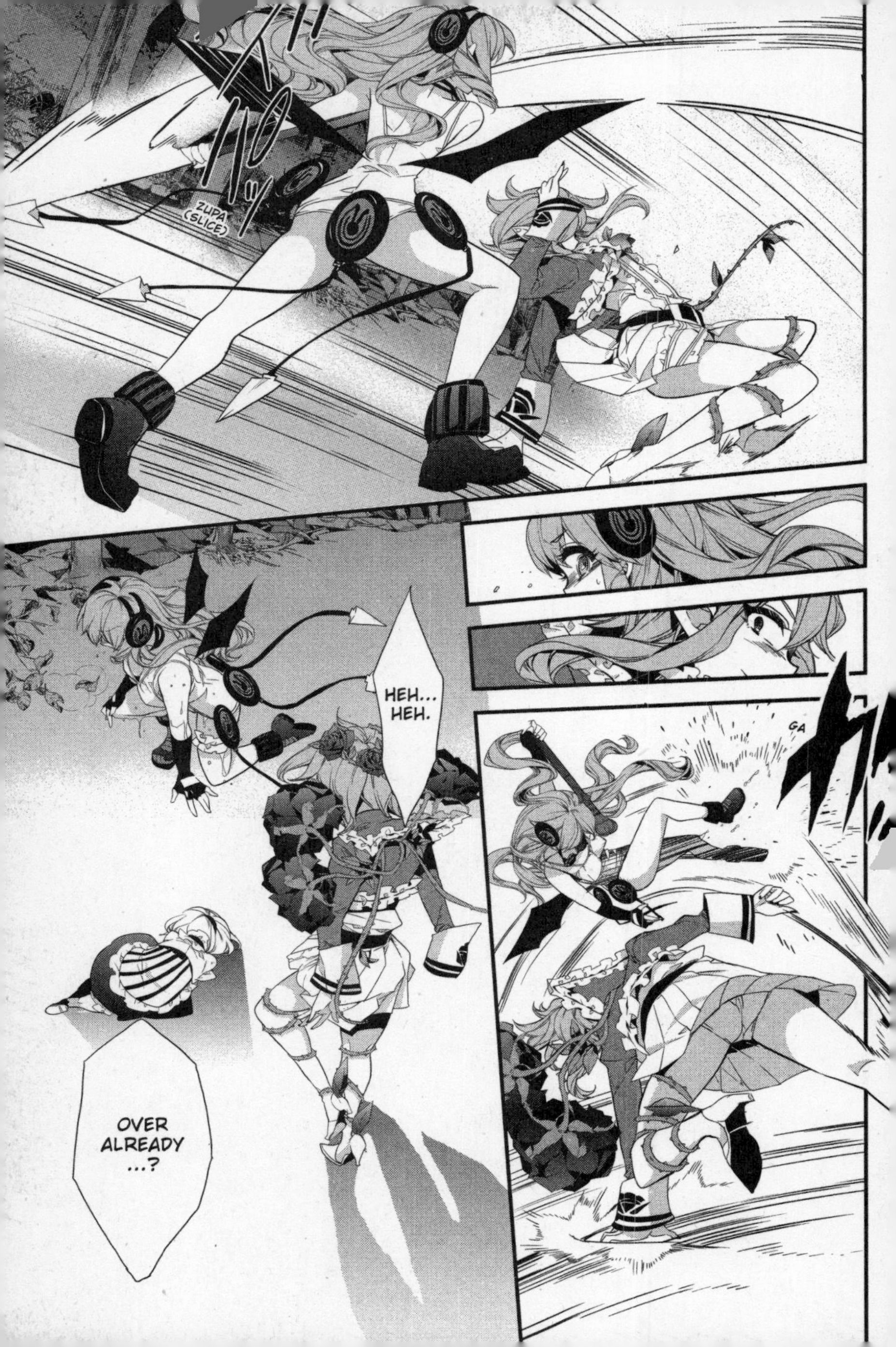
ZUPA
(SLICE)
GA
HEH... HEH.
OVER ALREADY ...?

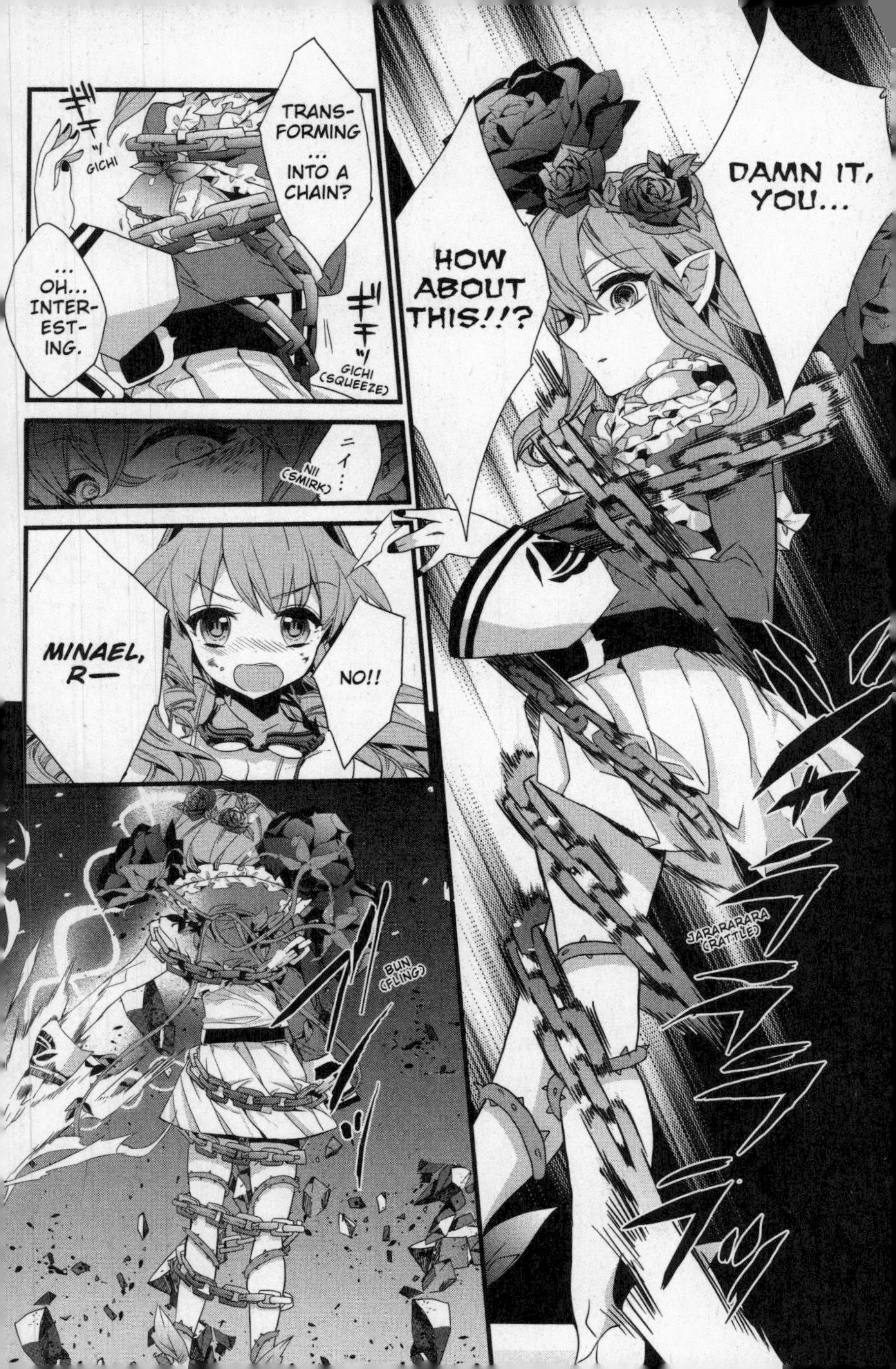
DAMN IT, YOU...
HOW ABOUT THIS!!?
JARARARARA (RATTLE)
TRANS-FORMING ... INTO A CHAIN?
ギチッ
GICHI
ギチッ
GICHI (SQUEEZE)
... OH... INTER-EST-ING.
ニィ…
NII (SMIRK)
MINAEL, R—
NO!!
BUN (FLING)

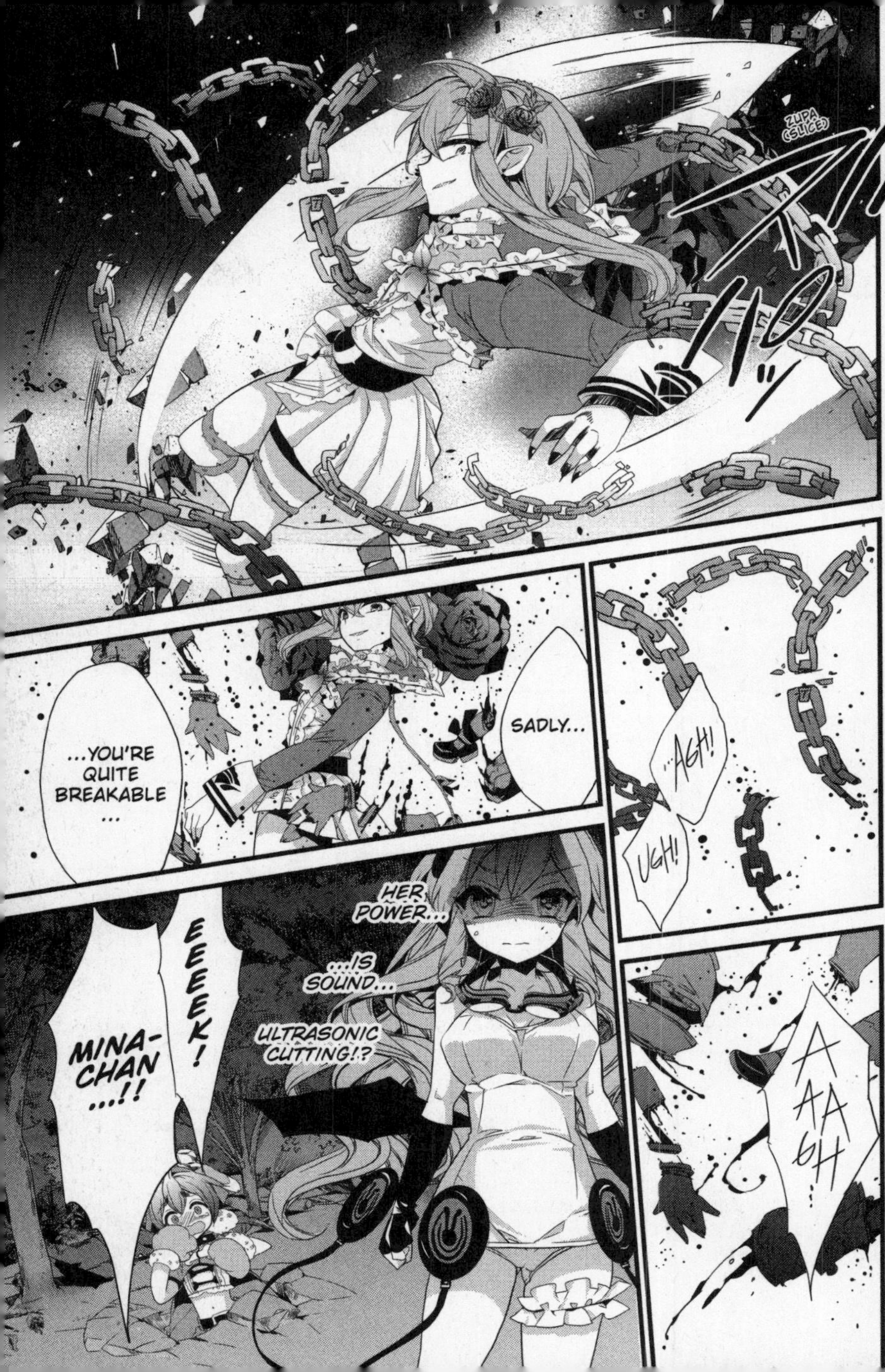
ZUPA (SLICE)
...AGH!
UGH!
SADLY...
...YOU'RE QUITE BREAKABLE ...
AAAGH
HER POWER...
...IS SOUND...
ULTRASONIC CUTTING!?
EEEEEK!
MINA-CHAN...!!

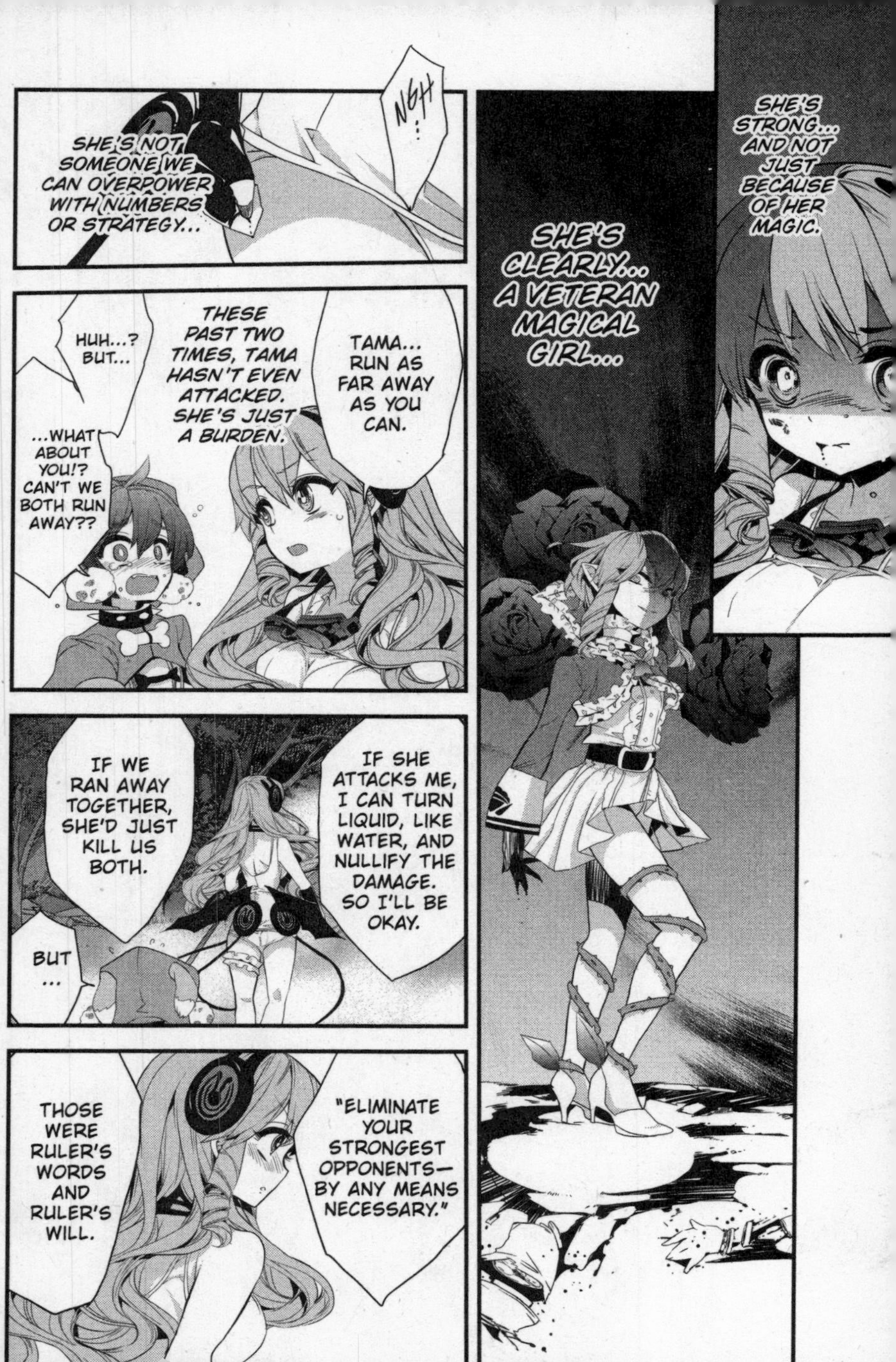
SHE'S STRONG... AND NOT JUST BECAUSE OF HER MAGIC.
SHE'S CLEARLY... A VETERAN MAGICAL GIRL...
NGH...
SHE'S NOT SOMEONE WE CAN OVERPOWER WITH NUMBERS OR STRATEGY...
TAMA... RUN AS FAR AWAY AS YOU CAN.
THESE PAST TWO TIMES, TAMA HASN'T EVEN ATTACKED. SHE'S JUST A BURDEN.
HUH...? BUT...
...WHAT ABOUT YOU!? CAN'T WE BOTH RUN AWAY??
IF SHE ATTACKS ME, I CAN TURN LIQUID, LIKE WATER, AND NULLIFY THE DAMAGE. SO I'LL BE OKAY.
IF WE RAN AWAY TOGETHER, SHE'D JUST KILL US BOTH.
BUT ...
"ELIMINATE YOUR STRONGEST OPPONENTS—BY ANY MEANS NECESSARY."
THOSE WERE RULER'S WORDS AND RULER'S WILL.

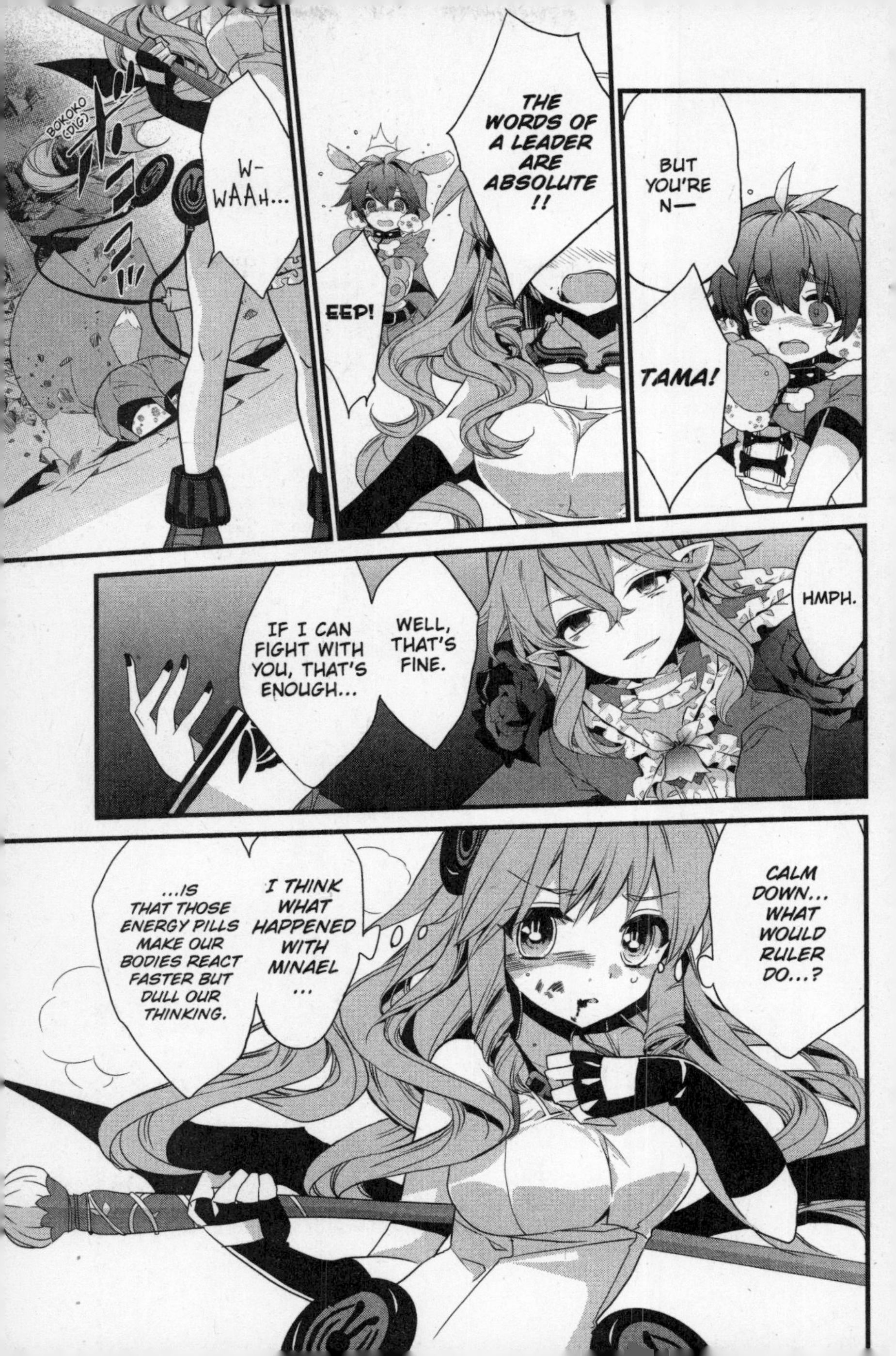
BUT YOU'RE N—
TAMA!
THE WORDS OF A LEADER ARE ABSOLUTE!!
EEP!
W-WAAH...
BOKOKO (DIG)
HMPH.
WELL, THAT'S FINE.
IF I CAN FIGHT WITH YOU, THAT'S ENOUGH...
CALM DOWN... WHAT WOULD RULER DO...?
I THINK WHAT HAPPENED WITH MINAEL ...
...IS THAT THOSE ENERGY PILLS MAKE OUR BODIES REACT FASTER BUT DULL OUR THINKING.

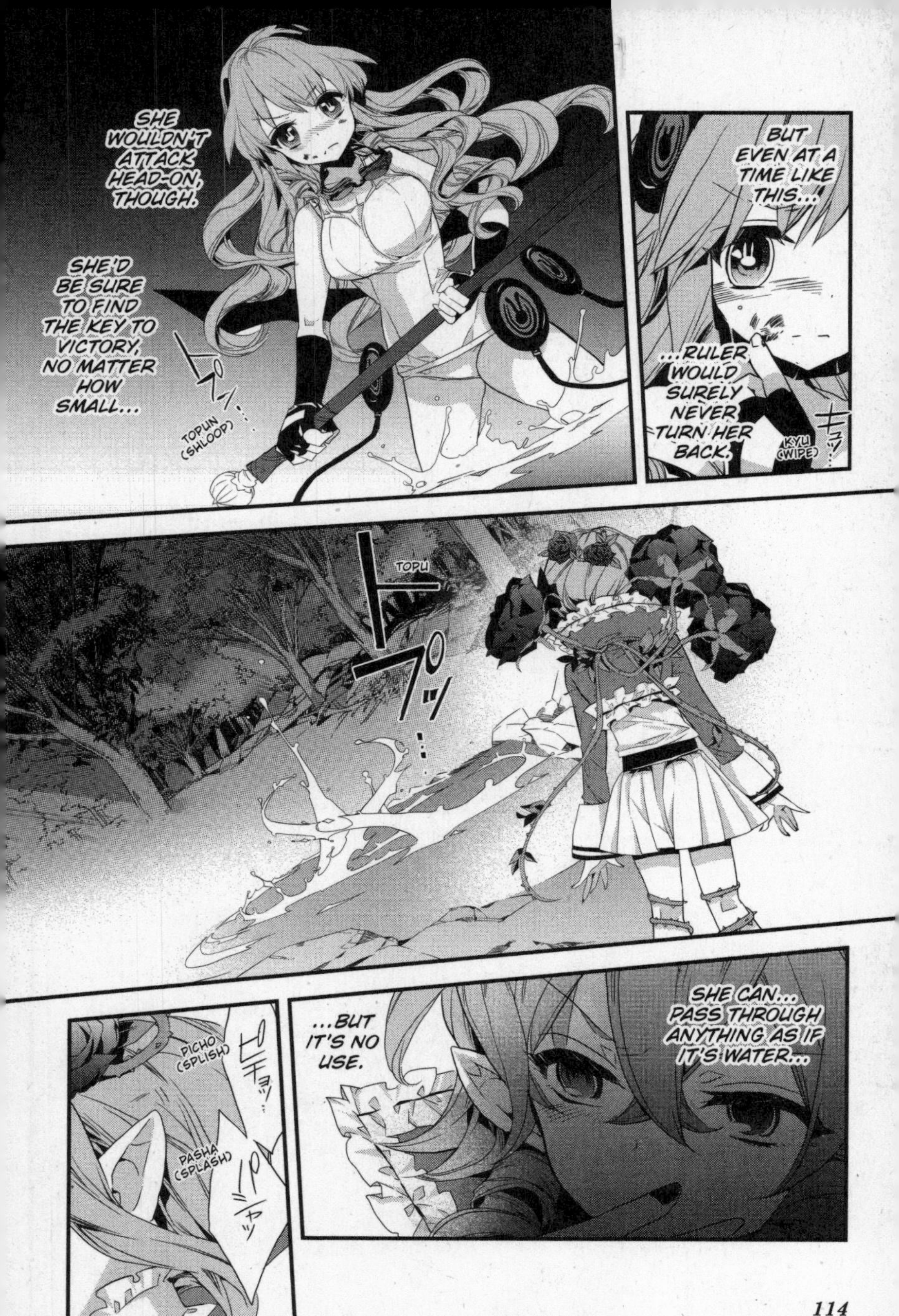
BUT EVEN AT A TIME LIKE THIS...
...RULER WOULD SURELY NEVER TURN HER BACK.
KYU (WIPE)
SHE WOULDN'T ATTACK HEAD-ON, THOUGH.
SHE'D BE SURE TO FIND THE KEY TO VICTORY, NO MATTER HOW SMALL...
TOPUN (SHLOOP)
TOPU
SHE CAN... PASS THROUGH ANYTHING AS IF IT'S WATER...
...BUT IT'S NO USE.
PICHO (SPLISH)
PASHA (SPLASH)

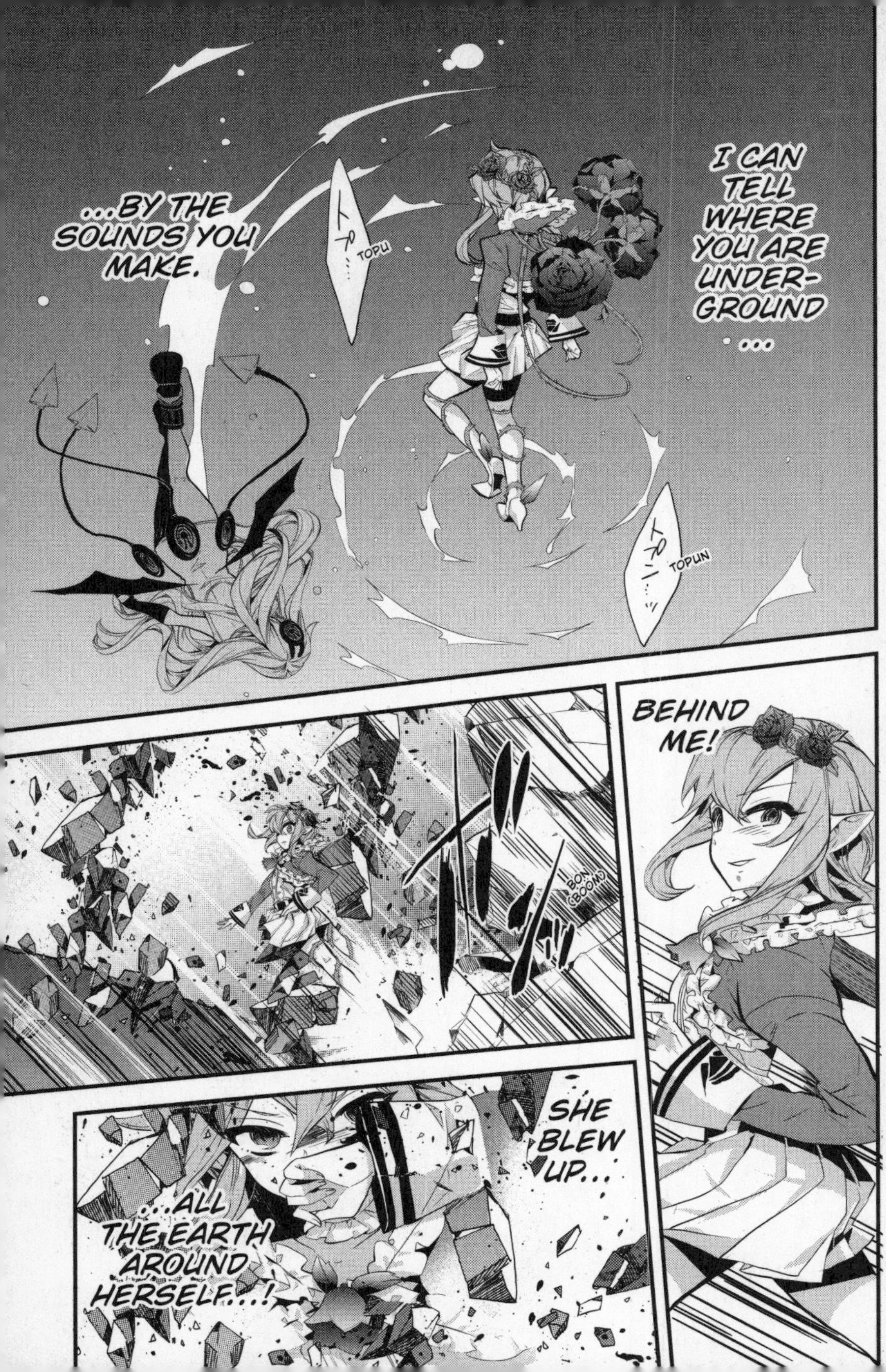
I CAN TELL WHERE YOU ARE UNDER-GROUND...
TOPU
...BY THE SOUNDS YOU MAKE.
TOPUN
BEHIND ME!
BON (BOOM)
SHE BLEW UP...
...ALL THE EARTH AROUND HERSELF...!

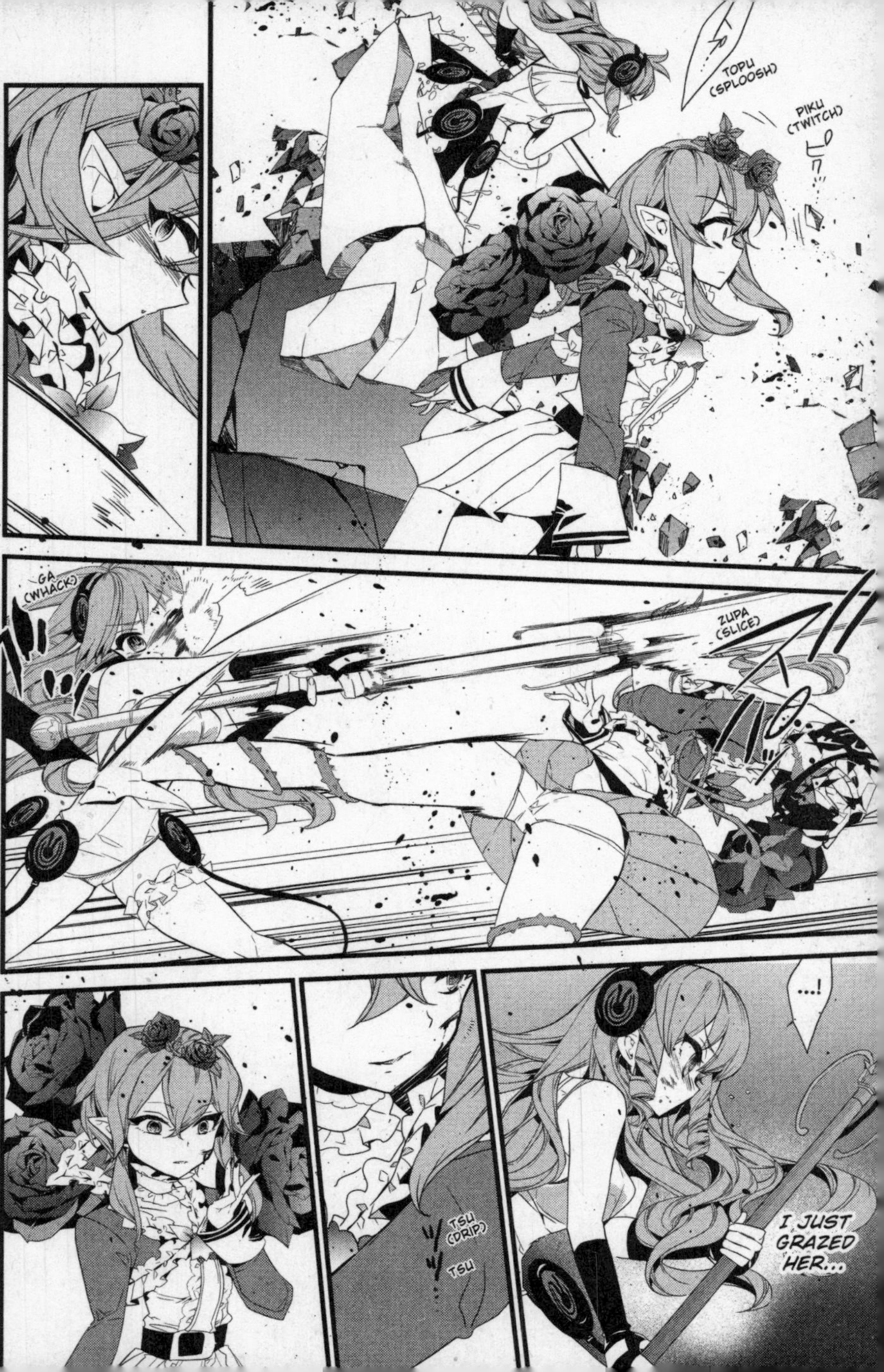
TOPU (SPLOOSH)
PIKU (TWITCH)
ZUPA (SLICE)
GA (WHACK)
...!
I JUST GRAZED HER...
TSU (DRIP)
TSU

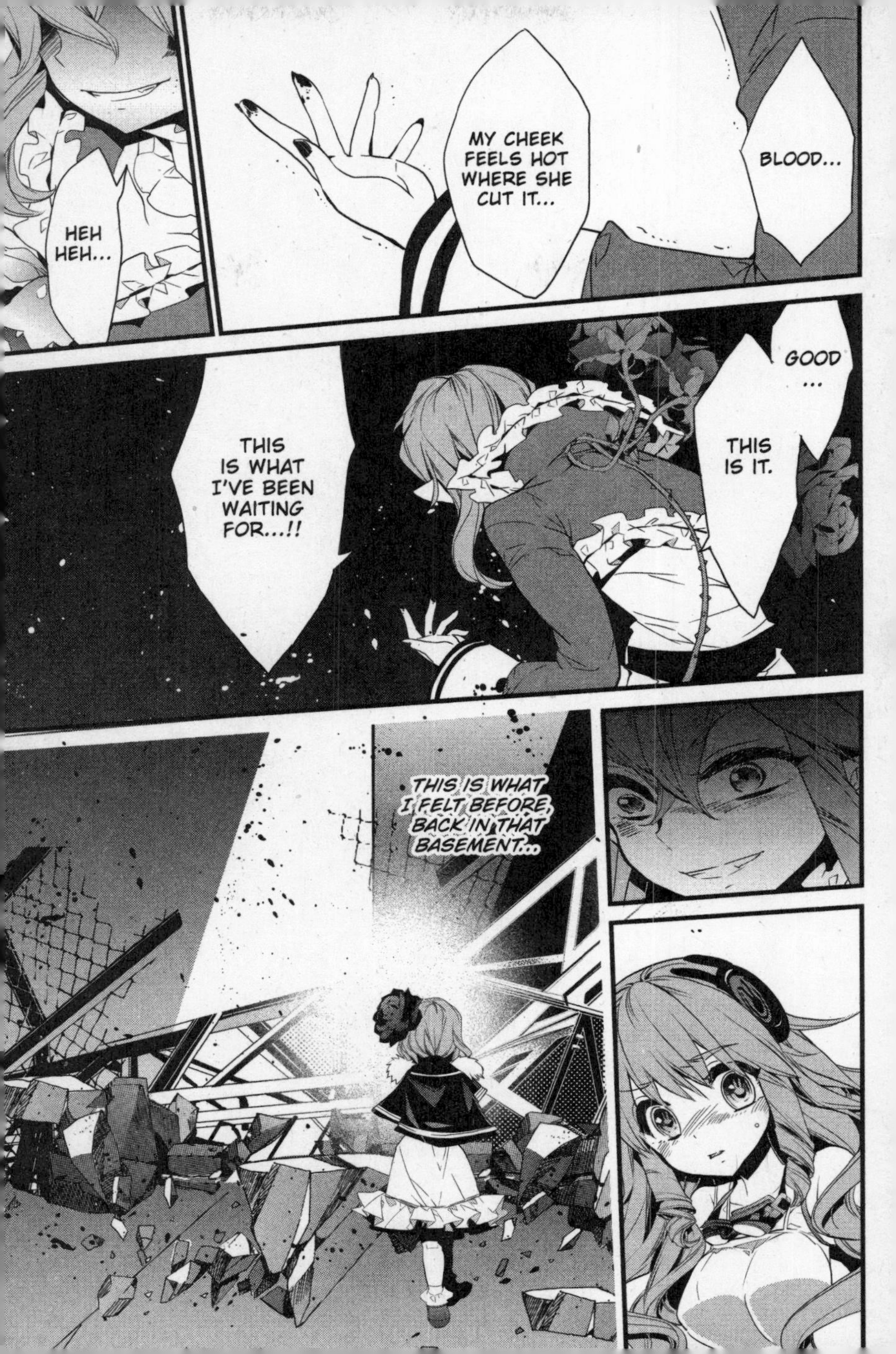
BLOOD...
MY CHEEK FEELS HOT WHERE SHE CUT IT...
HEH HEH...
GOOD...
THIS IS IT.
THIS IS WHAT I'VE BEEN WAITING FOR...!!
THIS IS WHAT I FELT BEFORE, BACK IN THAT BASEMENT...

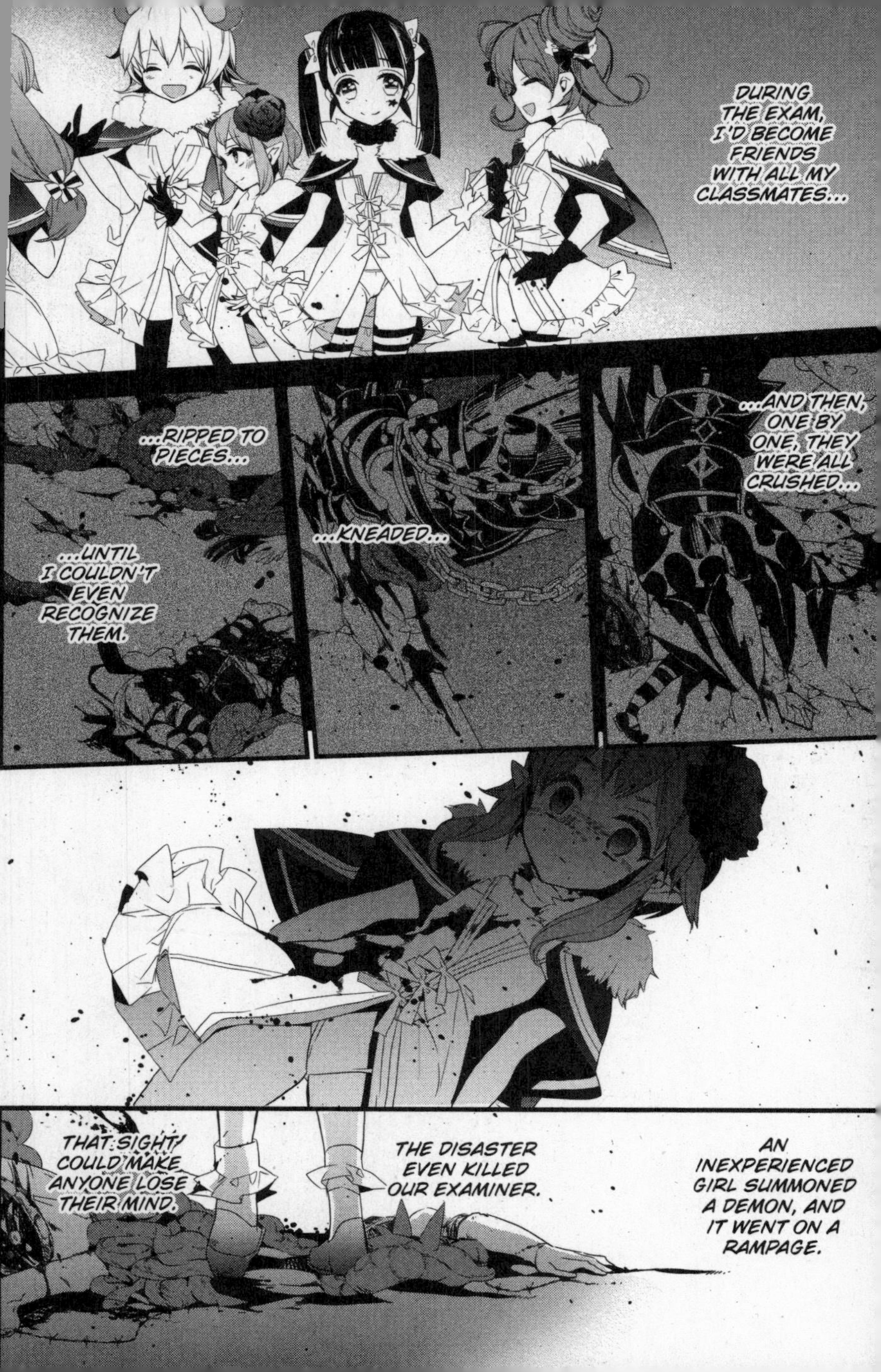
DURING THE EXAM, I'D BECOME FRIENDS WITH ALL MY CLASSMATES...
...AND THEN, ONE BY ONE, THEY WERE ALL CRUSHED...
...KNEADED...
...RIPPED TO PIECES...
...UNTIL I COULDN'T EVEN RECOGNIZE THEM.
AN INEXPERIENCED GIRL SUMMONED A DEMON, AND IT WENT ON A RAMPAGE.
THE DISASTER EVEN KILLED OUR EXAMINER.
THAT SIGHT COULD MAKE ANYONE LOSE THEIR MIND.

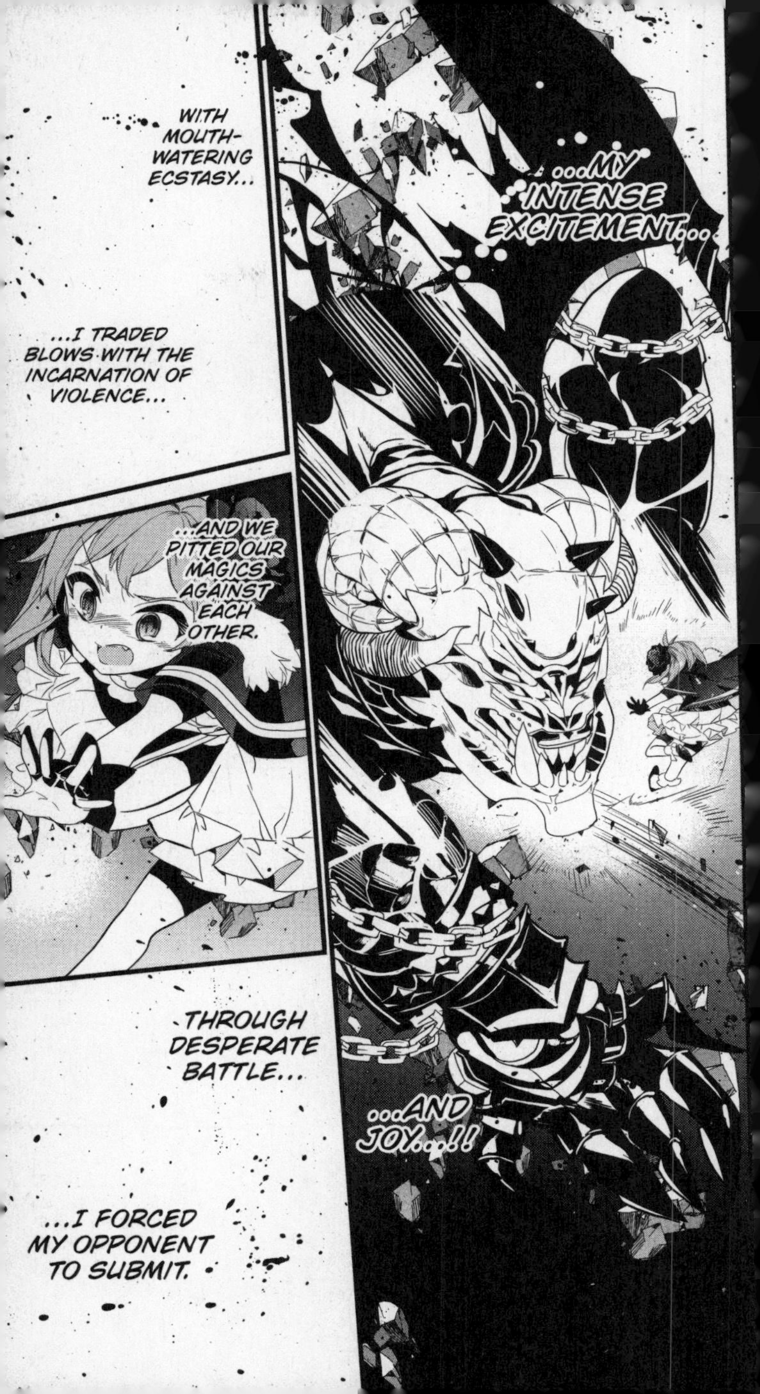
...MY INTENSE EXCITEMENT...
...AND JOY...!!
WITH MOUTH-WATERING ECSTASY...
...I TRADED BLOWS WITH THE INCARNATION OF VIOLENCE...
...AND WE PITTED OUR MAGICS AGAINST EACH OTHER.
THROUGH DESPERATE BATTLE...
...I FORCED MY OPPONENT TO SUBMIT.

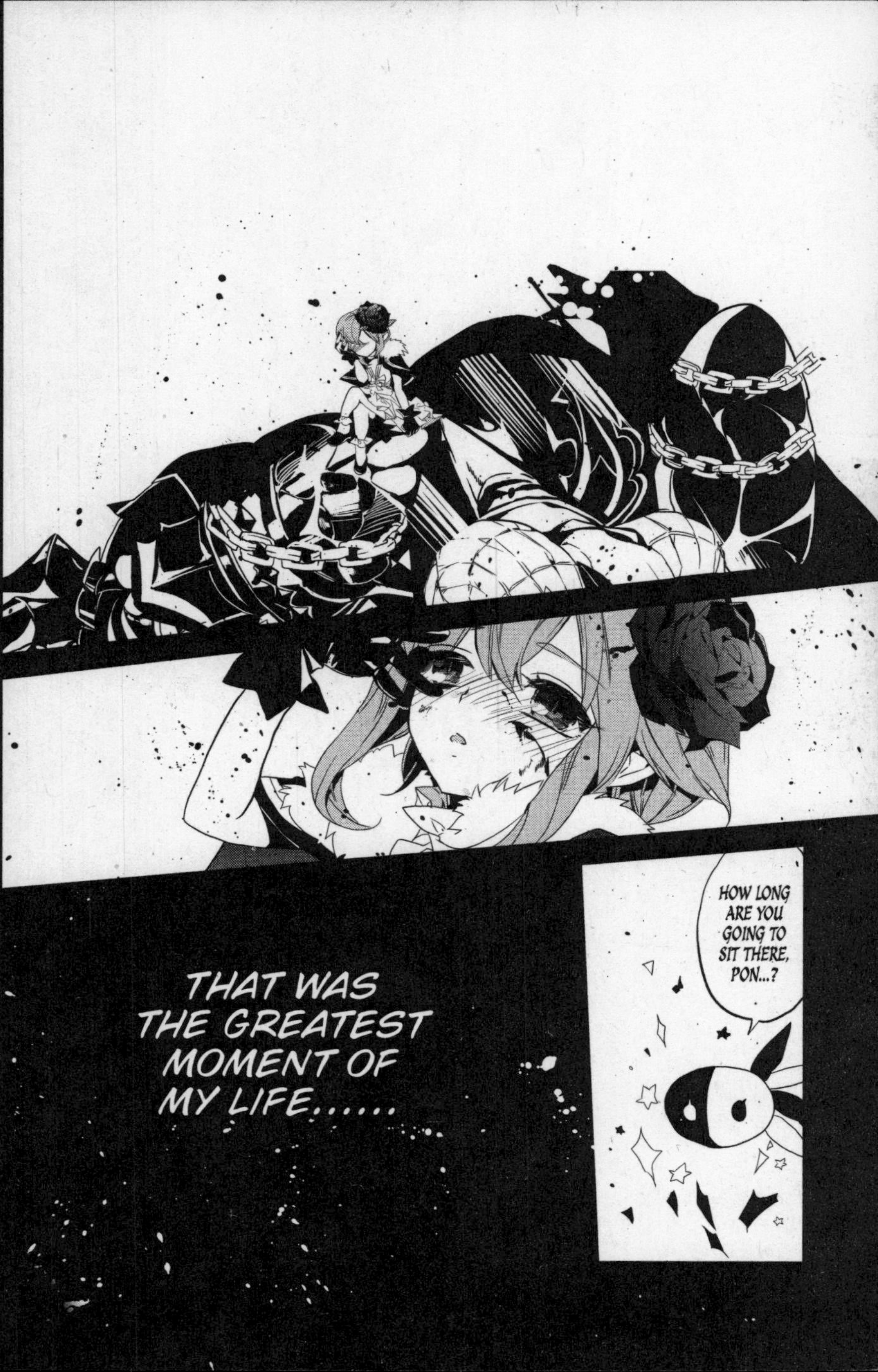
HOW LONG ARE YOU GOING TO SIT THERE, PON...?
THAT WAS THE GREATEST MOMENT OF MY LIFE......

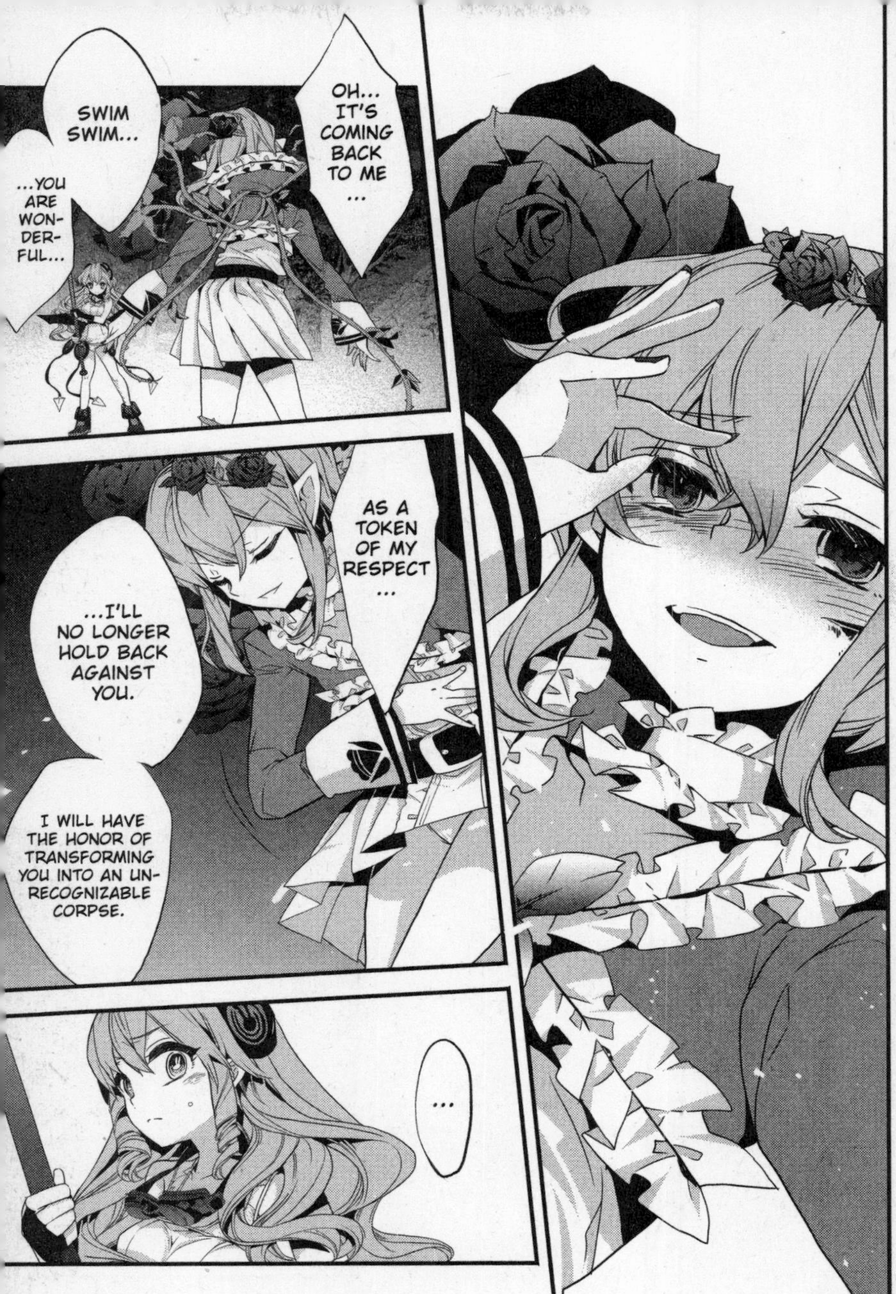
OH... IT'S COMING BACK TO ME...
SWIM SWIM...
...YOU ARE WONDERFUL...
AS A TOKEN OF MY RESPECT...
...I'LL NO LONGER HOLD BACK AGAINST YOU.
I WILL HAVE THE HONOR OF TRANSFORMING YOU INTO AN UNRECOGNIZABLE CORPSE.
...

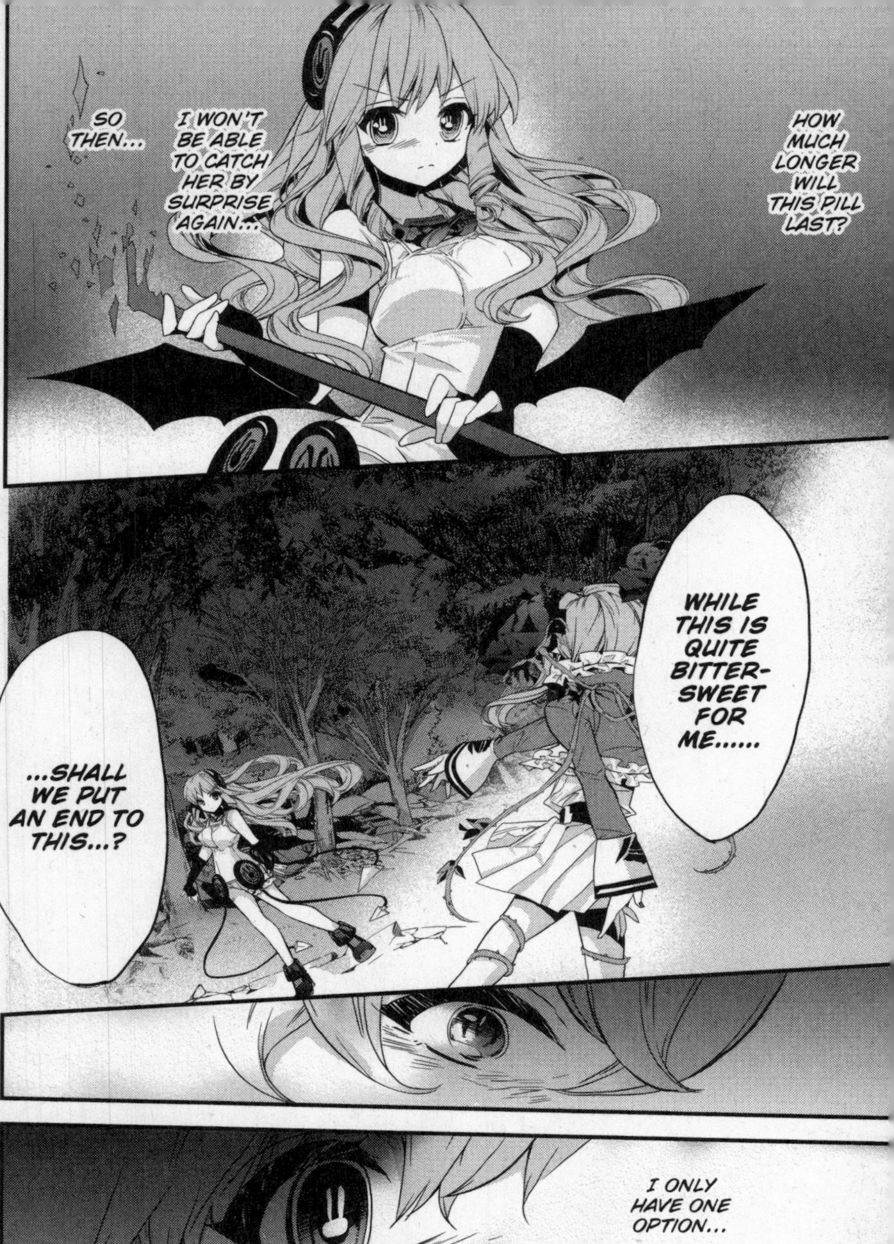
HOW MUCH LONGER WILL THIS PILL LAST?
I WON'T BE ABLE TO CATCH HER BY SURPRISE AGAIN...
SO THEN...
WHILE THIS IS QUITE BITTER-SWEET FOR ME......
...SHALL WE PUT AN END TO THIS...?
I ONLY HAVE ONE OPTION...

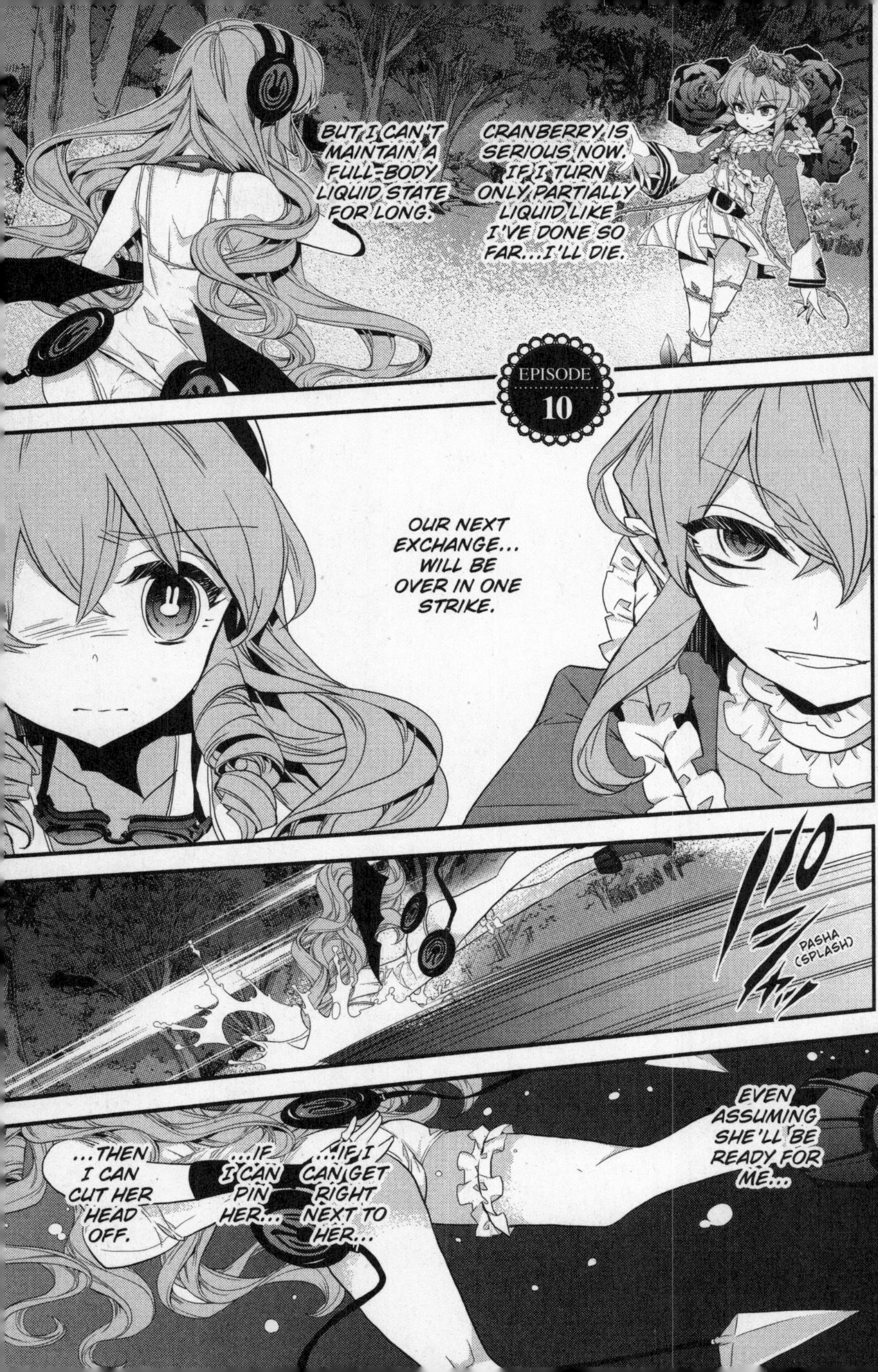
CRANBERRY IS SERIOUS NOW. IF I TURN ONLY PARTIALLY LIQUID LIKE I'VE DONE SO FAR...I'LL DIE.
BUT I CAN'T MAINTAIN A FULL-BODY LIQUID STATE FOR LONG.
EPISODE 10
OUR NEXT EXCHANGE... WILL BE OVER IN ONE STRIKE.
PASHA (SPLASH)
EVEN ASSUMING SHE'LL BE READY FOR ME...
...IF I CAN GET RIGHT NEXT TO HER...
...IF I CAN PIN HER...
...THEN I CAN CUT HER HEAD OFF.

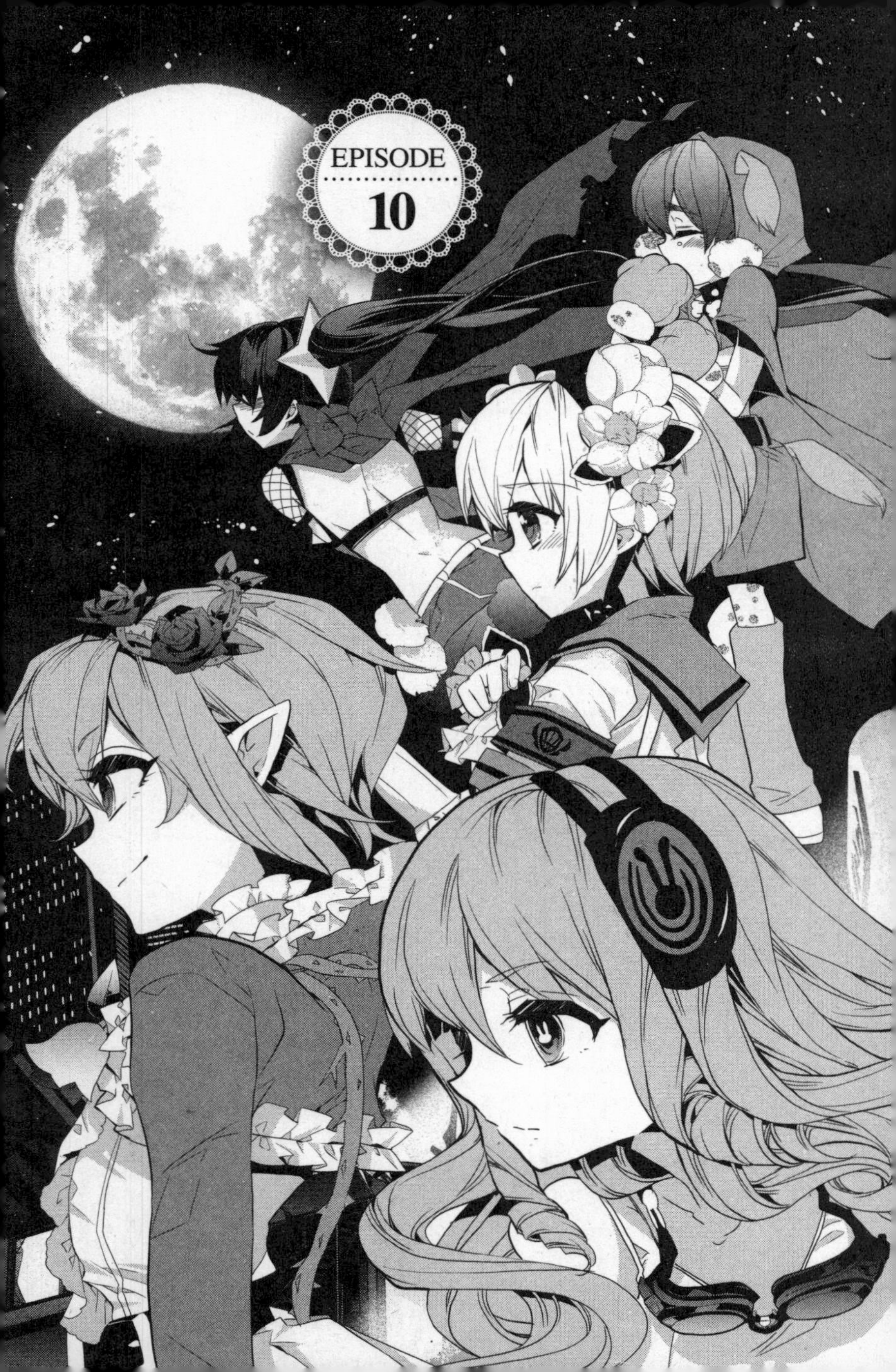
EPISODE
10

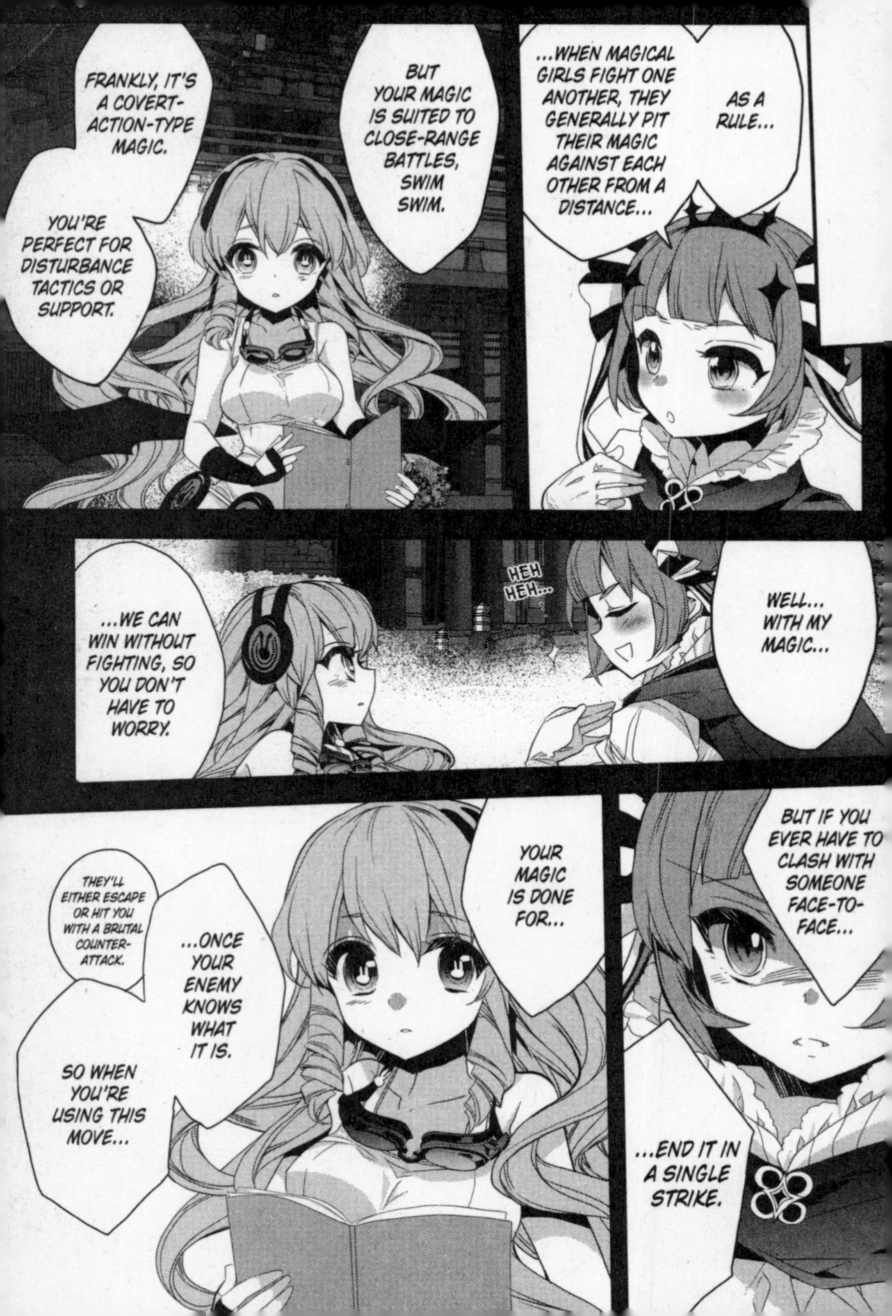
AS A RULE...
...WHEN MAGICAL GIRLS FIGHT ONE ANOTHER, THEY GENERALLY PIT THEIR MAGIC AGAINST EACH OTHER FROM A DISTANCE...
BUT YOUR MAGIC IS SUITED TO CLOSE-RANGE BATTLES, SWIM SWIM.
FRANKLY, IT'S A COVERT-ACTION-TYPE MAGIC.
YOU'RE PERFECT FOR DISTURBANCE TACTICS OR SUPPORT.
WELL... WITH MY MAGIC...
HEH HEH...
...WE CAN WIN WITHOUT FIGHTING, SO YOU DON'T HAVE TO WORRY.
BUT IF YOU EVER HAVE TO CLASH WITH SOMEONE FACE-TO-FACE...
...END IT IN A SINGLE STRIKE.
YOUR MAGIC IS DONE FOR...
...ONCE YOUR ENEMY KNOWS WHAT IT IS.
THEY'LL EITHER ESCAPE OR HIT YOU WITH A BRUTAL COUNTER-ATTACK.
SO WHEN YOU'RE USING THIS MOVE...

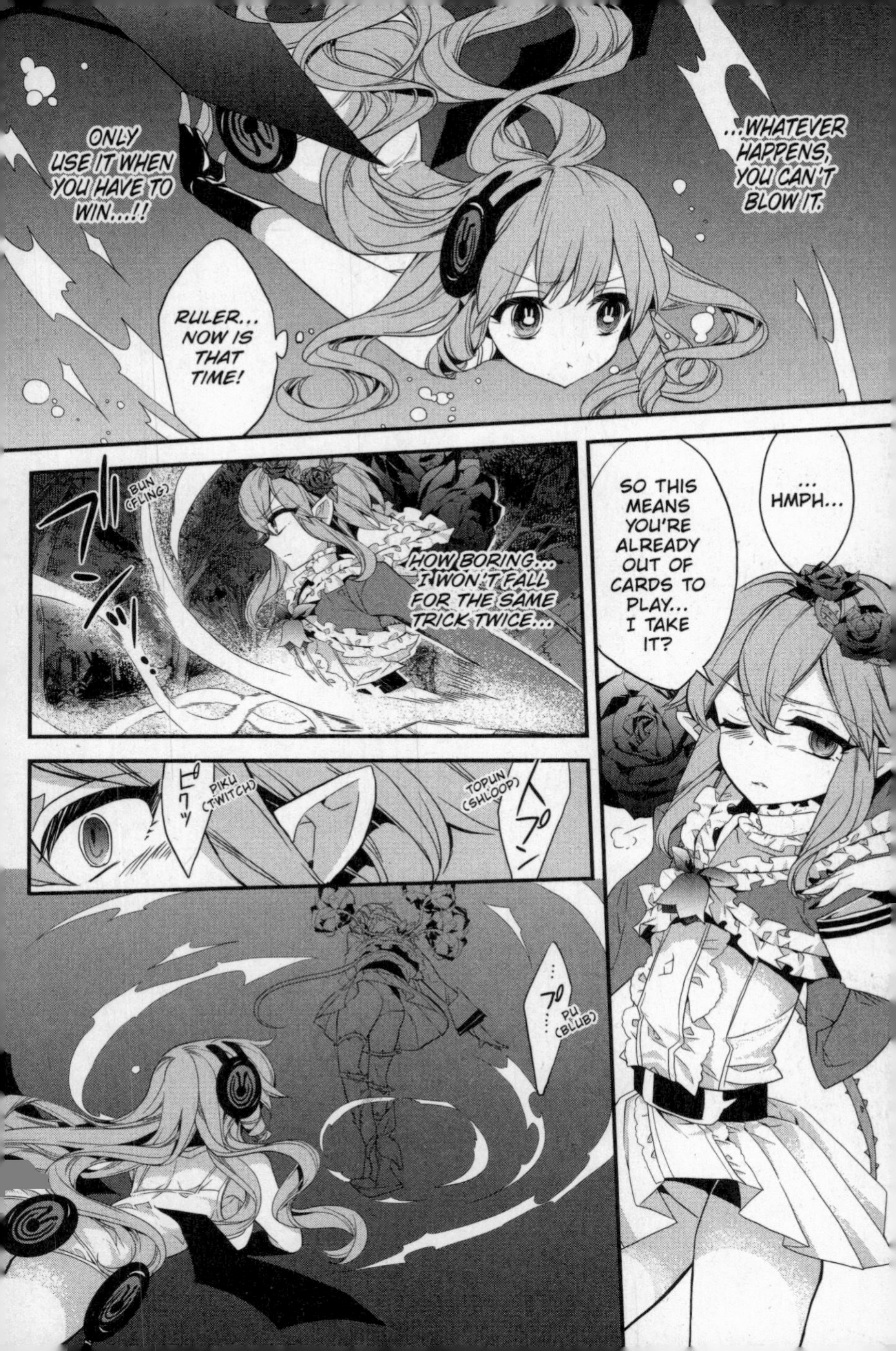
...WHATEVER HAPPENS, YOU CAN'T BLOW IT.
ONLY USE IT WHEN YOU HAVE TO WIN...!!
RULER... NOW IS THAT TIME!
... HMPH...
SO THIS MEANS YOU'RE ALREADY OUT OF CARDS TO PLAY... I TAKE IT?
BUN (FLING)
HOW BORING... I WON'T FALL FOR THE SAME TRICK TWICE...
TOPUN (SHLOOP)
PIKU (TWITCH)
PU (BLUB)

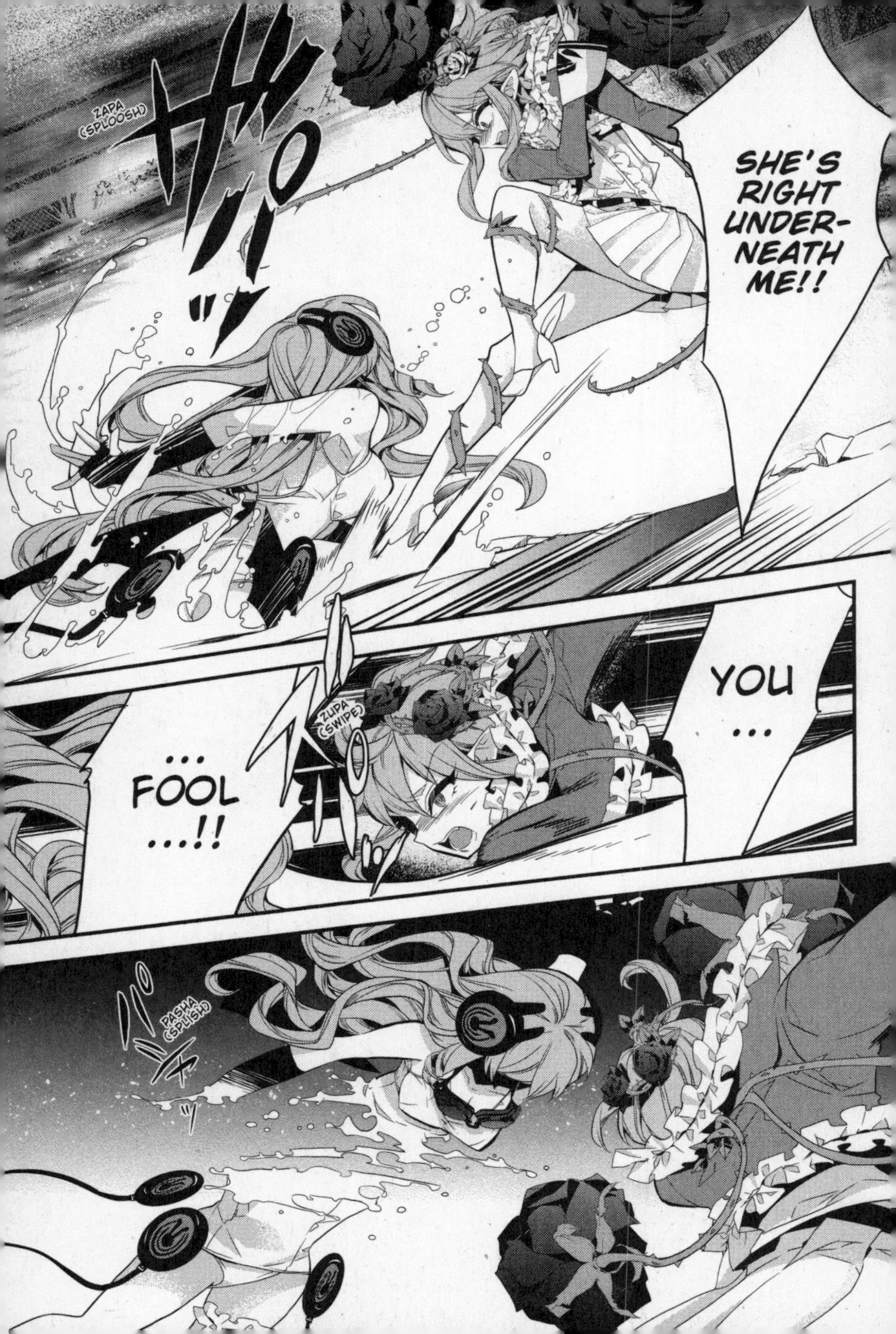
SHE'S RIGHT UNDER-NEATH ME!!
ZAPA (SPLOOSH)
YOU ...
ZUPA (SWIPE)
... FOOL ...!!
PASHA (SPLISH)

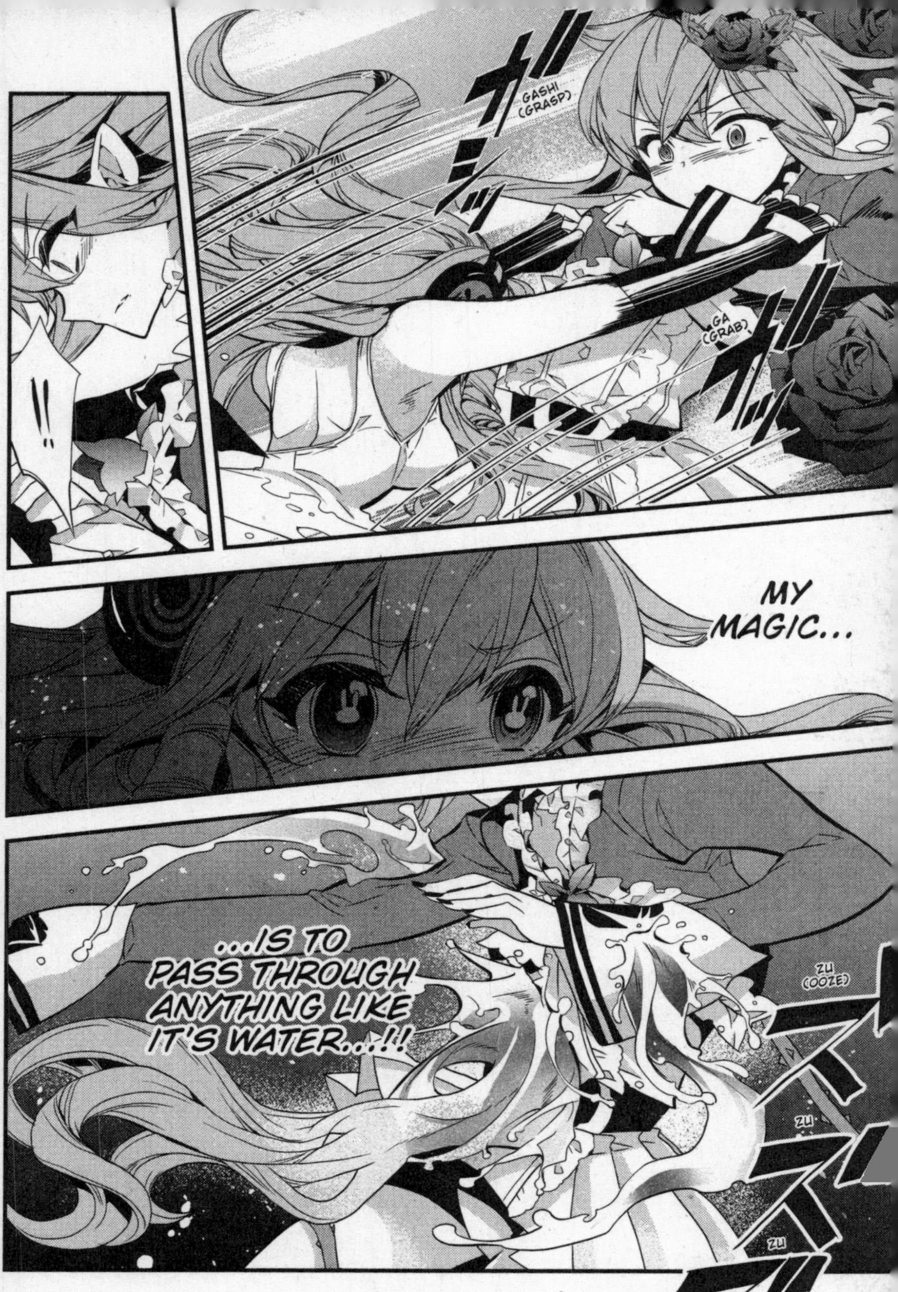
GASHI (GRASP)
GA (GRAB)
!!
MY MAGIC...
ZU (OOZE)
ZU
ZU
...IS TO PASS THROUGH ANYTHING LIKE IT'S WATER...!!

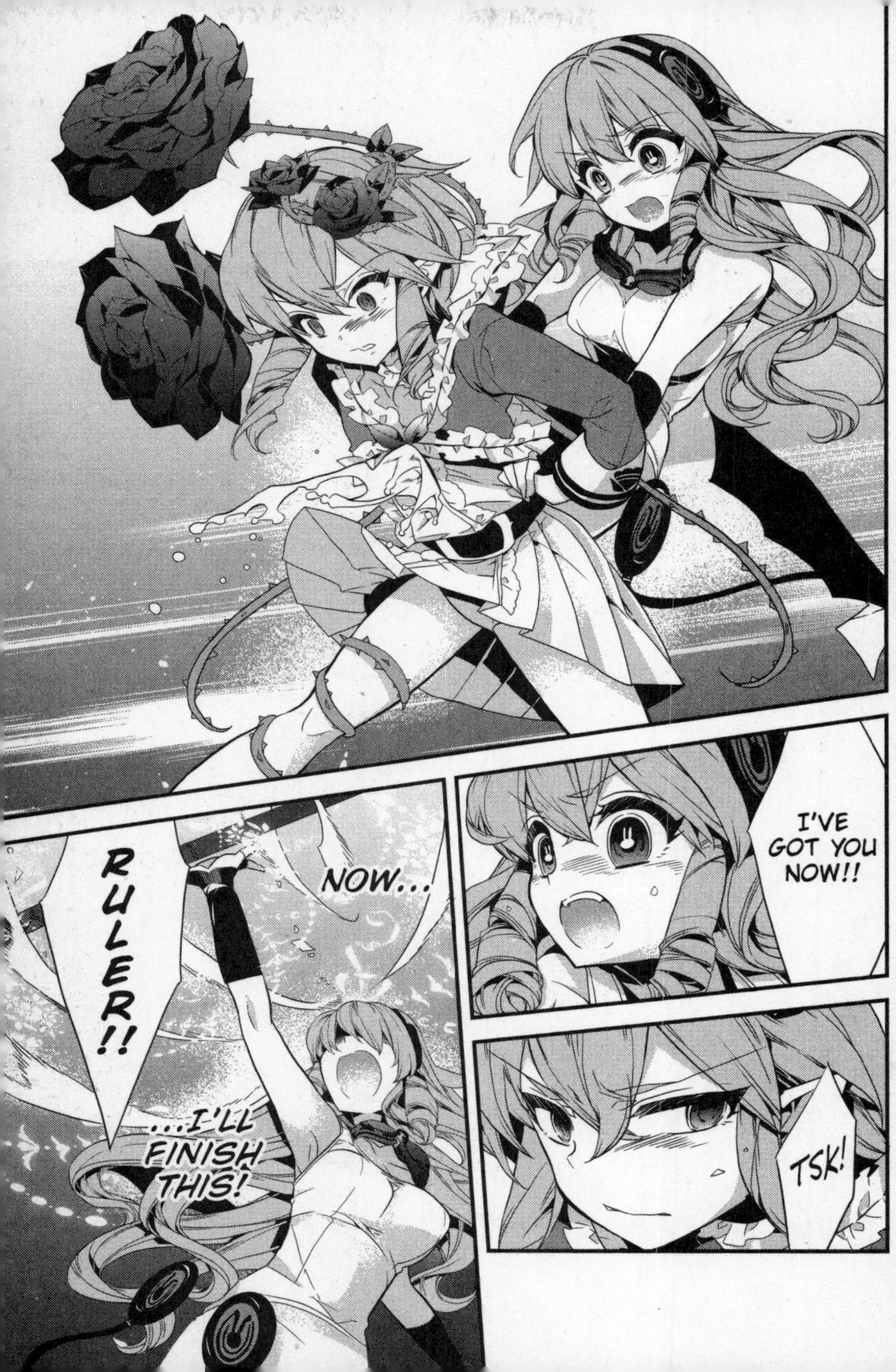
I'VE GOT YOU NOW!!
TSK!
NOW...
RULER!!
...I'LL FINISH THIS!

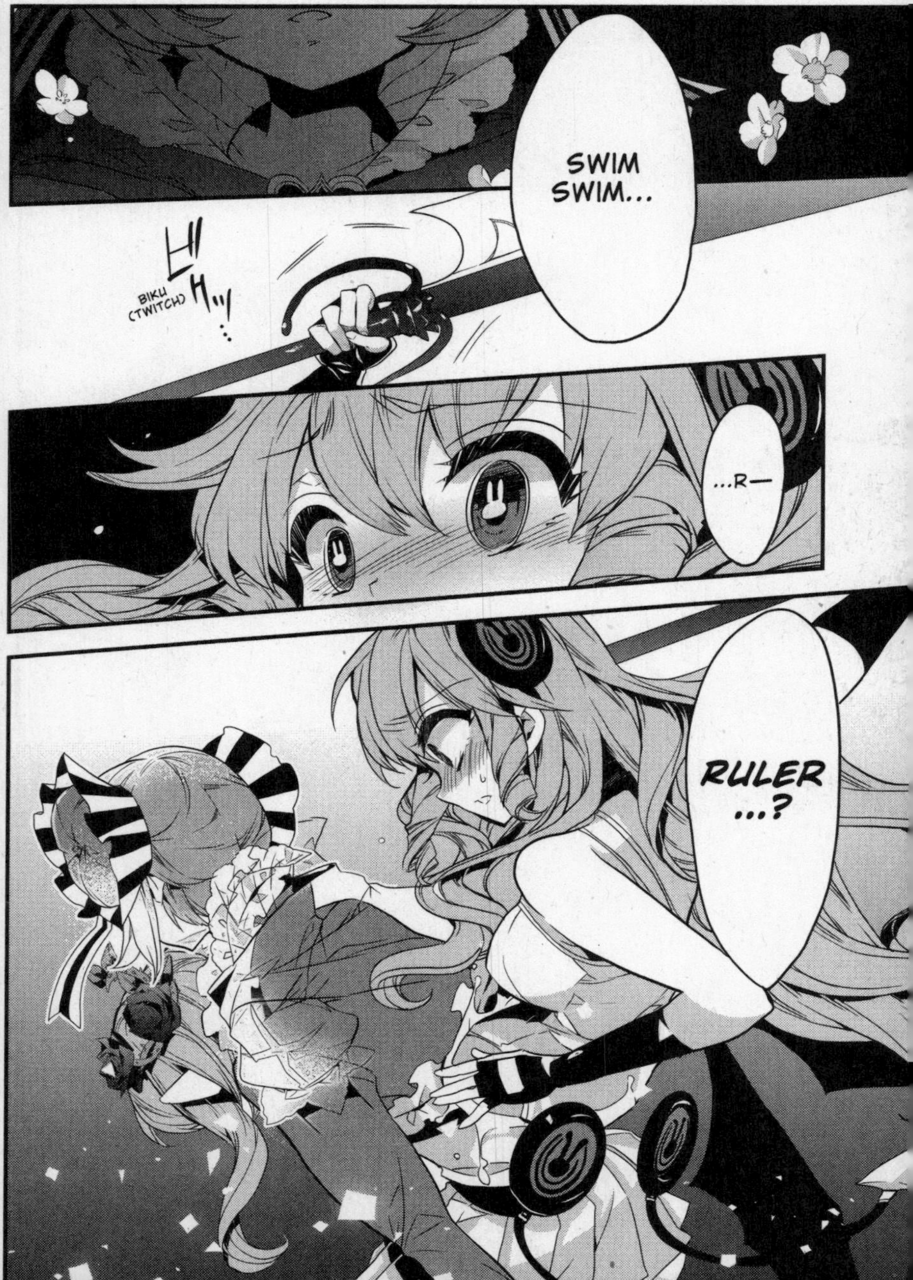
SWIM SWIM...
BIKU (TWITCH)
...R—
RULER ...?

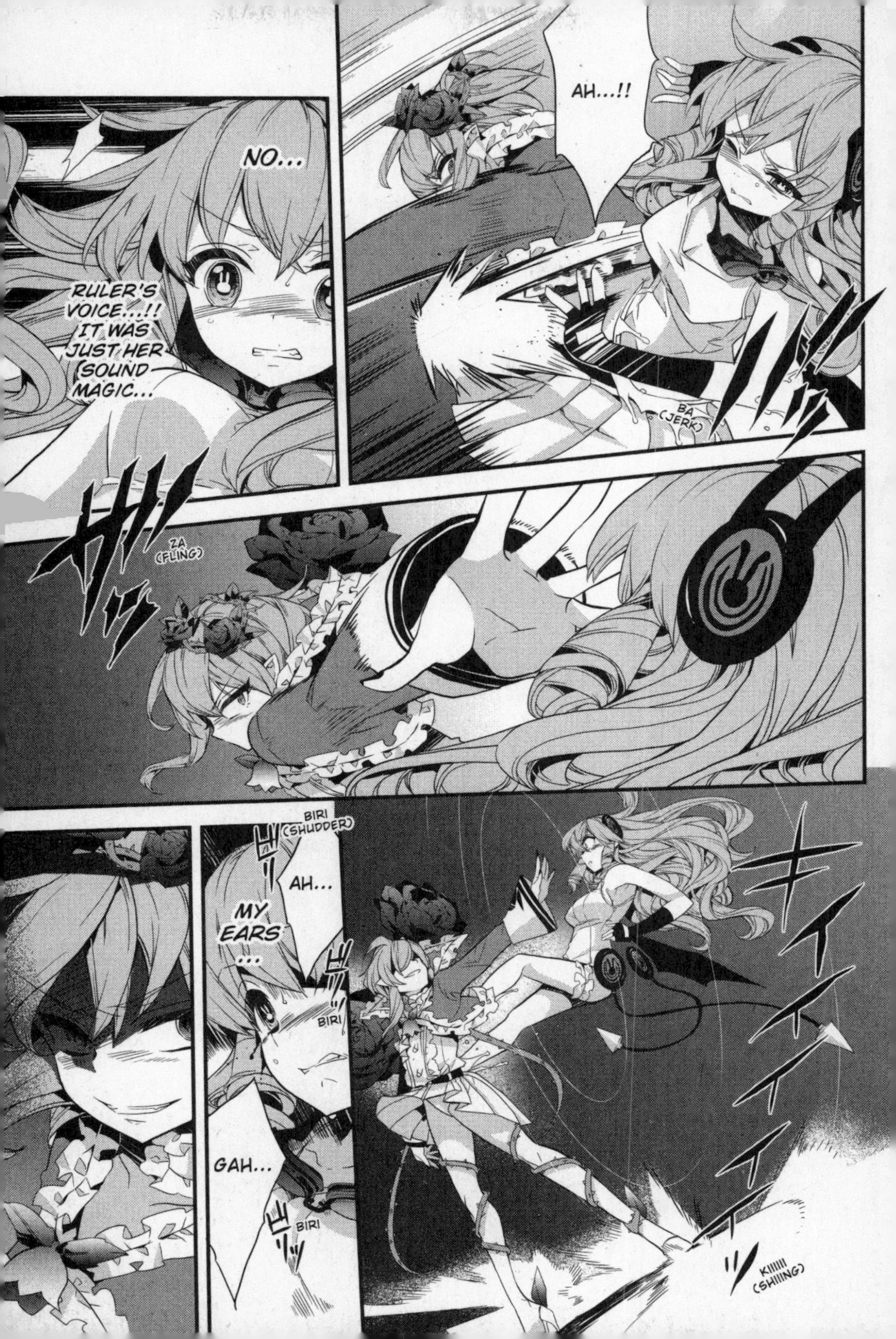
AH...!!
BA (JERK)
NO...
RULER'S VOICE...!! IT WAS JUST HER SOUND MAGIC...
ZA (FLING)
KIIIIII (SHIIIING)
BIRI (SHUDDER)
AH...
MY EARS ...
BIRI
GAH...
BIRI

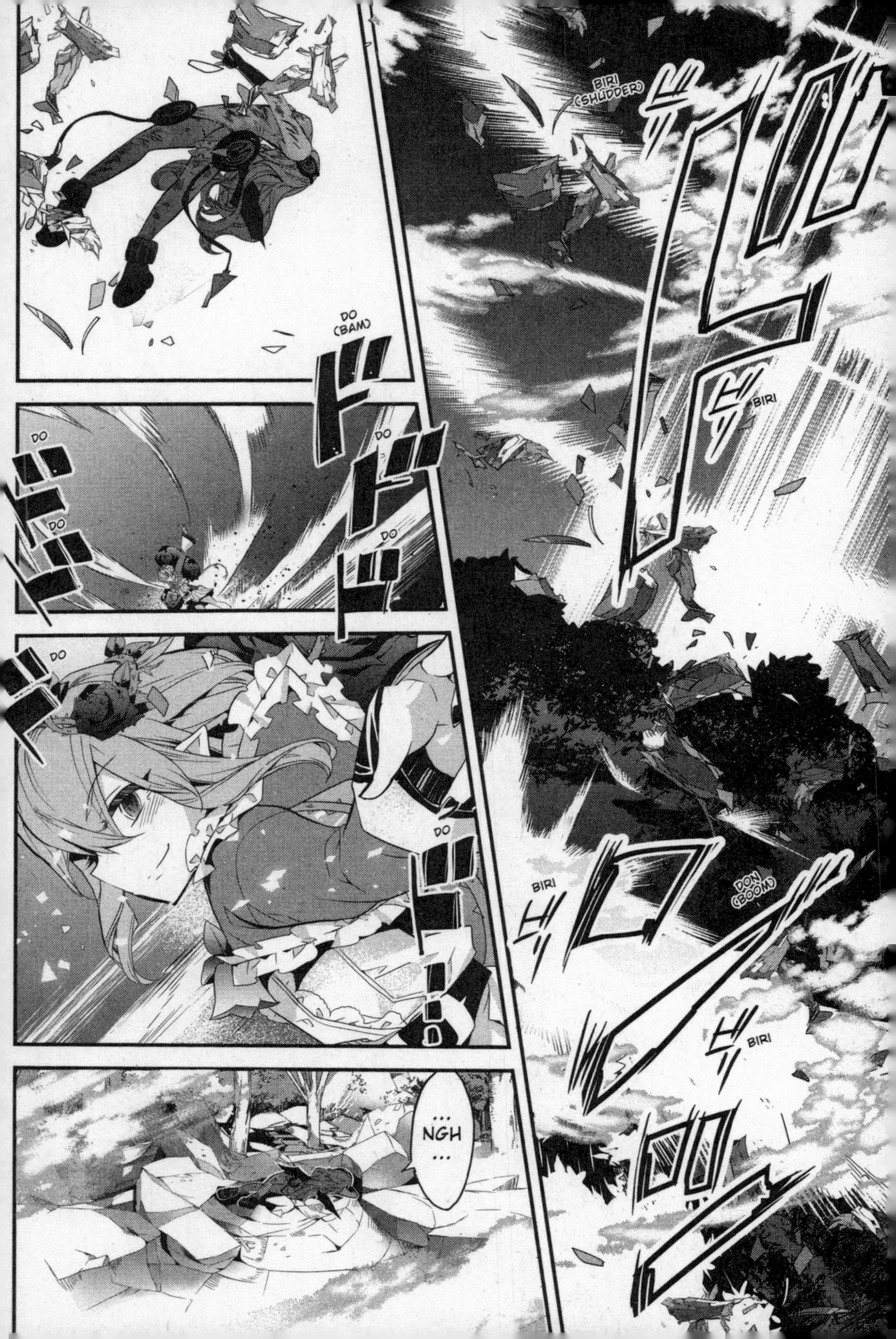
BIRI (SHUDDER)
BIRI
DON (BOOM)
BIRI
BIRI
DO (BAM)
DO
DO
DO
DO
DO
DO
... NGH ...

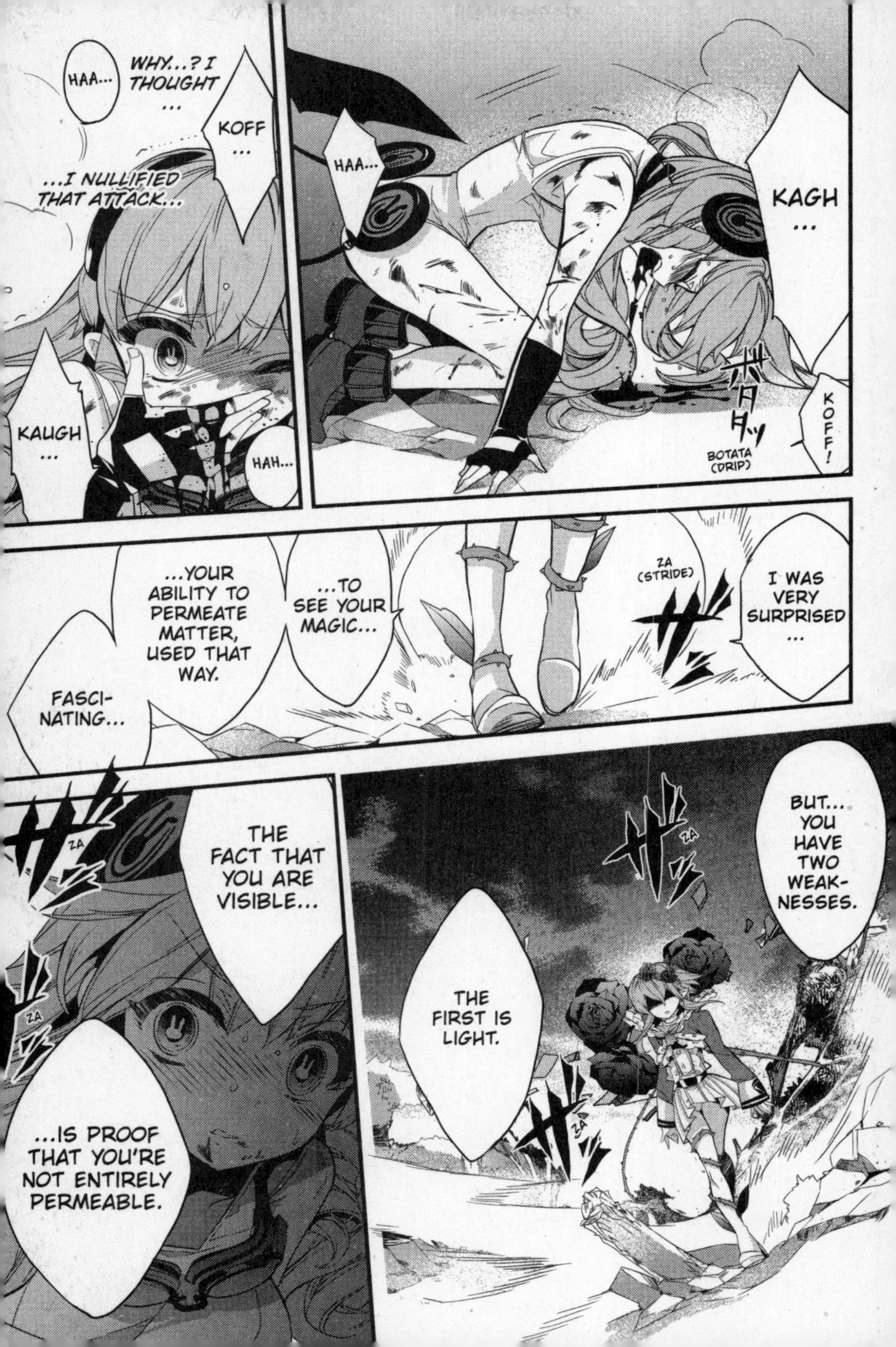
KAGH...
HAA...
KOFF!
BOTATA (DRIP)
WHY...? I THOUGHT...
HAA...
KOFF...
...I NULLIFIED THAT ATTACK...
HAH...
KAUGH...
I WAS VERY SURPRISED...
ZA (STRIDE)
...TO SEE YOUR MAGIC...
...YOUR ABILITY TO PERMEATE MATTER, USED THAT WAY.
FASCINATING...
BUT... YOU HAVE TWO WEAKNESSES.
ZA
THE FIRST IS LIGHT.
ZA
THE FACT THAT YOU ARE VISIBLE...
ZA
ZA
...IS PROOF THAT YOU'RE NOT ENTIRELY PERMEABLE.

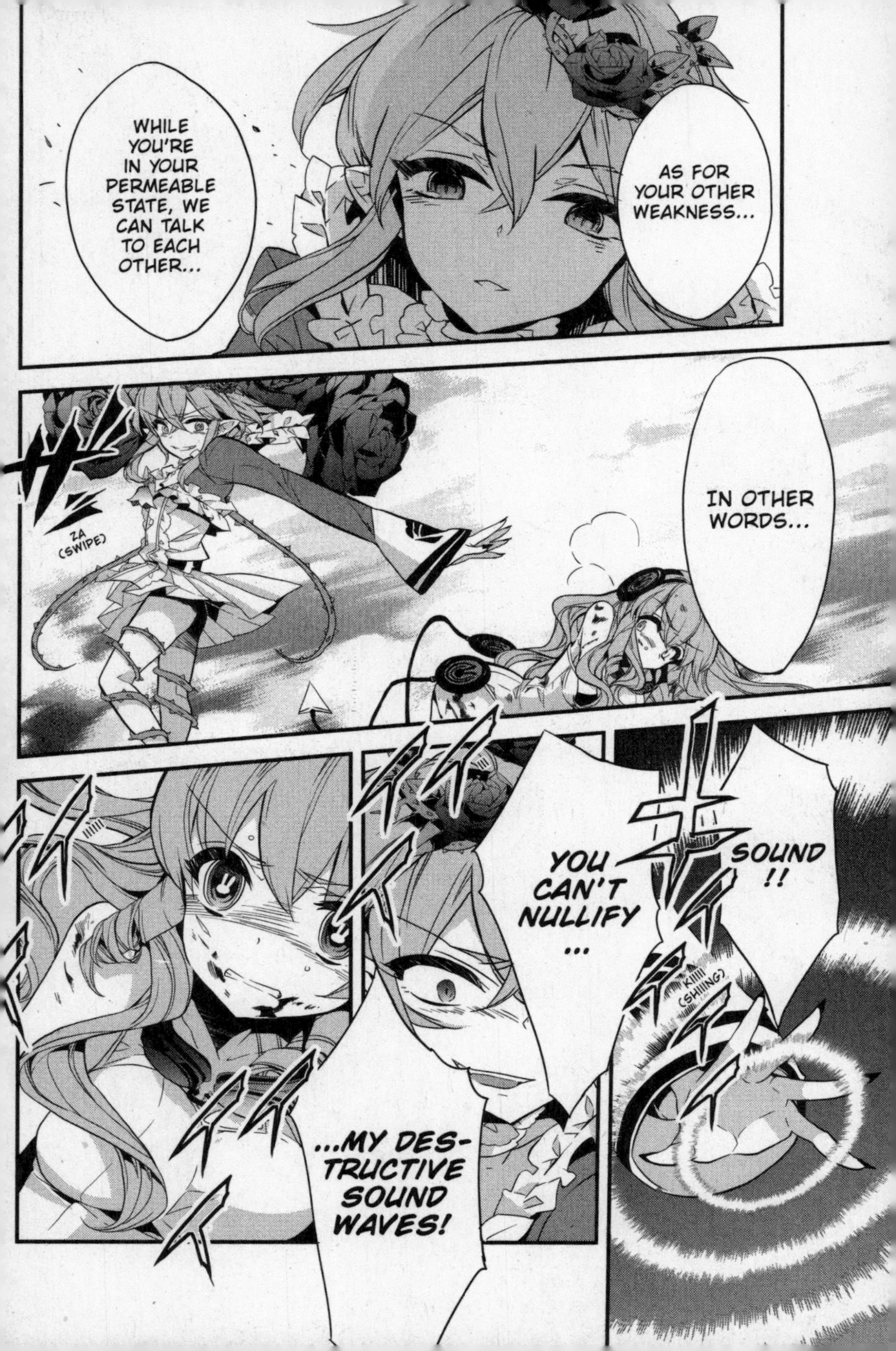
AS FOR YOUR OTHER WEAKNESS...
WHILE YOU'RE IN YOUR PERMEABLE STATE, WE CAN TALK TO EACH OTHER...
IN OTHER WORDS...
ZA (SWIPE)
SOUND!!
KIIIII (SHIIING)
YOU CAN'T NULLIFY...
...MY DES-TRUCTIVE SOUND WAVES!

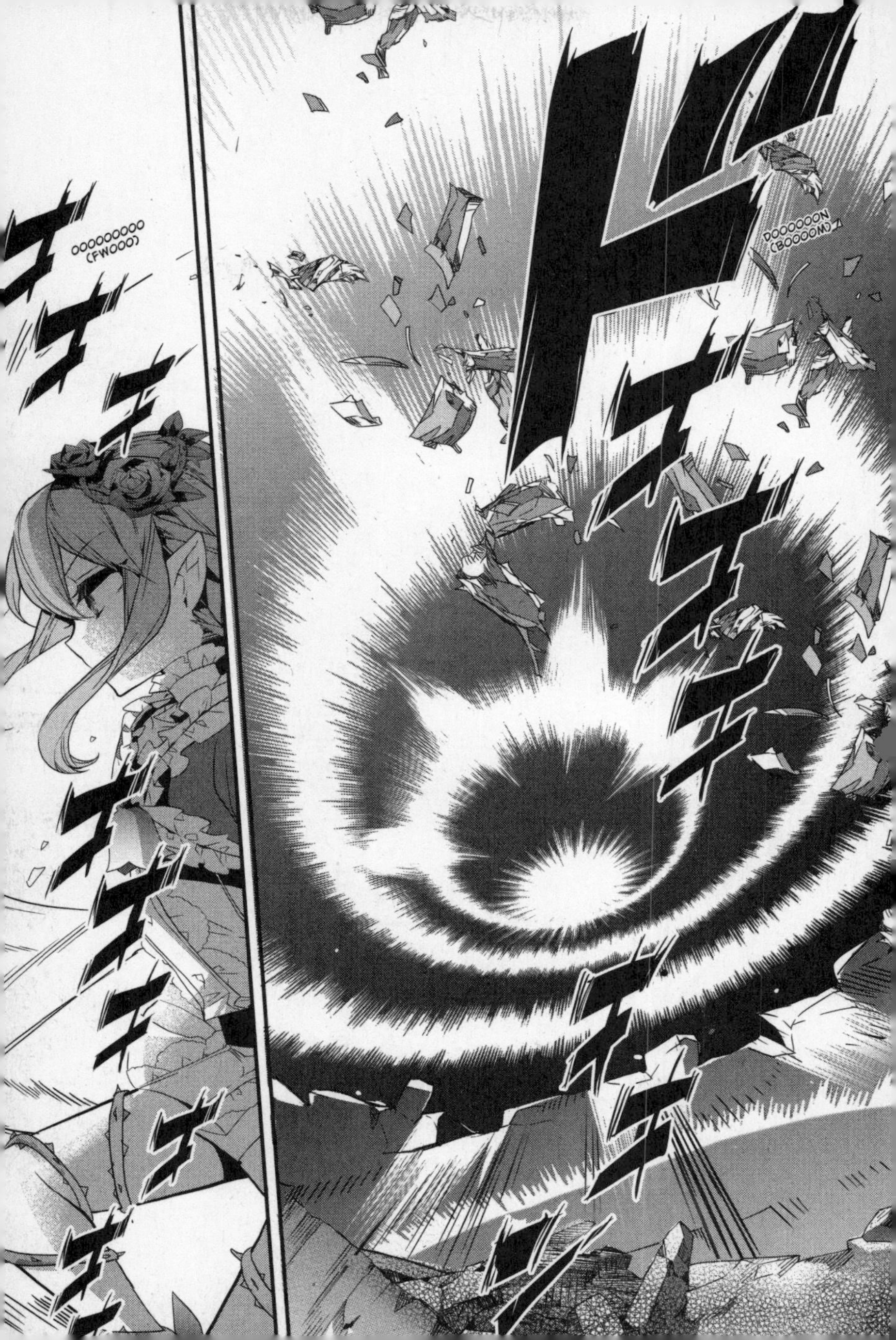
DOOOOOON
(BOOOOM)
OOOOOOOOO
(FWOOO)

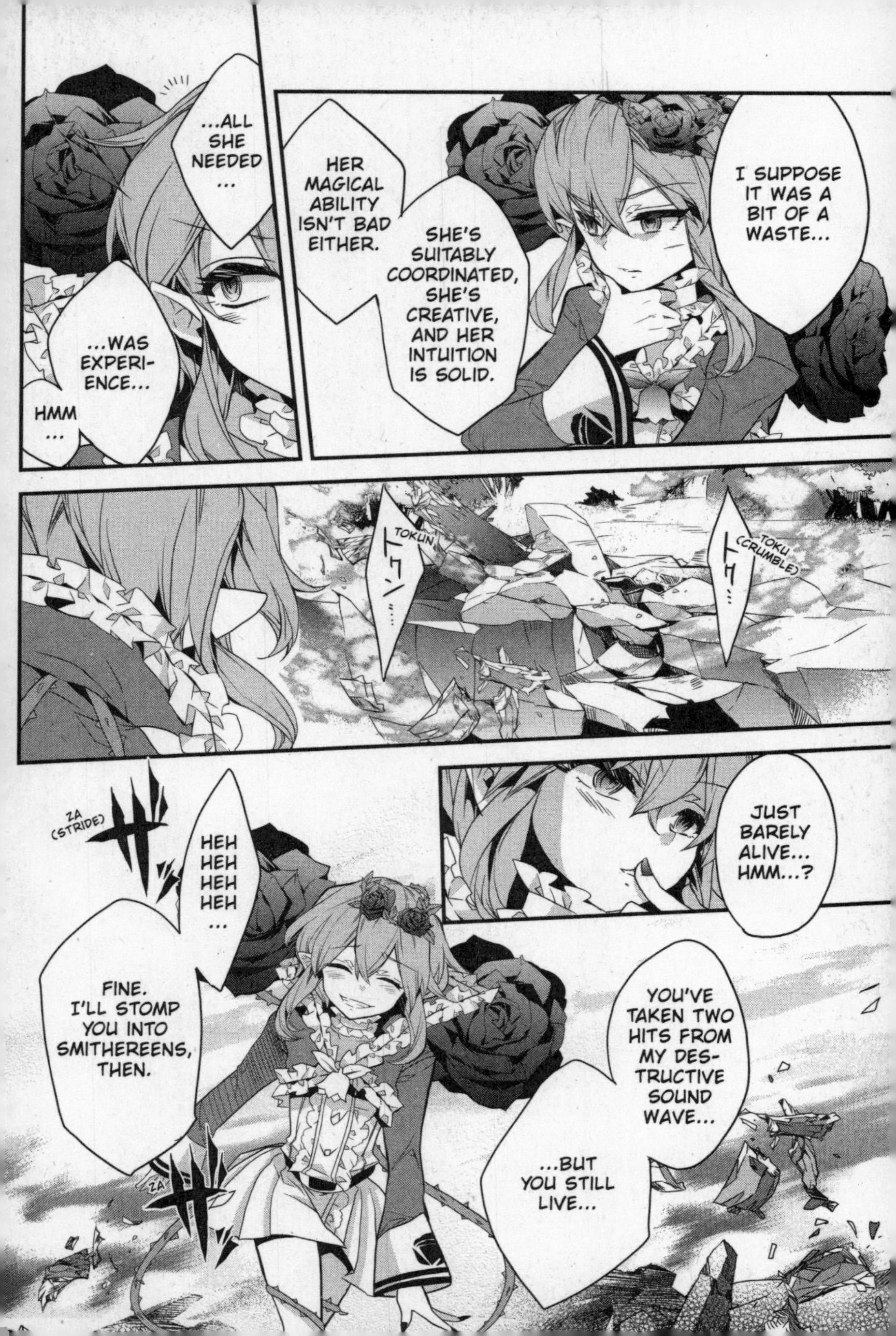
I SUPPOSE IT WAS A BIT OF A WASTE...
SHE'S SUITABLY COORDINATED, SHE'S CREATIVE, AND HER INTUITION IS SOLID.
HER MAGICAL ABILITY ISN'T BAD EITHER.
...ALL SHE NEEDED...
...WAS EXPERIENCE...
HMM...
TOKU (CRUMBLE)
TOKUN
JUST BARELY ALIVE... HMM...?
YOU'VE TAKEN TWO HITS FROM MY DESTRUCTIVE SOUND WAVE...
...BUT YOU STILL LIVE...
HEH HEH HEH HEH...
ZA (STRIDE)
FINE. I'LL STOMP YOU INTO SMITHEREENS, THEN.
ZA

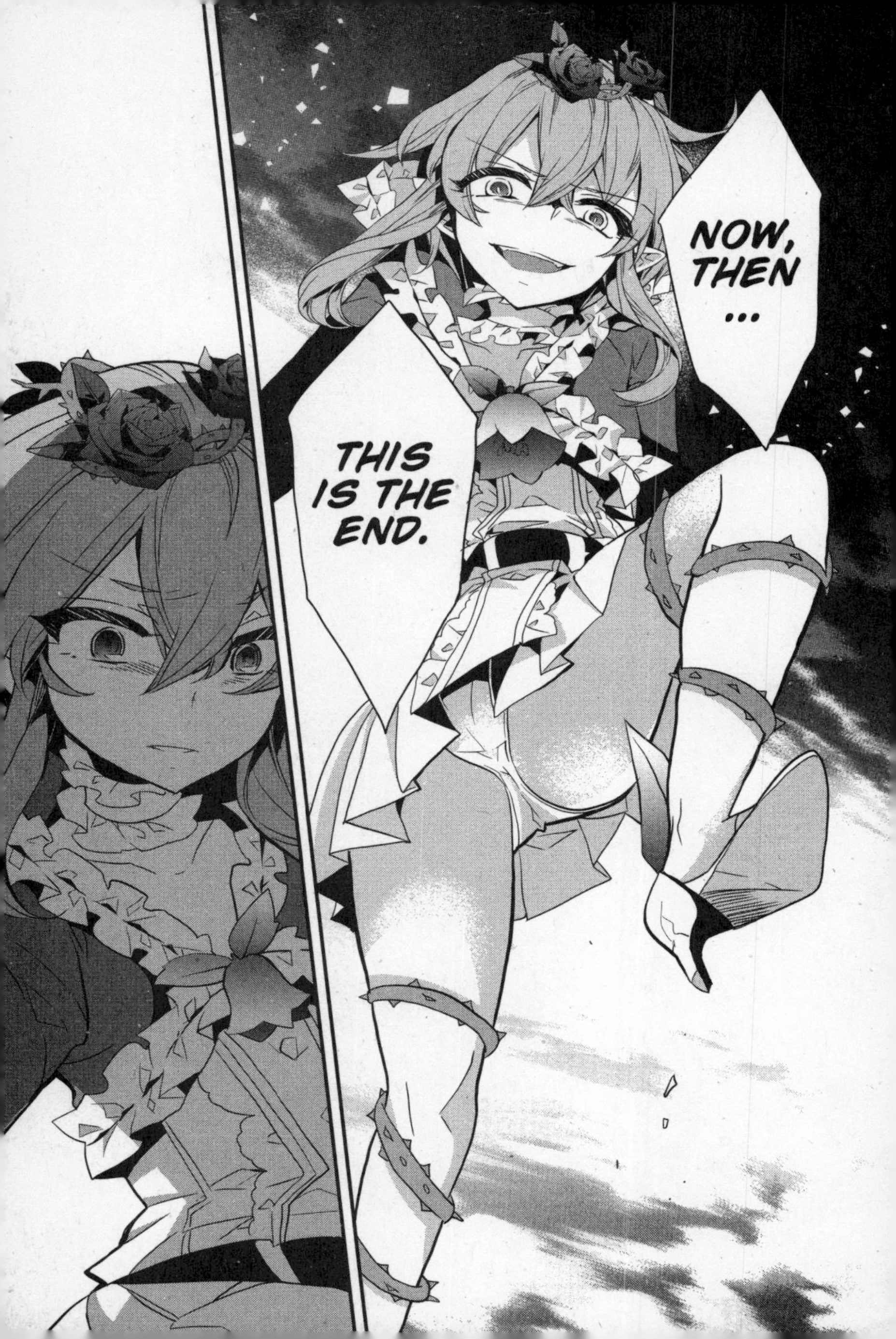
NOW, THEN ...
THIS IS THE END.

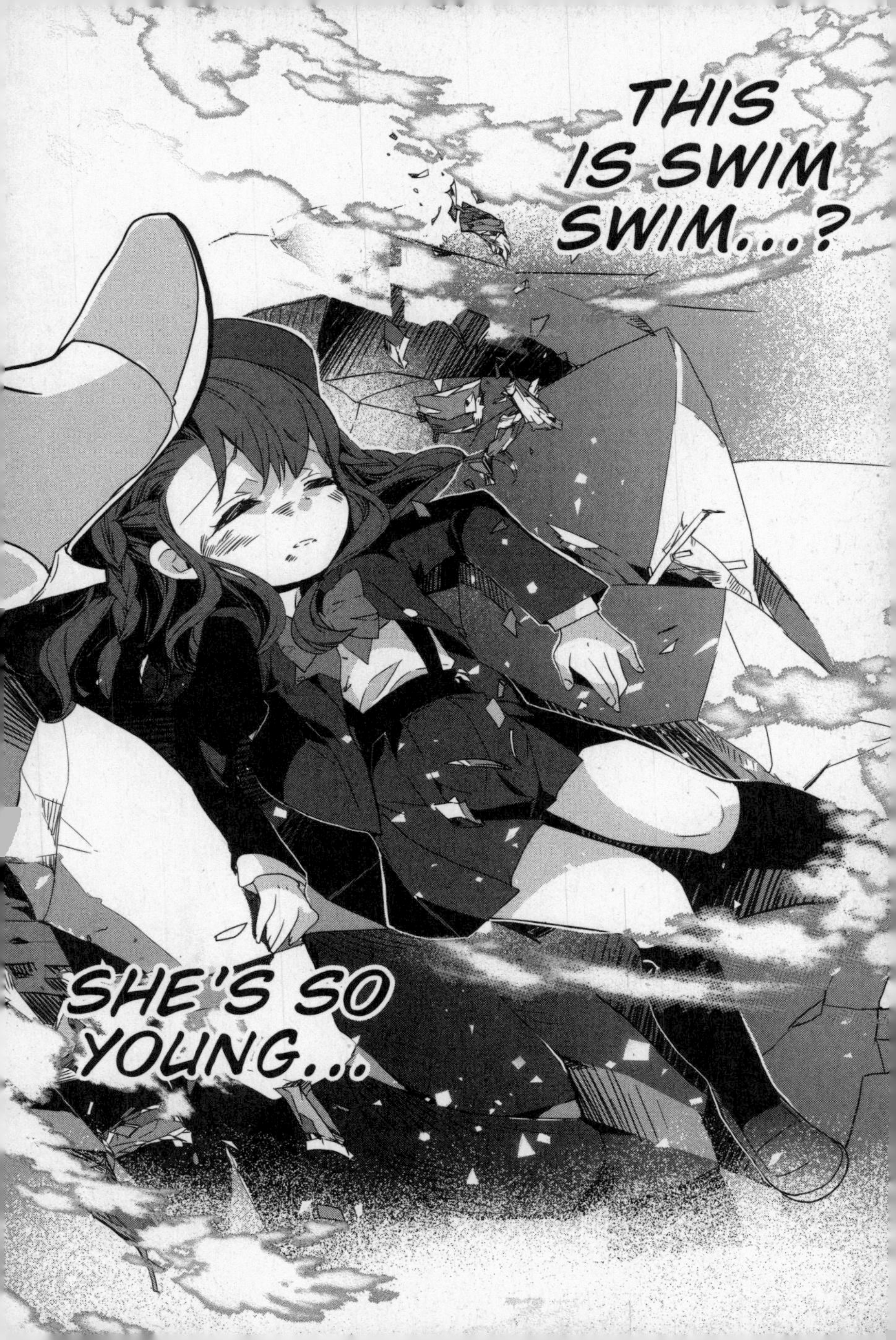
THIS IS SWIM SWIM...?
SHE'S SO YOUNG...

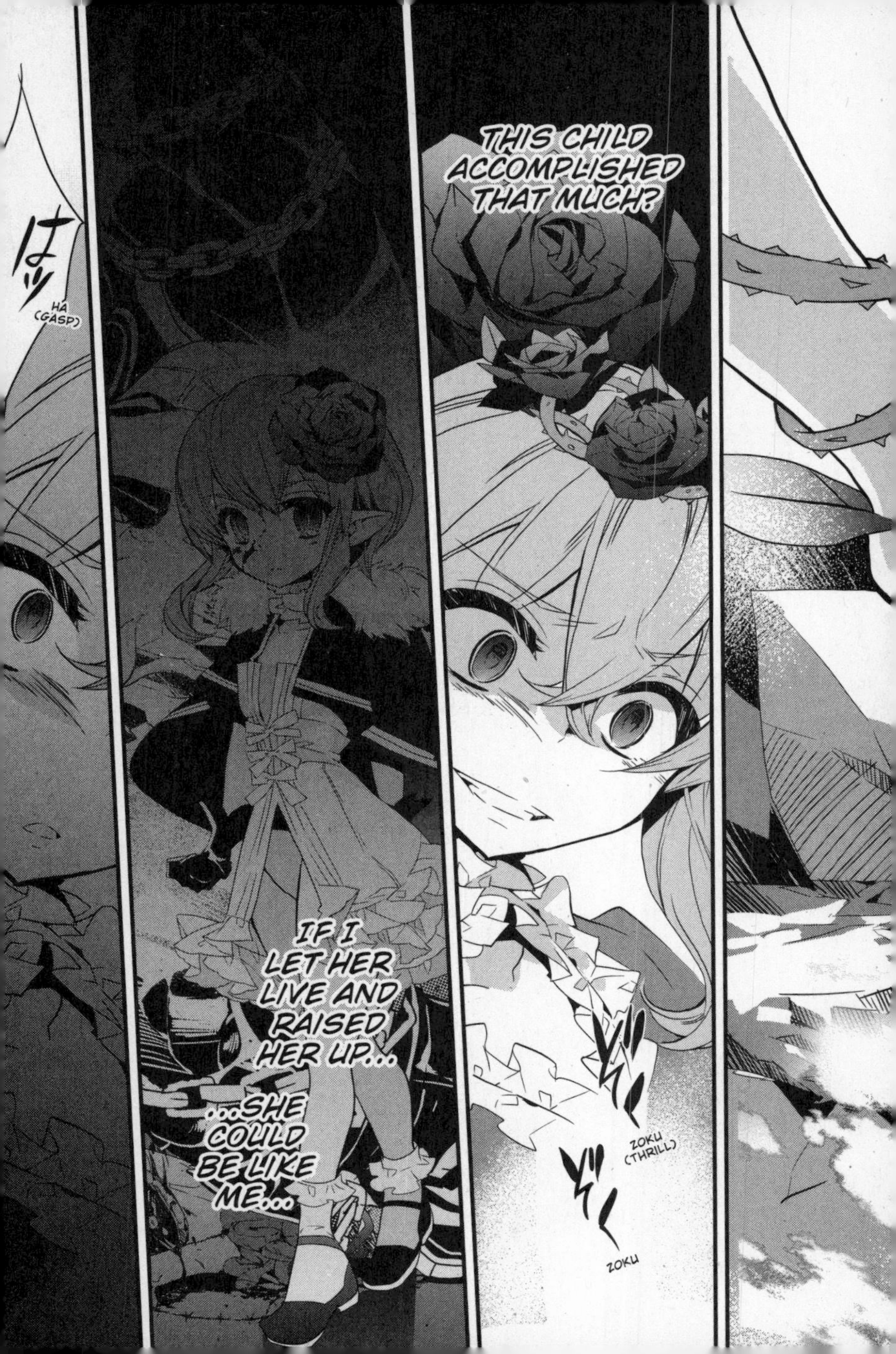
THIS CHILD ACCOMPLISHED THAT MUCH?
ZOKU (THRILL)
ZOKU
IF I LET HER LIVE AND RAISED HER UP...
...SHE COULD BE LIKE ME...
はッ
HA (GASP)

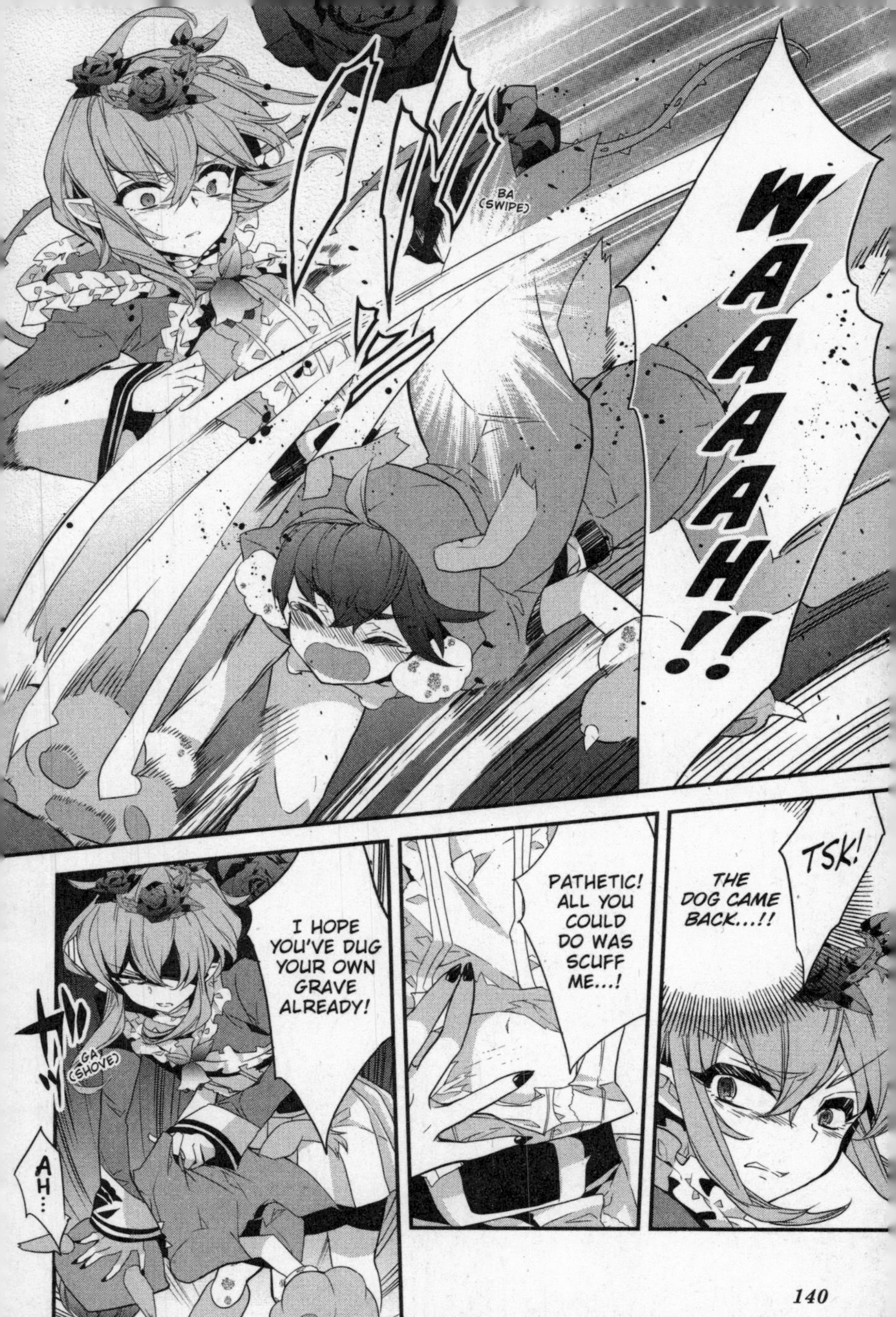
WAAAAAH!!
BA
(SWIPE)
TSK!
THE DOG CAME BACK...!!
PATHETIC! ALL YOU COULD DO WAS SCUFF ME...!
I HOPE YOU'VE DUG YOUR OWN GRAVE ALREADY!
GA
(SHOVE)
AH...

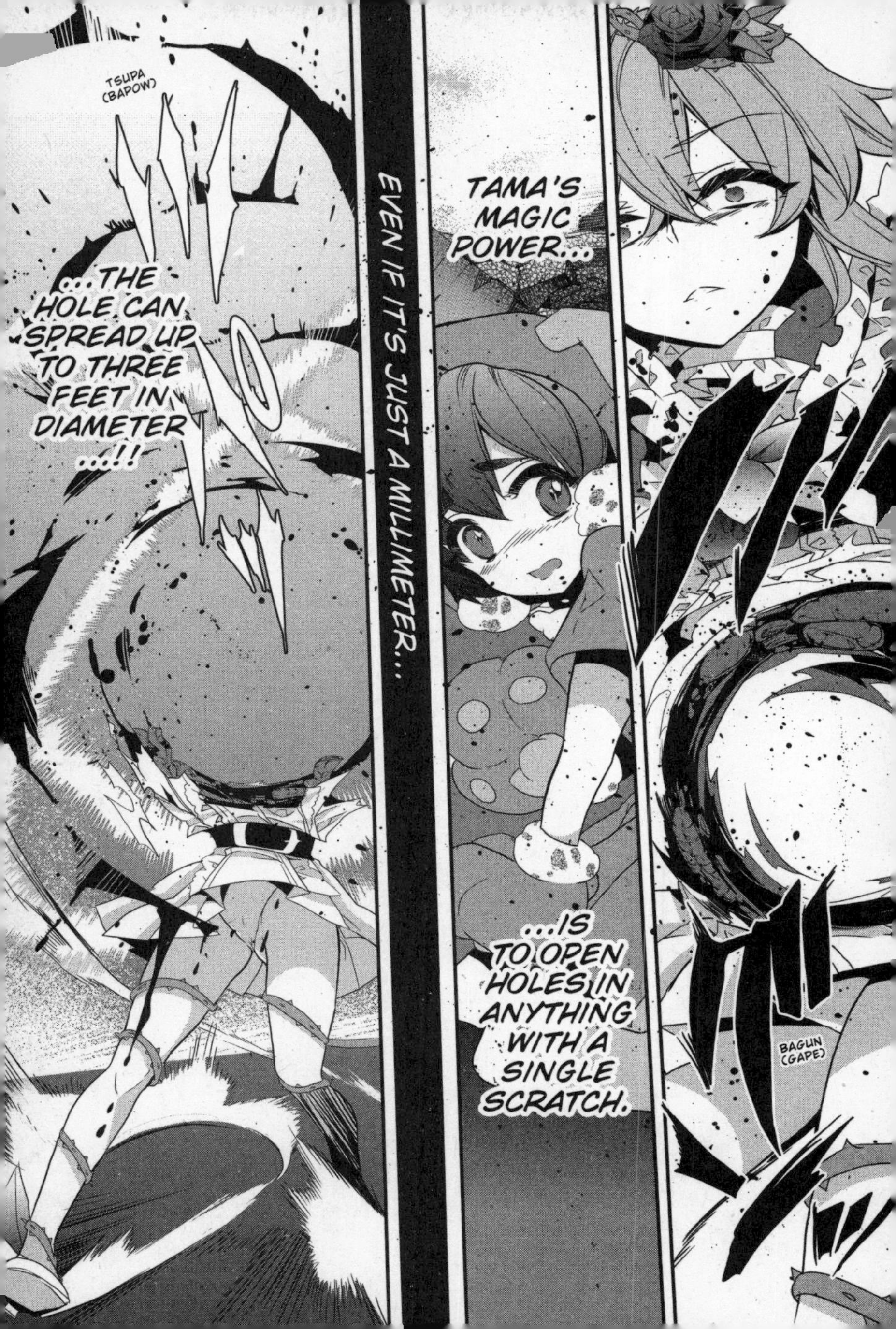
BAGUN (GAPE)
TAMA'S MAGIC POWER...
...IS TO OPEN HOLES IN ANYTHING WITH A SINGLE SCRATCH.
EVEN IF IT'S JUST A MILLIMETER...
TSUPA (BAPOW)
...THE HOLE CAN SPREAD UP TO THREE FEET IN DIAMETER...!!

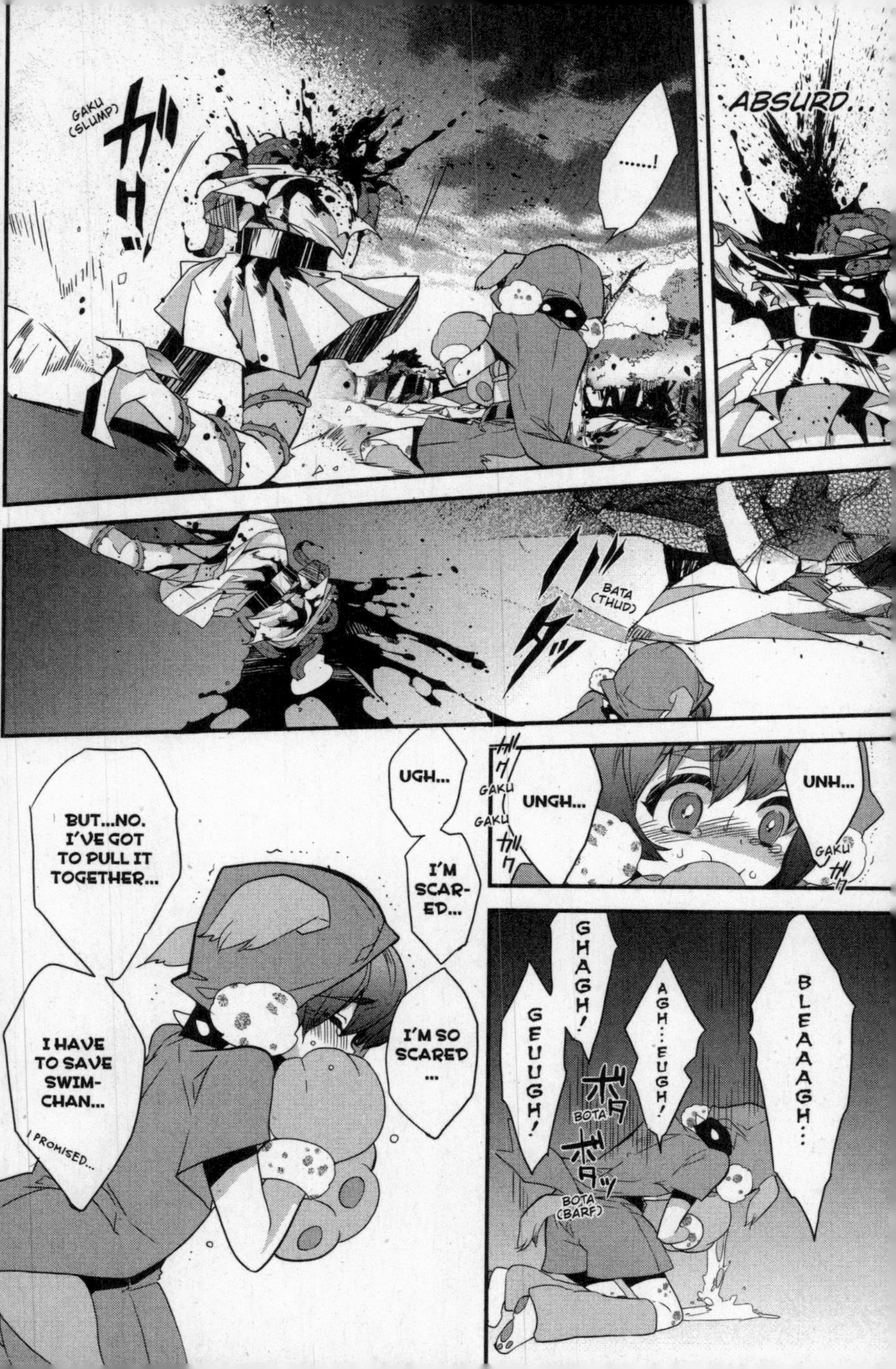
ABSURD...
......!
GAKU (SLUMP)
BATA (THUD)
UNH...
GAKU
UNGH...
GAKU
GAKU
BLEAAAGH...
AGH...EUGH!
GHAGH!
GEUUGH!
BOTA
BOTA (BARF)
UGH...
I'M SCARED...
BUT...NO. I'VE GOT TO PULL IT TOGETHER...
I'M SO SCARED...
I HAVE TO SAVE SWIM-CHAN...
I PROMISED...

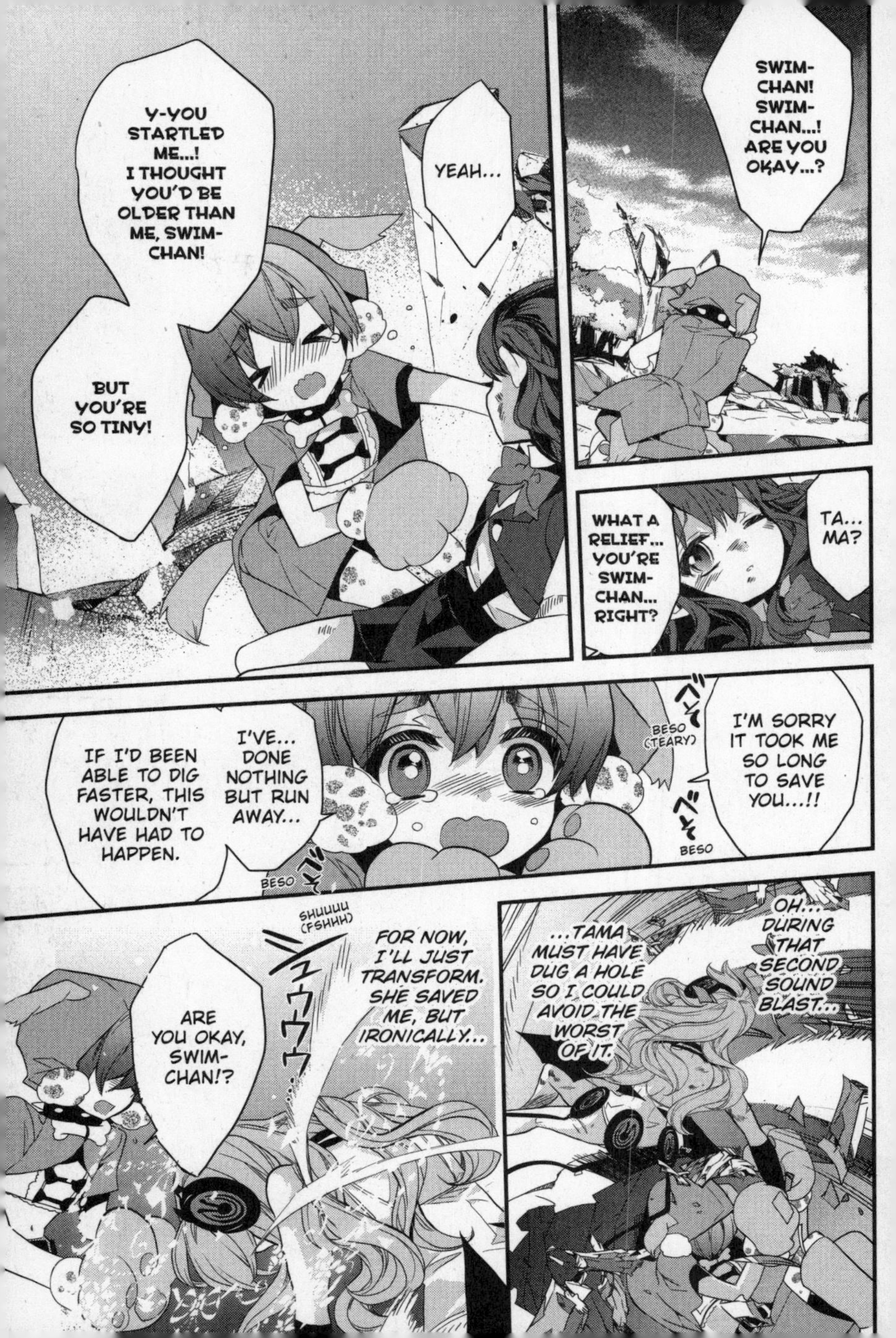
SWIM-CHAN! SWIM-CHAN...! ARE YOU OKAY...?
TA... MA?
WHAT A RELIEF... YOU'RE SWIM-CHAN... RIGHT?
YEAH...
Y-YOU STARTLED ME...! I THOUGHT YOU'D BE OLDER THAN ME, SWIM-CHAN!
BUT YOU'RE SO TINY!
BESO (TEARY)
I'M SORRY IT TOOK ME SO LONG TO SAVE YOU...!!
BESO
I'VE... DONE NOTHING BUT RUN AWAY...
IF I'D BEEN ABLE TO DIG FASTER, THIS WOULDN'T HAVE HAD TO HAPPEN.
BESO
OH... DURING THAT SECOND SOUND BLAST...
...TAMA MUST HAVE DUG A HOLE SO I COULD AVOID THE WORST OF IT.
FOR NOW, I'LL JUST TRANSFORM. SHE SAVED ME, BUT IRONICALLY...
SHUUUU (FSHHH)
ARE YOU OKAY, SWIM-CHAN!?

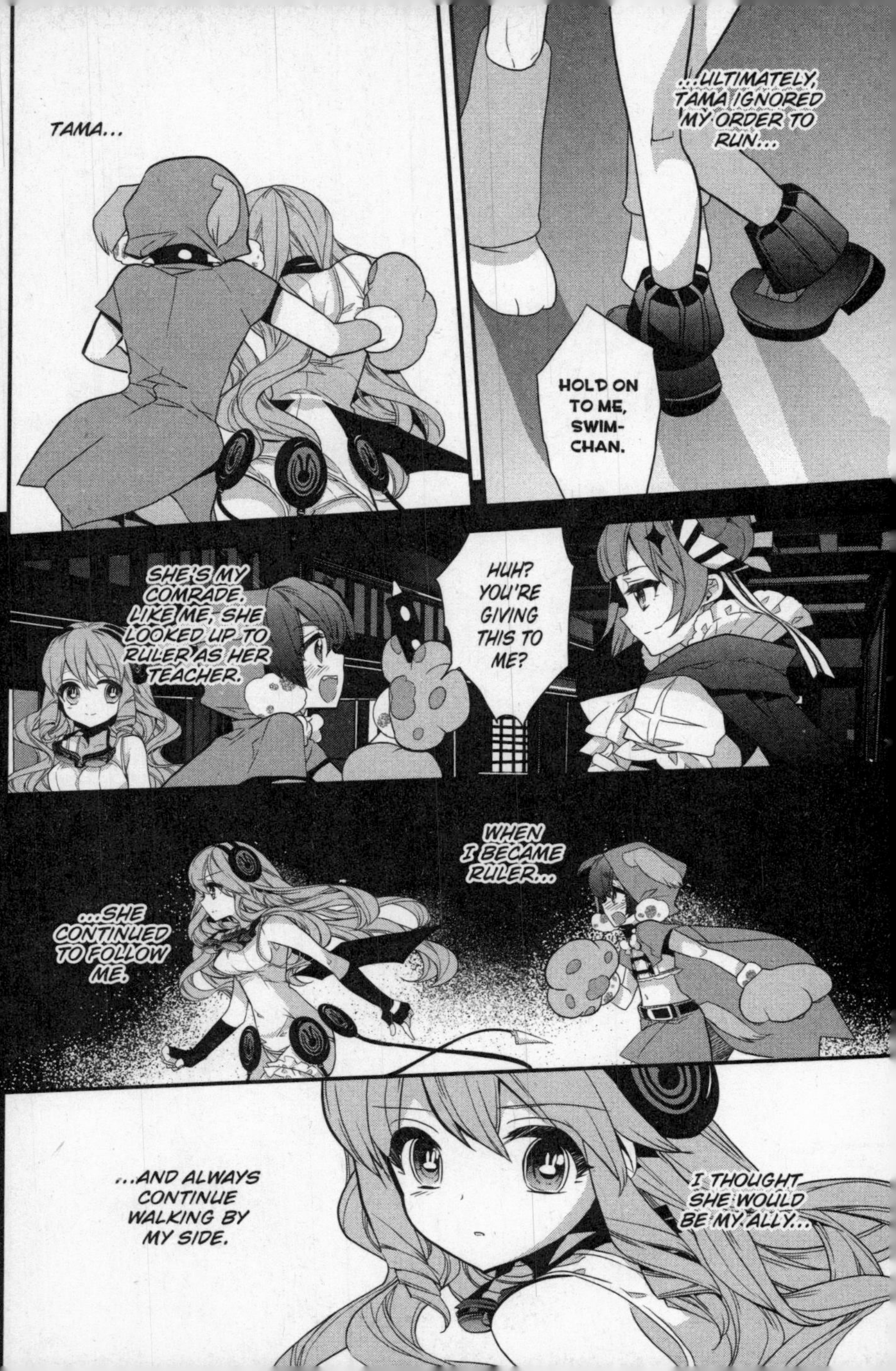
...ULTIMATELY, TAMA IGNORED MY ORDER TO RUN...
HOLD ON TO ME, SWIM-CHAN.
TAMA...
HUH? YOU'RE GIVING THIS TO ME?
SHE'S MY COMRADE. LIKE ME, SHE LOOKED UP TO RULER AS HER TEACHER.
WHEN I BECAME RULER...
...SHE CONTINUED TO FOLLOW ME.
I THOUGHT SHE WOULD BE MY ALLY...
...AND ALWAYS CONTINUE WALKING BY MY SIDE.

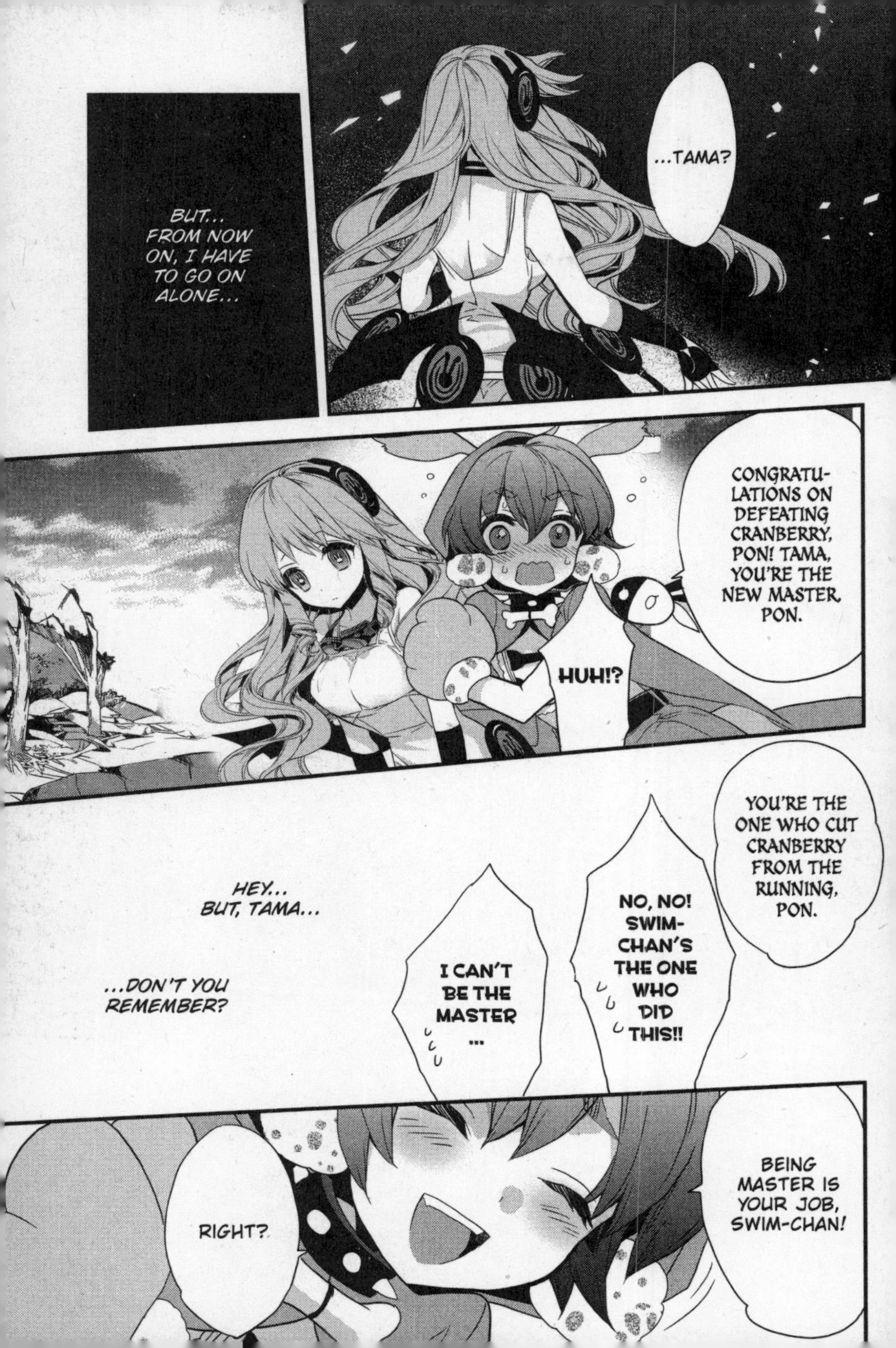
...TAMA?
BUT... FROM NOW ON, I HAVE TO GO ON ALONE...
CONGRATULATIONS ON DEFEATING CRANBERRY, PON! TAMA, YOU'RE THE NEW MASTER PON.
HUH!?
YOU'RE THE ONE WHO CUT CRANBERRY FROM THE RUNNING, PON.
NO, NO! SWIM-CHAN'S THE ONE WHO DID THIS!!
I CAN'T BE THE MASTER...
HEY... BUT, TAMA...
...DON'T YOU REMEMBER?
BEING MASTER IS YOUR JOB, SWIM-CHAN!
RIGHT?

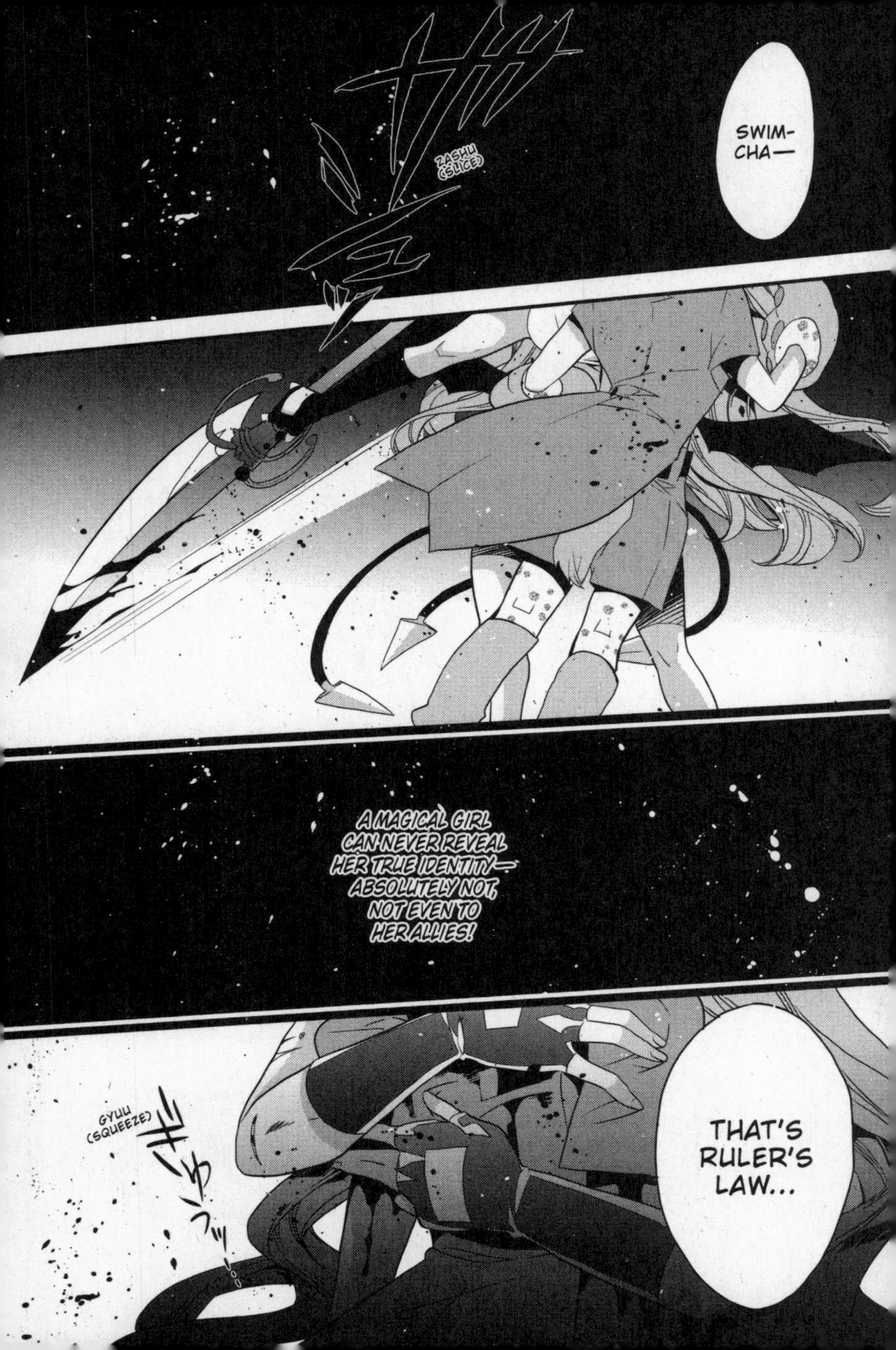
SWIM-CHA—
ZASHU (SLICE)
A MAGICAL GIRL CAN NEVER REVEAL HER TRUE IDENTITY—ABSOLUTELY NOT, NOT EVEN TO HER ALLIES!
THAT'S RULER'S LAW...
GYUU (SQUEEZE)

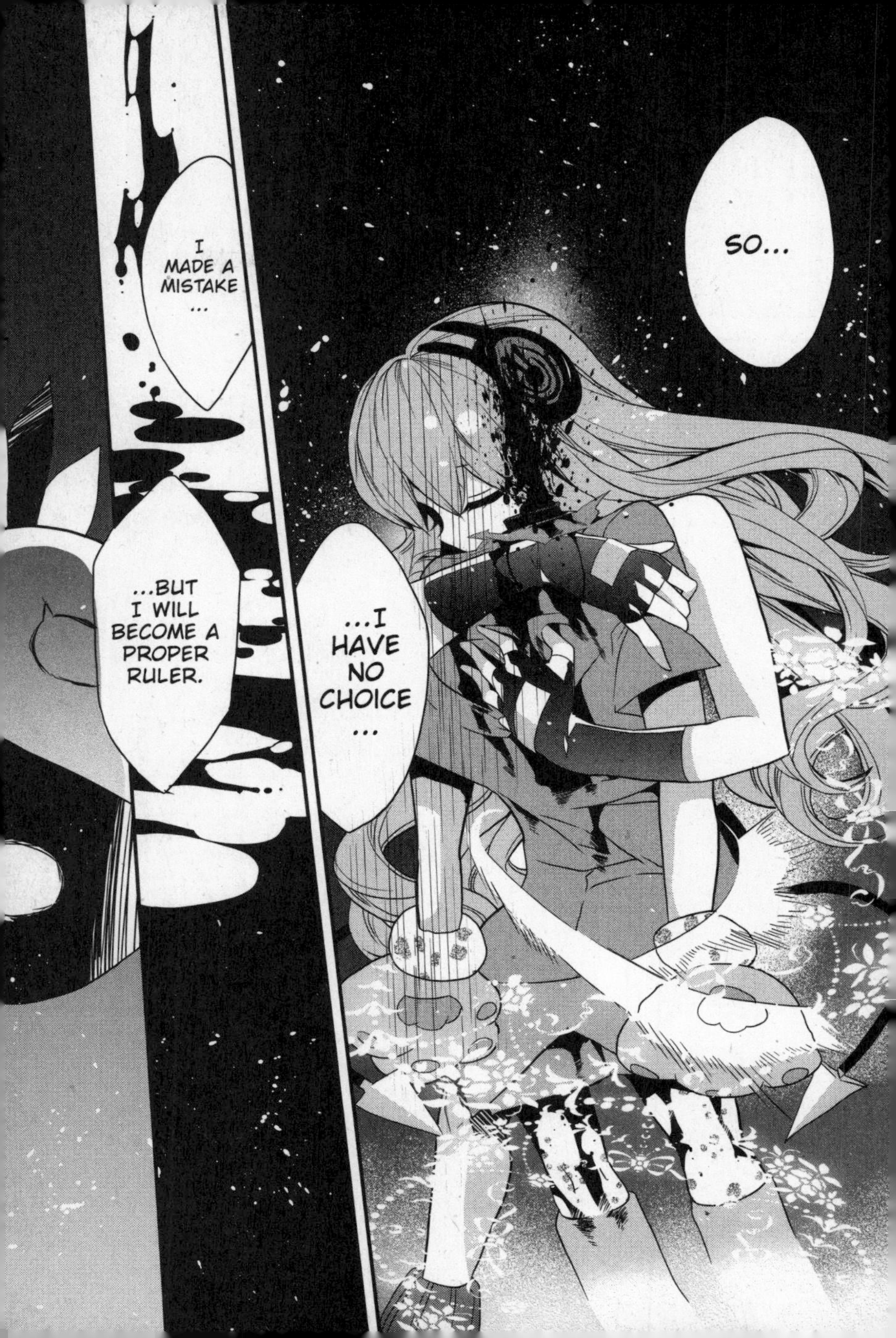
SO...
...I HAVE NO CHOICE...
I MADE A MISTAKE...
...BUT I WILL BECOME A PROPER RULER.

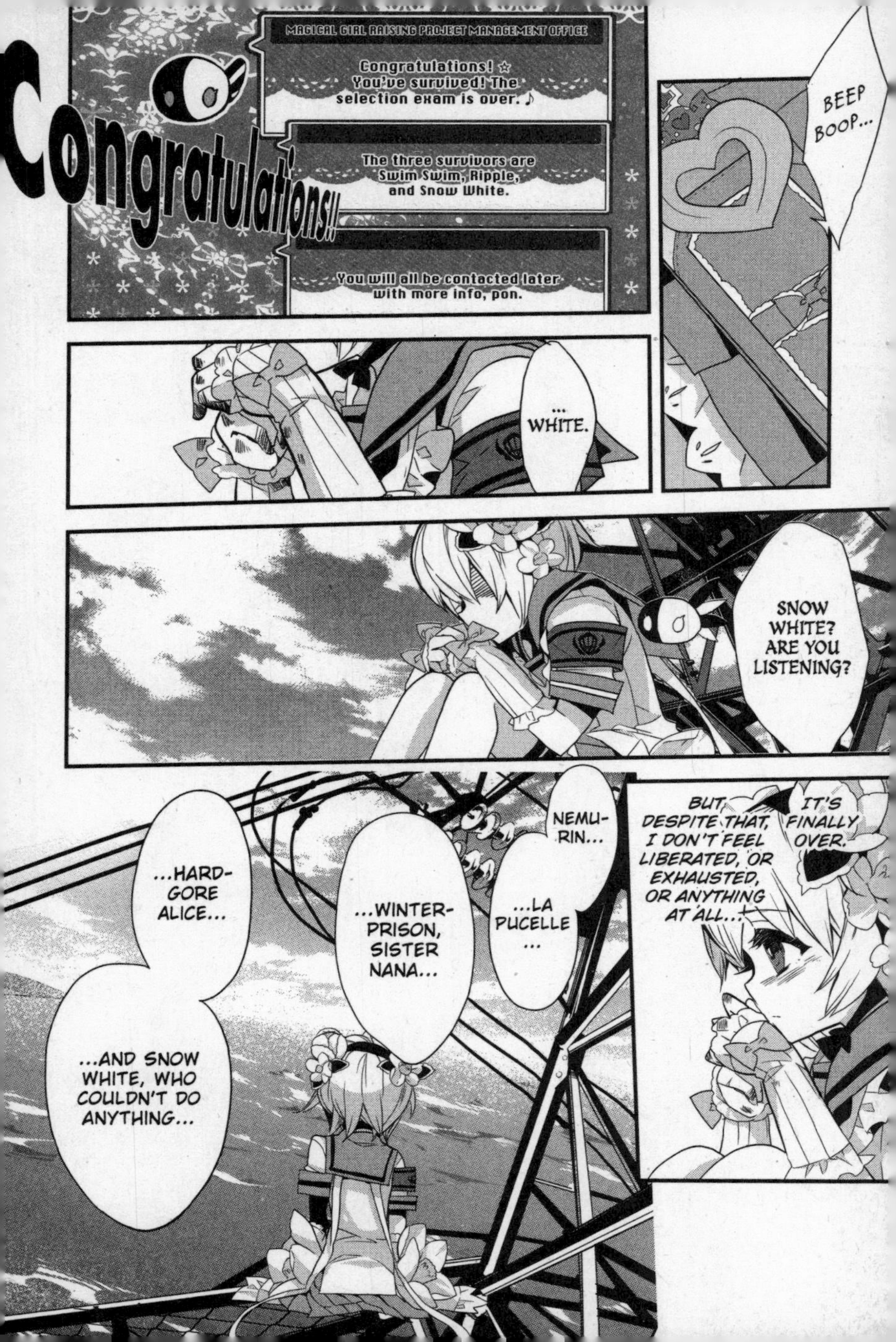
BEEP BOOP...
Congratulations!!
MAGICAL GIRL RAISING PROJECT MANAGEMENT OFFICE
Congratulations! ☆ You've survived! The selection exam is over. ♪
The three survivors are Swim Swim, Ripple, and Snow White.
You will all be contacted later with more info, pon.
... WHITE.
SNOW WHITE? ARE YOU LISTENING?
IT'S FINALLY OVER.
BUT, DESPITE THAT, I DON'T FEEL LIBERATED, OR EXHAUSTED, OR ANYTHING AT ALL...
NEMU-RIN...
...LA PUCELLE ...
...WINTER-PRISON, SISTER NANA...
...HARD-GORE ALICE...
...AND SNOW WHITE, WHO COULDN'T DO ANYTHING...

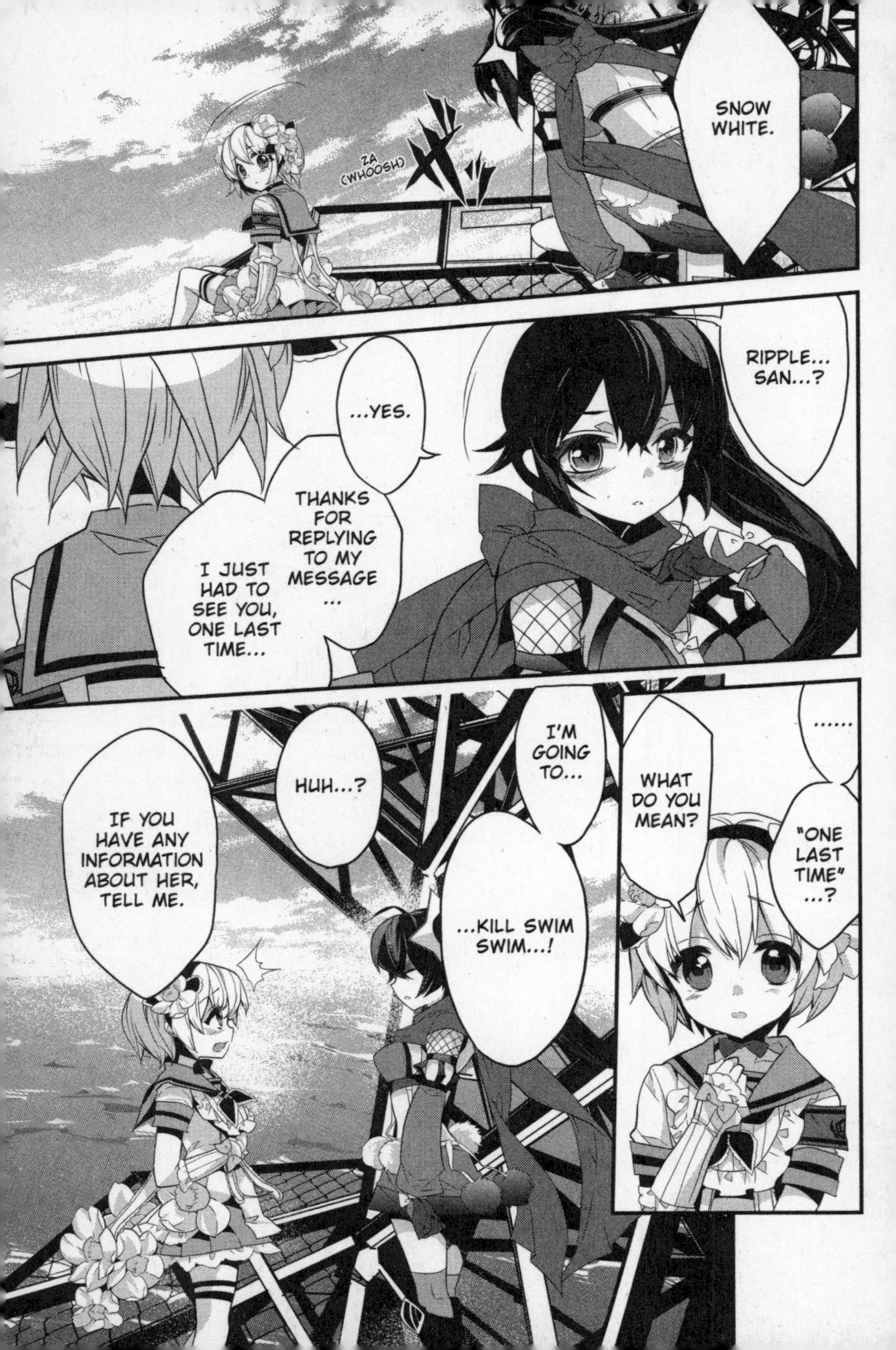
SNOW WHITE.
ZA (WHOOSH)
RIPPLE... SAN...?
...YES.
THANKS FOR REPLYING TO MY MESSAGE ...
I JUST HAD TO SEE YOU, ONE LAST TIME...
......
"ONE LAST TIME" ...?
WHAT DO YOU MEAN?
I'M GOING TO...
...KILL SWIM SWIM...!
HUH...?
IF YOU HAVE ANY INFORMATION ABOUT HER, TELL ME.

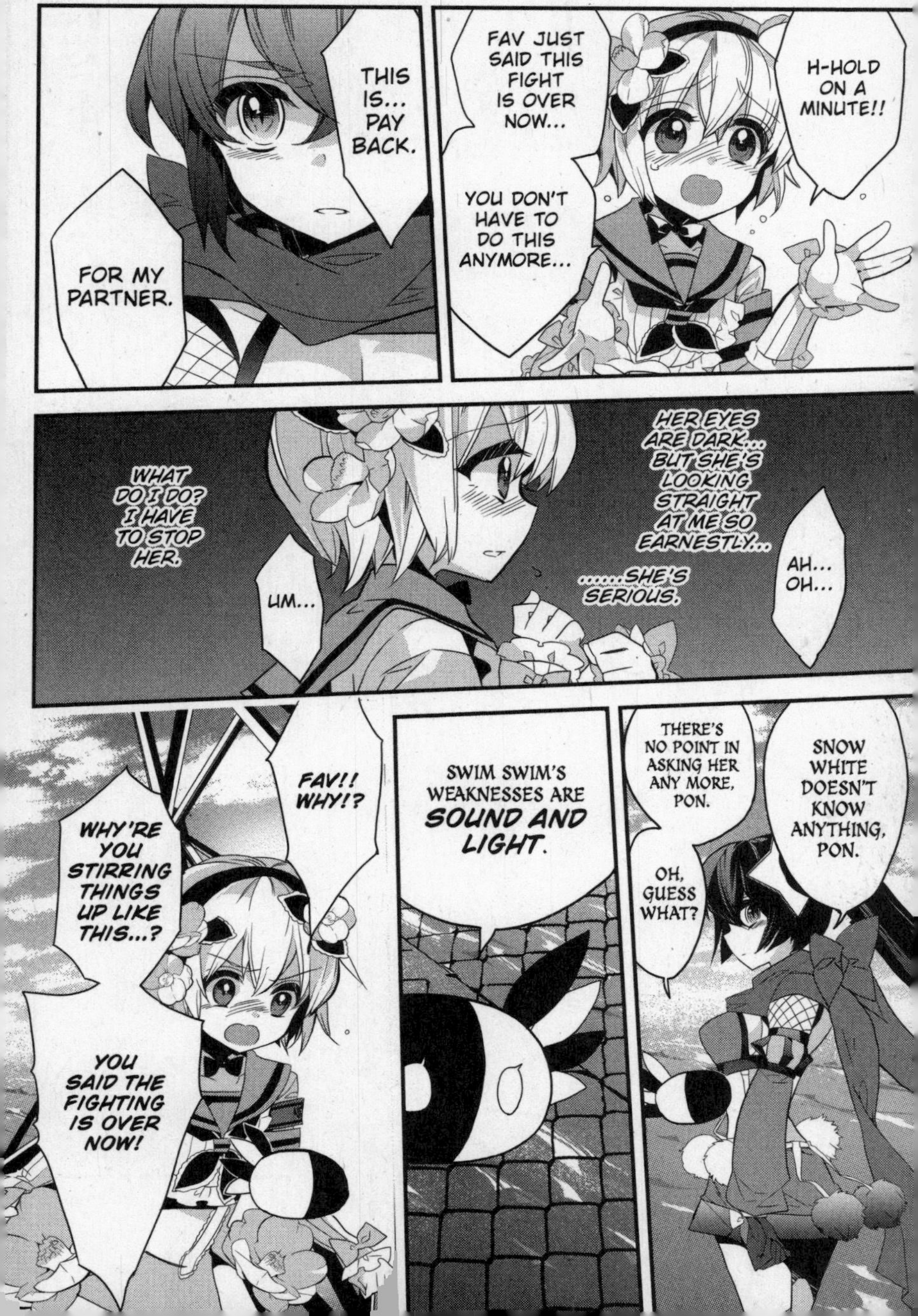
H-HOLD ON A MINUTE!!
FAV JUST SAID THIS FIGHT IS OVER NOW...
YOU DON'T HAVE TO DO THIS ANYMORE...
THIS IS... PAY BACK.
FOR MY PARTNER.
AH... OH...
HER EYES ARE DARK... BUT SHE'S LOOKING STRAIGHT AT ME SO EARNESTLY...
......SHE'S SERIOUS.
WHAT DO I DO? I HAVE TO STOP HER.
UM...
SNOW WHITE DOESN'T KNOW ANYTHING, PON.
THERE'S NO POINT IN ASKING HER ANY MORE, PON.
OH, GUESS WHAT?
SWIM SWIM'S WEAKNESSES ARE SOUND AND LIGHT.
FAV!! WHY!?
WHY'RE YOU STIRRING THINGS UP LIKE THIS...?
YOU SAID THE FIGHTING IS OVER NOW!

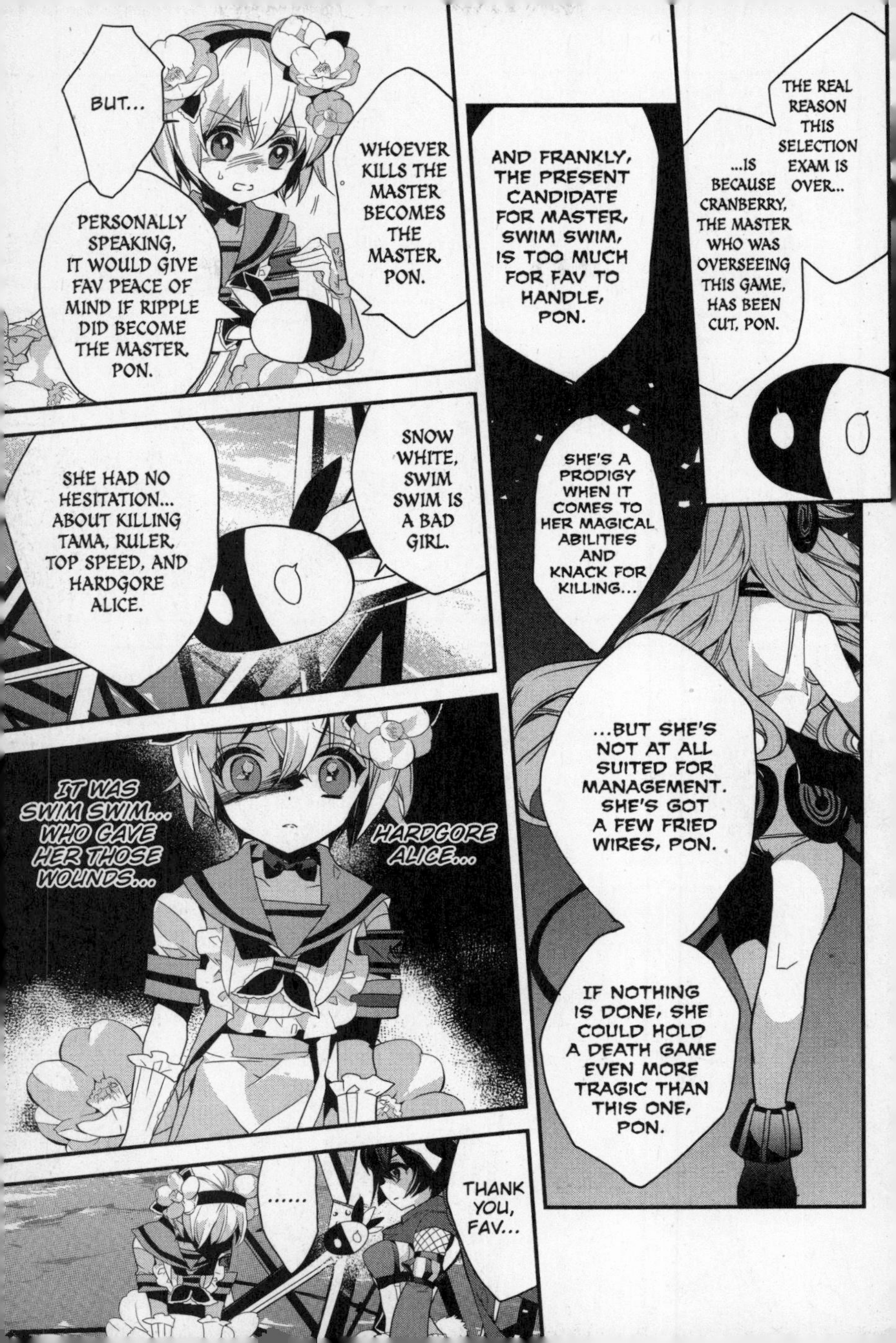
THE REAL REASON THIS SELECTION EXAM IS OVER...
...IS BECAUSE CRANBERRY, THE MASTER WHO WAS OVERSEEING THIS GAME, HAS BEEN CUT, PON.
AND FRANKLY, THE PRESENT CANDIDATE FOR MASTER, SWIM SWIM, IS TOO MUCH FOR FAV TO HANDLE, PON.
SHE'S A PRODIGY WHEN IT COMES TO HER MAGICAL ABILITIES AND KNACK FOR KILLING...
...BUT SHE'S NOT AT ALL SUITED FOR MANAGEMENT. SHE'S GOT A FEW FRIED WIRES, PON.
IF NOTHING IS DONE, SHE COULD HOLD A DEATH GAME EVEN MORE TRAGIC THAN THIS ONE, PON.
WHOEVER KILLS THE MASTER BECOMES THE MASTER, PON.
BUT...
PERSONALLY SPEAKING, IT WOULD GIVE FAV PEACE OF MIND IF RIPPLE DID BECOME THE MASTER, PON.
SNOW WHITE, SWIM SWIM IS A BAD GIRL.
SHE HAD NO HESITATION... ABOUT KILLING TAMA, RULER, TOP SPEED, AND HARDGORE ALICE.
HARDGORE ALICE...
IT WAS SWIM SWIM... WHO GAVE HER THOSE WOUNDS...
THANK YOU, FAV...
......

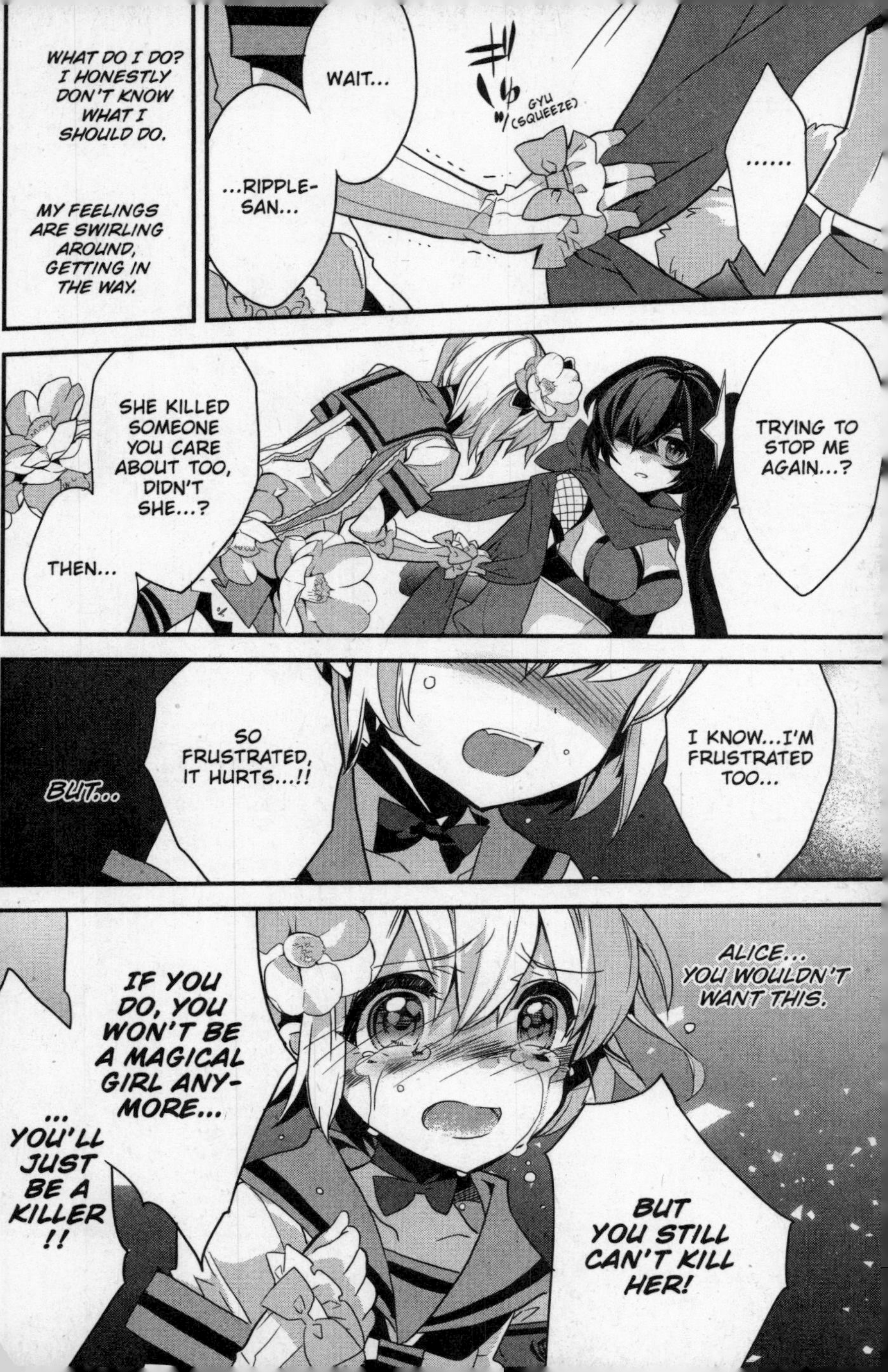
......
GYU (SQUEEZE)
WAIT...
...RIPPLE-SAN...
WHAT DO I DO? I HONESTLY DON'T KNOW WHAT I SHOULD DO.
MY FEELINGS ARE SWIRLING AROUND, GETTING IN THE WAY.
TRYING TO STOP ME AGAIN...?
SHE KILLED SOMEONE YOU CARE ABOUT TOO, DIDN'T SHE...?
THEN...
I KNOW...I'M FRUSTRATED TOO...
SO FRUSTRATED, IT HURTS...!!
BUT...
ALICE... YOU WOULDN'T WANT THIS.
BUT YOU STILL CAN'T KILL HER!
IF YOU DO, YOU WON'T BE A MAGICAL GIRL ANYMORE...
...YOU'LL JUST BE A KILLER!!

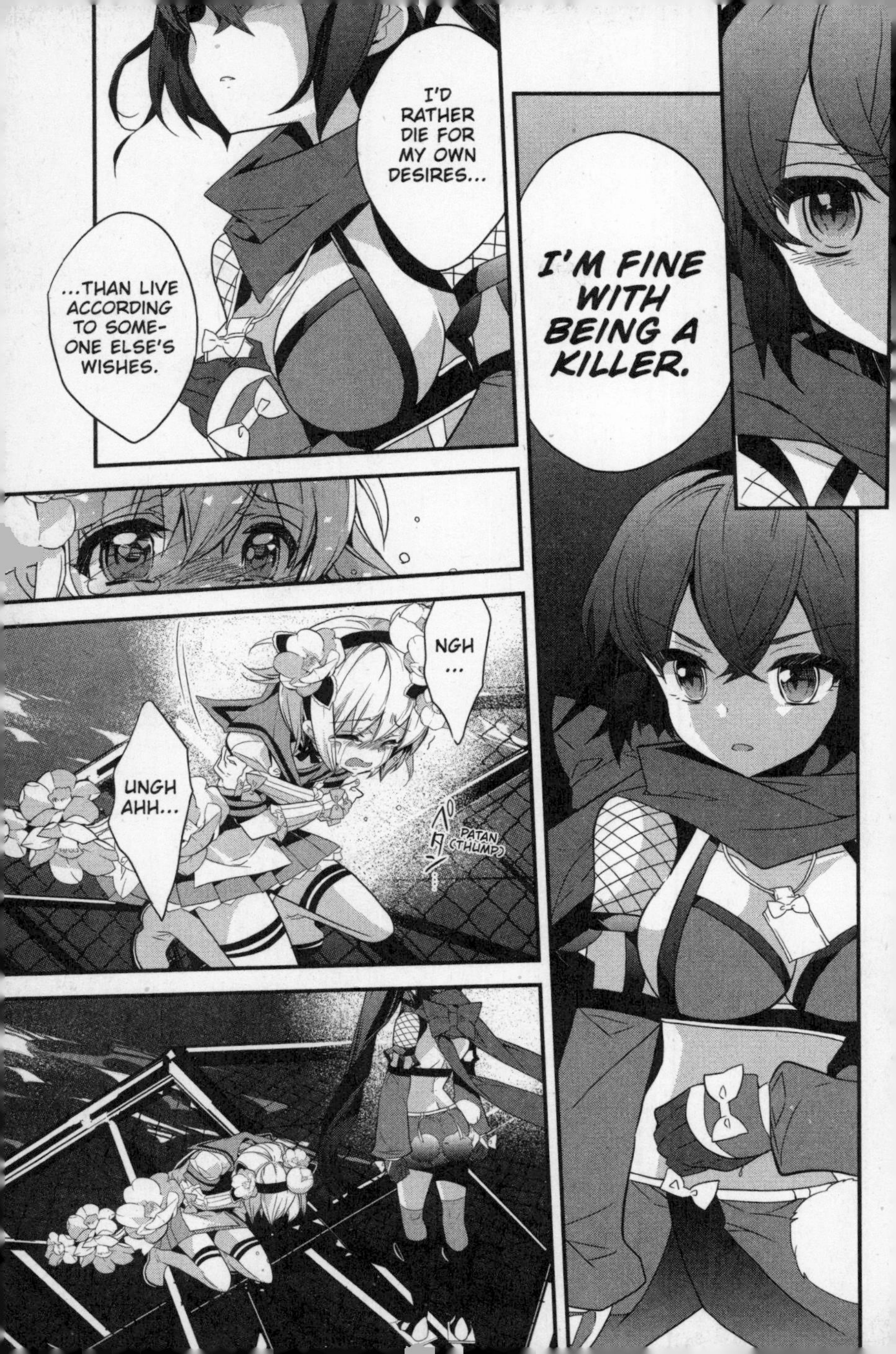
I'M FINE WITH BEING A KILLER.
I'D RATHER DIE FOR MY OWN DESIRES...
...THAN LIVE ACCORDING TO SOME-ONE ELSE'S WISHES.
NGH ...
PATAN (THUMP)
UNGH AHH...

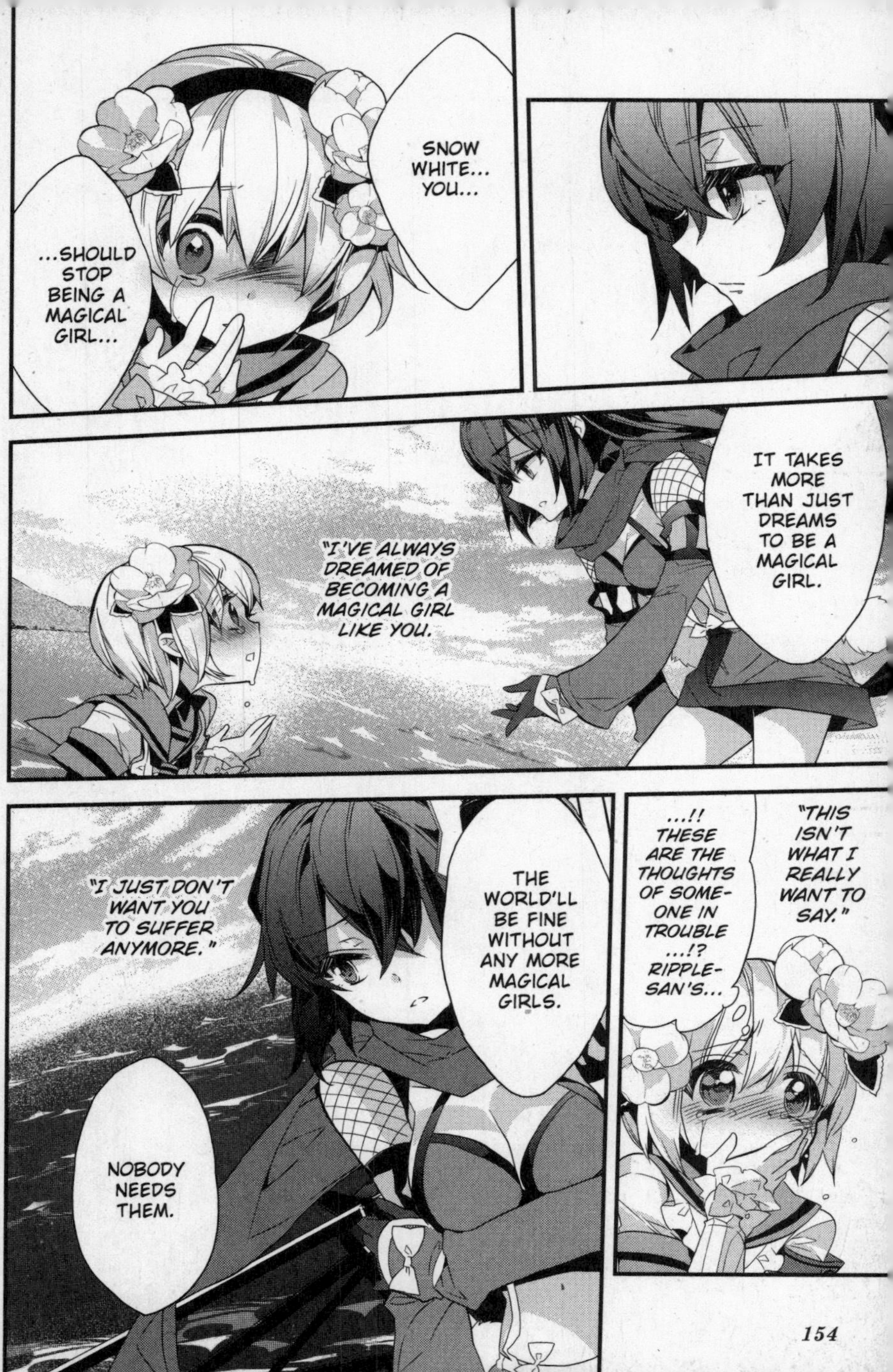
SNOW WHITE... YOU...
...SHOULD STOP BEING A MAGICAL GIRL...
IT TAKES MORE THAN JUST DREAMS TO BE A MAGICAL GIRL.
"I'VE ALWAYS DREAMED OF BECOMING A MAGICAL GIRL LIKE YOU.
"THIS ISN'T WHAT I REALLY WANT TO SAY."
...!! THESE ARE THE THOUGHTS OF SOME-ONE IN TROUBLE ...!? RIPPLE-SAN'S...
THE WORLD'LL BE FINE WITHOUT ANY MORE MAGICAL GIRLS.
"I JUST DON'T WANT YOU TO SUFFER ANYMORE."
NOBODY NEEDS THEM.

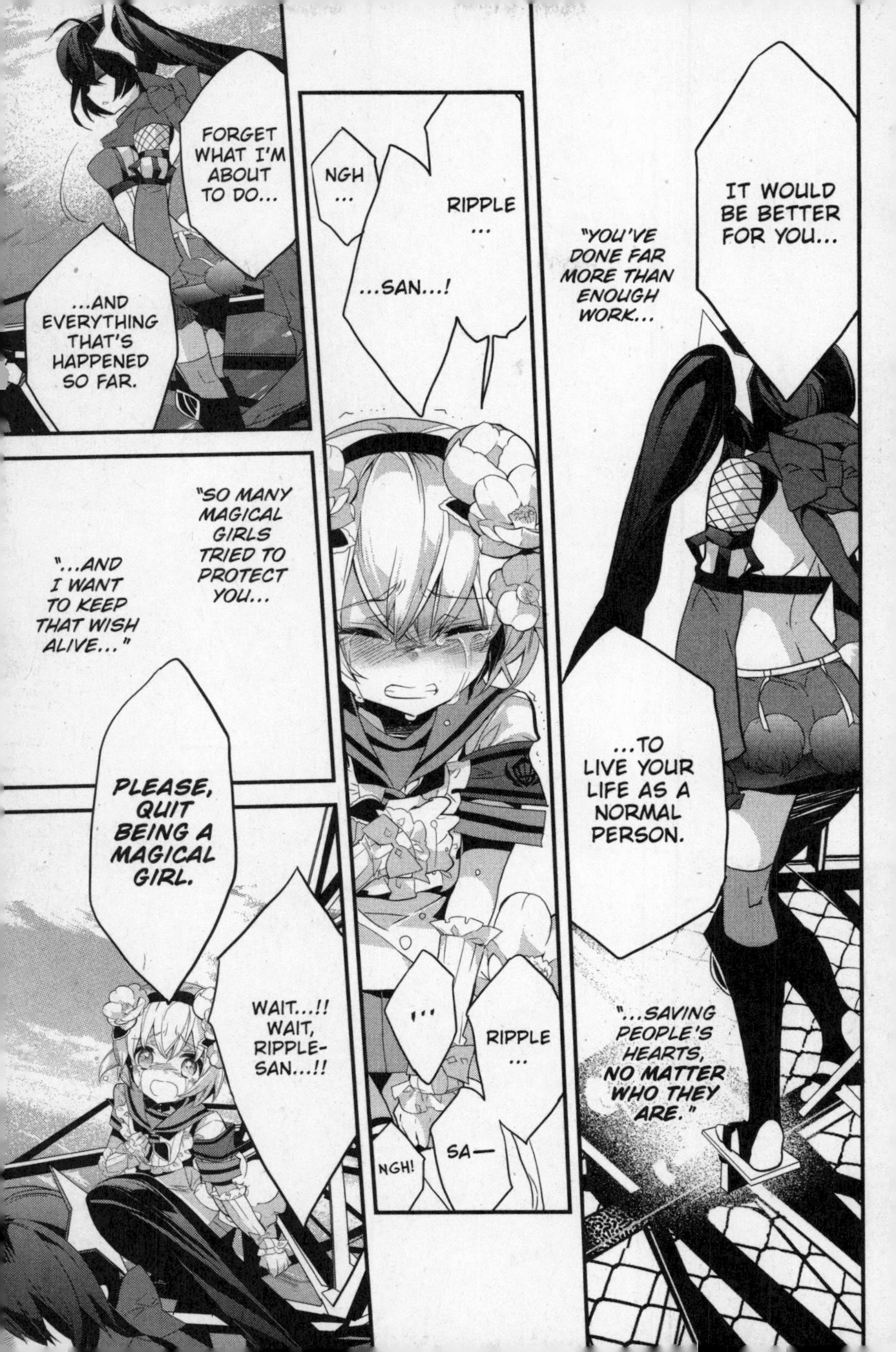
IT WOULD BE BETTER FOR YOU...
"YOU'VE DONE FAR MORE THAN ENOUGH WORK...
...TO LIVE YOUR LIFE AS A NORMAL PERSON.
"...SAVING PEOPLE'S HEARTS, NO MATTER WHO THEY ARE."
NGH ...
RIPPLE ...
...SAN...!
'...
RIPPLE ...
SA—
NGH!
FORGET WHAT I'M ABOUT TO DO...
...AND EVERYTHING THAT'S HAPPENED SO FAR.
"SO MANY MAGICAL GIRLS TRIED TO PROTECT YOU...
"...AND I WANT TO KEEP THAT WISH ALIVE..."
PLEASE, QUIT BEING A MAGICAL GIRL.
WAIT...!! WAIT, RIPPLE-SAN...!!

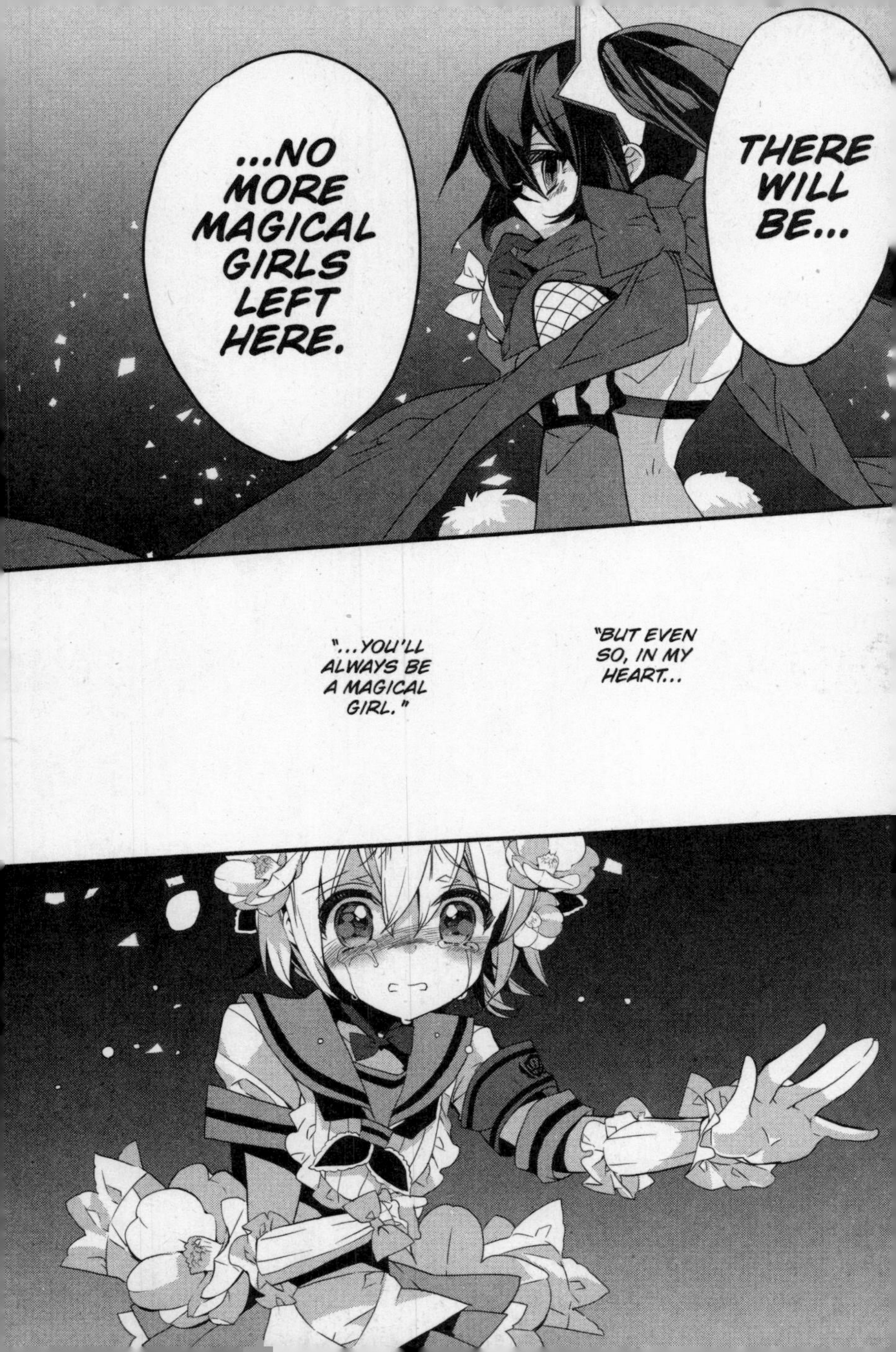
THERE WILL BE...
...NO MORE MAGICAL GIRLS LEFT HERE.
"BUT EVEN SO, IN MY HEART...
"...YOU'LL ALWAYS BE A MAGICAL GIRL."

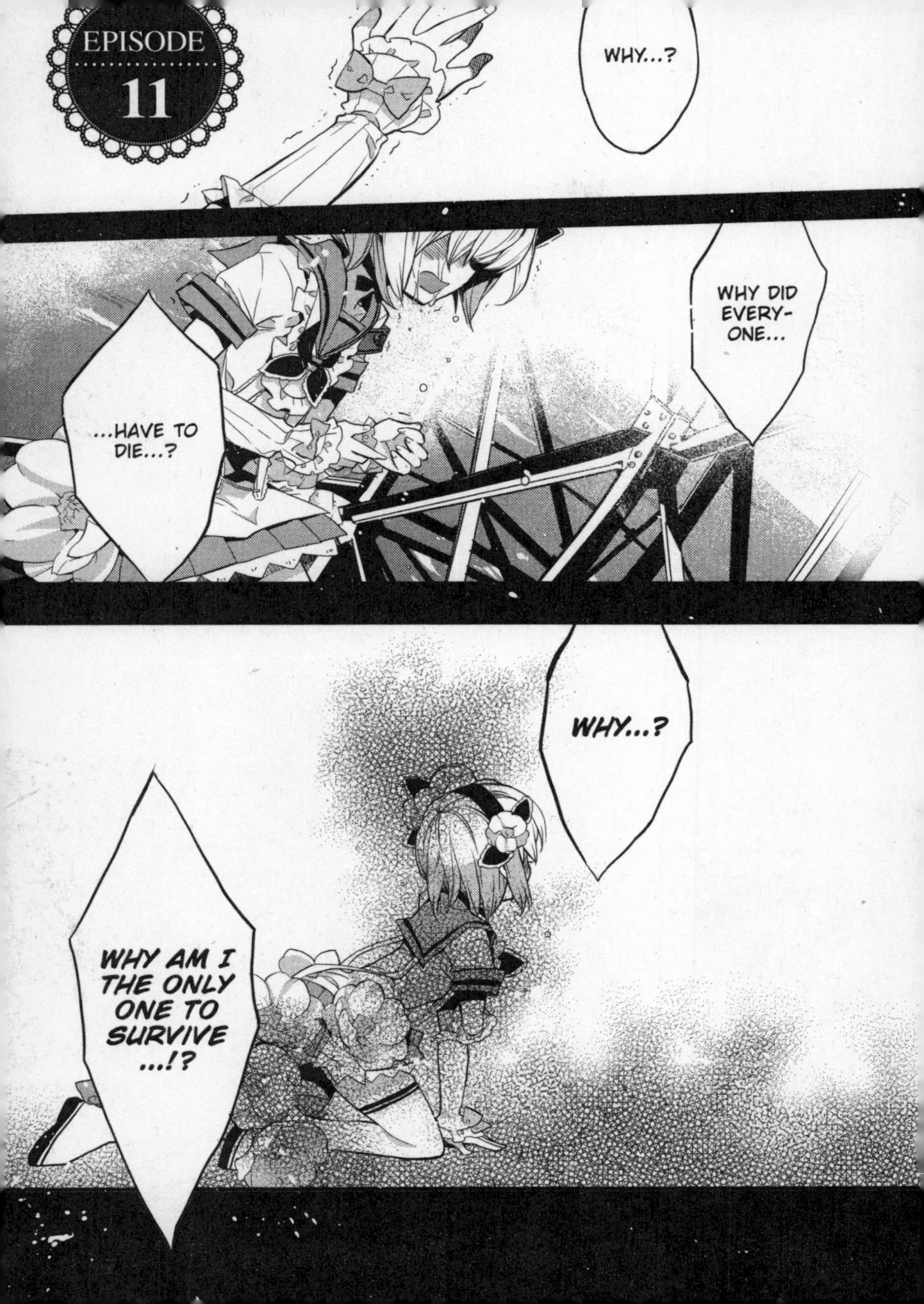
EPISODE 11
WHY...?
WHY DID EVERY-ONE...
...HAVE TO DIE...?
WHY...?
WHY AM I THE ONLY ONE TO SURVIVE ...!?

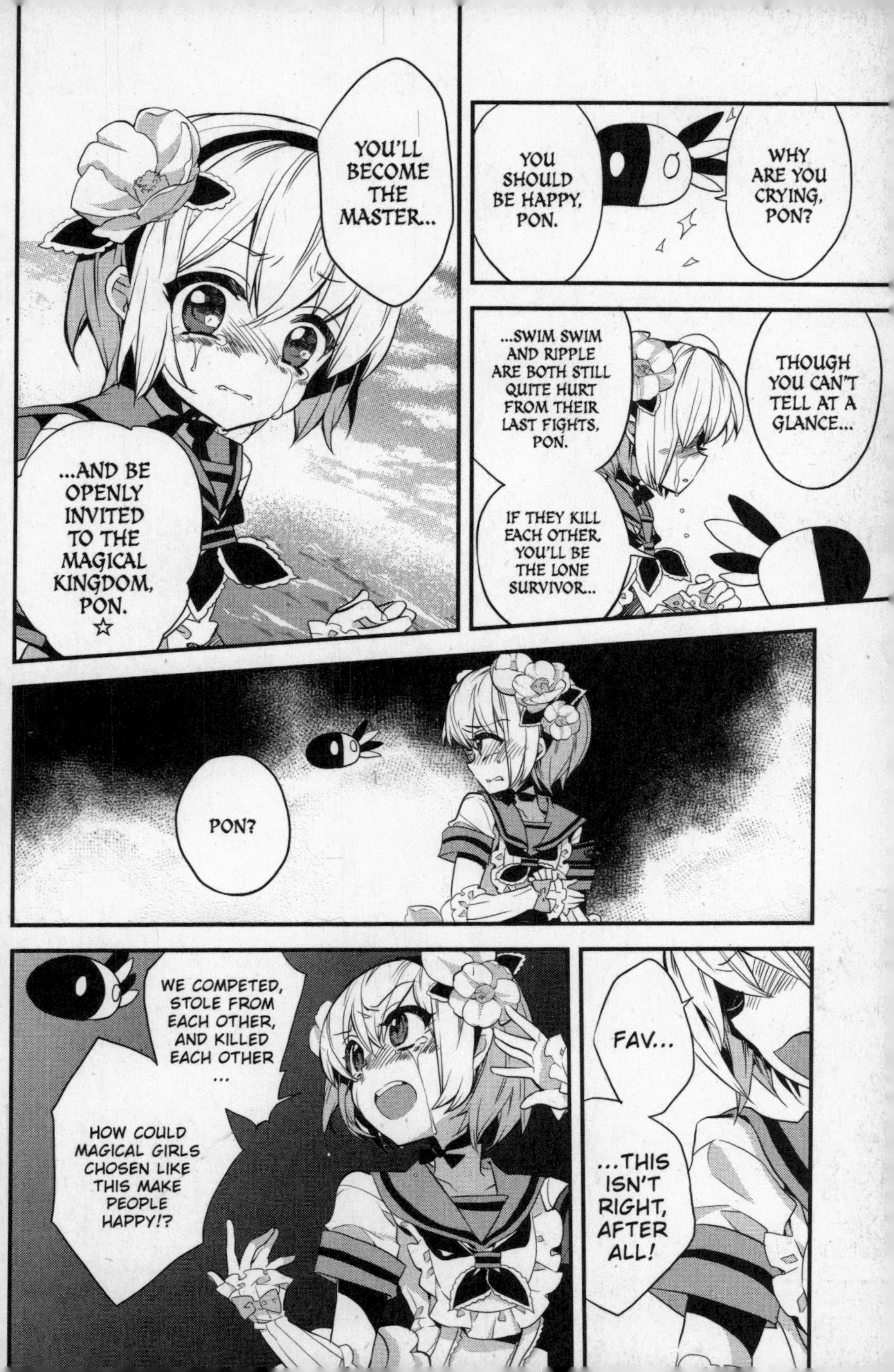
WHY ARE YOU CRYING, PON?
YOU SHOULD BE HAPPY, PON.
THOUGH YOU CAN'T TELL AT A GLANCE...
...SWIM SWIM AND RIPPLE ARE BOTH STILL QUITE HURT FROM THEIR LAST FIGHTS, PON.
IF THEY KILL EACH OTHER, YOU'LL BE THE LONE SURVIVOR...
YOU'LL BECOME THE MASTER...
...AND BE OPENLY INVITED TO THE MAGICAL KINGDOM, PON. ☆
PON?
FAV...
...THIS ISN'T RIGHT, AFTER ALL!
WE COMPETED, STOLE FROM EACH OTHER, AND KILLED EACH OTHER...
HOW COULD MAGICAL GIRLS CHOSEN LIKE THIS MAKE PEOPLE HAPPY!?

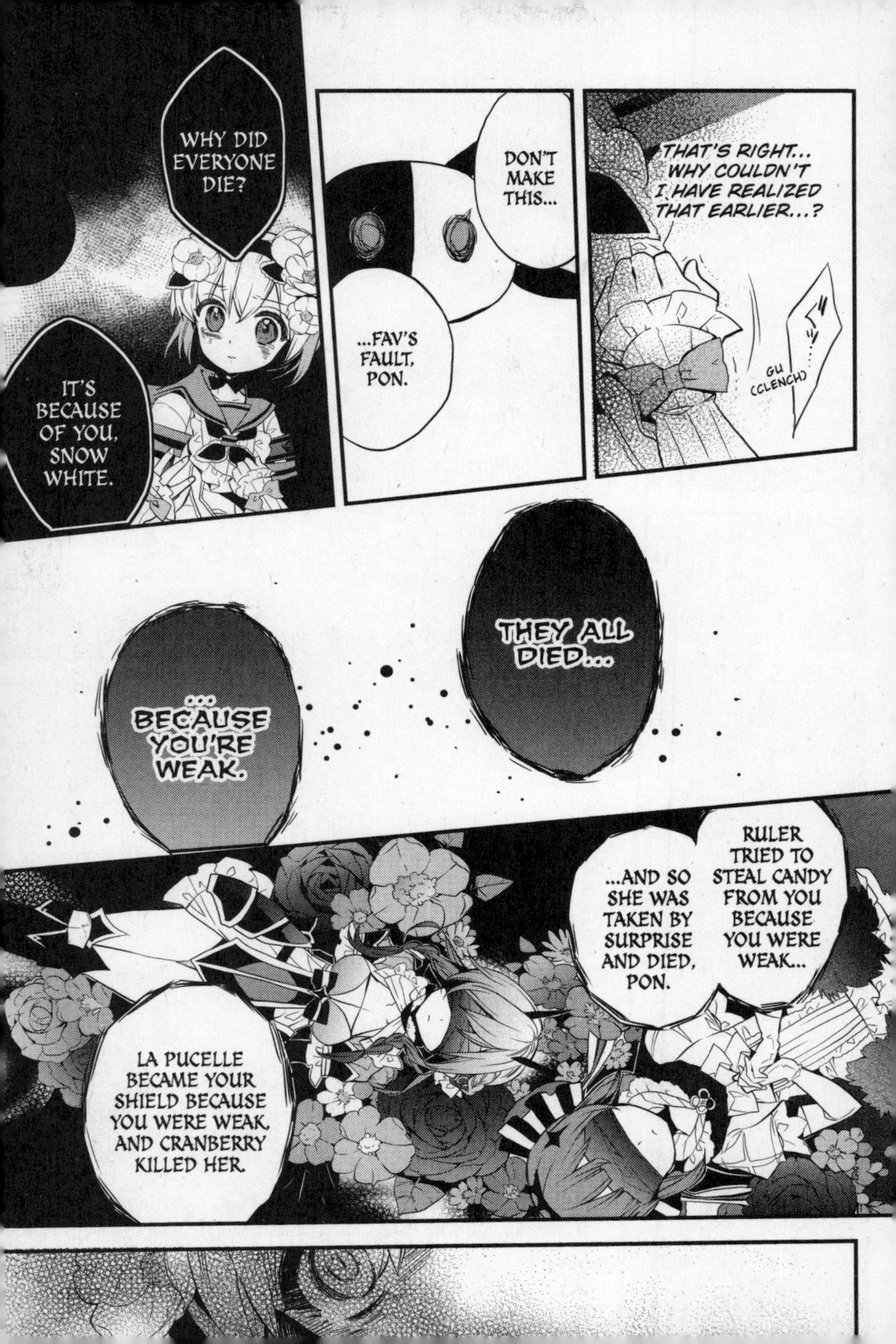
THAT'S RIGHT... WHY COULDN'T I HAVE REALIZED THAT EARLIER...?
GU (CLENCH)
DON'T MAKE THIS...
...FAV'S FAULT, PON.
WHY DID EVERYONE DIE?
IT'S BECAUSE OF YOU, SNOW WHITE.
THEY ALL DIED...
...BECAUSE YOU'RE WEAK.
RULER TRIED TO STEAL CANDY FROM YOU BECAUSE YOU WERE WEAK...
...AND SO SHE WAS TAKEN BY SURPRISE AND DIED, PON.
LA PUCELLE BECAME YOUR SHIELD BECAUSE YOU WERE WEAK, AND CRANBERRY KILLED HER.

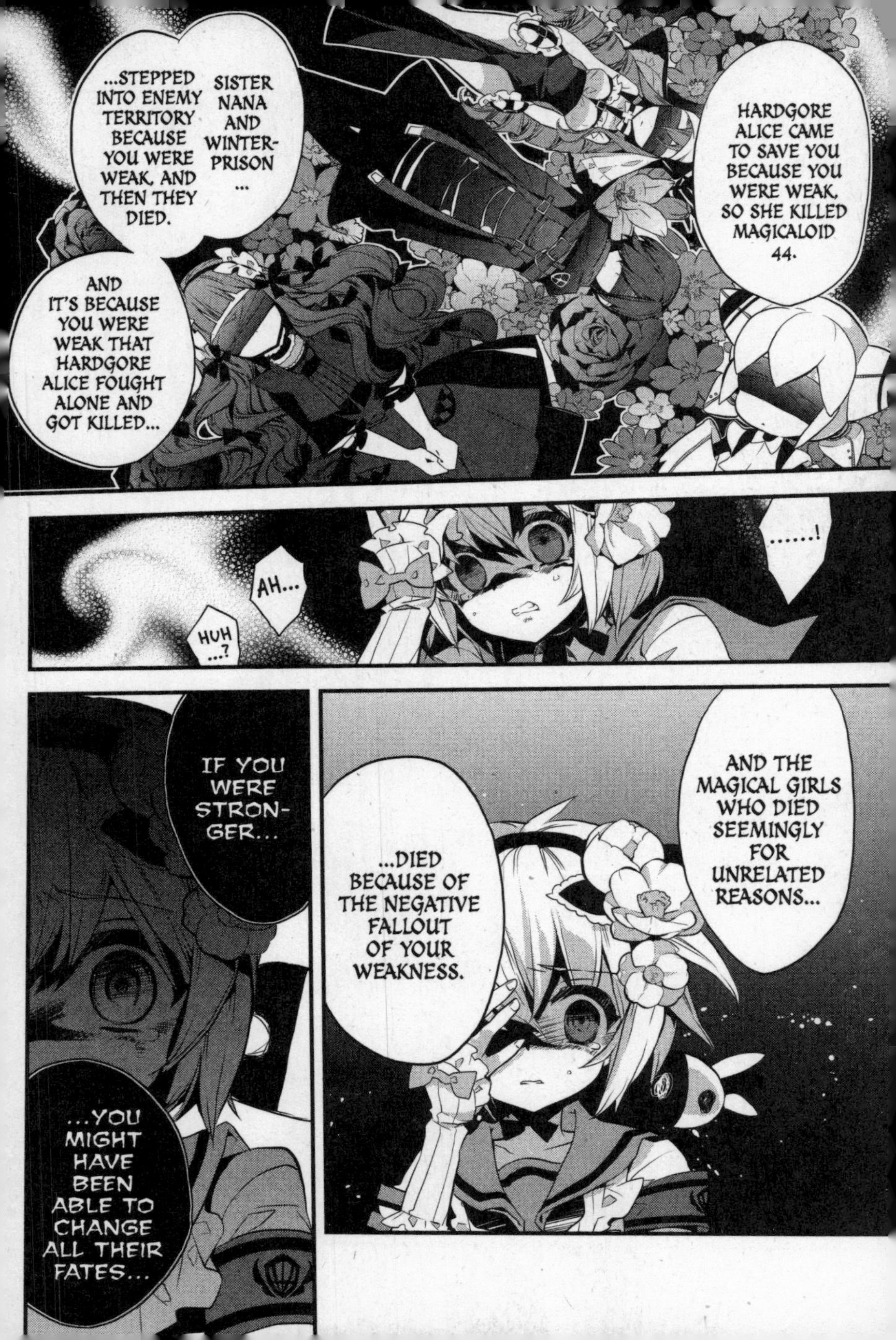
HARDGORE ALICE CAME TO SAVE YOU BECAUSE YOU WERE WEAK, SO SHE KILLED MAGICALOID 44.
SISTER NANA AND WINTER-PRISON...
...STEPPED INTO ENEMY TERRITORY BECAUSE YOU WERE WEAK, AND THEN THEY DIED.
AND IT'S BECAUSE YOU WERE WEAK THAT HARDGORE ALICE FOUGHT ALONE AND GOT KILLED...
......!
AH...
HUH...?
AND THE MAGICAL GIRLS WHO DIED SEEMINGLY FOR UNRELATED REASONS...
...DIED BECAUSE OF THE NEGATIVE FALLOUT OF YOUR WEAKNESS.
IF YOU WERE STRON-GER...
...YOU MIGHT HAVE BEEN ABLE TO CHANGE ALL THEIR FATES...

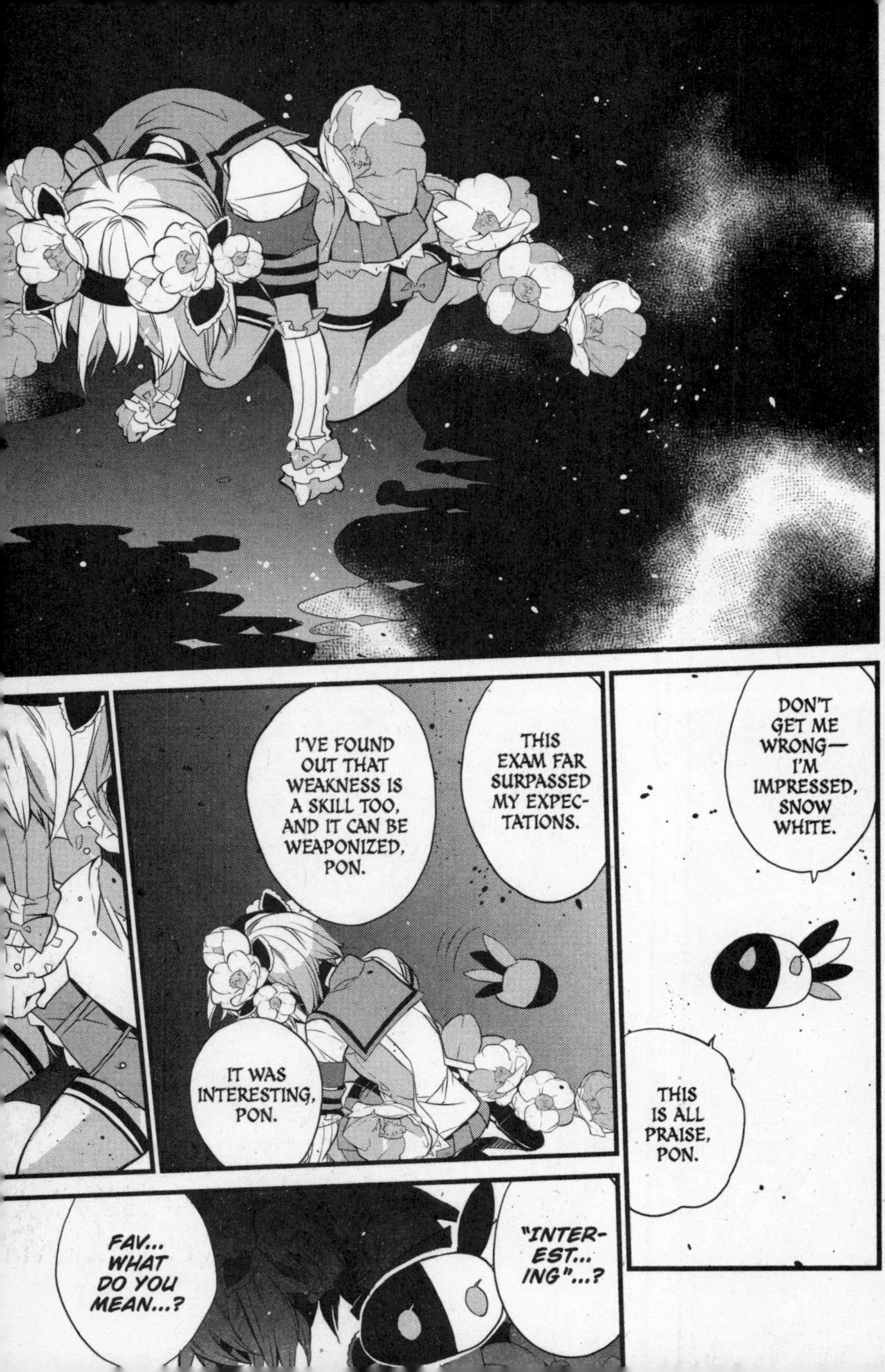
DON'T GET ME WRONG—I'M IMPRESSED, SNOW WHITE.
THIS IS ALL PRAISE, PON.
THIS EXAM FAR SURPASSED MY EXPECTATIONS.
I'VE FOUND OUT THAT WEAKNESS IS A SKILL TOO, AND IT CAN BE WEAPONIZED, PON.
IT WAS INTERESTING, PON.
"INTEREST... ING"...?
FAV... WHAT DO YOU MEAN...?

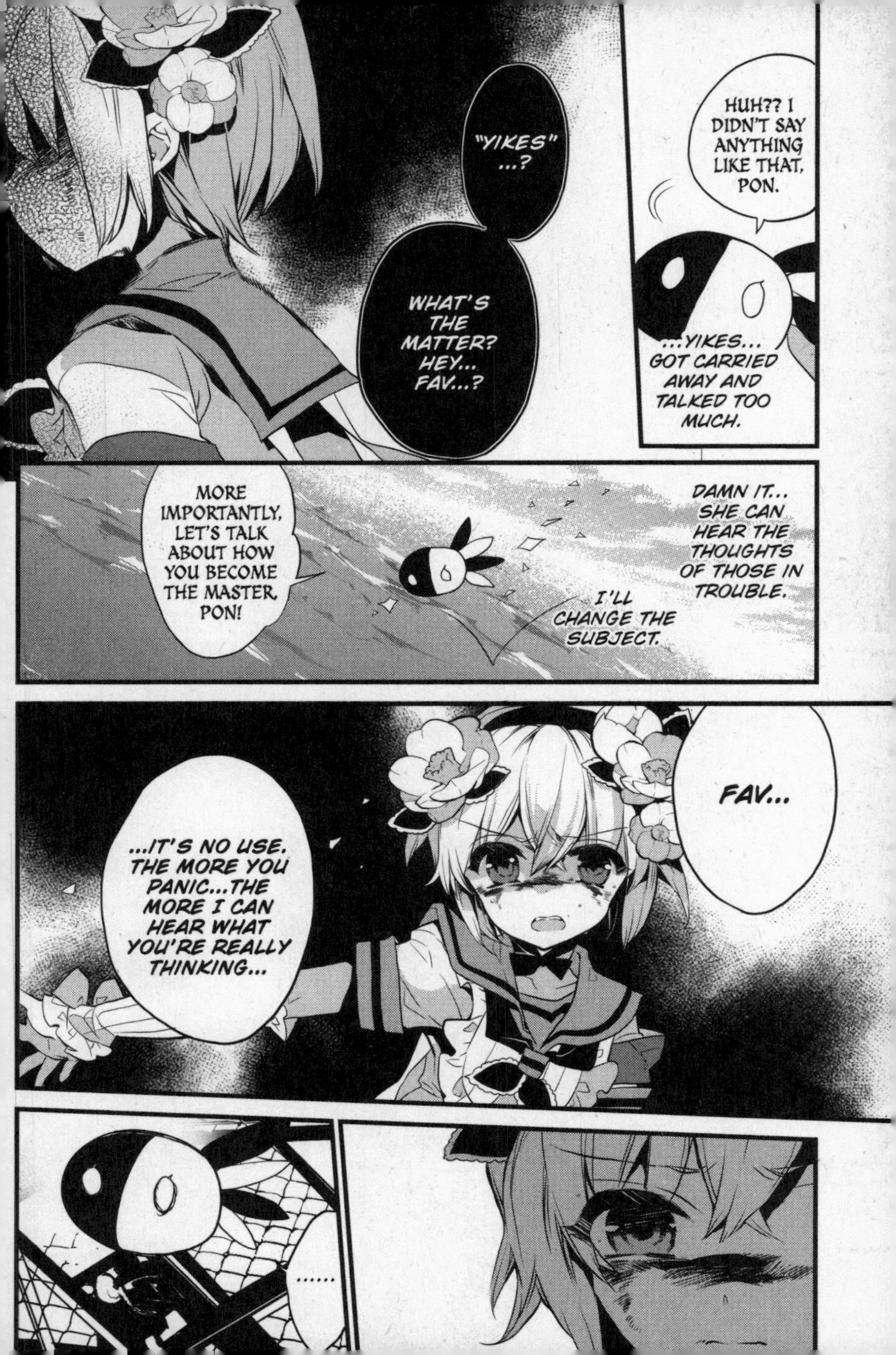
HUH?? I DIDN'T SAY ANYTHING LIKE THAT, PON.
...YIKES... GOT CARRIED AWAY AND TALKED TOO MUCH.
"YIKES" ...?
WHAT'S THE MATTER? HEY... FAV...?
DAMN IT... SHE CAN HEAR THE THOUGHTS OF THOSE IN TROUBLE.
I'LL CHANGE THE SUBJECT.
MORE IMPORTANTLY, LET'S TALK ABOUT HOW YOU BECOME THE MASTER, PON!
FAV...
...IT'S NO USE. THE MORE YOU PANIC...THE MORE I CAN HEAR WHAT YOU'RE REALLY THINKING...
......

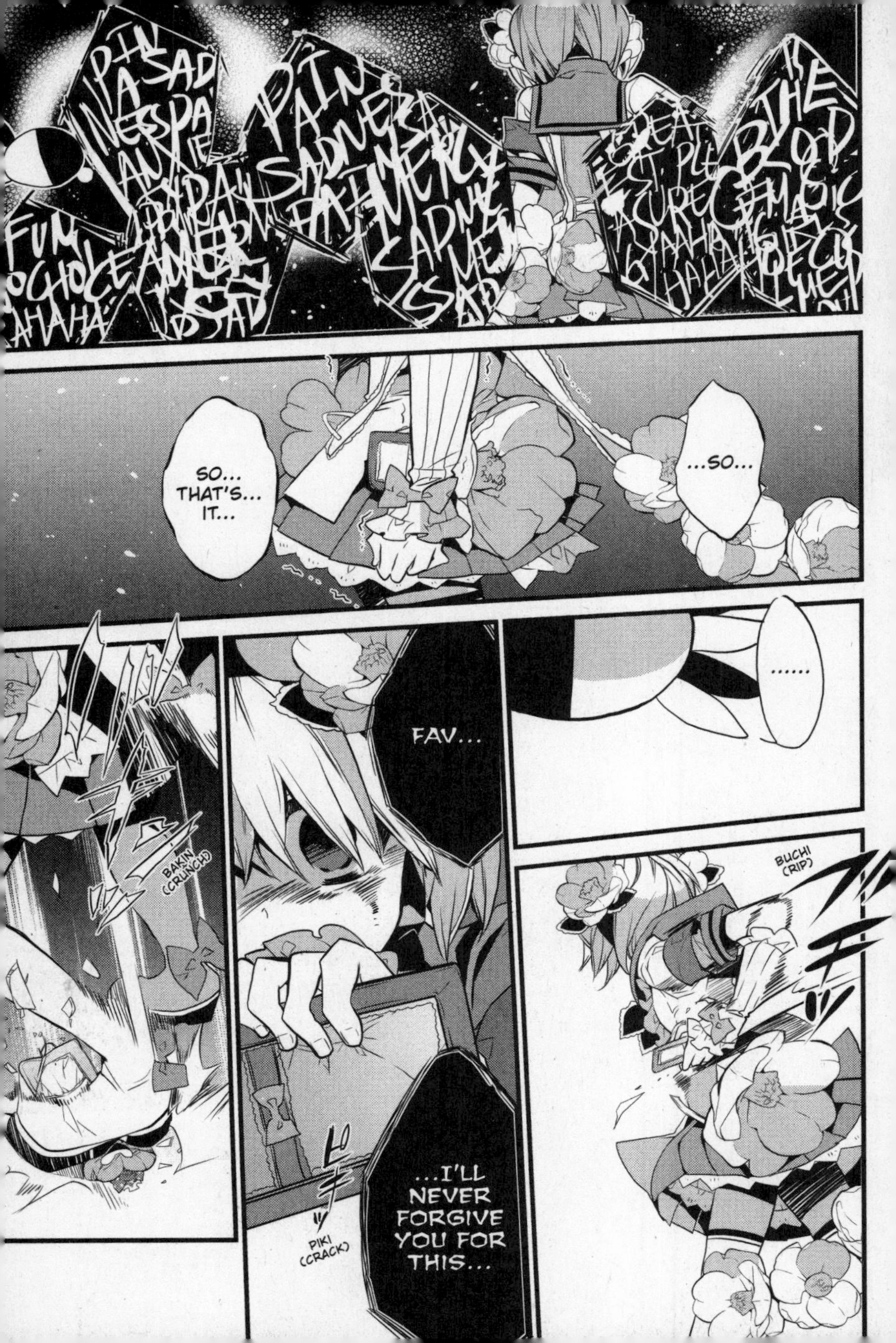
...SO...
SO... THAT'S... IT...
......
BUCHI (RIP)
FAV...
...I'LL NEVER FORGIVE YOU FOR THIS...
PIKI (CRACK)
BAKIN (CRUNCH)

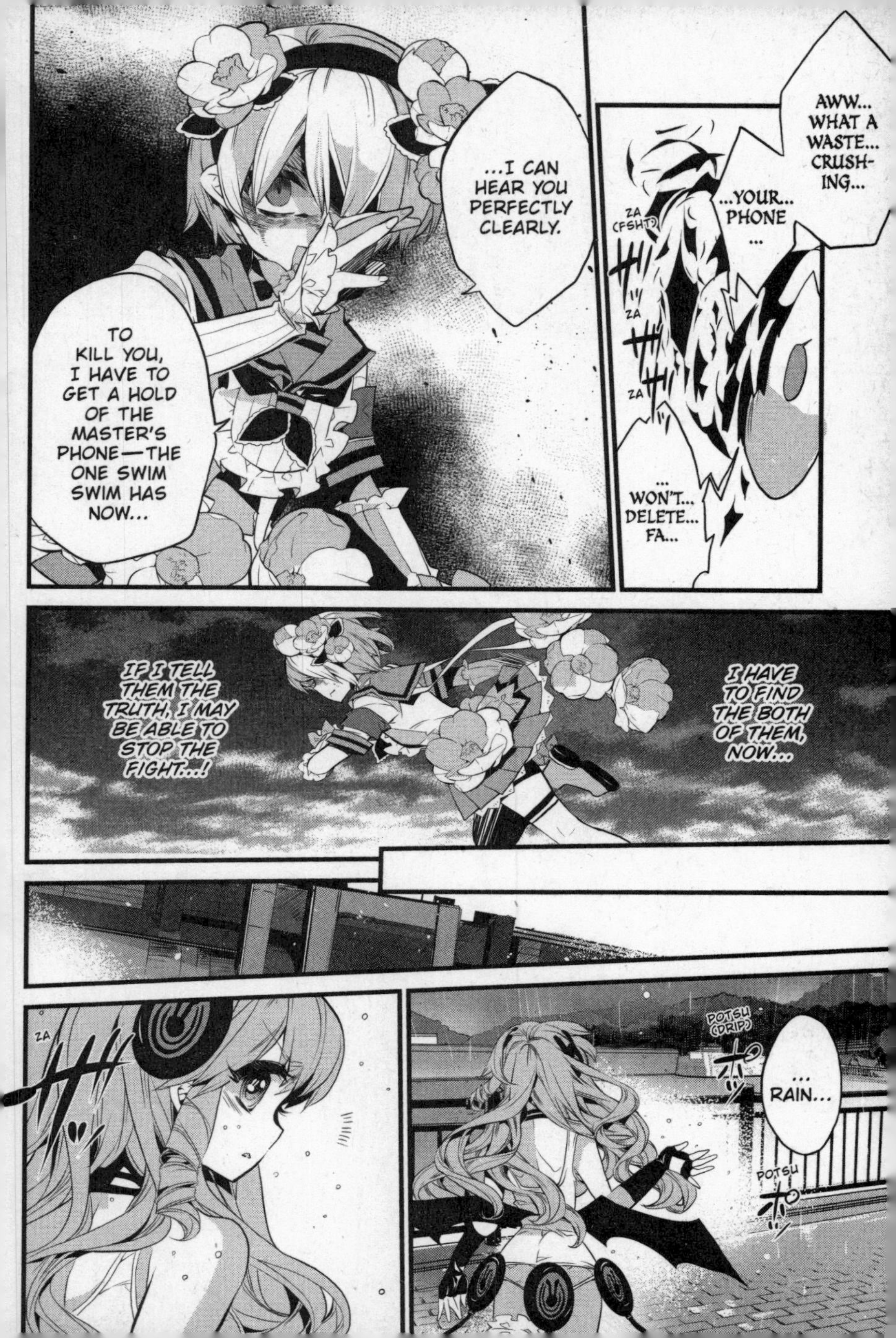
AWW... WHAT A WASTE... CRUSH-ING...
...YOUR... PHONE ...
ZA (FSHT)
ZA
ZA
... WON'T... DELETE... FA...
...I CAN HEAR YOU PERFECTLY CLEARLY.
TO KILL YOU, I HAVE TO GET A HOLD OF THE MASTER'S PHONE—THE ONE SWIM SWIM HAS NOW...
I HAVE TO FIND THE BOTH OF THEM, NOW...
IF I TELL THEM THE TRUTH, I MAY BE ABLE TO STOP THE FIGHT...!
POTSU (DRIP)
... RAIN...
POTSU
ZA

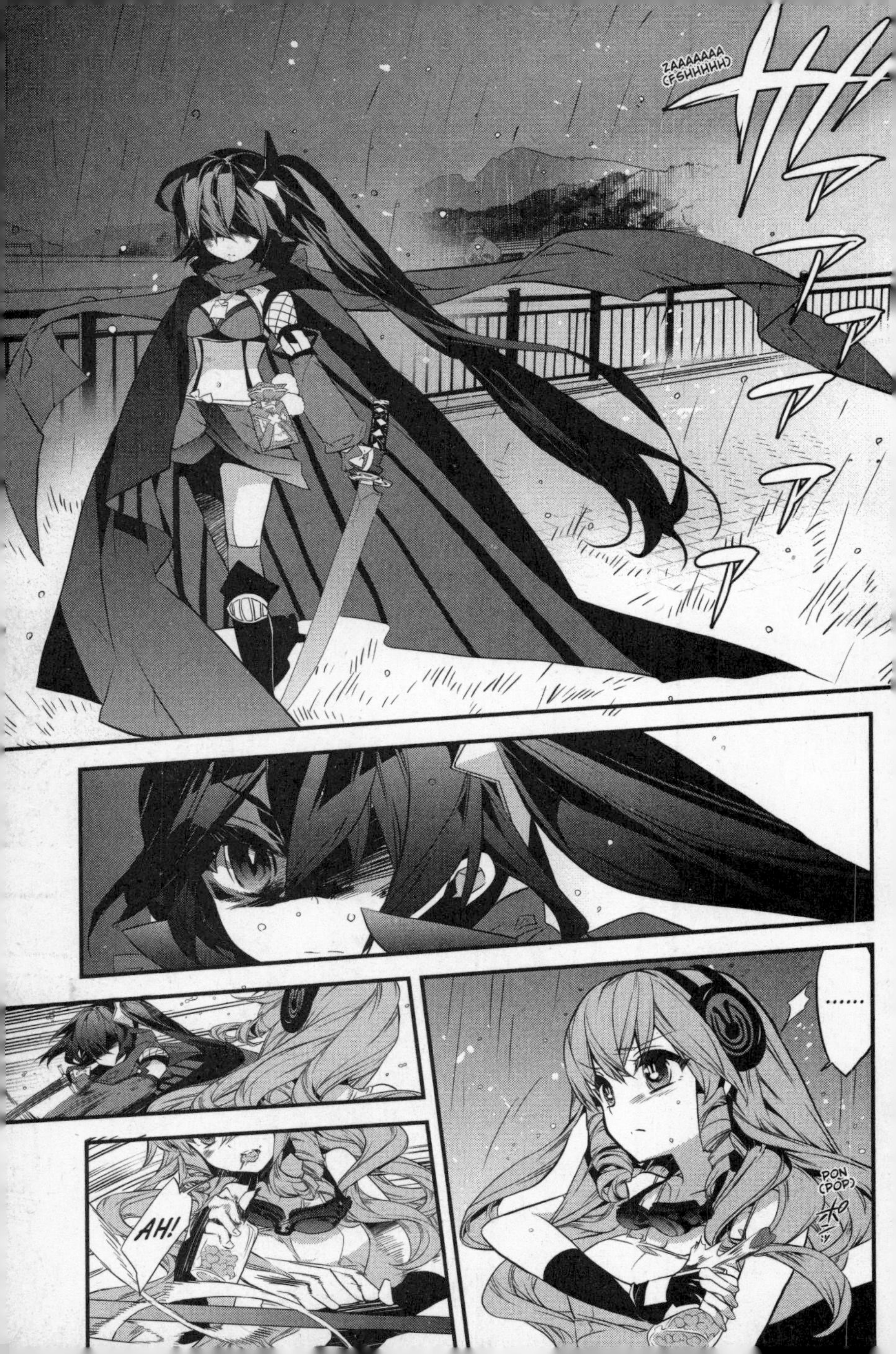
ZAAAAAAA
(FSHHHHH)
......
PON
(POP)
AH!

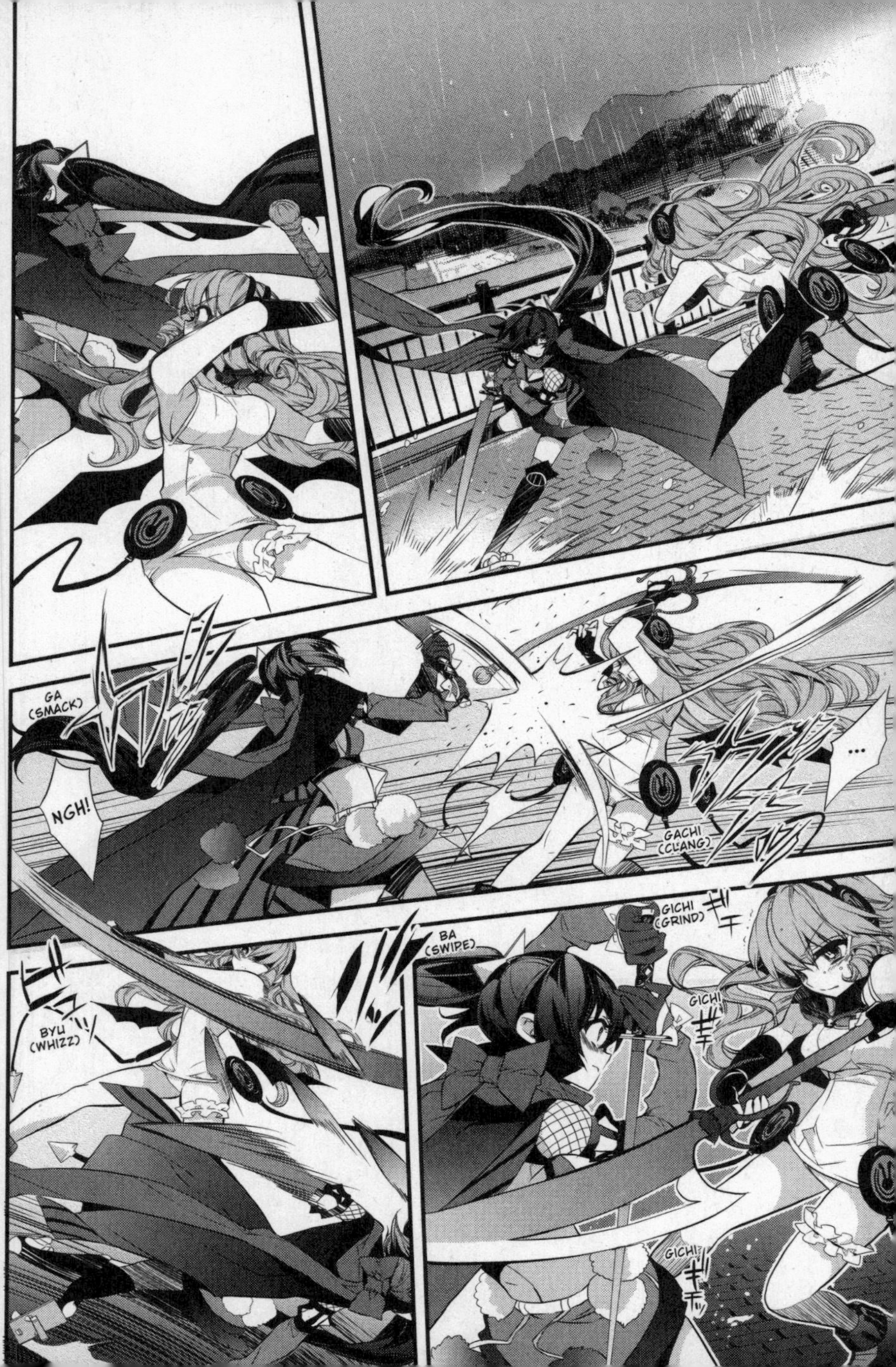
...
GACHI (CLANG)
GA (SMACK)
NGH!
GICHI (GRIND)
BA (SWIPE)
GICHI
GICHI
BYU (WHIZZ)

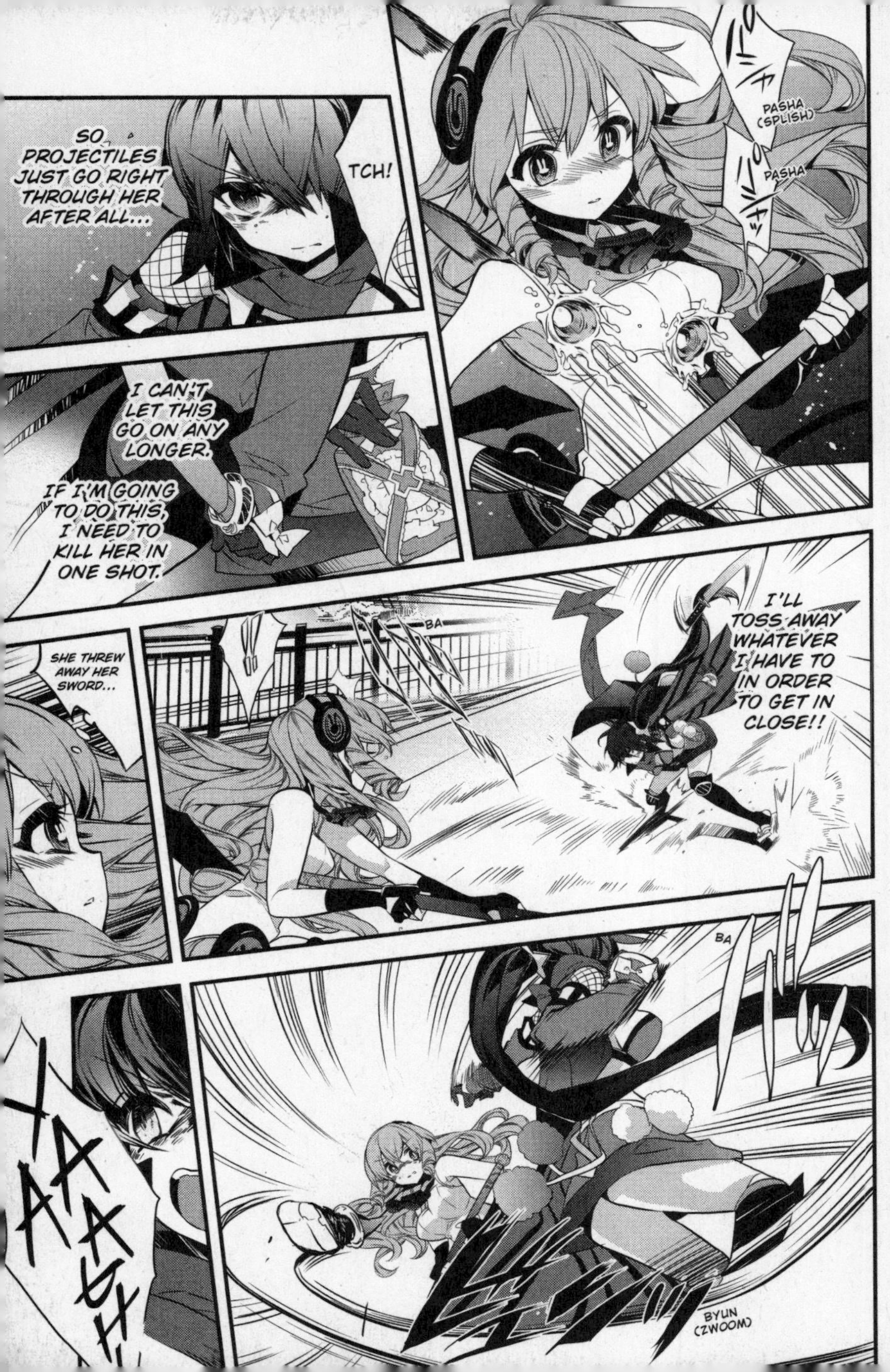
PASHA (SPLISH)
PASHA
TCH!
SO PROJECTILES JUST GO RIGHT THROUGH HER AFTER ALL...
I CAN'T LET THIS GO ON ANY LONGER.
IF I'M GOING TO DO THIS, I NEED TO KILL HER IN ONE SHOT.
I'LL TOSS AWAY WHATEVER I HAVE TO IN ORDER TO GET IN CLOSE!!
BA
SHE THREW AWAY HER SWORD...
BA
BYUN (ZWOOM)
YAAAAUGH

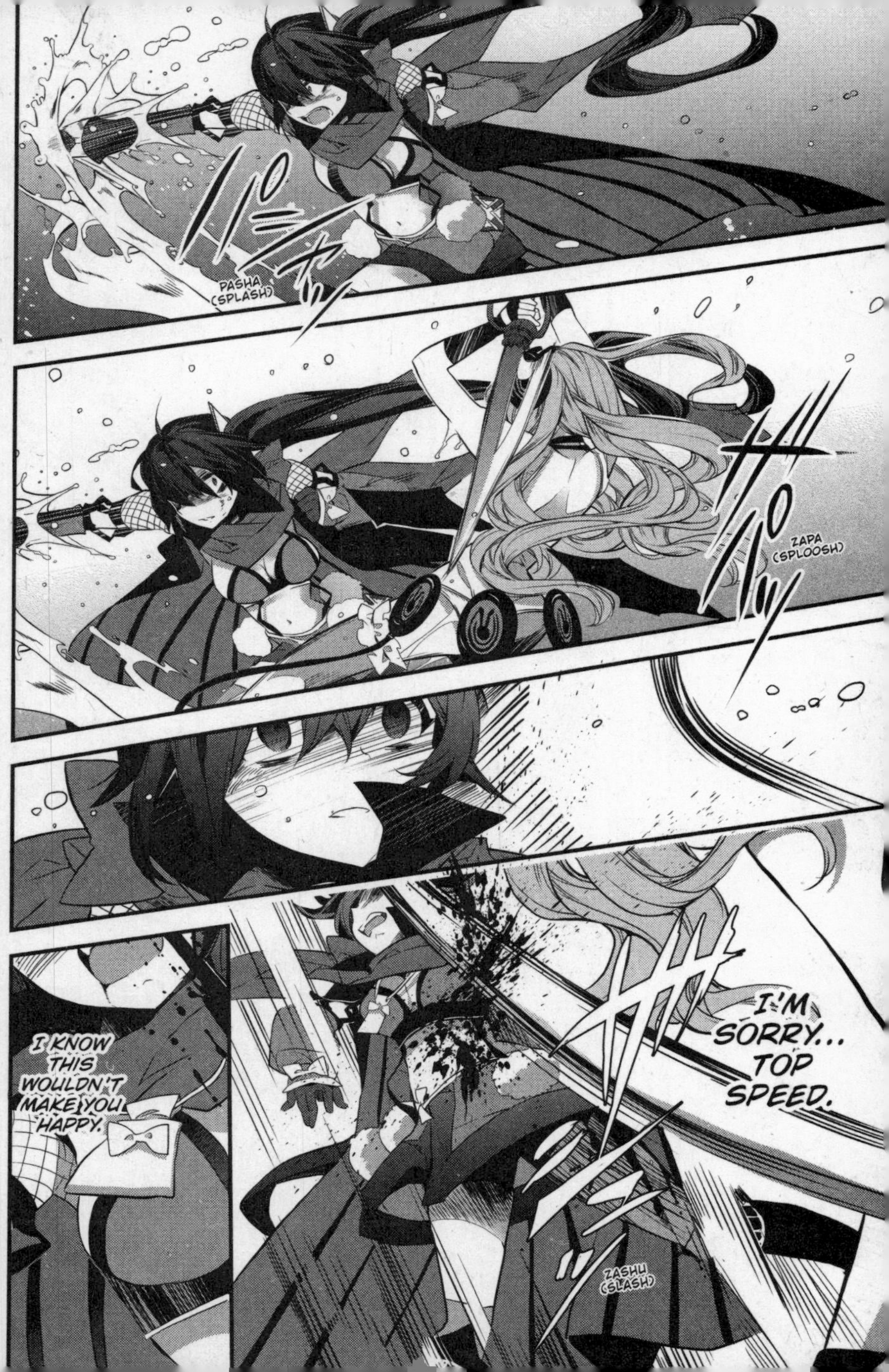
PASHA (SPLASH)
ZAPA (SPLOOSH)
I'M SORRY... TOP SPEED.
ZASHU (SLASH)
I KNOW THIS WOULDN'T MAKE YOU HAPPY.

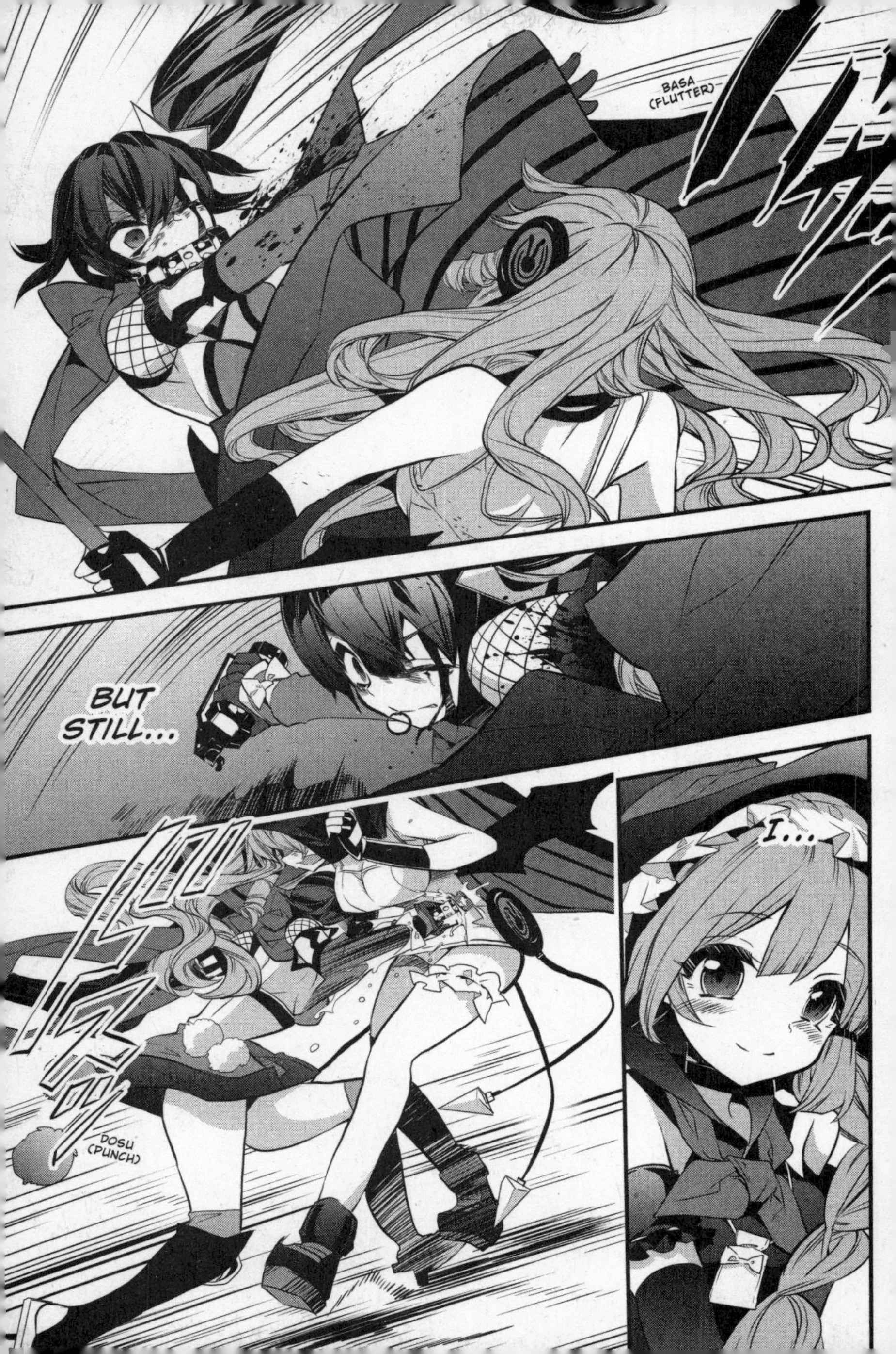
BASA
(FLUTTER)
BUT STILL...
I...
DOSU
(PUNCH)

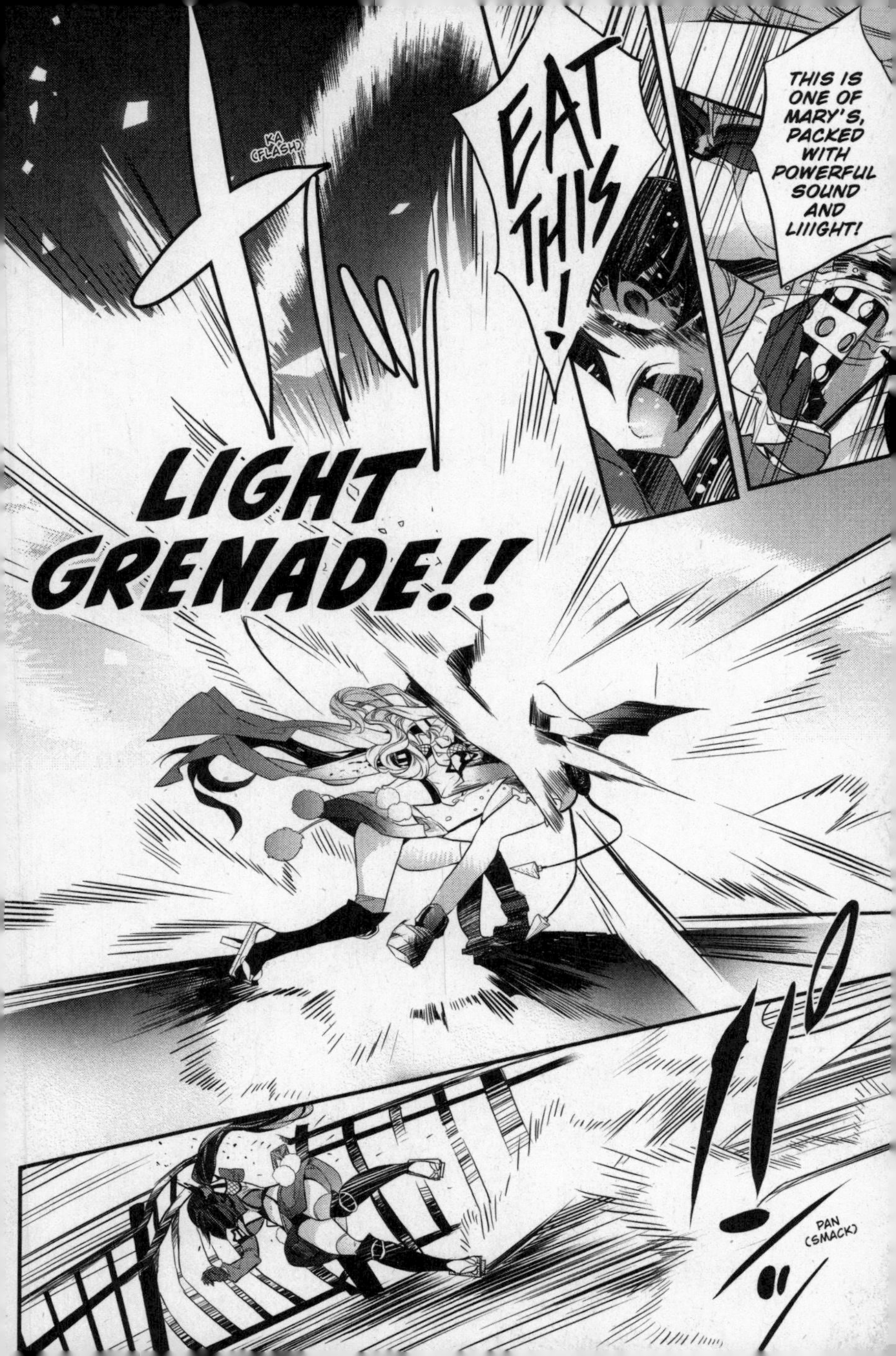
THIS IS ONE OF MARY'S, PACKED WITH POWERFUL SOUND AND LIIIGHT!
EAT THIS!
KA (FLASH)
LIGHT GRENADE!!
!!
PAN (SMACK)

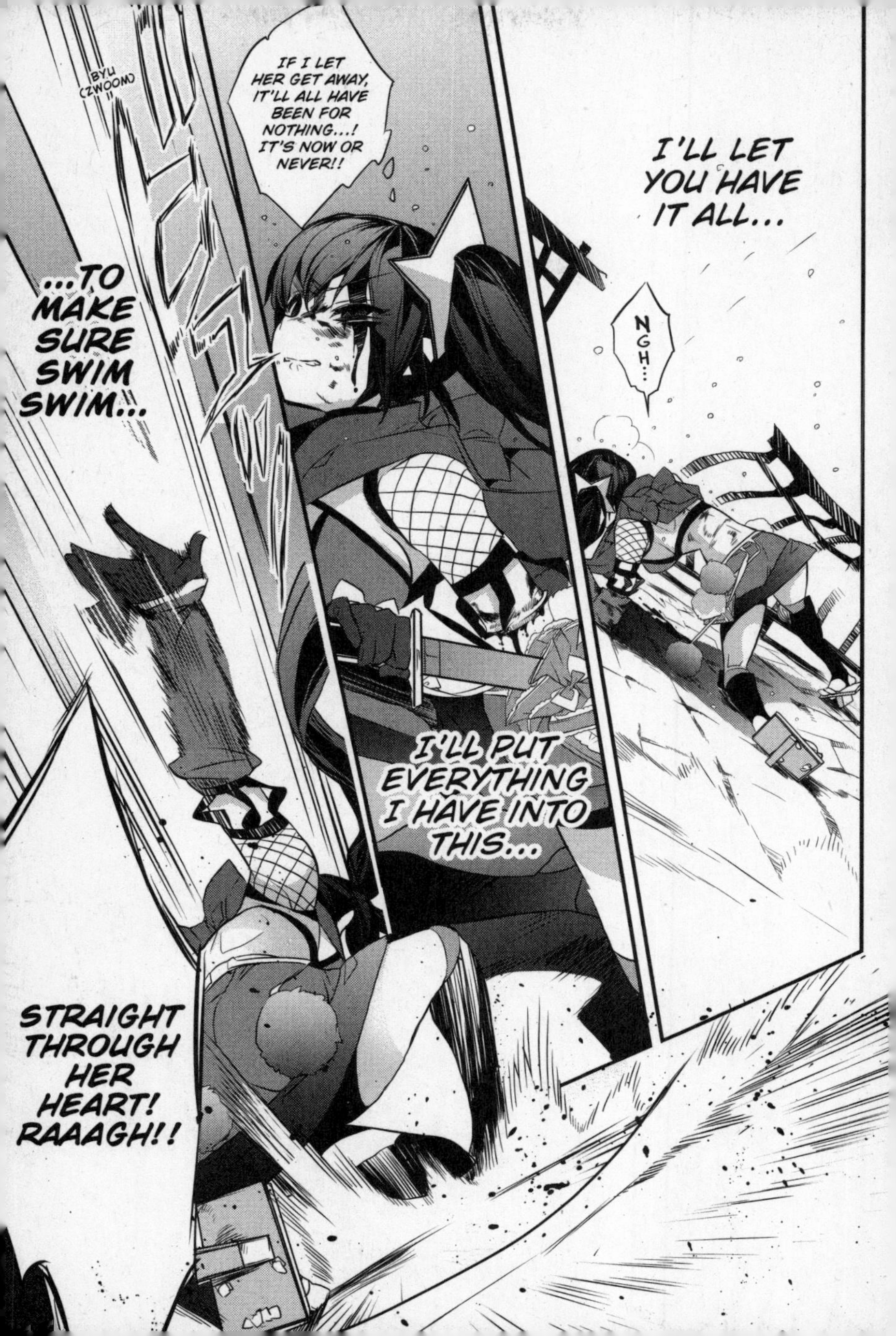
I'LL LET YOU HAVE IT ALL...
NGH...
IF I LET HER GET AWAY, IT'LL ALL HAVE BEEN FOR NOTHING...! IT'S NOW OR NEVER!!
I'LL PUT EVERYTHING I HAVE INTO THIS...
BYU (ZWOOM)
...TO MAKE SURE SWIM SWIM...
STRAIGHT THROUGH HER HEART! RAAAGH!!

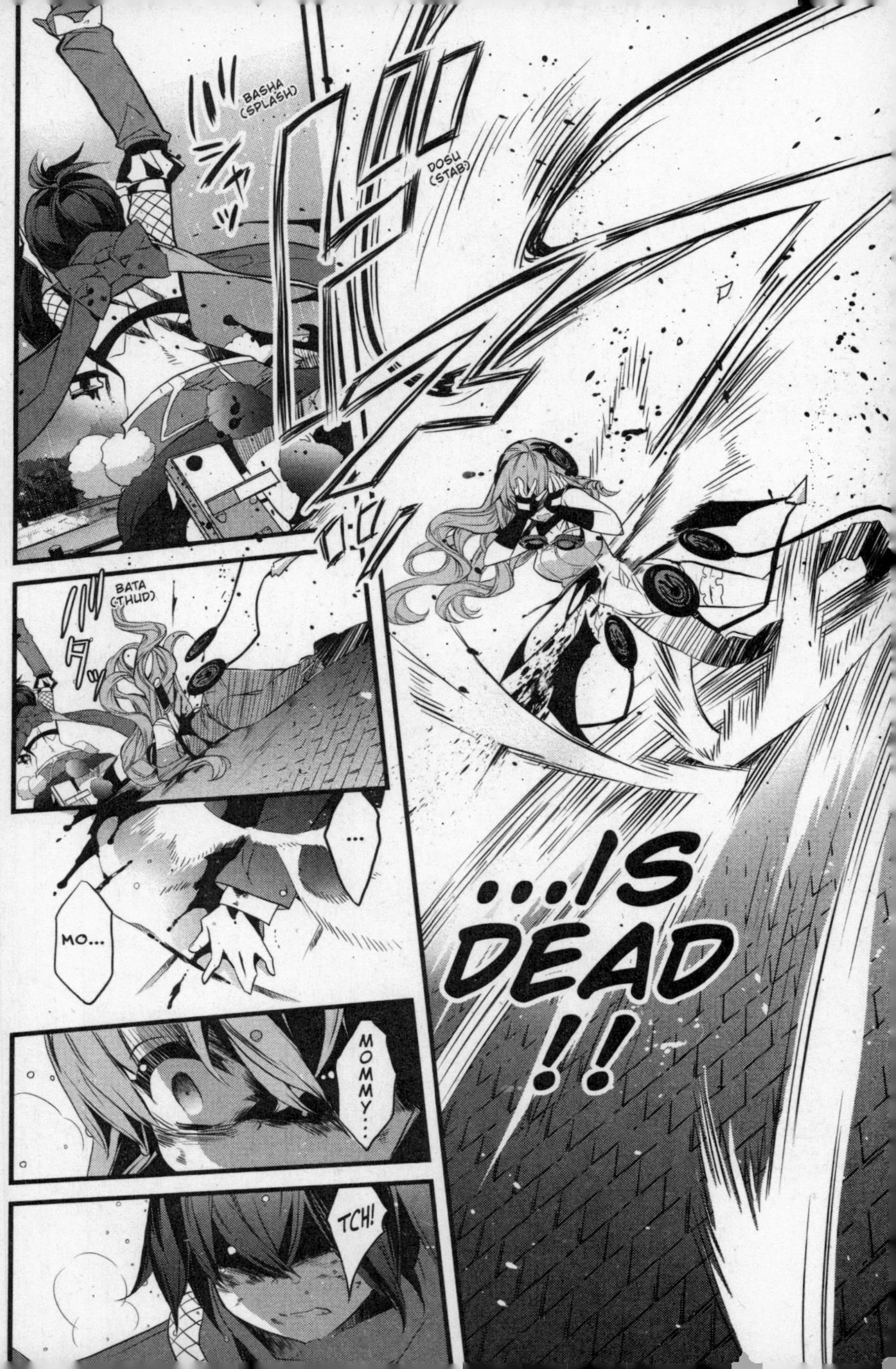
DOSU (STAB)
...IS DEAD!!
BASHA (SPLASH)
BATA (THUD)
...
MO...
MOMMY...
TCH!

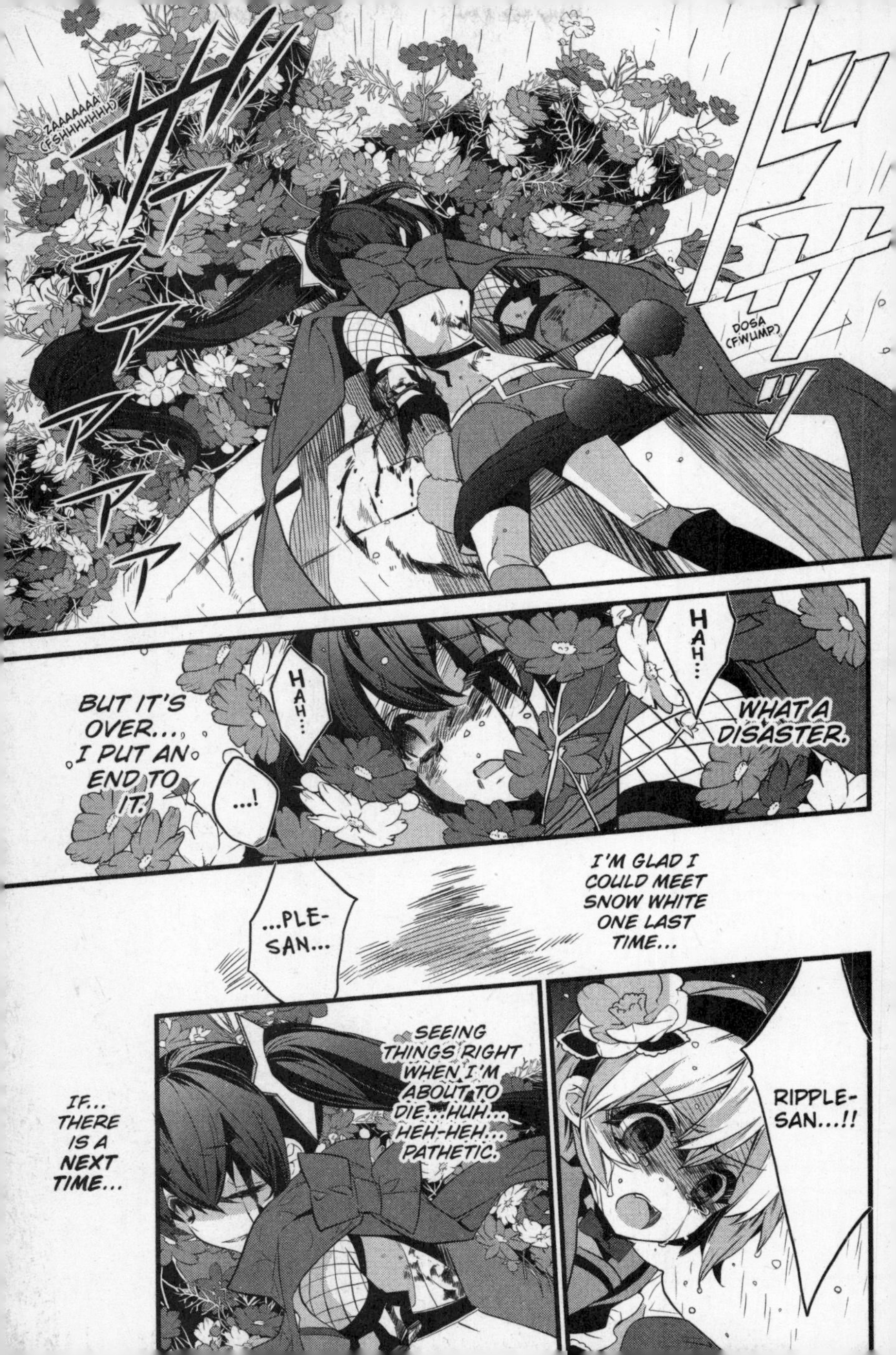
DOSA (FWUMP)
ZAAAAAAA (FSHHHHHHH)
HAH...
WHAT A DISASTER.
HAH...
...!
BUT IT'S OVER... I PUT AN END TO IT.
I'M GLAD I COULD MEET SNOW WHITE ONE LAST TIME...
...PLE-SAN...
RIPPLE-SAN...!!
SEEING THINGS RIGHT WHEN I'M ABOUT TO DIE...HUH... HEH-HEH... PATHETIC.
IF... THERE IS A NEXT TIME...

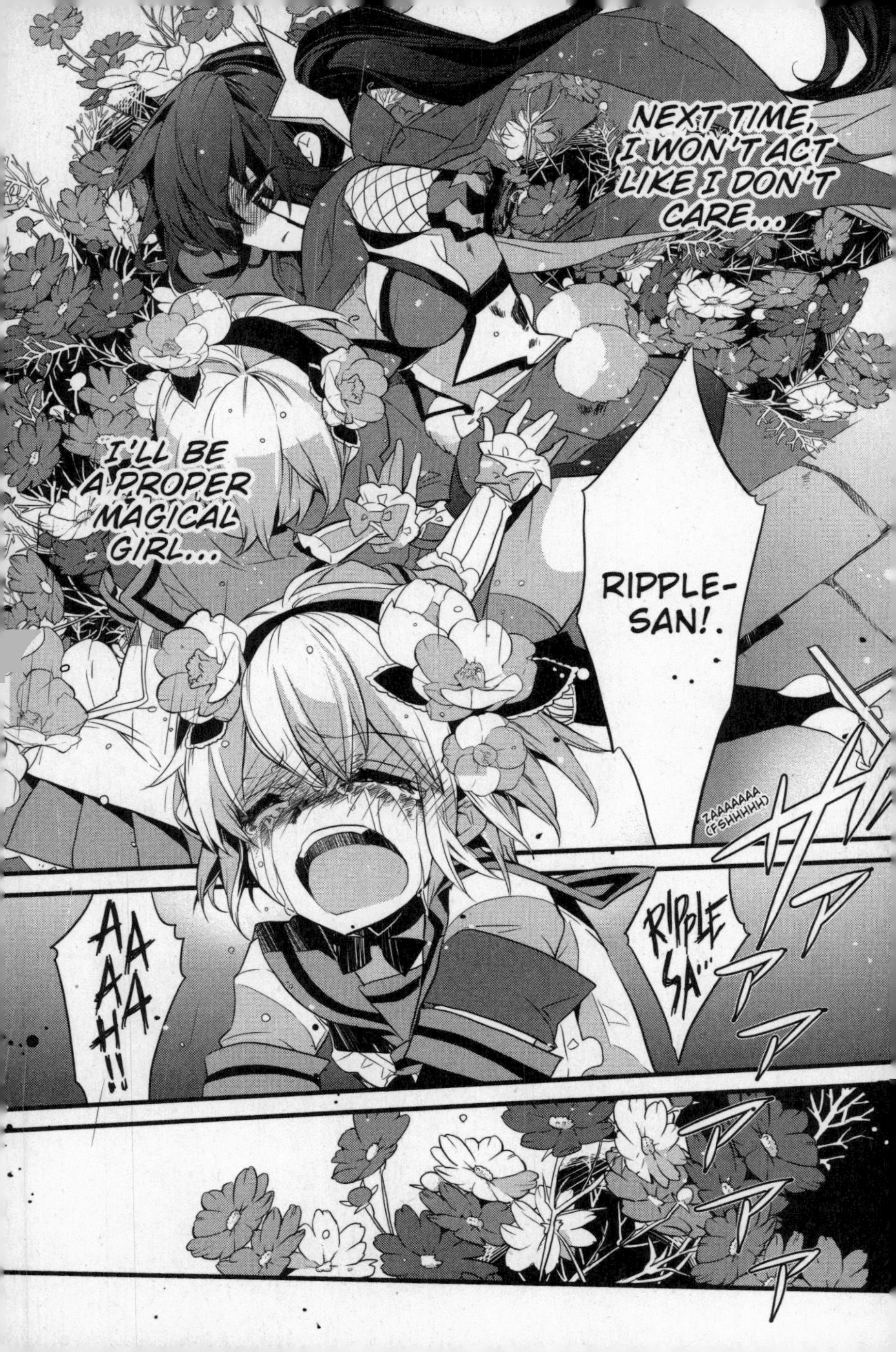
NEXT TIME, I WON'T ACT LIKE I DON'T CARE...
I'LL BE A PROPER MAGICAL GIRL...
RIPPLE-SAN!..
ZAAAAAAA (FSHHHHH)
RIPPLE SA...
AAAAH!!

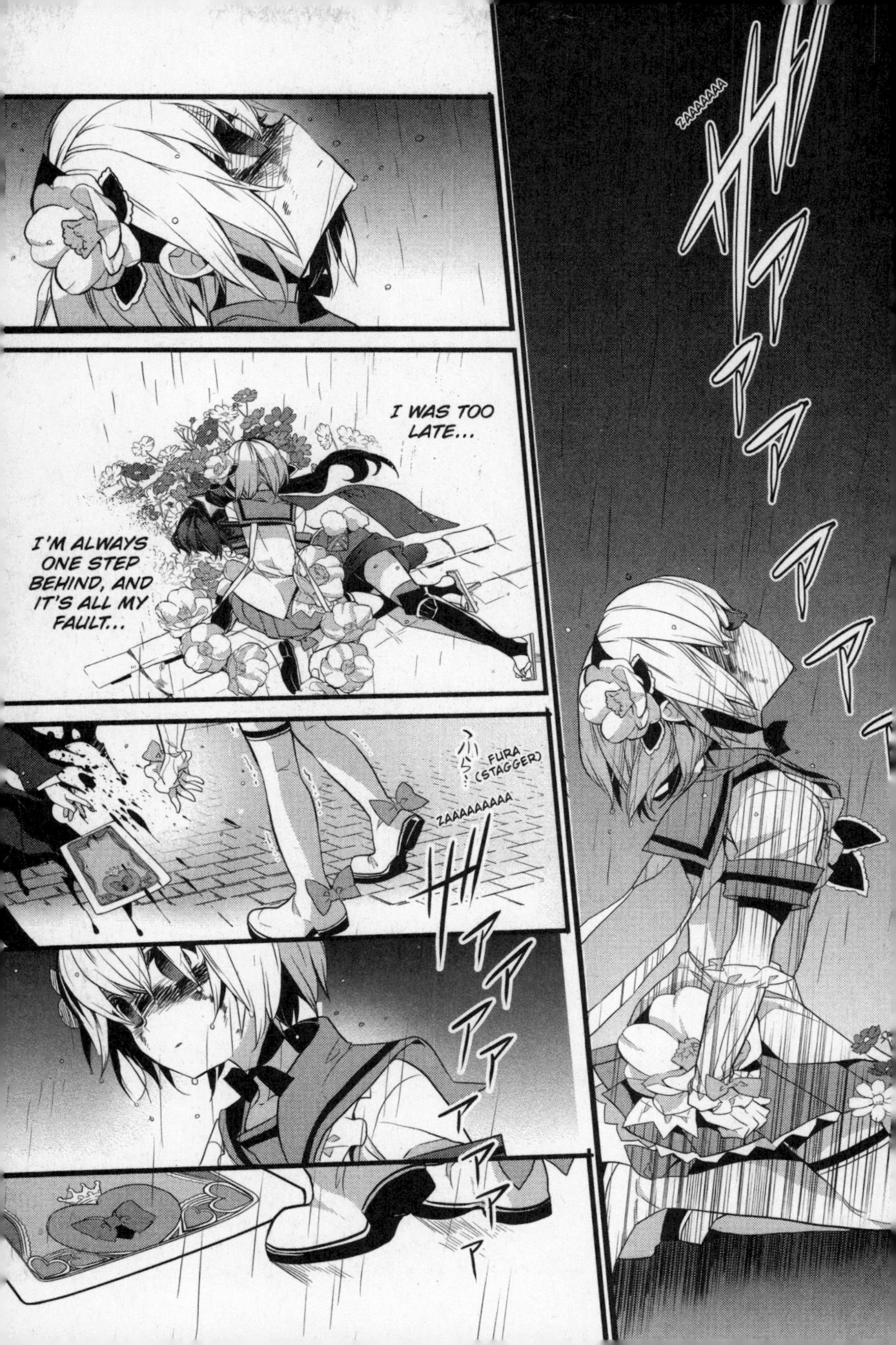
ZAAAAAAA
I WAS TOO LATE...
I'M ALWAYS ONE STEP BEHIND, AND IT'S ALL MY FAULT...
ふら
FURA (STAGGER)
ZAAAAAAAAA

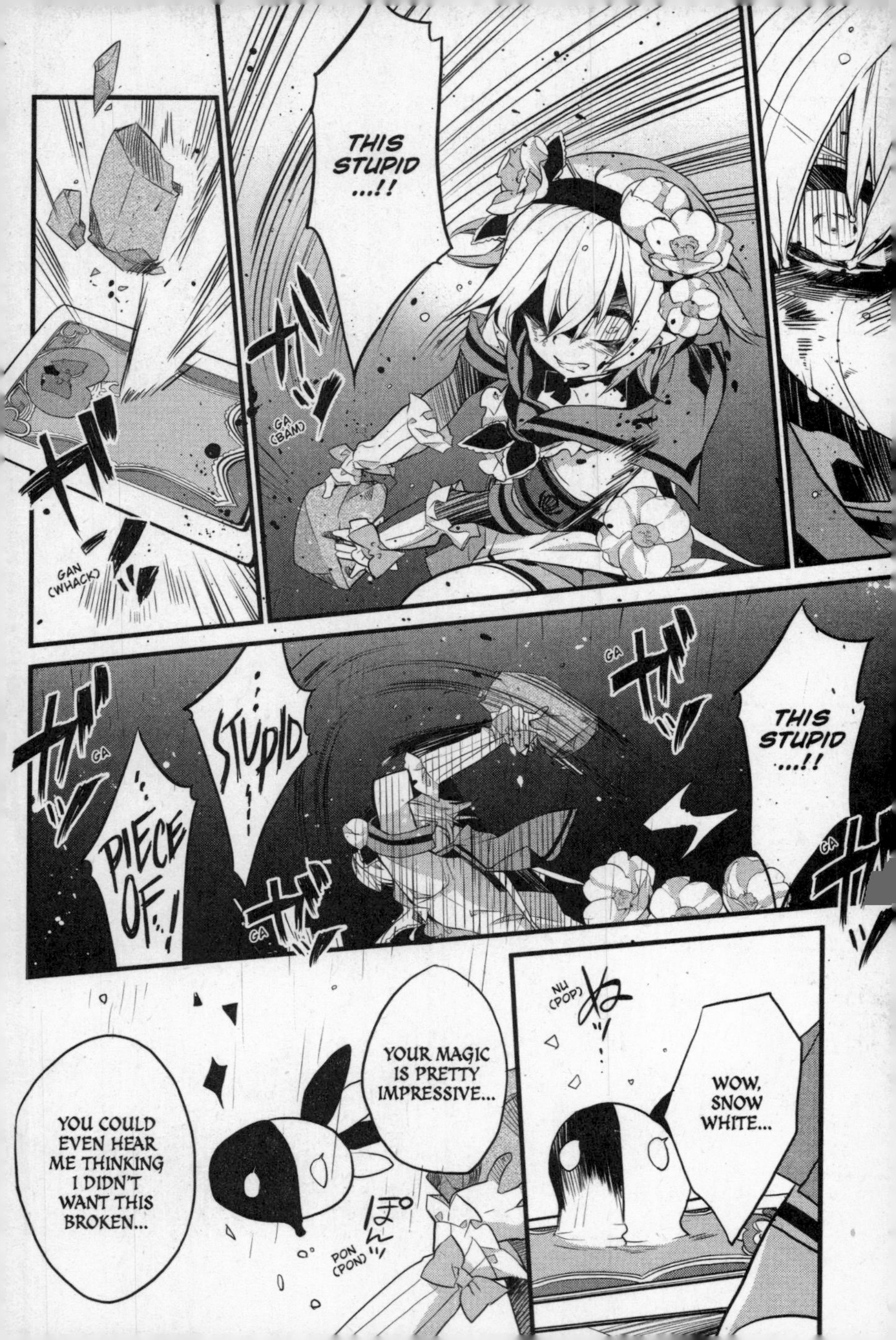
THIS STUPID ...!!
GA (BAM)
GAN (WHACK)
GA
THIS STUPID ...!!
GA
STUPID
PIECE OF...!
GA
GA
NU (POP)
WOW, SNOW WHITE...
YOUR MAGIC IS PRETTY IMPRESSIVE...
YOU COULD EVEN HEAR ME THINKING I DIDN'T WANT THIS BROKEN...
PON (PON)

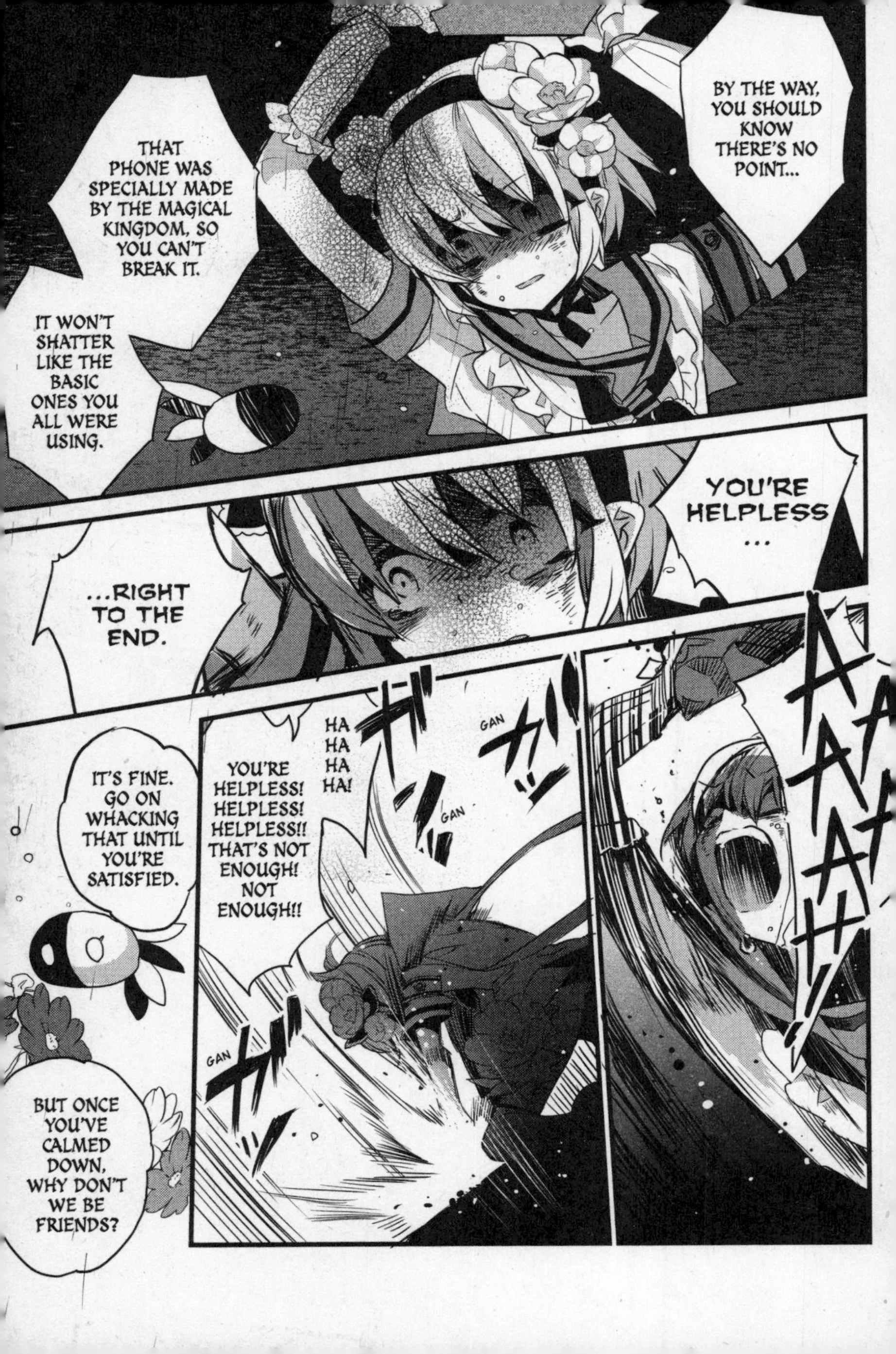
BY THE WAY, YOU SHOULD KNOW THERE'S NO POINT...
THAT PHONE WAS SPECIALLY MADE BY THE MAGICAL KINGDOM, SO YOU CAN'T BREAK IT.
IT WON'T SHATTER LIKE THE BASIC ONES YOU ALL WERE USING.
YOU'RE HELPLESS ...
...RIGHT TO THE END.
HA HA HA HA!
GAN
YOU'RE HELPLESS! HELPLESS! HELPLESS!! THAT'S NOT ENOUGH! NOT ENOUGH!!
GAN
GAN
IT'S FINE. GO ON WHACKING THAT UNTIL YOU'RE SATISFIED.
BUT ONCE YOU'VE CALMED DOWN, WHY DON'T WE BE FRIENDS?

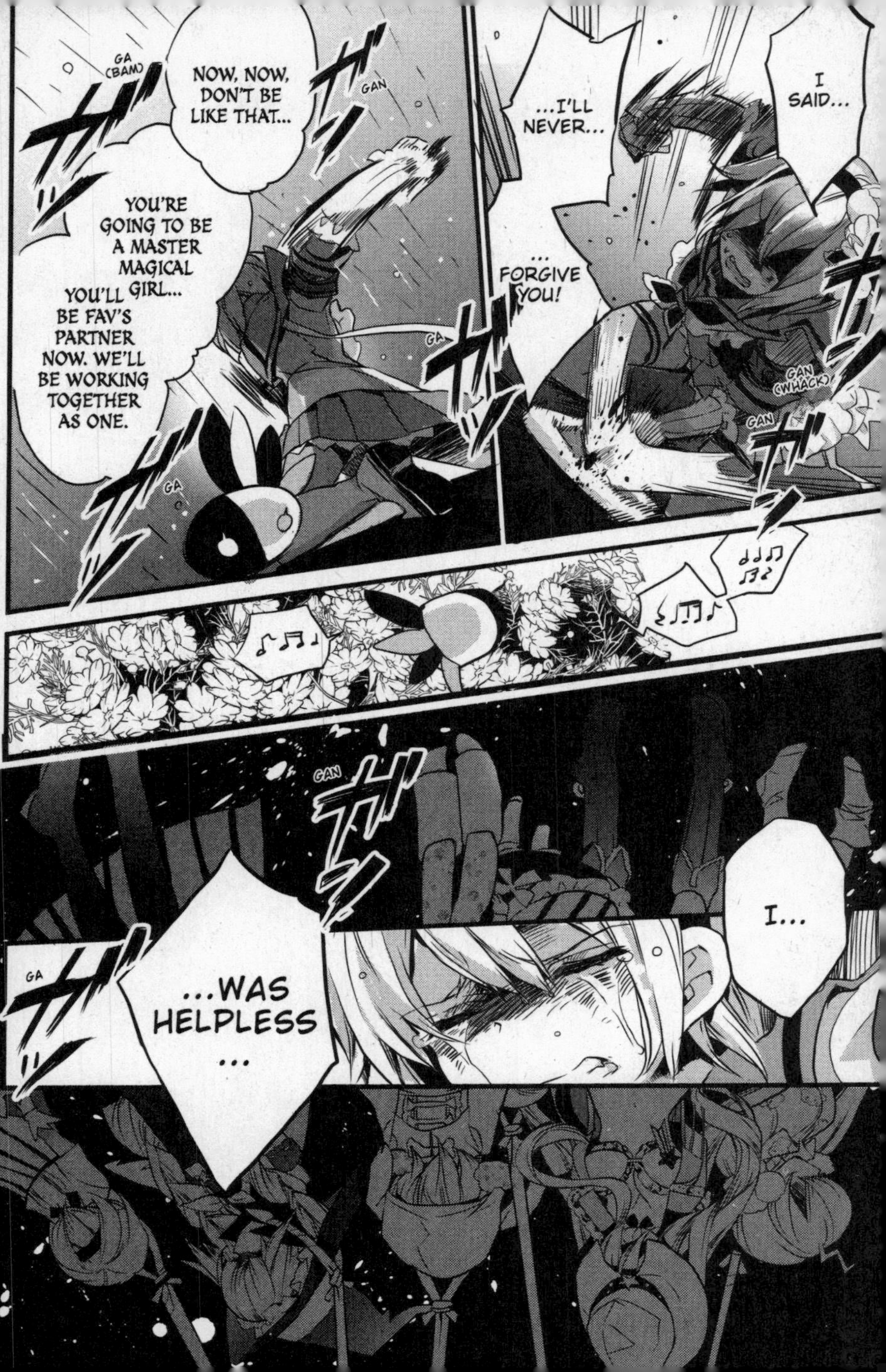
I SAID...
...I'LL NEVER...
...FORGIVE YOU!
GAN (WHACK)
GAN
GA
GA (BAM)
GAN
NOW, NOW, DON'T BE LIKE THAT...
YOU'RE GOING TO BE A MASTER MAGICAL GIRL...
YOU'LL BE FAV'S PARTNER NOW. WE'LL BE WORKING TOGETHER AS ONE.
GA
GAN
I...
...WAS HELPLESS ...
GA

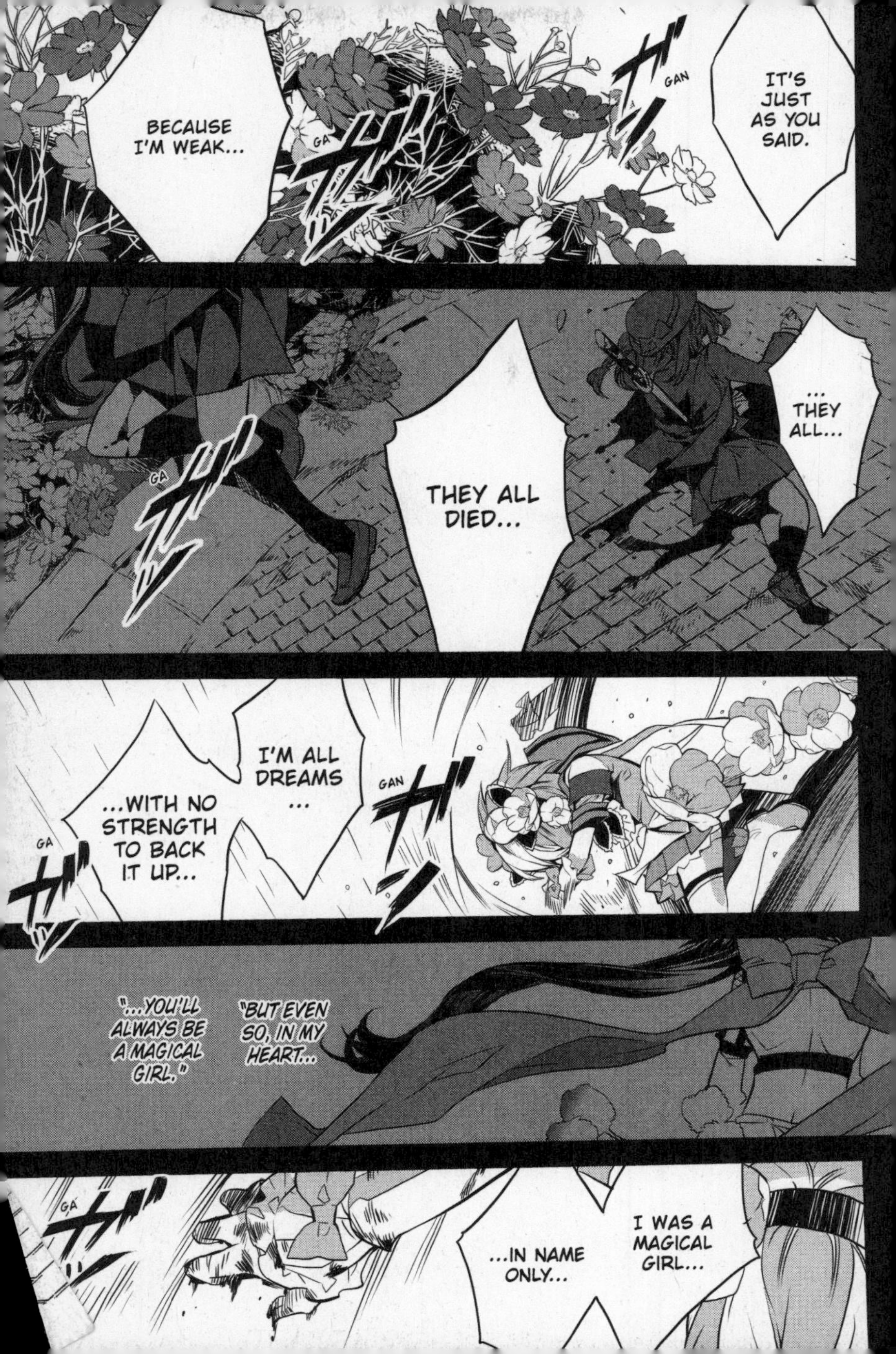
IT'S JUST AS YOU SAID.
GAN
GA
BECAUSE I'M WEAK...
...THEY ALL...
THEY ALL DIED...
GA
GAN
I'M ALL DREAMS ...
...WITH NO STRENGTH TO BACK IT UP...
GA
"BUT EVEN SO, IN MY HEART...
"...YOU'LL ALWAYS BE A MAGICAL GIRL."
I WAS A MAGICAL GIRL...
...IN NAME ONLY...
GA

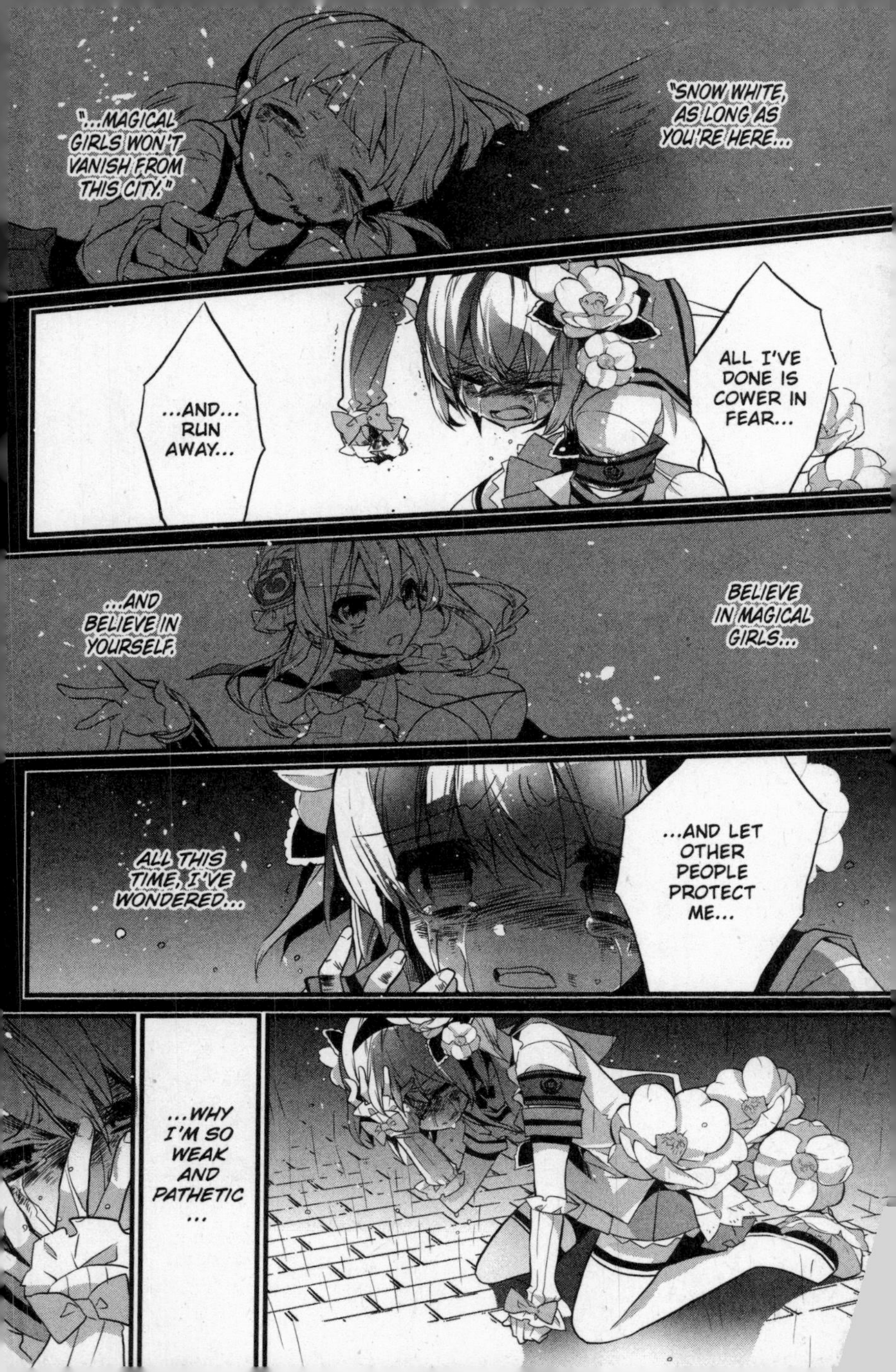
"SNOW WHITE, AS LONG AS YOU'RE HERE...
"...MAGICAL GIRLS WON'T VANISH FROM THIS CITY."
ALL I'VE DONE IS COWER IN FEAR...
...AND... RUN AWAY...
BELIEVE IN MAGICAL GIRLS...
...AND BELIEVE IN YOURSELF.
...AND LET OTHER PEOPLE PROTECT ME...
ALL THIS TIME, I'VE WONDERED...
...WHY I'M SO WEAK AND PATHETIC ...

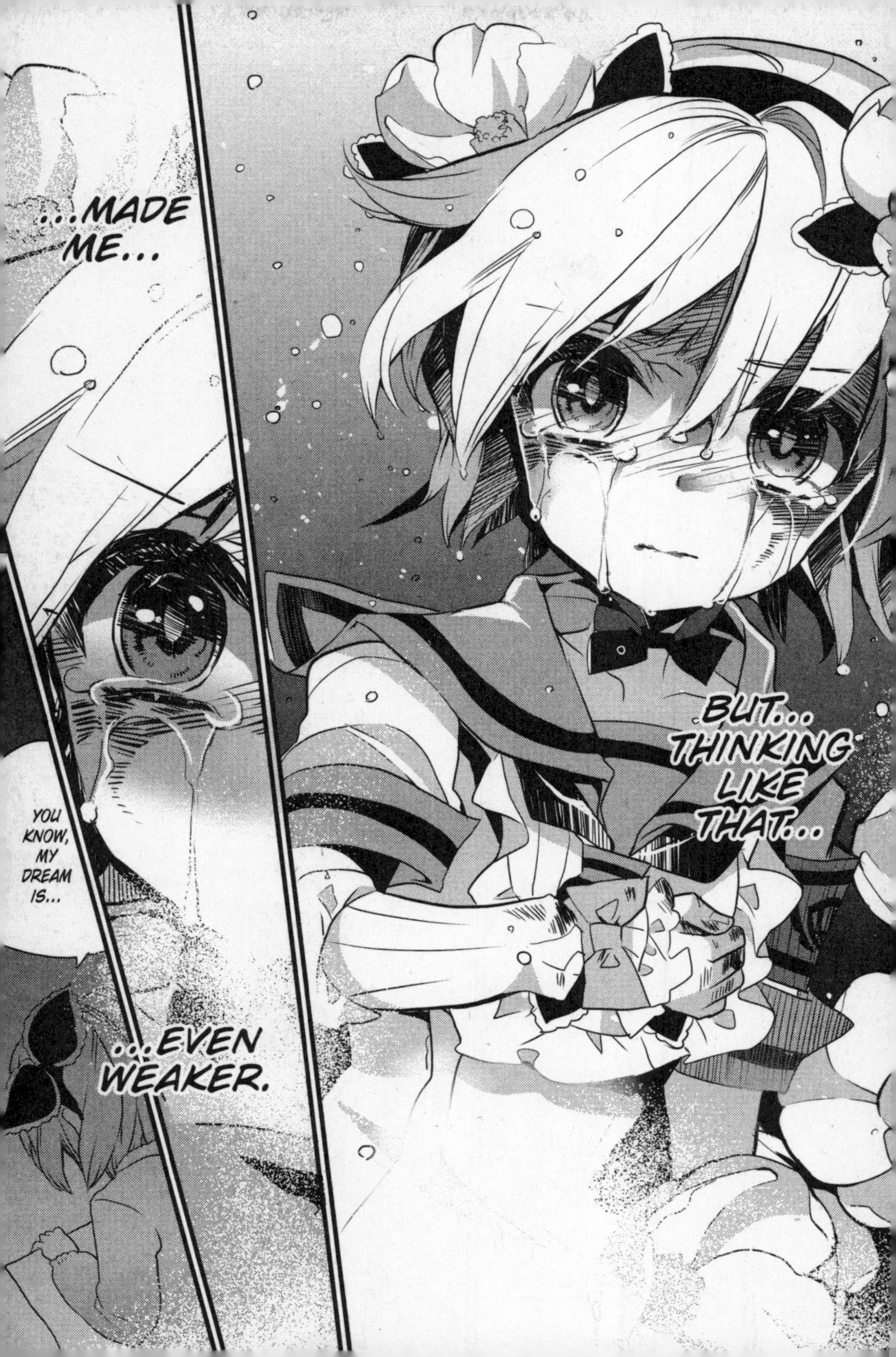
BUT... THINKING LIKE THAT...
...MADE ME...
YOU KNOW, MY DREAM IS...
...EVEN WEAKER.

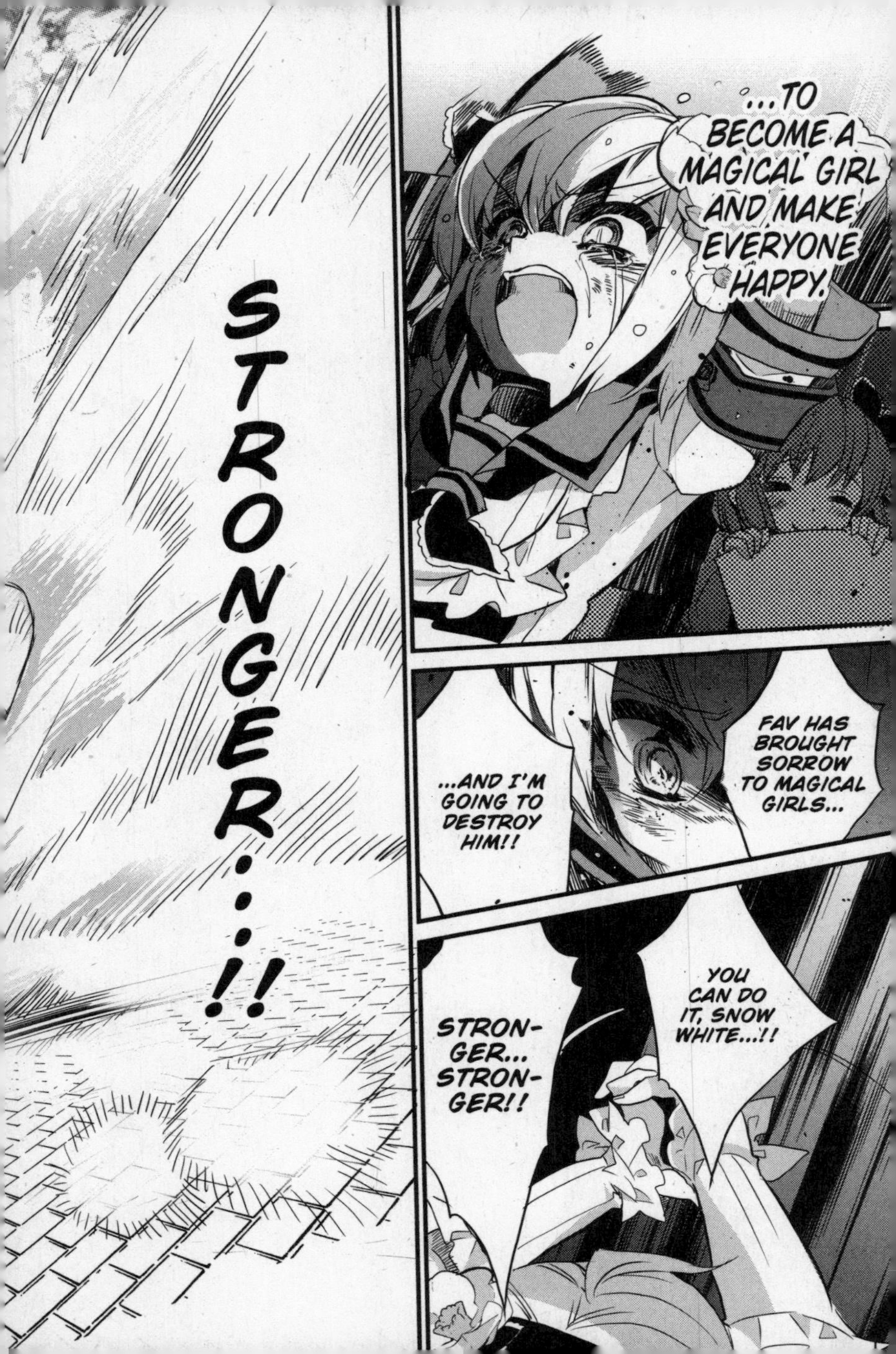
...TO BECOME A MAGICAL GIRL AND MAKE EVERYONE HAPPY.
FAV HAS BROUGHT SORROW TO MAGICAL GIRLS...
...AND I'M GOING TO DESTROY HIM!!
YOU CAN DO IT, SNOW WHITE...!!
STRON-GER... STRON-GER!!
STRONGER...!!

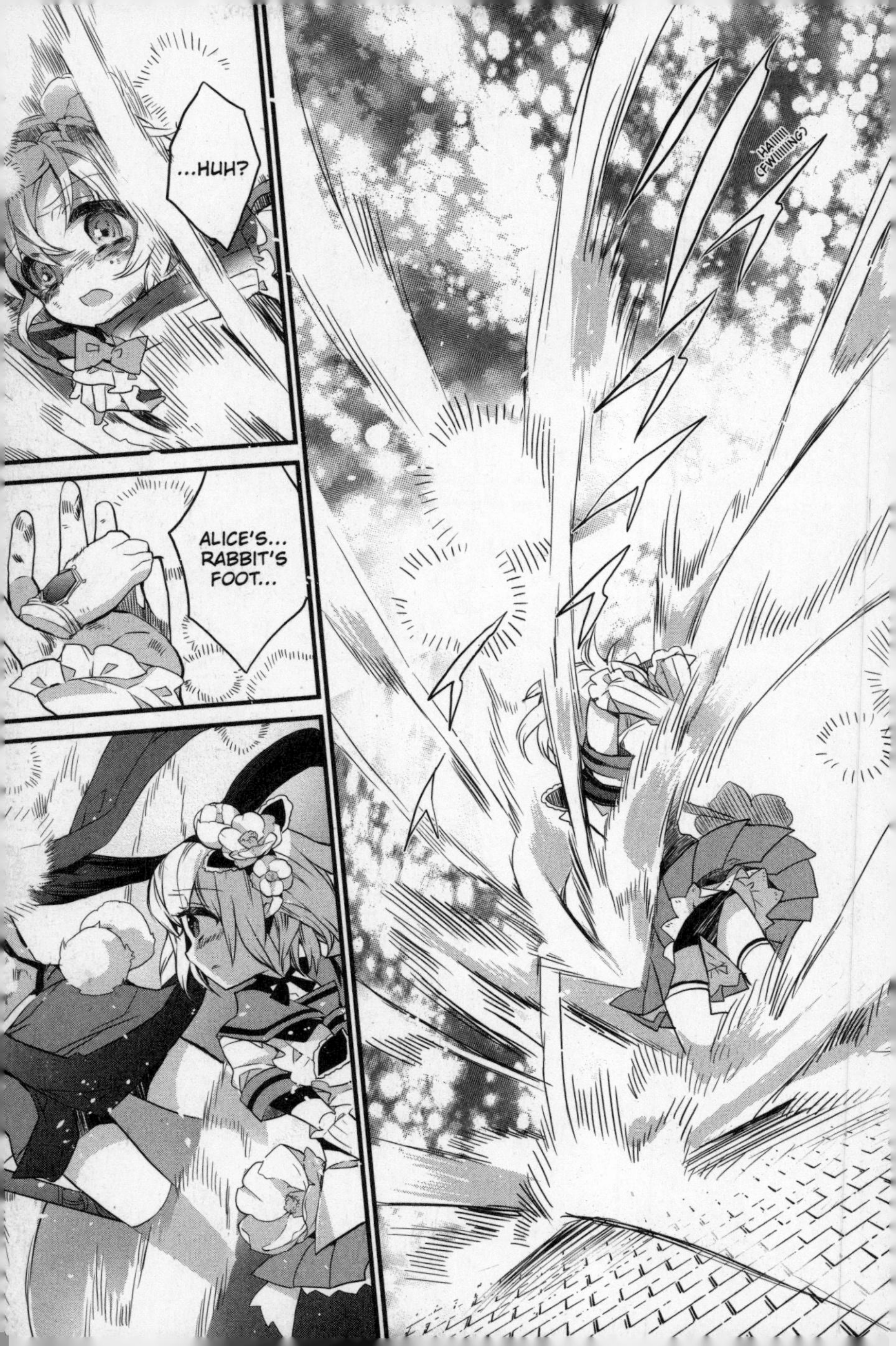
HAIIIIII
(FWIIIIIING)
...HUH?
ALICE'S... RABBIT'S FOOT...

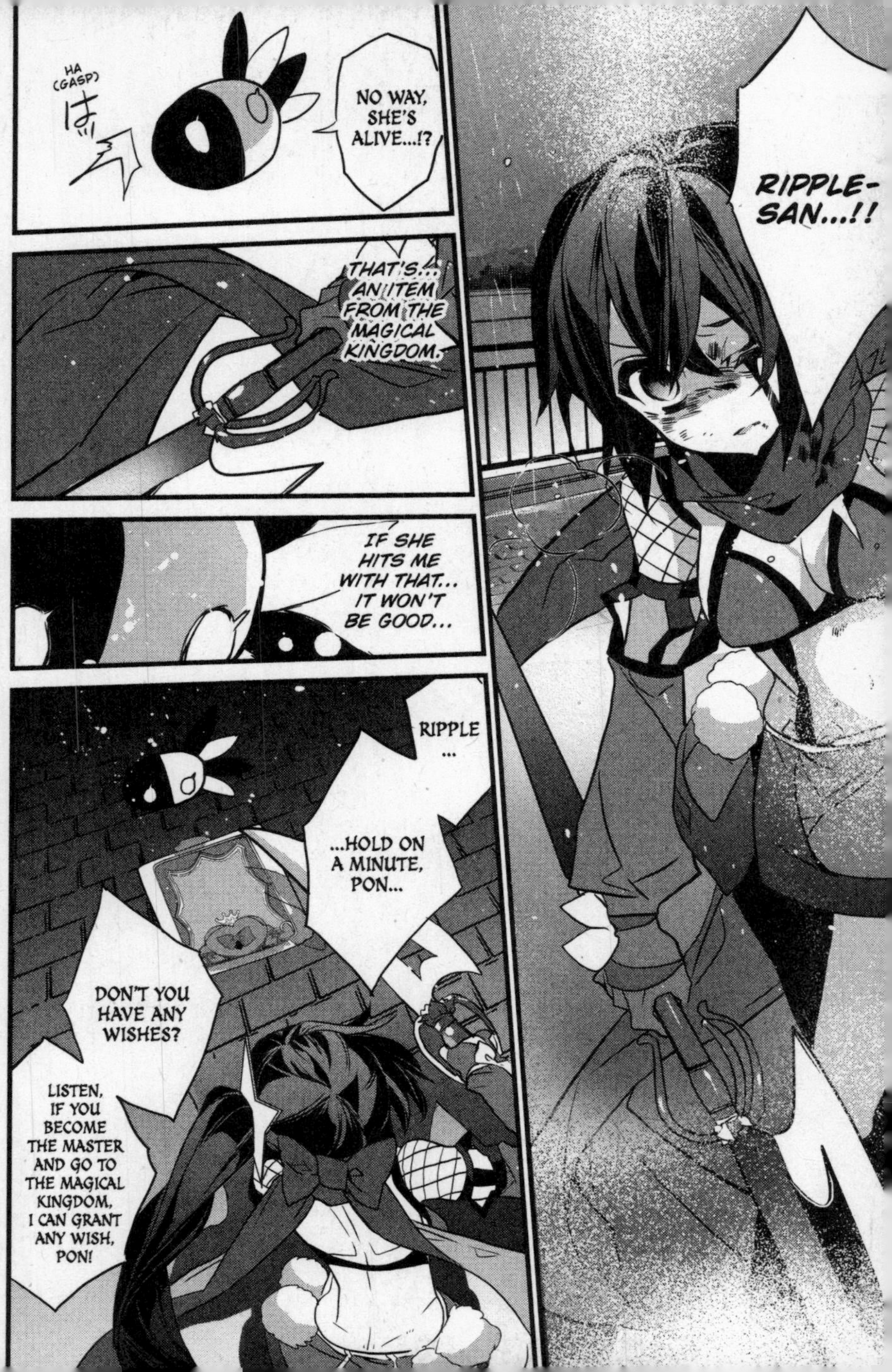

RIPPLE-SAN...!!
NO WAY, SHE'S ALIVE...!?
HA (GASP)
は
THAT'S... AN ITEM FROM THE MAGICAL KINGDOM.
IF SHE HITS ME WITH THAT... IT WON'T BE GOOD...
RIPPLE ...
...HOLD ON A MINUTE, PON...
DON'T YOU HAVE ANY WISHES?
LISTEN, IF YOU BECOME THE MASTER AND GO TO THE MAGICAL KINGDOM, I CAN GRANT ANY WISH, PON!

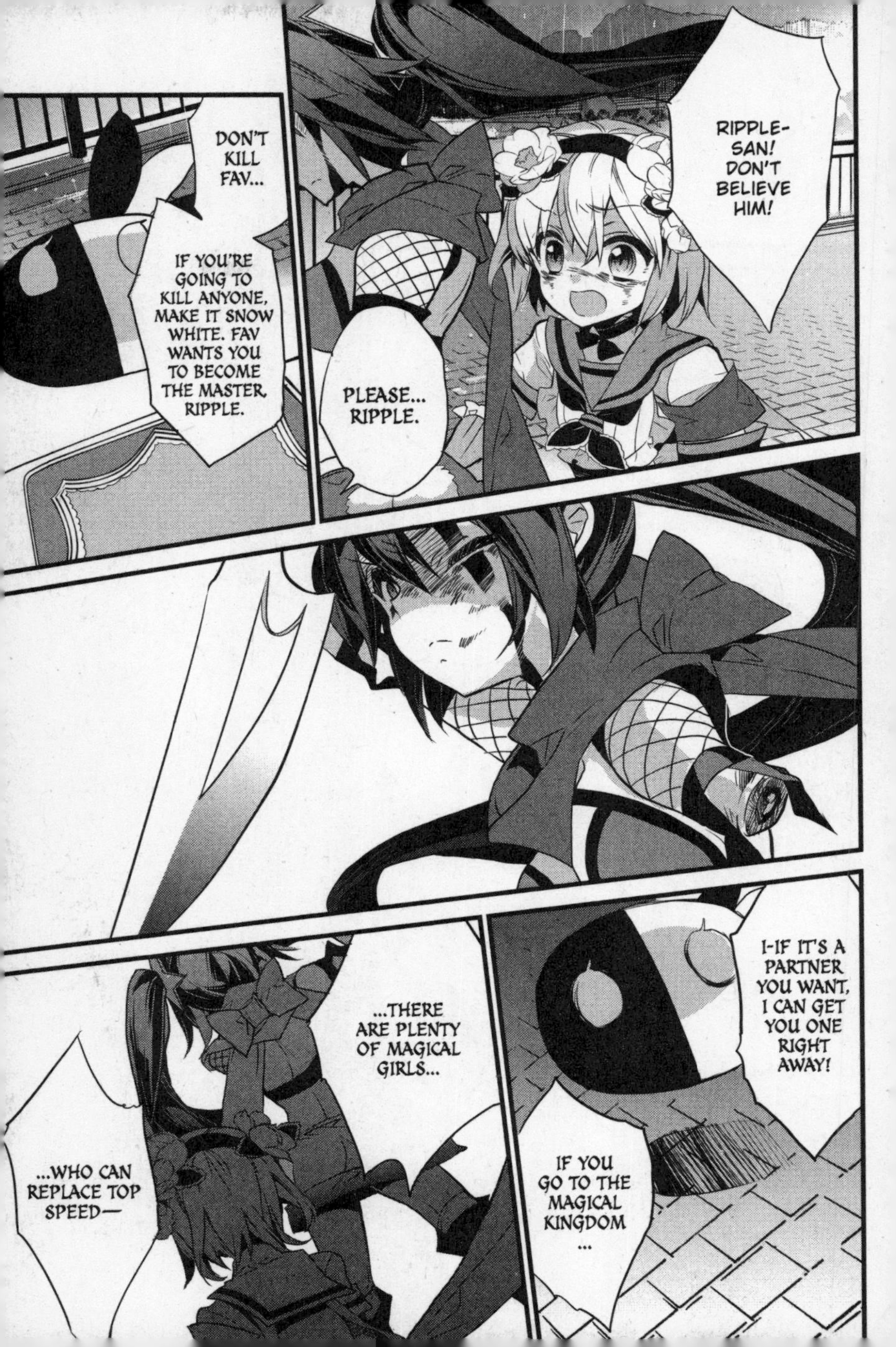
RIPPLE-SAN! DON'T BELIEVE HIM!
PLEASE... RIPPLE.
DON'T KILL FAV...
IF YOU'RE GOING TO KILL ANYONE, MAKE IT SNOW WHITE. FAV WANTS YOU TO BECOME THE MASTER, RIPPLE.
I-IF IT'S A PARTNER YOU WANT, I CAN GET YOU ONE RIGHT AWAY!
IF YOU GO TO THE MAGICAL KINGDOM ...
...THERE ARE PLENTY OF MAGICAL GIRLS...
...WHO CAN REPLACE TOP SPEED—

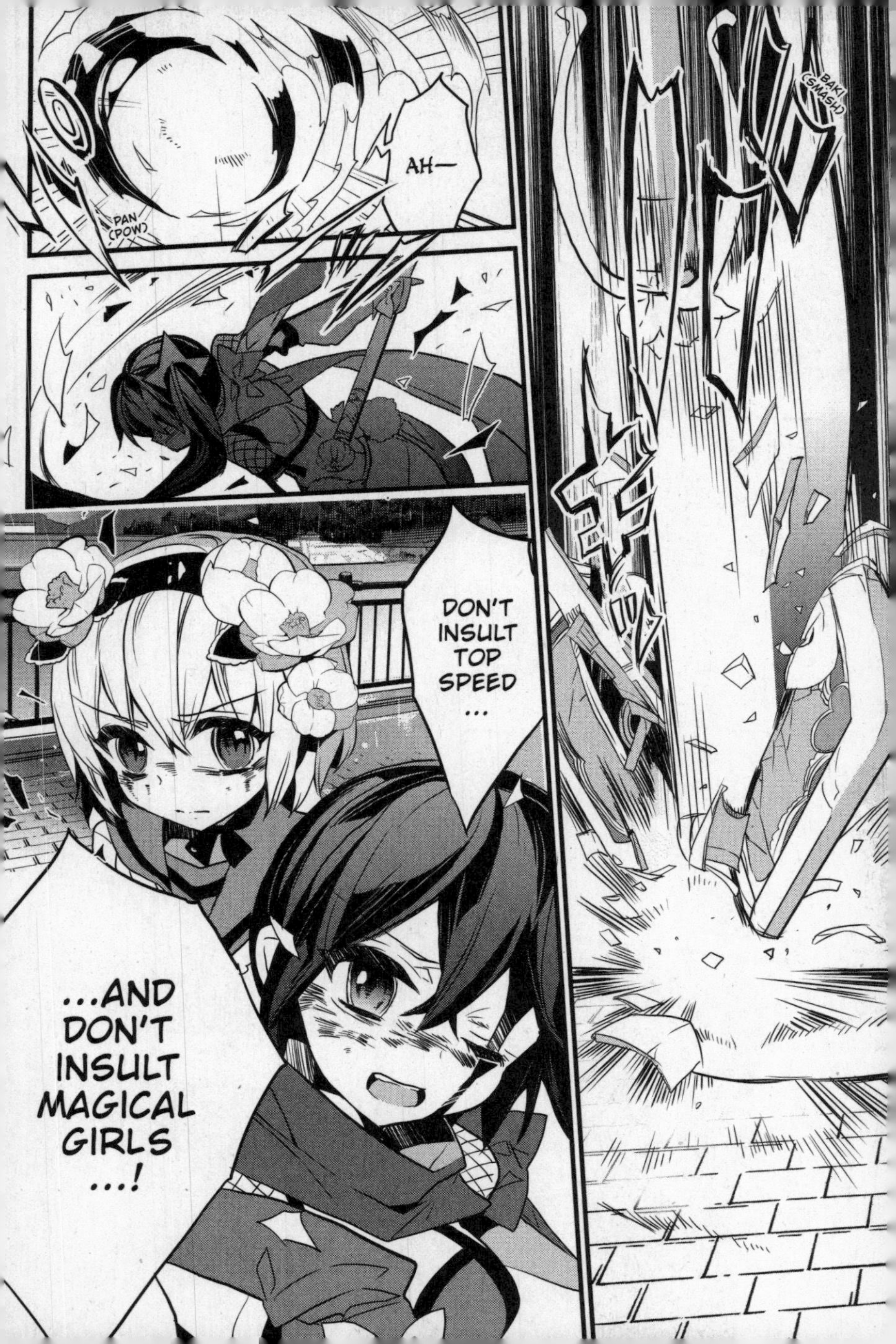

BAKI (SMASH)
AH—
PAN (POW)
DON'T INSULT TOP SPEED ...
...AND DON'T INSULT MAGICAL GIRLS ...!

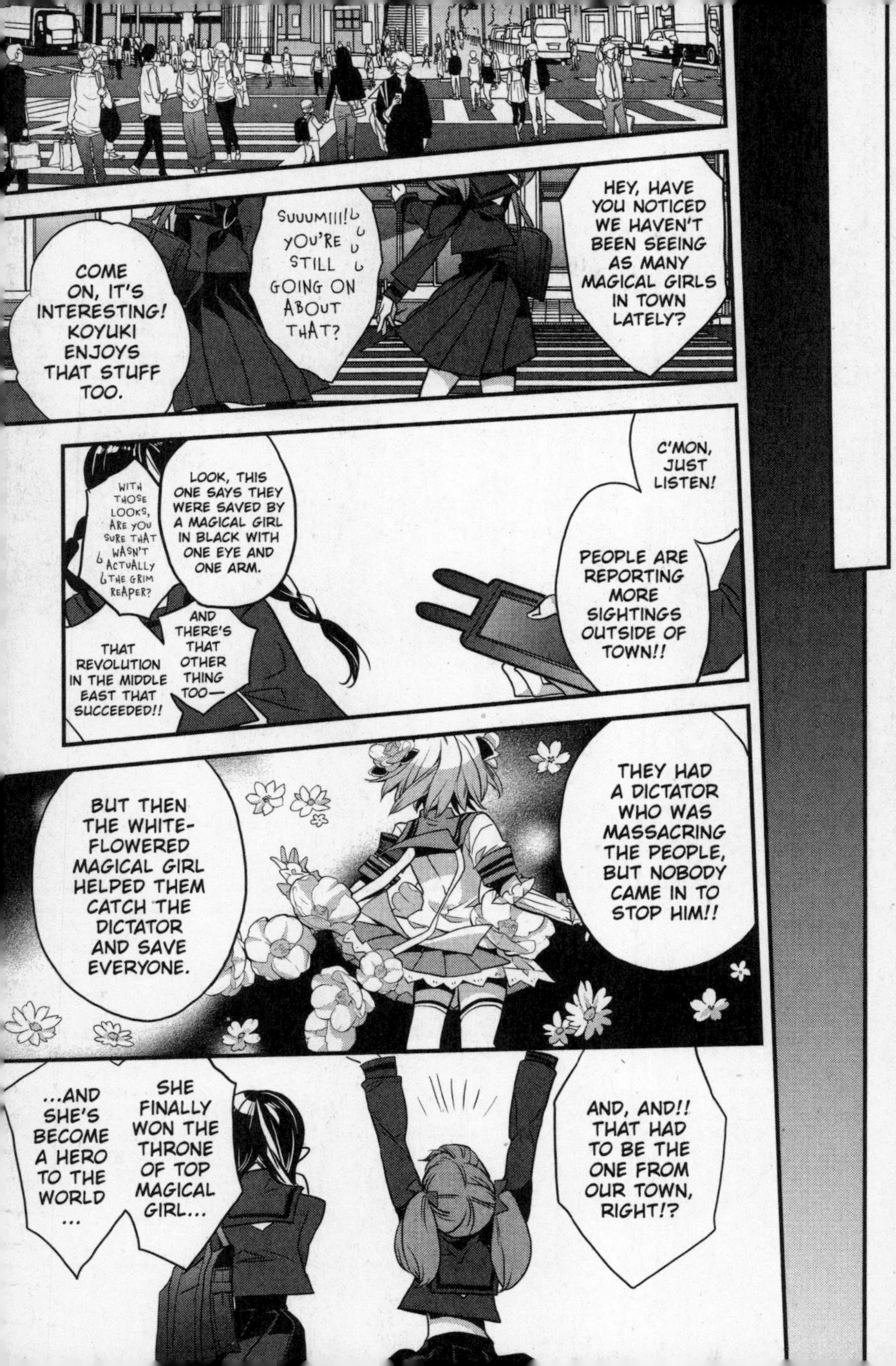
HEY, HAVE YOU NOTICED WE HAVEN'T BEEN SEEING AS MANY MAGICAL GIRLS IN TOWN LATELY?
SUUUMIII!! YOU'RE STILL GOING ON ABOUT THAT?
COME ON, IT'S INTERESTING! KOYUKI ENJOYS THAT STUFF TOO.
C'MON, JUST LISTEN!
PEOPLE ARE REPORTING MORE SIGHTINGS OUTSIDE OF TOWN!!
LOOK, THIS ONE SAYS THEY WERE SAVED BY A MAGICAL GIRL IN BLACK WITH ONE EYE AND ONE ARM.
WITH THOSE LOOKS, ARE YOU SURE THAT WASN'T ACTUALLY THE GRIM REAPER?
AND THERE'S THAT OTHER THING TOO—
THAT REVOLUTION IN THE MIDDLE EAST THAT SUCCEEDED!!
THEY HAD A DICTATOR WHO WAS MASSACRING THE PEOPLE, BUT NOBODY CAME IN TO STOP HIM!!
BUT THEN THE WHITE-FLOWERED MAGICAL GIRL HELPED THEM CATCH THE DICTATOR AND SAVE EVERYONE.
AND, AND!! THAT HAD TO BE THE ONE FROM OUR TOWN, RIGHT!?
SHE FINALLY WON THE THRONE OF TOP MAGICAL GIRL...
...AND SHE'S BECOME A HERO TO THE WORLD...

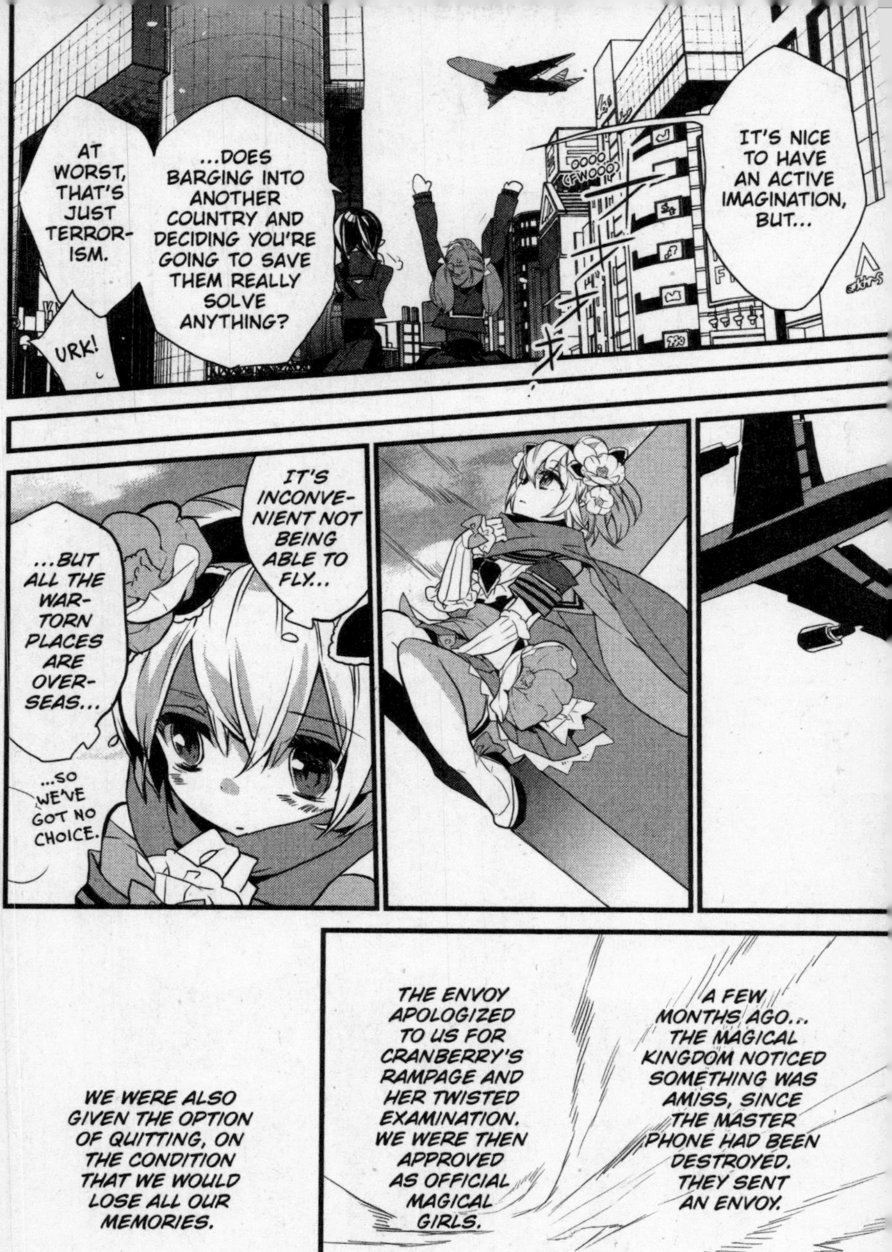
IT'S NICE TO HAVE AN ACTIVE IMAGINATION, BUT...
...DOES BARGING INTO ANOTHER COUNTRY AND DECIDING YOU'RE GOING TO SAVE THEM REALLY SOLVE ANYTHING?
AT WORST, THAT'S JUST TERRORISM.
URK!
IT'S INCONVENIENT NOT BEING ABLE TO FLY...
...BUT ALL THE WAR-TORN PLACES ARE OVERSEAS...
...SO WE'VE GOT NO CHOICE.
A FEW MONTHS AGO... THE MAGICAL KINGDOM NOTICED SOMETHING WAS AMISS, SINCE THE MASTER PHONE HAD BEEN DESTROYED. THEY SENT AN ENVOY.
THE ENVOY APOLOGIZED TO US FOR CRANBERRY'S RAMPAGE AND HER TWISTED EXAMINATION. WE WERE THEN APPROVED AS OFFICIAL MAGICAL GIRLS.
WE WERE ALSO GIVEN THE OPTION OF QUITTING, ON THE CONDITION THAT WE WOULD LOSE ALL OUR MEMORIES.

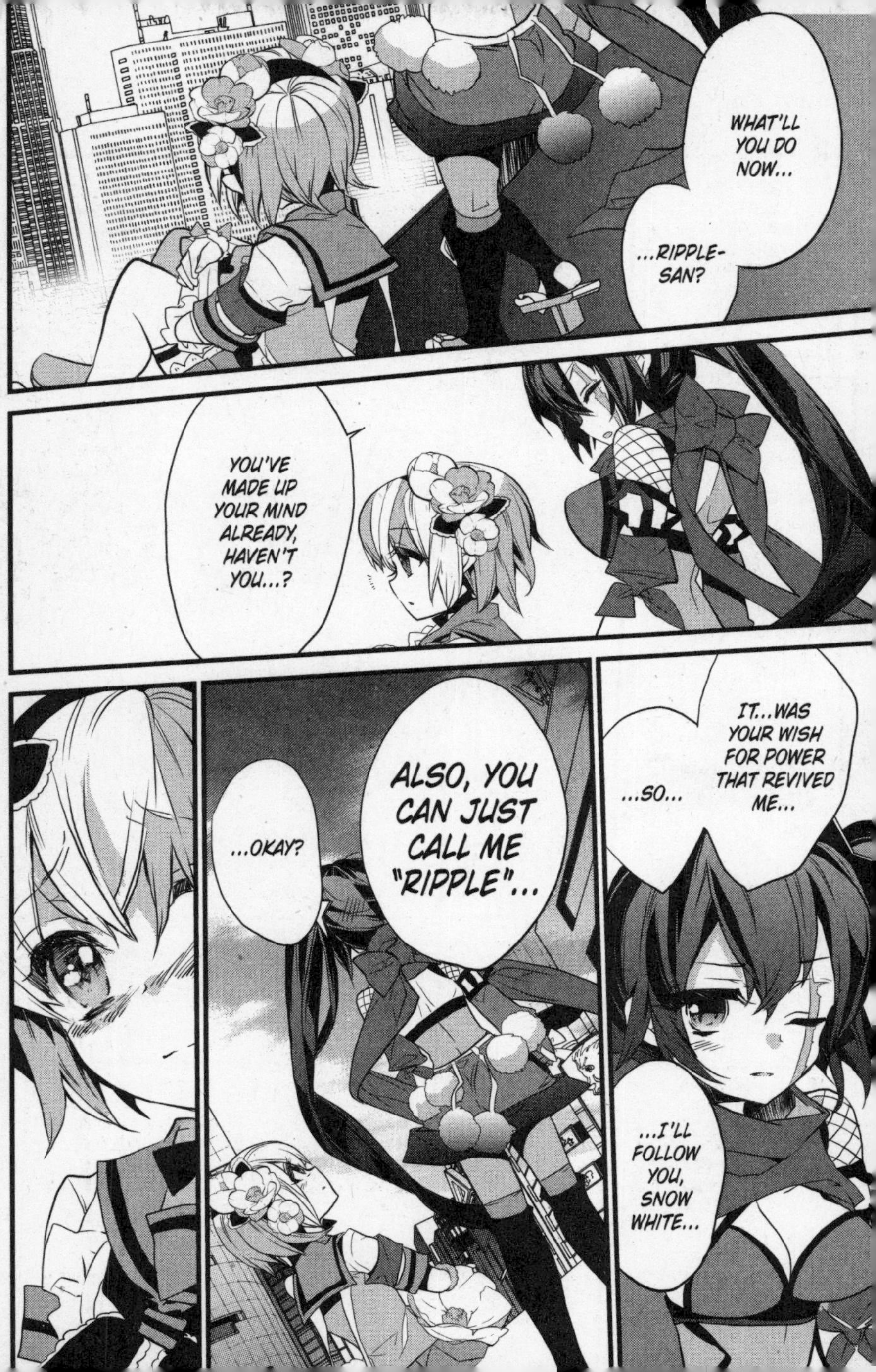
WHAT'LL YOU DO NOW...
...RIPPLE-SAN?
YOU'VE MADE UP YOUR MIND ALREADY, HAVEN'T YOU...?
IT...WAS YOUR WISH FOR POWER THAT REVIVED ME...
...SO...
...I'LL FOLLOW YOU, SNOW WHITE...
ALSO, YOU CAN JUST CALL ME "RIPPLE"...
...OKAY?

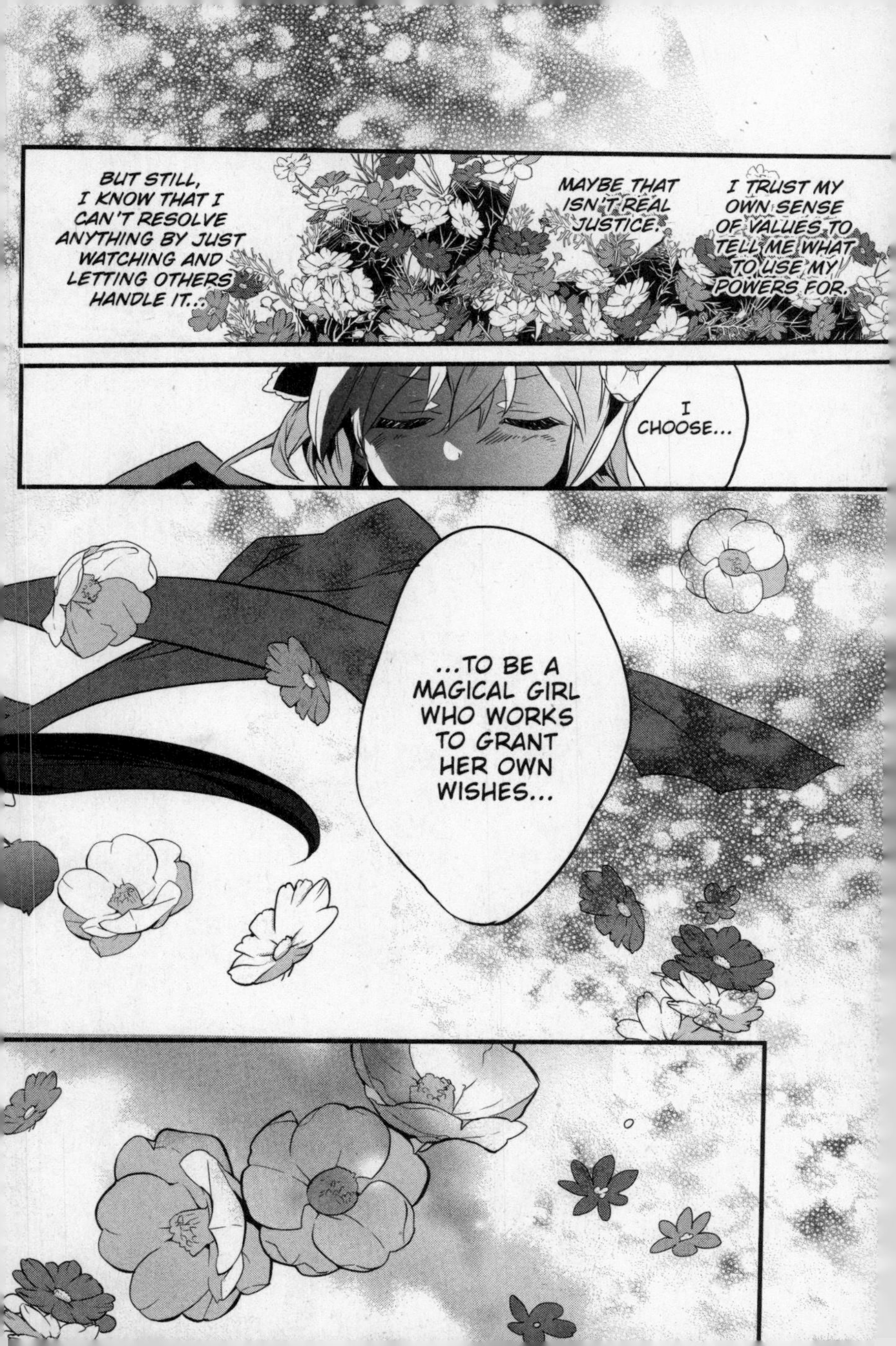
I TRUST MY OWN SENSE OF VALUES TO TELL ME WHAT TO USE MY POWERS FOR.
MAYBE THAT ISN'T REAL JUSTICE.
BUT STILL, I KNOW THAT I CAN'T RESOLVE ANYTHING BY JUST WATCHING AND LETTING OTHERS HANDLE IT...
I CHOOSE...
...TO BE A MAGICAL GIRL WHO WORKS TO GRANT HER OWN WISHES...

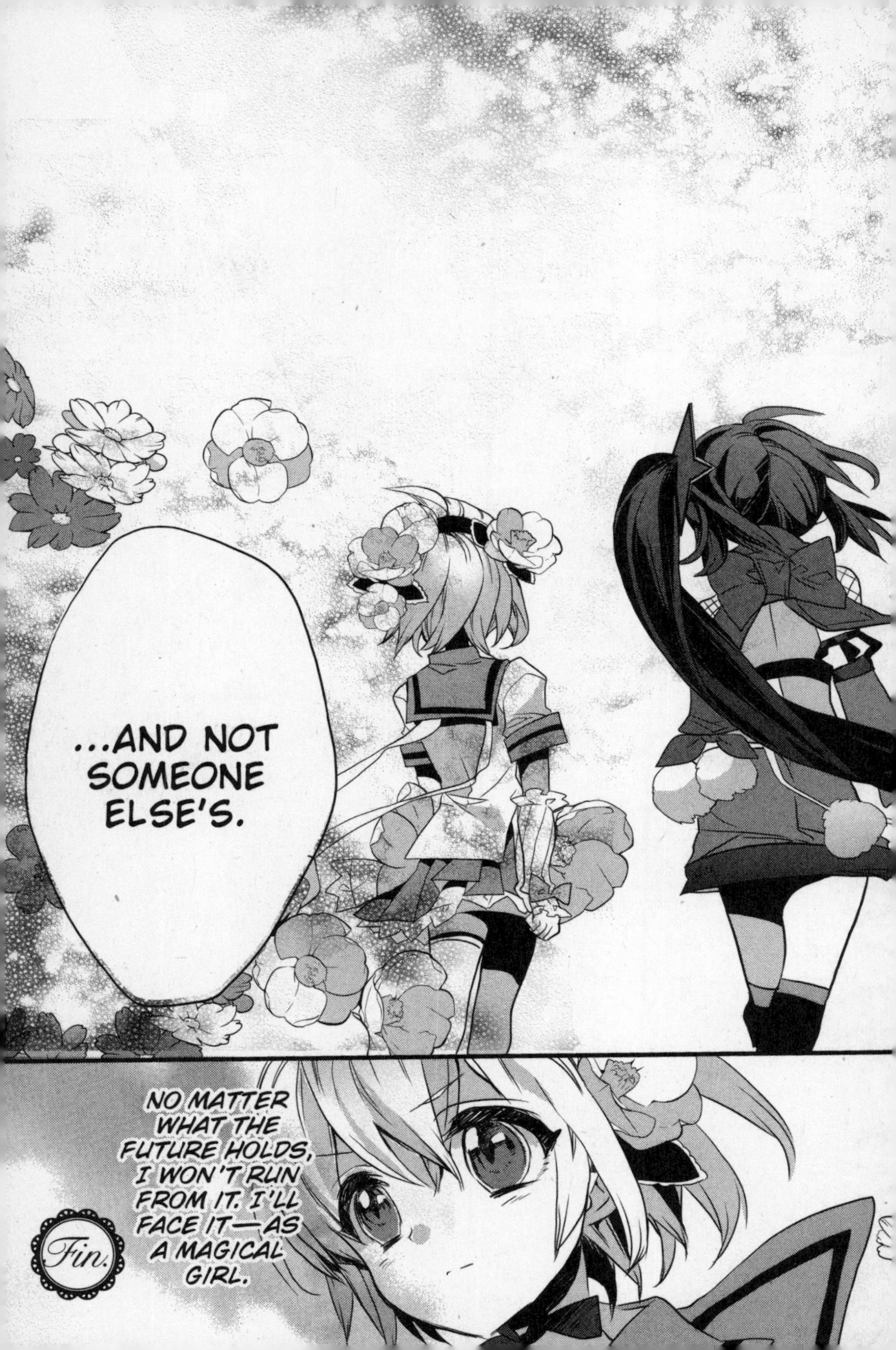
...AND NOT SOMEONE ELSE'S.
NO MATTER WHAT THE FUTURE HOLDS, I WON'T RUN FROM IT. I'LL FACE IT—AS A MAGICAL GIRL.
Fin.

Magical Girl Raising Project
2

Art:
Edoya POCHI

Original story:
Asari Endou

Translation: Jennifer Ward
Lettering: Rochelle Gancio

Character design:
Marui-no

MAHO SHOJO IKUSEI KEIKAKU Volume 2
© Asari Endou · Marui-no / Takarajimasha, Inc.
© Edoya POCHI 2016
First published in Japan in 2016 by KADOKAWA CORPORATION, Tokyo.
English translation rights arranged with KADOKAWA CORPORATION, Tokyo, through Tuttle-Mori Agency, Inc., Tokyo.

English translation © 2018 by Yen Press, LLC

Yen Press
1290 Avenue of the Americas
New York, NY 10104

Visit us at yenpress.com
facebook.com/yenpress
twitter.com/yenpress
yenpress.tumblr.com
instagram.com/yenpress

First Yen Press Edition: April 2018

Yen Press is an imprint of Yen Press, LLC.
The Yen Press name and logo are trademarks of Yen Press, LLC.

The publisher is not responsible for websites (or their content) that are not owned by the publisher.

Library of Congress Control Number: 2017954137

ISBNs: 978-0-316-52131-4 (paperback)
       978-0-316-52132-1 (ebook)

10 9 8 7 6 5 4 3 2 1

WOR

Printed in the United States of America

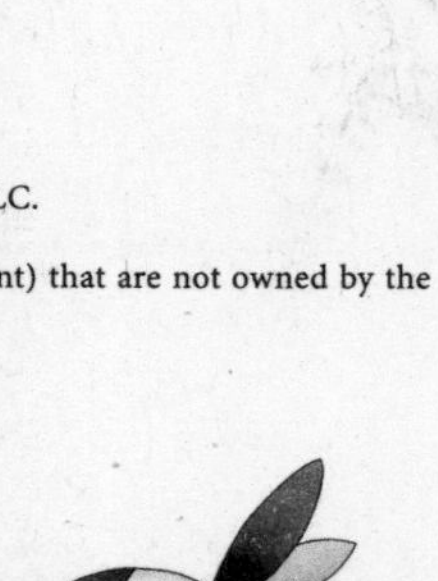